This new guide to the coast path from Plymouth to Poole (217¼ miles) covers the third part, the South Devon and Dorset section, of the 630-mile South-West Coast Path and is the final book in this series. It was walked, researched and written by **Henry Stedman** (top, left) and **Joel Newton** (right) accompanied by **Daisy**.

JOEL NEWTON took his first footsteps on the South-West Coast Path (SWCP) in 2007. With ill-fitting shoes and a bag that was far too heavy he set off from Minehead, eventually arriving in Falmouth five weeks later with a far lighter bag and an injured foot. That journey was over but it was to become the inspiration for many more including Offa's Dyke Path, West Highland Way, Great Glen Way, Hadrian's Wall Path, Cotswold Way, and sections of The Pennine Way – in addition to finishing the SWCP. He finally reached Poole Harbour whilst co-authoring this, his third book for Trailblazer.

Born in Chatham, Kent, **HENRY STEDMAN** has been writing guidebooks for over fifteen years and is the author or co-author of half a dozen titles, including Trailblazer's *Kilimanjaro – The Trekking Guide to Africa's Highest Mountain*, *Dolomites Trekking*, *Coast to Coast Path* and *Hadrian's Wall Path*, as well as *The Bradt Guide to Palestine* and the *Rough Guides* to *Indonesia* and *Southeast Asia*.

When not travelling or writing, Henry lives in England editing other people's guidebooks, maintaining his Kilimanjaro website and arranging climbs on the mountain through his company, Climb Mount Kilimanjaro.

DAISY is Henry's dog, though any assumption that ownership equates with control is entirely wrong in this instance. Two parts trouble to one part Parson's Jack Russell, together with her two human companions Daisy managed to walk the entire trail – indeed, for every five miles that they completed, Daisy did about ten. This is her third book.

Authors

Dorset & South Devon Coast Path (SWCP Part 3)

First edition: 2013

Publisher Trailblazer Publications
The Old Manse, Tower Rd, Hindhead, Surrey, GU26 6SU, UK
info@trailblazer-guides.com, www.trailblazer-guides.com

British Library Cataloguing in Publication Data
A catalogue record for this book is available from the British Library

ISBN 978-1-905864-45-4

© **Trailblazer 2013**: Text and maps

Series Editor: Anna Jacomb-Hood
Editor: Anna Jacomb-Hood   **Proof-reading**: Jane Thomas   **Cartography**: Nick Hill
Layout: Anna Jacomb-Hood   **Index**: Anna Jacomb-Hood
Photographs (flora): © Bryn Thomas   **All other photographs**: © Henry Stedman

The maps in this guide were prepared from out-of-Crown-
copyright Ordnance Survey maps amended and updated by Trailblazer.

Acknowledgements

Thanks, as always, to everyone at Trailblazer for their Herculean efforts in turning our text
into this book: Anna Jacomb-Hood for editing and compiling the index; Jane Thomas for
proof-reading; Nick Hill for the maps; and, as ever, to Bryn, for keeping us in work. We're
also grateful to Roderick Leslie for checking the bird text.
    Henry would also like to thank Joel and Daisy for their company on the trail – and the
latter for the handwarming service she provided every morning

A request

The authors and publisher have tried to ensure that this guide is as accurate and up to date
as possible. Nevertheless, things change. If you notice any changes or omissions that should
be included in the next edition of this book, please write to Trailblazer (address above) or
email us at ⌨ info@trailblazer-guides.com. A free copy of the next edition will be sent to
persons making a significant contribution.

Warning: coastal walking and long-distance walking can be dangerous

Please read the notes on when to go (pp13-16) and on outdoor safety (pp66-9). Every effort
has been made by the author and publisher to ensure that the information contained herein
is as accurate and up to date as possible. However, they are unable to accept responsibility
for any inconvenience, loss or injury sustained by anyone as a result of the advice and information given in this guide.

Updated information will be available on: ⌨ **www.trailblazer-guides.com**

Photos – Opposite and front cover: Looking down on Durdle Door
Overleaf: The White Cliffs at Old Harry Rocks, Studland Hill
© Henry Stedman 2013

Printed on chlorine-free paper by D'Print (☎ +65-6581 3832), Singapore

Dorset &
South Devon
COAST PATH

SW COAST PATH PART 3 – PLYMOUTH TO POOLE

88 large-scale maps & guides to 48 towns and villages

PLANNING – PLACES TO STAY – PLACES TO EAT

HENRY STEDMAN & JOEL NEWTON

TRAILBLAZER PUBLICATIONS

Contents

PART 4: ROUTE GUIDE AND MAPS

APPENDICES

Contents

ABOUT THIS BOOK

This guidebook contains all the information you need. The hard work has been done for you so you can plan your trip from home without the usual pile of books, maps and guides.

When you're all packed and ready to go, there's comprehensive public transport information to get you to and from the trail and 88 detailed route maps and 29 town plans to help you find your way along it.

The guide includes:

● All standards of accommodation with reviews of campsites, hostels, B&Bs, guesthouses and hotels
● Walking companies if you want an organised tour and baggage-carrying services if you just want your luggage carried
● Itineraries for all levels of walkers
● Answers to all your questions: when to go, degree of difficulty, what to pack, and how much the whole walking holiday will cost
● Walking times in both directions and GPS waypoints
● Cafés, pubs, tearooms, takeaways, restaurants and shops for buying supplies
● Rail, bus and taxi information for all places along the path
● Street plans of the main towns both on and off the path
● Historical, cultural and geographical background information

MINIMUM IMPACT FOR MAXIMUM INSIGHT

Man has suffered in his separation from the soil and from other living creatures ... and as yet he must still, for security, look long at some portion of the earth as it was before he tampered with it. **Gavin Maxwell**, *Ring of Bright Water*, 1960

Why is walking in wild and solitary places so satisfying? Partly it is the sheer physical pleasure: sometimes pitting one's strength against the elements and the lie of the land. The beauty and wonder of the natural world and the fresh air restore our sense of proportion and the stresses and strains of everyday life slip away. Whatever the character of the countryside, walking in it benefits us mentally and physically, inducing a sense of well-being, an enrichment of life and an enhanced awareness of what lies around us.

All this the countryside gives us and the least we can do is to safeguard it by supporting rural economies, local businesses, and low-impact methods of farming and land-management, and by using environmentally sensitive forms of transport – walking being pre-eminent.

In this book there is a detailed and illustrated chapter on the wildlife and conservation of the region and a chapter on minimum-impact walking, with ideas on how to tread lightly in this fragile environment; by following its principles we can help to preserve our natural heritage for future generations.

INTRODUCTION

This book covers the last 217¼ miles (350km) of the South-West Coast Path (SWCP), Britain's longest national trail. The walk described begins on the Devon–Cornwall border, at Plymouth and, having navigated Devon's entire southern coastline, enters the **This book covers the last 217¼ miles of the 630-mile South-West Coast Path** county of Dorset at Lyme Regis, before finishing at South Haven Point, overlooking Poole Harbour. Together with the two other books in this series, the entire 630 miles of the SWCP is covered.

There are few, if any, stretches of the British coastline that can offer the walker such variety, such interest – and such beauty – as this third and final leg of the coast path. From sun-drenched promenades to wild, remote cliff-tops, through ancient 'apple-pie' villages, tiny thatched hamlets and smart, friendly Georgian resorts, this path has it all. Indeed it is difficult to think of another section of any national trail that so comprehensively lives up to that well-worn cliché of the travel industry: that there is something for everyone. For historians the trail begins – most appropriately, given the many

The most photographed milepost in the UK? On the way to Lulworth Cove.

On the coast path in South Devon, looking west towards East Prawle, near Start Point.

famous journeys that have departed from the same spot – at the Mayflower Steps, in Plymouth's timeless Barbican district, and passes through such fascinating towns as medieval Dartmouth, home to the UK's only Royal Naval college, and Teignmouth, the last place in mainland England to be successfully invaded by a foreign power. Castles, caves, barrows, burial mounds, ships, stone circles, historic harbours and old hostelries – all lie on the path, and all offer something to intrigue and captivate the history buff.

Similarly, geologists also have plenty that they'll find engrossing – and indeed you don't need to be an expert in stone or strata to enjoy them. Not only is the English Riviera (see box p153) the home of a Global Geopark but across the River Exe there's The Jurassic Coast World Heritage Site, where the very rocks you step on can take you on a 185-million-year geological journey. Steep and precipitous cliffs of orange, grey and white change their hue with each passing geological era; and if these don't 'rock' your world, within these very cliffs are the fossils of strange and unfamiliar beasts that once dominated the Earth: a long-vanished land of soaring pterodactyls rather than swooping peregrines, where plesiosaurus, not porpoise, cruised the seas, and the endemic scelidosaurus once roamed where sheep now ruminate.

The wildlife of today is not without its merits either, from the lovely deer of Lulworth to otters in Axmouth. And while man has done more than his fair share of shaping and utilising the land you pass through, he has also been careful to protect it too, with numerous Sites of Special Scientific Interest, several nature reserves and no fewer than three Areas of Outstanding Natural Beauty – with each encompassing mile after mile of epic panoramas, jagged sea stacks, and bountiful, beckoning beaches. There are also such spectacular delights as the curious Undercliffs, moulded by landslides and decorated by the free hand of nature into a truly English jungle; the south coast's highest point, Golden Cap; and the iconic natural architecture of Durdle Door, Stair Hole and Lulworth Cove.

But if all the above sounds a bit too worthy, for those after less cerebral pleasures the path also cuts through such quintessential seaside resorts as Exmouth, Sidmouth and the English Riviera (Torquay, Paignton and Brixham) – a land of doughnuts and dodgems, arcades and amusements, candy floss and crazy golf.

Another joy of the coast path is the food, with fish in Brixham so fresh you can taste the salt of the ocean. Crab sandwiches, pints of real ale and cream teas galore can be savoured all along the path, especially in the thatched villages of Beer, Abbotsbury and West Lulworth, all of which prove that nature doesn't have the monopoly on beauty and defy you not to change your plans and spend a night in their cosy embrace.

Of course such rewards aren't gained without a fight, and there are a couple of tough stretches of walking that must be completed before you can say that you've conquered the path. But those of you who started in Minehead, the beginning of the SWCP, will know that, whatever the hardships faced, the treasures of this wonderful, endlessly fascinating path, are always – always! – worth any effort expended.

❏ The South-West Coast Path

Typing 'Minehead to South Haven Point, Dorset' into Googlemaps, reveals that travelling between the two can be completed in a matter of 3 hours 37 minutes by car, along a distance of 96.6 miles. Even walking, along the most direct route, takes only around 29 hours, so Googlemaps says, with the path an even shorter one at just 89.3 miles.

It is these two points that are connected by the South-West Coast Path (SWCP). This most famous – and infamous – of national trails is, however, a good deal longer than 89.3 miles. Though estimates as to its exact length vary – and to a large part are determined both by which of the alternative paths one takes at various stages and also by changes in the path caused by erosion and other factors – the most widely accepted estimate is that the path is about 630 miles (1014km) long.

So why, when you could walk from Minehead to South Haven Point in just 29 hours, do most people choose to take 6-8 weeks? The answer is simple: the SWCP is one of the most beautiful trails in the UK. Around 70% of those 630 miles are spent either in national parks or regions that have been designated an Area of Outstanding Natural Beauty. The variety of places crossed by the SWCP is extraordinary too: from sunkissed beaches to sandy burrows, holiday parks to fishing villages, esplanade to estuary, on top of windswept cliffs and under woodland canopy, the scenery that one travels through has to be the most diverse of any of the national trails. Maintaining such a monumental route is no easy task. A survey in 2000 stated that the trail could boast 2473 signposts and waymarks, 302 bridges, 921 stiles, and 26,719 steps. These figures are, of course, out of date now, though they do still give an idea of both how long the trail is and how much is involved in building and maintaining it to such a high standard. The task of looking after the trail falls to a dedicated team from the official body, Natural England (see p71). Another important organisation, and one that looks after the rights of walkers, is the South West Coast Path Association (see p46), a charity that fights for improvements to the path and offers advice, information and support to walkers. They also campaign against many of the proposed changes to the path, and help to ensure that England's right-of-way laws which ensure that the footpath is open to the public – even though it does, on occasion, pass through private property – are fully observed. *(cont'd overleaf)*

❏ The South-West Coast Path *(cont'd from p9)*

History of the path

In 1948 a government report recommended the creation of a footpath around the entire South-West peninsula to improve public access to the coast which, at that time, was pretty dire. It took until 1973 for the Cornwall Coast Path to be declared officially open and another five years for the rest of the South-West Coast Path to be completed. The section covered in this book, Dorset & South Devon, is the third part that most coastal walkers complete, though it was one of the earliest sections opened to the public, back in 1974.

The origins of the path, however, are much older than its official designation. Originally, the paths were established – or at least adopted, there presumably being coastal paths from time immemorial that connected the coastal villages – by the local coastguards in the 19th century, who needed a path that hugged the shoreline closely to aid them in their attempts to spot and prevent smugglers from bringing contraband into the country. The coastguards were unpopular in the area as they prevented the locals from exploiting a lucrative if illegal activity, to the extent that it was considered too dangerous for them to stay in the villages; as a result, the authorities were obliged to build special cottages for the coastguards that stood (and, often, still stand) in splendid isolation near the path – but well away from the villages.

The lifeboat patrols also used the path to look out for craft in distress (and on one famous occasion used the path to drag their boat to a safe launch to rescue a ship in distress). When the coastguards' work ended in 1856, the Admiralty took over the task of protecting England's shoreline and thus the paths continued to be used.

The route – Minehead (Somerset) to Poole Harbour (Dorset)

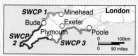

The SWCP officially begins at Minehead in Somerset (its exact starting point marked by a sculpture that celebrates the trail), heads west right round the bottom south-west corner of Britain then shuffles back along the south coast to South Haven Point, overlooking Poole Harbour in Dorset.

On its lengthy journey around Britain's south-western corner the SWCP crosses national parks such as Exmoor as well as regions that have been designated Areas of Outstanding Natural Beauty (including North, South and East Devon AONB and the Cornwall and Dorset AONBs) or Sites of Special Scientific Interest (Braunton Burrows being just one example – an area that also enjoys a privileged status as a UNESCO Biosphere Reserve), and even two UNESCO World Heritage sites: the Jurassic Coast of East Devon and Dorset, and the old mining landscape of Cornwall and West Devon. Other features passed on the way include the highest cliffs on mainland Britain (at Great Hangman – also the highest point on the coast path at 318m/1043ft, with a cliff-face of 244m), the largest sand-dune system in England (at Braunton Burrows), England's most westerly point (at Land's End) and Britain's most southerly (at the Lizard), the 18-mile barrier beach of Chesil Bank, one of the world's largest natural harbours at Poole, and even the National Trust's only official naturist beach at Studland!

The path ends at South Haven Point, its exact finish marked by a second SWCP sculpture. The path also takes in four counties – Somerset, Devon, Cornwall and Dorset – and connects with over 15 other long-distance trails; the southern section from Plymouth to Poole also forms part of the 3125-mile long European E9 Coastal Path that runs on a convoluted route from Portugal to Estonia.

How difficult is the path?

INTRODUCTION

The South-West Coast Path is just a (very, very) long walk, so there's no need for crampons, ropes, ice axes, oxygen bottles or any other climbing paraphernalia, because there's no climbing involved. All you need to complete the walk is some suitable clothing, a bit of money, a rucksack full of determination and a half-decent pair of calf muscles.

The part of the SWCP that is covered by this book is perhaps the one with the most variety. Topographically speaking, there are plenty of steep ups-and-downs as well as large flat areas of walking on seaside promenades. While the Riviera (see box p153) provides walkers with an unbroken swathe of civilisation, this book is bookended by two remote sections where settlements are scarce and amenities are few and far between. These two sections, from Mount Batten Point to Salcombe and from Lulworth Cove to Swanage, require a little advanced planning to ensure you have something to eat and somewhere to rest your head for the night. Still, with the path well signposted (see p12) all the way along and the sea keeping you company for the entire stretch, it's difficult to get lost (though it's always a good idea to take a compass or GPS unit, just in case).

As with any walk, you can minimise the risks by preparing properly. Your greatest danger on the walk is likely to be from the weather, which can be so unpredictable in this corner of the world, so it is vital that you dress for inclement conditions and always carry a set of dry clothes with you. Not pushing yourself too hard is important too, as over-exertion leads to exhaustion and all its inherent dangers (see pp66-9), so plan an itinerary that matches your abilities rather

---

Walking the South-West Coast Path

In terms of difficulty, there are those people who, having never undertaken such a trail before, are under the illusion that coastal walking is a cinch; that all it involves is a simple stroll along mile after mile of golden, level beach, the walker needing to pause only to kick the sand out from his or her flipflop or buy another ice cream.

The truth, of course, is somewhat different, for coastal paths tend to stick to the cliffs above the beaches rather than the beaches themselves (which is actually something of a relief, given how hard it is to walk across sand or shingle). These cliffs make for some spectacular walking but – given the undulating nature of Britain's coastline, and the fact the course of the SWCP inevitably crosses innumerable river valleys, each of which forces the walker to descend rapidly before climbing back up again almost immediately afterwards – some exhausting walking too. Indeed, it has been estimated that anybody who completes the entire SWCP will have climbed more than four times the height of Everest (35,031m to be precise, or 114,931ft) by the time they finish!

Given these figures, it is perhaps hardly surprising that most people take around eight weeks to complete the whole route, and few do so in one go; indeed, it is not unusual for people to take years or even decades to complete the whole path, taking a week or two here and there to tackle various sections until the whole trail is complete.

INTRODUCTION

Signposting is good: look for the acorn symbol

than your (over-) ambitions. In terms of orientation, the South-West Coast Path is very well signposted, so you shouldn't lose your way. However, we think that the distances the signposts have written on them can be of questionable accuracy and so not always to be trusted; indeed sometimes even the spelling on the signposts is wrong ('Porlock Wier' is one spelling we saw more than once). But in terms of helping you find your way, the signposts on the SWCP do a terrific job and the trail authorities are to be congratulated both on this and on the maintenance of the trail in general.

Golden Cap (see p248), at 191m (627ft) the highest point on the south coast of England.

INTRODUCTION

How long do you need?

People take an average of around 18 days to complete the walk; count on three weeks in total to give you time to travel there and back. Of course, if you're fit there's no reason why you can't go a little faster, if that's what you want to do, and finish the walk in 15 days

People take an average of around 18 days to complete the walk

or even less, though you will end up having a different sort of trek from most of the other people on the trail. For whilst theirs is a fairly relaxing holiday, yours will be more of a sport. What's more, you won't have much time to laze in the sun on the beaches, scoff scones in tearooms, visit an attraction or two, or sup local beers under the shade of a pub parasol – which does rather beg the question as to why you've come here in the first place!

There's nothing wrong with this approach, of course – *chacun à son goût*, as the French probably say. However, what you **mustn't do is try to push yourself too fast, or too far.** That road leads only to exhaustion, injury or, at the absolute least, an unpleasant time.

When deciding how long to allow for the trek, those intending to camp and carry their own luggage

See pp33-4 for some suggested itineraries covering different walking speeds

shouldn't underestimate just how much a heavy pack can slow them down. On pp33-4 there are some suggested itineraries covering different walking speeds. If you have only a few days, don't try to walk it all; concentrate instead on one area such as the coast path through Dorset, the Riviera (see box p153), or the less demanding section from Plymouth to Salcombe or Dartmouth.

When to go

SEASONS

'My shoes are clean from walking in the rain.' **Jack Kerouac**

Britain is a notoriously wet country and South-West England does nothing to crush that reputation. Few walkers manage to complete the walk without suffering at least one downpour; two or three per walk are more likely, even in summer. That said, it's equally unlikely that you'll spend a week in the area and not see any sun at all, and even the most cynical of walkers will have to admit that, during the **walking season** at least, there are more sunny days than showery ones.

The season, by the way, starts at Easter and builds to a crescendo in August, before steadily tailing off in October. Few people attempt the entire path after the end of October though there are still plenty of people on day walks. Many places close in November for the winter.

There is one further point to consider when planning your trip. Firstly, remember that most people set off on the trail at a weekend. This means that you'll find the trail quieter **during the week** and as a consequence you may find it easier to book accommodation.

Spring

Find a dry fortnight in springtime (around the end of March to mid-June) and you're in for a treat. The wild flowers are coming into bloom, lambs are skipping in the meadows and the grass is green and lush.

Of course, finding a dry week in spring is not easy but occasionally there's a mini-heatwave at this time. Another advantage with walking at this time is that there will be fewer walkers and finding accommodation is relatively easy, though do check that the hostels and B&Bs are open. Easter is the exception; the first major holiday in the year when people flock to the coast.

Summer

Summer, on the other hand, can be a bit *too* busy, at least in the towns and tourist centres, and over a weekend in August can be both suffocating and insufferable. Still, the chances of a prolonged period of sunshine are of course higher at this time of year than any other, the days are longer, and all the facilities and public transport are operating. Our advice is this: if you're flexible and want to avoid seeing too many people on the trail, avoid the school holidays, which basically means ruling out the tail end of July, all of August and the first few days of September. Alternatively, if you crave the company of other walkers, summer will provide you with the opportunity of meeting plenty, though do remember that you **must book your accommodation in advance**, especially if staying in B&B-style accommodation. Despite the higher than average chance of sunshine, take clothes for any eventuality – it will probably still rain at some point.

Autumn

September is a wonderful time to walk; many tourists have returned home and the path is clear. The weather is usually reliably sunny too, at least at the beginning of September, though we admit we don't have any figures to back this claim. The first signs of winter will be felt in October but there's nothing really to deter the walker. In fact there's still much to entice you, such as the colours of the heathland, which come into their own in autumn; a magnificent blaze of brilliant purples and pinks, splashed with the occasional yellow flowers of gorse (it is more usual in spring but can thrive in autumn). By the end of October, however, the weather will begin to get a little wilder and the nights will start to draw in. Most campsites and some B&Bs and hostels may close.

Winter

November can bring crisp clear days which are ideal for walking, although you'll definitely feel the chill when you stop on the cliff tops for a break. Winter temperatures rarely fall below freezing but the incidence of gales and storms definitely increases. You need to be fairly hardy to walk in December and January and you may have to alter your plans

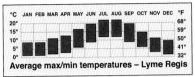

Average max/min temperatures – Lyme Regis

because of the weather. By February the daffodils and primroses are already appearing but even into March it can still be decidedly chilly if the sun is not out.

While winter is definitely the low season with many places closed, this can be more of an advantage than a disadvantage. Very few people walk at this time of year, giving you long stretches of the trail to yourself. When you do stumble across other walkers they are as happy as you to stop and chat. Finding B&B accommodation is easier as you will rarely have to book more than a night ahead (though it is still worth checking in advance as some B&Bs close out of season), but if you are planning to camp, or are on a small budget, you will find places to stay much more limited.

WEATHER

Before departing on your walk, tell yourself this: at some point on my walk it is going to **rain**. That's not to say it will, but at least if it does you won't be too disappointed and will hopefully have come prepared for this, clothes-wise. Besides,

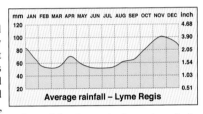

Average rainfall – Lyme Regis

walking in the rain can be fun, at least for a while: the gentle drumming of rain on hood can be quite relaxing, the path is usually quiet, and if it really does chuck it down at least it provides an excuse to linger in tearooms and have that extra scone. And as long as you dress accordingly and take note of the safety advice given on pp66-9, walking in moderate rain is no more dangerous than walking at any other time – though do be careful, particularly on exposed sections, if the path becomes slippy or the wind picks up.

DAYLIGHT HOURS

If walking in winter, autumn or even early spring, you must take account of how far you can walk in the available light. It won't be possible to cover as many miles as you would in summer. Conversely, in the summer months there is enough available light until at least 9pm –

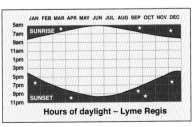

Hours of daylight – Lyme Regis

so don't use that as an excuse for finishing your day's walk early! Remember, too, that you will get a further 30-45 minutes of usable light before sunrise and after sunset depending on the weather.

❏ FESTIVALS AND ANNUAL EVENTS

April
● **Budleigh Salterton Jazz Festival** (💻 www.budleighjazzfestival.org)

May
● **Dart Music Festival, Dartmouth** (💻 www.dartmusicfestival.co.uk)
● **Brixham Pirate & Shanty Festival** (💻 www.brixhampiratefestival.co.uk) Live music, historic re-enactments and possibly the 'biggest gathering of pirates'.
● **Lyme Regis Fossil Festival** (💻 www.fossilfestival.com; mostly free) A weekend of fossil-hunting walks, talks, displays and a fossil fair.
● **Lyme Regis Jazz Festival** (💻 www.lymeregisjazzfestival.co.uk)

June
● **Exmouth Festival** (💻 www.exmouthfestival.org.uk) Annual nine-day festival of music, theatre, film and dance, showcasing local talent.
● **Teignmouth Folk Festival** (💻 www.teignmouthfolk.co.uk)
● **Dawlish Arts Festival** (💻 www.dawlish.com/event/details?eventdateid=2528) Month-long festival of arts, crafts, theatre, classical music, gospel and jazz.
● **Shaldon Festival** (💻 www.shaldonfestival.co.uk) Weekend of classical music featuring established professionals as well as choral workshops for amateurs.
● **Wessex Folk Festival, Weymouth** (💻 www.wessexfolk.co.uk)

July
● **Barbican International Jazz & Blues Festival, Plymouth** (💻 www.barbicanjazz andbluesfestival.com) Held at the same time as the Plymouth Classic Boat Rally and Port of Plymouth Regatta.
● **Dorset Seafood Festival, Weymouth** (💻 www.dorsetseafood.co.uk)
● **Camp Bestival, Lulworth Castle** (💻 www.campbestival.net) Music, comedy and many other events held over a long weekend in late July.
● **Swanage Jazz Festival** (💻 www.swanagejazz.org).
● **Torbay Carnival, Paignton** (💻 www.torbaycarnival.com) Nine days of events including a procession, fireworks, classic car show.
● **Square and Compass Stone Carving Festival, Worth Matravers** (☎ 01929-439229, 💻 www.squareandcompasspub.co.uk) Over two weeks; runs into August.

August
● **British Firework Championships, Plymouth** (💻 www.britishfireworks.co.uk)
● **Sidmouth Folk Week** (💻 www.sidmouthfolkweek.co.uk)
● **Burton Bradstock Festival of Music & Art** (💻 www.burtonbradstockfestival.com)

September
● **Budleigh Salterton Literary Festival** (💻 www.budlitfest.org.uk)
● **Swanage Folk Festival** (💻 www.swanageff.co.uk) Annual shindig with numerous musicians, dance & music workshops.
● **Agatha Christie Festival** (💻 www.englishriviera.co.uk/agathachristie/agatha-christie-festival) Week-long celebration of the author's works in and around Torquay.

October
● **Dartmouth Food Festival** (💻 www.dartmouthfoodfestival.com)
● **Torbay Festival of Poetry** (💻 www.torbaypoetryfestival.co.uk) Torquay & Brixham.
● **Beer Rhythm & Blues Festival** (💻 www.steppinout.info)

November
● **Teignmouth Jazz Festival** (💻 www.teignmouthjazz.org)

PLANNING YOUR WALK

1

Practical information for the walker

ROUTE FINDING

For most of its length the coast path is well signposted. At confusing
junctions the route is usually indicated by a finger-post sign with

'coast path' written on it. At other points,
where there could be some confusion,
there are wooden waymark posts with an
acorn symbol and a yellow arrow to indicate in which direction you should head.
The waymarking is the responsibility of
the local authorities along the trail who have a duty to maintain the
path. Generally they do a good job but occasionally you will come
across sections of the trail where waymarking is ambiguous, or even
non-existent, but with the detailed trail maps and directions in this
book and the fact that you always have the sea to one side it would
be hard to get really lost.

Using GPS with this book

Given the above, modern Wainwrights may scoff while more open-
minded walkers will accept that GPS technology can be an inexpen-
sive, well-established if non-essential, navigational aid. In no time at
all a GPS receiver with a clear view of the sky will establish your
position and altitude in a variety of formats, including the British OS
grid system, to within a few metres.

The maps in the route guide include numbered waypoints; these
correlate to the list on pp325-7, which gives the latitude/longitude
position in a decimal minute format as well as a description. Where
the path is vague, or there are several options, you will find more
waypoints. You can download the complete list of these waypoints
for free as a GPS-readable file (that doesn't include the text descriptions) from the Trailblazer website: 🖳 www.trailblazer-guides.com
(click on GPS waypoints).

It's also possible to buy state-of-the-art digital mapping to import
into your GPS unit, assuming that you have sufficient memory
capacity, but it's not the most reliable way of navigating and the
small screen on your pocket-sized unit will invariably fail to put
places into context or give you the 'big picture'.

Bear in mind that the vast majority of people who tackle this path do so perfectly well without a GPS unit. Instead of rushing out to invest in one, consider putting the money towards good-quality footwear or waterproofs instead.

ACCOMMODATION

The trail guide (Part 4) lists a fairly comprehensive selection of places to stay along the length of the trail. You have three main options: camping, using B&Bs/guesthouses/hotels, or staying in hostels and bunkhouses/camping barns. Few people stick to just one of these options the whole way, preferring, for example, to camp most of the time but spend every third night in a guesthouse, or perhaps use hostels where possible (as there are only a few on this stretch of the path) but splash out on a B&B where necessary.

Note that when booking accommodation that is far from the path, remember to ask if a pick-up and drop-off service is available (usually only B&Bs provide this service); at the end of a tiring day it's nice to know a lift is available to take you to your accommodation rather than having to traipse another two or three miles off the path to get to your bed for the night. (This is particularly true at the beginning of the walk, around Wembury/Hope, and even more so at the end around Lulworth Cove/Kimmeridge, where there are only a few B&Bs and they are usually a fair walk from the path – and the walking is arduous enough as it is on this section!)

The facilities' table on pp38-9 provides a quick snapshot of what type of accommodation is available in each of the towns and villages along the way, while the tables on p33-4 provide some suggested itineraries. The following is a brief introduction to what to expect from each type of accommodation.

Camping

There are campsites all the way along the South-West Coast Path. That said, there are few people who choose to camp every night on the trail. You're almost bound to get at least one night where the rain falls relentlessly, soaking equipment and sapping morale, and it is then that most campers opt to spend the next night drying out in a hostel or B&B. There are, however, many advantages with camping. It's more economical, for a start, with many campsites charging somewhere around £5-10pp (though we have found places that charge £40 in high season, with a three-night minimum stay over bank holiday weekends too!). There's rarely any need to book either, except possibly in the very high season, and even then you'd be very unlucky not to find somewhere.

Campsites vary; some are just a quiet corner of a farmer's field, while others are full-blown holiday parks with a few spaces put aside for tents. Showers are usually available, occasionally for a fee though more often than not for free. Note that **wild camping** (ie not in a regular campsite) is not allowed.

Camping is not an easy option; the route is wearying enough without carrying your accommodation around with you. Should you decide to camp, therefore, we advise you to look into employing a baggage-carrying company (see p28), though this does, of course, mean it will cost more and that you will lose a certain amount of freedom as you have to tell the company, at least a day before, of your next destination – and stick to it – so that you and your bag can be reunited every evening.

Bunkhouses
The term 'bunkhouse' can mean many different things, though usually it's nothing more than a converted barn in a farmer's field with a couple of wooden benches to sleep on. Sleeping bags are usually necessary in these places. While not exactly the lap of luxury, a night in a bunkhouse is probably the nearest non-campers will get to sleeping outside, while at the same time providing campers with shelter from the elements should the weather look like taking a turn for the worse. Some of the better bunkhouses provide a shower and simple kitchen with running water and perhaps a kettle, and occasionally pots, pans, cutlery and crockery.

There is only one **bunkhouse** close to this stretch of the SWCP, at East Soar Farm near Salcombe – though there are rumours of a camping barn being built at Bigbury-on-Sea. (Weymouth's Bunkhouse Plus is excluded, as this, in all honesty, is more of a hostel than anything else.)

Hostels
It isn't really feasible to plan to stay in a hostel every night on this walk as there are only three independent hostels (Plymouth, Weymouth and Swanage) and five **YHA hostels** (at Salcombe, Beer, Portland, West Lulworth and Swanage). However, they are worth considering, especially as they are good places to meet fellow walkers, swap stories and compare blisters.

If you associate YHA hostels with cold, crowded dorms, uncomfortable beds and lousy food be prepared to think again. Many hostels provide good meals (breakfast is usually served 7.30-9am and evening meals 6-8pm) and a number are also licensed, but if you prefer to self-cater most have a fully equipped kitchen and some have a shop selling emergency groceries, snacks and souvenirs. In addition they now have a whole range of additional facilities from drying rooms to televisions and internet access.

Dorms usually have bunk beds sleeping 4-6 people but a couple of hostels on this route have 2-bedded rooms. Toilet and shower facilities are still shared (few hostels have a bath) but YHA Beer has a 6-bedded room that is en suite.

The curfew (usually 11pm) is annoying but many YHA hostels now utilise access codes on their doors to offer residents more freedom.

Most of the hostels on this path are open all year but in the winter months at certain times YHA Beer, Lulworth Cove, Portland and Swanage are only open to prebooked sole-use groups. In fact at any time of the year they may be fully booked with schools or other groups so contact the YHA or the relevant hostel to check the situation. Finally, the cost of staying in a hostel (£16-23pp; with a £3 per night discount for members) is in most instances not that much cheaper than staying in a B&B, especially once breakfast has been added on.

Booking a hostel Despite the name, anybody of any age can join the YHA. This can be done at any hostel or by contacting the **Youth Hostels Association of England and Wales** (☎ 01629-592700, ☎ 0800-019 1700, 🖥 www.yha.org.uk).

Membership costs £15.95 per year (£9.95 for anyone under 26; small discounts if paying by direct debit). Having secured your membership, YHA hostels are easy to book, either online or by ringing each hostel direct.

Bed and breakfast accommodation

Bed and Breakfasts (**B&Bs**) are a great British institution and many of those along the South-West Coast Path are absolutely charming. Nearly all the B&Bs on this route have either en suite rooms or rooms with private facilities. (In this book we have stated where a B&B has rooms with shared facilities, so rare are they on the trail.)

The rooms usually contain either a double bed (known as a double room), or two single beds (known as a twin room, though these are sometimes pushed together to create a double bed). Triple rooms are for three people and family rooms are for three or more. Triple/family rooms usually contain a double bed and either a single bed or a bunk bed; occasionally there are three or four single beds.

Note that in winter some B&Bs close; for those that stay open, make sure beforehand that they will have their heating in your room turned on!

An evening meal (usually around £15-20) is often provided at the more remote or bigger places, at least if you book in advance. (Note that if you have

PLANNING YOUR WALK

❏ **Should you book your accommodation in advance?**
When walking any section of the South-West Coast Path it's essential that you have your night's accommodation booked by the time you set off in the morning, whether you're planning to stay in a hostel or a B&B. Nothing is more deflating than to arrive at your destination at the day's end only to find that you've then got to walk a further five miles or so, or even take a detour, because everywhere is booked. For this reason, it would pay to cast an eye over the list of festivals and events (see box pp15-16) in towns and villages on the path as accommodation will be particularly hard to find at those times. Note that, as well as the annual events mentioned, a number of the towns, especially those near estuaries such as Dartmouth, host regattas, during which time they can also become very busy.

Outside the high season (ie the summer period coinciding with the long school holidays in the UK), and particularly in April/May or September, as long as you're flexible and willing to take what's offered, with maybe even a night or two in a hostel if that's all there is, you should get away with booking **B&B-style accommodation** just a few nights in advance, or indeed just the night before. If planning to walk in the high season (and also over a weekend) you should book as soon as you can, especially if you want to stay in a particular place. However, many places don't accept advance bookings for one night in the peak season/weekends so actually for this route it may be hard to book in advance for a single-night stay; it would only be possible for two nights or more.

If planning to stay in **hostels**, it's worth checking in advance that they will be open, though most on this route are open all year. It's also well worth phoning at least one night before, and well before that if it's a weekend or the peak season, to make sure the hostel isn't fully booked.

Campers, however, have more flexibility and can often just turn up and find a space there and then, though ringing in advance can't hurt.

any dietary requirements – eg if you're vegetarian, or have to have a gluten-free diet – you need to tell the B&B owner beforehand!) Alternatively, if you want to eat out, there's nearly always a pub or restaurant nearby or, if it's far, the B&B owner may give you a lift to and from the nearest place with food.

The difference between a B&B and a **guesthouse** is minimal, though some of the better guesthouses are more like hotels, offering evening meals and a lounge for guests. **Pubs** and **inns** also offer bed and breakfast accommodation and prices are no more than in a regular B&B.

Hotels usually *do* cost more than B&Bs, however, and some might be a little incensed with a bunch of smelly trekkers turning up and treading mud into their carpet. Most on the South-West Coast Path, however, are used to seeing trekkers and welcome them warmly.

Rates Proprietors quote their **tariffs** either on a **per person** (pp) basis or **per room**, assuming two people are sharing; rates are also sometimes given for single occupancy of a room where there are no single rooms.

Accommodation in this guide starts at around £20pp for the most basic B&Bs rising to around £50pp for the most luxurious places. Most charge around £25-35pp. Rates in hotels start at around £35pp; however, sometimes they don't include breakfast.

Solo walkers should note: single rooms are not easy to find and you will often end up in a double/twin room and are likely therefore to have to pay a single occupancy supplement (£5-15), or even the full room rate in peak season.

Some places have their own website and offer online/email **booking** but for the majority you will need to phone. Most places ask for a deposit (about 50%) which is generally non-refundable if you cancel at short notice. Some places may charge 100% if the booking is for one night only; they may also charge a single-night supplement or require a stay of at least two nights. Always let the owner know as soon as possible if you have to cancel your booking so they can offer the bed to someone else.

Larger places take credit or debit cards. Most smaller B&Bs only accept cheques by post or payment by bank transfer for the deposit; the balance can be settled with cash or a cheque.

FOOD AND DRINK

Stay in a B&B and you'll be filled to the gills with a cooked **English breakfast**. This usually consists of a bowl of cereal followed by a plateful of eggs, bacon, sausages, mushrooms, tomatoes and possibly baked beans or black pudding, with toast and butter, and all washed down with coffee, tea and/or juice. Enormously satisfying the first time you try it, by the fourth or fifth morning you may start to prefer a lighter continental breakfast.

If you have had enough of these cooked breakfasts and/or plan an early start, ask if you can have a packed lunch instead of breakfast. Your landlady or hostel can usually provide a **packed lunch** at an additional cost (unless it's in lieu of breakfast), though of course there's nothing to stop you preparing your own lunch (a penknife will be essential), or going to a pub (see p22) or café.

PLANNING YOUR WALK

❏ **Traditional food in Devon and Dorset**
As a major centre of farming and fishing, it's not surprising that the South-West is an important supplier of food to the rest of Britain and can boast some pretty fine local specialities.

Say 'Devon' to most Brits and in addition to images of sparkling coastlines and rolling hills, the county's name will also conjure up the delights of **clotted cream** – best enjoyed as part of a traditional **cream tea** with a scone or two and some whortle-berry jam. This is certainly a speciality, **whortleberry** being the local name for the wild bilberry (though they go by several other names including blueberry, heidelber-ry, huckleberry, hurtleberry and wimberry) and locally they're called 'worts' or 'urts'.

Dairy products as a whole are plentiful in this corner of the country including delicious yoghurts and ice-cream. **Blue Vinney** is Dorset's most renowned cheese, best eaten with some **Dorset knob biscuits** (today made by only one producer, Moores Biscuits, in Bridport), or for something sweeter you could try **Dorset apple cake** – and, just to make sure that no artery is left unclogged, enjoy it with a dollop of Dorset clotted cream.

From the sea, **South Devon crab** is reputed to be the tastiest in the world and smoked eels are a speciality in these parts too. The county's mature farmhouse cheeses, ice-creams and cottage loaves ensure that, no matter how hard you push yourself on the walk, you won't lose too much weight. Even if you're on a tight budg-et the ubiquitous fish & chips can be satisfying if cooked with fresh fish. At the other end of the scale there are plenty of restaurants around the coast offering mouth-watering dishes concocted from locally caught fish.

Whatever you do for lunch, don't forget to leave some room for a **cream tea** (see box above) or two, a morale, energy and cholesterol booster all rolled into one delicious package. To describe it as simply a pot of tea accompanied by scones served and with cream and jam is to totally ignore the history, cere-mony and joy of this Titan of teatime. The jury is out on whether you should put the jam on first or the cream – but either way, do not miss the chance of at least one cream tea.

Pubs are as much a feature of the walk as seagulls and sheep, and in some cases the pub is as much a tourist attraction as any castle or cove. Most pubs have become highly attuned to the desires of trekkers and offer lunch and evening meals (often with a couple of local dishes and usually some vegetarian options), some locally brewed beers, a garden to relax in on hot days and a roar-ing fire to huddle around on cold ones. The standard of the food varies widely, though is usually served in big portions, which is often just about all trekkers care about at the end of a long day. In many of the villages the pub is the only place to eat out. Note that pubs may close in the afternoon, especially in the winter months, so check in advance if you are hoping to visit a particular one, and also if you are planning lunch there as food serving hours can change.

That other great British culinary institution, the **fish 'n' chip shop**, can be found in virtually every town on the trail.

As well as these, there are **restaurants** and **takeaways** in the larger towns en route and also in some of the villages.

Opening hours

The opening hours for pubs, restaurants and cafés mentioned in Part 4 are as accurate as possible but often if the weather is bad, or there is no demand, places will close early or not open at all so it is worth checking in advance, especially if there are few eating places in the area. See box p26.

Self-catering

There is a shop of some description in most of the places along the route, though most are small (and often combined with the post office) and whether you'll be able to find precisely what you went in for is uncertain. If self-catering, therefore, your menu for the evening will depend upon what you found in the store that day. Part 4 details what shops are on the path.

❏ **Recommended places for food and drink**
The following are some of our favourite cafés, pubs and tearooms on the route. It's by no means an exhaustive list – there are plenty of great ones we didn't include – but nevertheless we hope you find this list useful.

● **Slapton:** *The Queens Arms* Great walking food served up in a friendly atmosphere; the kind of pub in which strangers share stories of the road walked thus far.
● **Stoke Fleming:** *The Green Dragon* A wonderful spot for lunch or dinner; relax in the beer garden or allow yourself to sink into one of the sofas indoors.
● **Dartmouth**: *Dartmouth Castle Tearooms* Just a lovely location, especially early in the morning or late in the day when the crowds have gone.
● **Paignton:** *TJ's The Restaurant by The Harbour* Our favourite of the Riviera cafés, with nice views and an imaginative menu.
● **Exmouth:** *The Beach* Smashing food, great beers, dog friendly, right on the path... as one can imagine, a popular place!
● **Beer**: *Captain's Cottage* Lovely food and friendly, chatty people.
● **Seatown:** *The Anchor Inn* Worth a stop for its location alone!
● **Abbotsbury**: *Abbey House Tea Rooms* Just a lovely place to sit and watch the ducks while gorging on a delightful tea.
● **Weymouth:** *Sandsfoot Garden Café* After a long day's walk, a snack, lunch or simply a drink may be more than welcome at this peaceful little spot before you continue into Weymouth.
● **Osmington Mills:** *The Smugglers* With an SWCP sign right outside its front door, the beer garden is the perfect place to stop for lunch or a shandy as you contemplate the brutal ascents and descents that will most likely make up the rest of your day's journey to Lulworth.
● **West Lulworth:** *The Castle Inn* Ciders galore and a walker-friendly menu as well as a remarkable attitude towards dogs – humans are definitely an after-thought here – the only issue may be the wait for a table: get there early!
● **Kimmeridge:** *Clavell's* As pretty much the only place to eat for miles around you haven't much choice but to eat here – so thank goodness the menu's large and the food is good!
● **Worth Matravers:** *Square and Compass* Brimming with character as well as award-winning beers and ciders, well worth the short diversion from the coast.
● **Studland Beach**: *Joe's Café* Ramshackle, informal, and basic – but there's something lovely about drinking hot chocolate while curling your toes in the sand.

PLANNING YOUR WALK

Drinking water

Be careful: on a hot day in some of the remoter parts after a steep climb or two you'll quickly dehydrate, which is at best highly unpleasant and at worst mightily dangerous. Always carry some water with you and in hot weather drink 3-4 litres a day. Don't be tempted by the water in the streams; if the cow or sheep

❏ **LOCAL BEER AND CIDER**

Beer

The process of brewing beer is believed to have been in Britain since the Neolithic period and is an art local brewers have been perfecting ever since. Real ale is beer that has been brewed using traditional methods. Real ales are not filtered or pasteurised, a process which removes and kills all the yeast cells, but instead undergo a secondary fermentation at the pub which enhances the natural flavours and brings out the individual characteristics of the beer. It's served at cellar temperature with no artificial fizz added unlike keg beer which is pasteurised and has the fizz added by injecting nitrogen dioxide.

● **Devon** Devon is currently thought to have approximately 30 breweries and microbreweries operating within its borders. Amongst the more celebrated is the **Dartmoor Brewery** (🖳 www.dartmoorbrewery.co.uk), family owned, situated in the centre of the national park and the highest brewery in England (at 1400ft/427m above sea level). From this vantage point they brew their famous Jail Ale (4.8%), as well as Dartmoor IPA (4%). Closer to the coast at Honiton, **Otter Brewery** (🖳 www.otter brewery.com) produces five regular brews including Otter Ale (4.5%) and Otter Amber (4%) as well as speciality beers such as MacOtter (5%). Meanwhile, based near Kingsbridge, **South Hams Brewery** (🖳 www.southhamsbrewery.co.uk) brews, amongst others, Devon Pride (3.8%) and Wild Blonde (4.4%).

Located in Newton Abbot, **Teignworthy Brewery** (🖳 www.teignworthybrewery .com) produces six regular ales including Beachcomber (4.5%) and Reel Ale (4%) as well as a further 16 seasonal ales. For the brave, their dark Russian Imperial Porter is a staggering 13%! Based in Paignton and having begun brewing in 2007, products from **Bays Brewery** (🖳 www.baysbrewery.co.uk), such as Gold (4.3%) and Breaker (4.7%), can also be found in pubs and off-licences about the South-West. Dolphin Inn, Dartmouth, serves beers from its brewery – **Bridgetown Brewery** (🖳 www.ven ture-inns.com/the-brewery.html).

● **Dorset** Beer-o-philes are just as well catered for over the border in Dorset. Scattered along the coast path you will come across **Hall & Woodhouse** (🖳 www .hall-woodhouse.co.uk) pubs, which stock several of their own-brewed Badger Ales, including Tanglefoot (4.9%) and Badger First Gold (4%).

Beginning just over the Devon–Dorset border, Lyme Regis has two breweries: **Mighty Hop Brewery** (🖳 www.mightyhopbrewery.co.uk) and **Town Mill Brewery** (🖳 www.townmillbrewery.com). Both produce beers named after local landmarks such as the former's Golden Cap Bitter (4%) and the latter's Cobb (3.9%) and Black Ven (5%).

Heading east, **Palmers Brewery** (🖳 www.palmersbrewery.com), based in Bridport, has been perfecting ale for over 200 years. Calling on such experience they produce five fine ales including Palmers Best Bitter (4.2%), Dorset Gold (4.5%) and Tally Ho! (5.5%), which was first brewed in 1949. Weymouth's **Dorset Brewing Company**'s (🖳 www.dbcales.com) award-winning products include ales such as Durdle Door (5%), bitters such as Jurassic (4.2%), and even a lager titled Chesil (4.1%).

faeces in the water don't make you ill, the chemicals from the pesticides and fertilisers used on the farms almost certainly will.

Using iodine or another purifying treatment will help to combat the former, though there's little you can do about the latter. It's a lot safer to fill up from taps instead.

Still further east, **Art Brew** (🖥 www.artbrew.co.uk) is a 'boutique' brewery based near Chideock and produces Art Nouveau (3.9%) and the far stronger Monkey IPA (6.4%). They also produce a version of the latter that consists of adding root ginger and chilli to the cask: the results of which one can only imagine! Meanwhile, nearer to the end of your hike, in Swanage the small **Dorset Piddle Brewery** (🖥 www .dorsetpiddlebrewery.co.uk) produces Piddle (4.1%) as well as the lager-style Silent Slasher (5.1%); and with five core beers, The **Isle of Purbeck Brewery** (🖥 ja25 32.wix.com/purbeckbrewery) produces the ominously named Fossil Fuel (4.1%) as well as Purbeck IPA (4.8%).

Cider
A pint of cider on this section of the walk is pretty much as obligatory as blisters. **Scrumpy**, or rough cider, is a particular form of cider, easy to differentiate from the weaker, more mass-market keg ciders, being cloudy, fizz-free and with bits floating in it too! The only thing to remember before drinking scrumpy is that it should be done so in moderation – it's powerful stuff. After you've drunk it, you'll be lucky to remember anything at all.
● **Devon** Look out for products from **Sandford Orchards** (🖥 www.sandfordor chards.co.uk), such as the cloudy Devon Scrumpy (6%), and their biggest seller, the sparkling and clear Devon Red (4.5%), as well as the eponymous Hunt's Cider (6%), made at Hunt's Farm on the outskirts of Paignton.
● **Dorset** Meanwhile, from Dorset, keep a sober eye open for glasses full of fizz and froth that have emanated from **Dorset Cider Company** (🖥 www.dorsetcidercom pany.co.uk), including the dry Angels (6.7%), the medium Number 6 (6.5%), and the medium-sweet Smoke Oak (6.7%), all of which are made with at least 12 varieties of local apple, and also those fermented at **Marshwood Vale Cider** (🖥 www.marsh woodvalecider.com), such as, the bottled and sweet, Dorset Kingfisher (7%) and the medium Dorset Tit (7%).

A must for cider aficionados is **The Castle Inn** at Lulworth. Committed to supporting traditional local cider makers they stock 12 traditional draught ciders and perries (produced from perry pears as opposed to apples) from Dorset, Somerset, Hampshire and Herefordshire. Pressed and ripened in Dorset they stock the popular Cider by Rosie (6.5%; 🖥 www.ciderbyrosie.co.uk), whilst favourites from the surrounding counties include beverages produced by Westons Cider such as Westons Old Rosie Scrumpy (7.3%) and Westons Country Perry (4.5%) from Herefordshire, and the Light (4.2%), Dry and Medium (both 6%) ciders produced by Orchard Pig in Somerset.

The Square and Compass, Worth Matravers, is also very proud of the cider they stock, and with good reason. Brewed in their back garden, six ciders are available, the most popular – and produced with 15 types of apple – being, the sweet Kiss Me Kate, the medium Eve's Idea and the dry Sat Down Becider, percentage-wise, all of which vary, depending on the barrel (6-6.5%). They also produce three single variety – meaning that they have been produced from just the one type of apple – ciders.

MONEY

There are several **banks** on the trail, most equipped with an **ATM** (cash machine). You'll also find cash machines in many shops and stores though these tend to charge around £1.75-2 to withdraw money. The longest stretch without a cash machine is between Salcombe and Strete (which both have at least one ATM, though there is nothing in between them).

Another way of getting money in your hand is to use the **cashback** system: find a store that will accept a debit card and ask them to advance cash against the card.

PLANNING YOUR WALK

☐ **Information for foreign visitors**
● **Currency** The British pound (£) comes in notes of £100, £50, £20, £10 and £5, and coins of £2 and £1. The pound is divided into 100 pence (usually referred to as 'p', pronounced 'pee') which comes in silver coins of 50p, 20p, 10p and 5p, and copper coins of 2p and 1p.
● **Money** Up-to-date **rates of exchange** can be found on 🖳 www.xe.com/ucc, at some post offices, or at any bank or travel agent. **Travellers' cheques** are hardly used now but can be cashed only at banks, foreign exchanges and some of the large hotels; it is probably better to pay with a debit/credit card or cash.
● **Business hours** Most shops and main post offices are open at least from Monday to Friday 9am-5pm and Saturday 9am-12.30pm but many shops open earlier and close later, some open on Sunday as well. Occasionally, especially in rural areas, you'll come across a local shop that closes at midday during the week, usually a Wednesday or Thursday. Many supermarkets remain open 12 hours a day; the Spar chain usually displays '8 till late' on the door. Banks typically open at 9.30am Monday to Friday and close at 3.30pm or 4pm, but of course ATM machines are open all the time (if they are outside). Pub hours are less predictable; although many open daily 11am-11pm, often in rural areas, and particularly in winter months, opening hours are 11am-3pm and 6-11pm Monday-Saturday, 11am/noon-3pm and 7-11pm on Sunday. Last entry to tourist attractions is often an hour before the closing time.
● **National holidays** Most businesses in the South-West are shut on 1st January, Good Friday (March/April), Easter Monday (March/April), first and last Monday in May, last Monday in August, 25th December and 26th December.
● **School holidays** State-school holidays in England are generally as follows: a one-week break late October, two weeks over Christmas and the New Year, a week mid February, two weeks around Easter, one week at the end of May/early June (to coincide with the bank holiday at the end of May) and five to six weeks from late July to early September. Private-school holidays fall at the same time, but tend to be slightly longer.
● **Documents** If you are a member of a National Trust organisation in your country bring your membership card as you should be entitled to free entry to National Trust properties and sites in the UK.
● **EHICs and travel insurance** Although Britain's National Health Service (NHS) is free at the point of use, that is only the case for residents. All visitors to Britain should be properly insured, including comprehensive health coverage. The European Health Insurance Card (EHIC) entitles EU nationals (on production of the EHIC card so ensure you bring it with you) to necessary medical treatment under the NHS while on a temporary visit here. For details, contact your national social security institution.

However, with few local stores, pubs or B&Bs accepting credit or debit cards, and few places where you can get money out along the way, it is essential to carry plenty of **cash** with you, though do keep it safe and out of sight (preferably in a moneybelt).

A **chequebook** could prove very useful as back-up, so that you don't have to keep on dipping into your cash reserves, especially as most B&Bs don't accept credit/debit cards.

However, this is not a substitute for proper medical cover on your travel insurance for unforeseen bills and for getting you home should that be necessary.

Also consider cover for loss and theft of personal belongings, especially if you are camping or staying in hostels, as there will be times when you'll have to leave your luggage unattended.

● **Weights and measures** The European Commission is no longer attempting to ban the pint or the mile: so, in Britain, milk can be sold in pints (1 pint = 568ml), as can beer in pubs, though most other liquid including petrol (gasoline) and diesel is sold in litres. Distances on road and path signs will continue to be given in miles (1 mile = 1.61km) rather than kilometres, and yards (1yd = 0.9m) rather than metres. The population remains divided between those who still use inches (1 inch = 2.5cm), feet (1ft = 0.3m) and yards and those who are happy with millimetres, centimetres and metres; you'll often be told that 'it's only a hundred yards or so' to somewhere, rather than a hundred metres or so.

Most food is sold in metric weights (g and kg) but the imperial weights of pounds (lb: 1lb = 453g) and ounces (oz: 1oz = 28g) are frequently displayed too. The weather – a frequent topic of conversation – is also an issue: while most forecasts predict temperatures in Celsius (C), many people continue to think in terms of Fahrenheit (F; see the temperature chart on p15 for conversions).

● **Smoking** The ban on smoking in public places relates not only to pubs and restaurants, but also to B&Bs, hostels and hotels. These latter have the right to designate one or more bedrooms where the occupants can smoke, but the ban is in force in all enclosed areas open to the public – even if they are in a private home such as a B&B. Should you be foolhardy enough to light up in a no-smoking area, which includes pretty well any indoor public place, you could be fined £50, but it's the owners of the premises who carry the can if they fail to stop you, with a potential fine of £2500.

● **Time** During the winter, the whole of Britain is on Greenwich Mean Time (GMT). The clocks move one hour forward on the last Sunday in March, remaining on British Summer Time (BST) until the last Sunday in October.

● **Telephone** The international country access code for Britain is ☎ 44 followed by the area code minus the first 0, and then the number you require. Within Britain, to call a landline number with the same code as the landline phone you are calling from, the code can be omitted: dial the number only. If you're using a mobile phone that is registered overseas, consider buying a local SIM card to keep costs down. Sadly now many phone boxes don't accept coins; you will need to have a phone, or a debit, card.

● **Emergency services** For police, ambulance, fire or coastguard dial ☎ 999 or ☎ 112.

Getting cash at post offices

Several banks have agreements with the Post Office allowing customers to make cash withdrawals free of charge using a debit card at branches throughout the country. Given that many towns and villages have post offices but may not have banks, this is a very useful facility. However, check with the Post Office Helpline (☎ 08457-223344, 🖥 www.postoffice.co.uk) that the post offices en route are still open.

If using the website, go to 🖥 www.postoffice.co.uk/making-withdrawals-in-branch for a full list of participating banks and for a list of post office branches with an ATM.

OTHER SERVICES

There is **public internet access** in the libraries along the trail as well as in several shops and other private enterprises. Many pubs, restaurants and B&Bs also have wi-fi for those who've brought their own laptop and/or mobile phone. Towns have at least one **supermarket** and most villages have a **grocery store**. You'll usually find a **phone box** near these shops, though you will almost definitely need a phone card (or debit/credit card) as many phone boxes no longer accept coins.

There are **outdoor equipment shops** in Plymouth, Torquay, Exmouth, Sidmouth, Weymouth and Swanage.

WALKING COMPANIES

It is, of course, possible to turn up with your boots and backpack at Plymouth and just start walking, with little planned save for your accommodation (see box on p20). The following companies, however, are in the business of making your holiday as stress-free and enjoyable as possible.

Baggage carriers

For those who don't fancy being burdened while on the path, it is possible to arrange to have your luggage transferred to the end of each day's destination. The main baggage company on the SWCP is the aptly named **Luggage Transfers** (☎ 01326-567247, 🖥 www.luggagetransfers.co.uk), who cover the whole of the path. Rates depend on the distance by road but the minimum charge is £13 and this covers up to two bags.

Alternatively, some of the taxi companies listed in this guide can provide a similar service within a local area if you want a break from carrying your bags for a day or so. Also, don't rule out the possibility of your B&B/guesthouse owner taking your bags ahead for you; plenty of them are glad to do so. Depending on the distance they may make no charge at all, or charge £10-15; this may be less than a taxi so is worth enquiring about.

Self-guided holidays

Useful for those who simply don't have the time to organise their trip, several companies now offer what are known as self-guided holidays, where your accommodation, transport at the start/end of the walk and baggage transportation along the trail are arranged for you. Detailed information and maps are also provided as a matter of course, thereby allowing you to just turn up and start marching!

The companies below offer **tailor-made holidays** as well as the packages mentioned. It may also be possible to negotiate with these companies to see if they will provide just one or two parts of their service, such as transporting your luggage from one point to the next.

● **Budget Walking** (☎ 01326-565114, 🖳 www.budgetwalking.co.uk; Cornwall) Claim to be the cheapest self-guided walking holidays along the SWCP. They offer budget and standard holidays on the entire SWCP, and arrange dog-friendly walking too. They also provide an accommodation-booking service for a fee of £7pp per night. Their website also has good day-by-day descriptions.

● **Celtic Trails** (☎ 01291-689774, 🖳 www.celtic-trails.com; Chepstow) Long-established company that offers treks all over the UK including the SWCP, which they divide into nine sections. The path covered by this book is divided into four sections: Plymouth to Brixham (seven nights, six days), Brixham to Lyme Regis (seven nights, six days), Lyme Regis to Poole (eight nights, seven days) and Exmouth to Poole (ten nights, nine days).

● **Contours** (☎ 01629-821900, 🖳 www.contours.co.uk; Derbyshire) Provide holidays for the SWCP, just as they do for just about every national trail and long-distance path in the country. For the SWCP they divide the path into ten sections and offer treks from three days to four weeks and more. The section covered in this book is divided into four parts: South Devon (Plymouth to Brixham), Tor Bay and Babbacombe Bay (Brixham to Exmouth), East Devon (Exmouth to Lyme Regis) and Dorset (Lyme Regis to Poole).

● **Encounter Walking Holidays** (☎ 01208-871066, 🖳 encounterwalkingholidays.com; Cornwall) Organise everything for the walker operating on every section of the path including the South Dorset Ridgeway option. Short breaks and week-long holidays through to two-month treks. Will help everyone from individual walkers to large groups and specialise in assisting overseas walkers along the route

● **Explore Britain** (☎ 01740-650900, 🖳 www.explorebritain.com; Co Durham) Organises several treks around the South-West peninsula including Sidmouth to Portesham, a six-night, inn-to-inn walking tour including two nights at Lyme Regis. They also offer a seven-night six-day walk from Upwey, near Dorchester, to Bournemouth.

● **Footpath Holidays** (☎ 01985-840049, 🖳 www.footpath-holidays.com; Wiltshire) Operate a range of walking holidays including inn-to-inn holidays for the whole path and single-centre holidays from the Purbeck peninsula, Dartmouth and Sidmouth. They also offer short breaks or one-week holidays. Baggage transfer is included as part of inn-to-inn holidays.

● **Footscape** (☎ 0777-295 4454, 🖳 www.footscape.co.uk; Dorchester) Offer bespoke independent and vehicle-supported walking holidays along the Jurassic coast and through Dorset's Inland Heritage from two nights to two weeks.

PLANNING YOUR WALK

● **Jurassic Coast Tours & Holidays** (☎ 01297-24415, 🖳 www.jurassiccoast tours.com; Beer, Devon) Based at Belmont House (see pp226-7) in Beer, trips of between two and five days can be arranged covering the path between Exmouth and Lyme Regis. They also offer transfers from Exeter Airport and local railway stations. Caters for the discerning traveller, offers the true Devon experience. Strong local knowledge.

● **Let's Go Walking!** (☎ 01837-880075, 🖳 www.letsgowalking.com; North Tawton, Devon) Offer walks on several of the national trails but being based in Devon they have a good knowledge of the SWCP. Holidays (seven nights, six days) include Salcombe to Starcross, Exmouth to Weymouth, and Weymouth to South Haven Point.

● **Load Off Your Back** (🖳 www.loadoffyourback.co.uk; Herts) Part of Ramblers Worldwide Holidays; offer Exmouth to Lyme Regis in four nights, Lyme Regis to Weymouth in four nights, Exmouth to Poole in ten to eleven nights, Lyme Regis to Poole in seven nights.

● **Macs Adventure** (☎ 0141-530 8886, 🖳 www.macsadventure.com; Glasgow) Have walks covering the whole SWCP including Plymouth to Brixham, Exmouth to Lyme Regis, Lyme Regis to Poole, with varying itineraries to suit.

● **Sherpa Expeditions** (☎ 020-8577 2717, 🖳 www.sherpa-walking-holidays. co.uk; Middlesex) Offer eight-day holidays from Lyme Regis to Lulworth Cove.

● **South Devon Walking Holidays** (☎ 01752-897034, 🖳 www.southdevon walkingholidays.co.uk; Devon) Specialise in walks between Plymouth and Dartmouth. Holidays include Plymouth to Dawlish Warren for nine nights and Plymouth to Dartmouth for six nights.

● **The Discerning Traveller** (☎ 01865-515618, 🖳 www.discerningtraveller .co.uk; Oxford) Offer walks along what they consider to be the finest part of the East Devon and Dorset Coast Path National Trail from Exmouth to Lyme Regis and Exmouth to Lulworth Cove for five or eight nights. They also offer a separate 'Purbeck' tour between Lulworth Cove and Studland.

● **Westcountry Walking Holidays** (☎ 0845-094 3848, 🖳 www.westcountry-walking-holidays.com; Middlesex) Arrange tours from Plymouth to Seaton (approx eleven days) and Seaton to Poole Harbour (approx eight days) as well as short breaks (two nights) for any two consecutive stages of the SWCP. Families and people looking to walk with their dog(s) are welcome.

Group/guided walking tours

No matter how much information is provided by the self-guided companies – or indeed this book – the chances are you will learn and appreciate much more in the company of an experienced and knowledgeable guide. Guided walking tours are ideal for those who want the extra safety, security and companionship that comes with walking in a group.

Accommodation, meals, transport to and from the trail, baggage transfer – all of these are usually included in the price. Be warned, however, that the standards of accommodation, the distances walked each day and the age of the clients that companies attract often vary widely, so do check each company carefully to make sure you choose that one that is right for you.

● **Footpath Holidays** (see p29) Offer fully guided tours in South Devon.
● **HF Holidays** (☎ 0845-470 8558, 🖥 www.hfholidays.co.uk; Herts) Offer seven-night 'Dorset Coast Path' holidays walking along the Jurassic Coast, from the Golden Cap near Lyme Regis to Studland Bay, and also centre-based walking holidays from their country houses at Haytor and Lulworth Cove.
● **Trexx Walking Holidays** (☎ 01305-783129, 🖥 rob@trexx.co.uk; Weymouth), established in 2012, provides guided walks (Oct-Mar) led by the owner of The Esplanade (see p286), a local man who has been visiting the area's beauty spots all of his life. Two- or three-day tours are available covering the coast between Charmouth and Lulworth Cove (and including the South Dorset Ridgeway) although other sites can also be visited and itineraries can be tailor-made. Food, accommodation and transport back to the hotel each night are all taken care of for you. For up-to-date prices check the website.

Budgeting

England is not a cheap place to go travelling and the accommodation providers on the South-West Coast Path are more than used to seeing tourists and charge accordingly. You may think before you set out that you are going to try to keep your budget to a minimum by camping every night and cooking your own food but it's a rare trekker who sticks to this rule. Besides, the B&Bs and pubs on the route are amongst the path's major attractions and it would be a pity not to sample the hospitality in at least some of them.

   If the only expenses of this walk were accommodation and food, budgeting for the trip would be a piece of cake. Unfortunately, in addition there are all the little extras that push up the cost: beer, cream teas, stamps and postcards, internet use, buses here and there, baggage carriers, phone calls, laundry, film, souvenirs, entrance fees... it's surprising how much all of these things add up.

CAMPING

You can survive on less than £15 per person if you use the cheapest campsites, don't visit a pub, avoid all museums and tourist attractions, cook all your own food from staple ingredients and generally have a pretty miserable time of it. Even then, unforeseen expenses will probably nudge your daily budget above this figure. Include the occasional pint, and perhaps a pub meal every now and then, and the figure will be nearer £20-25 a day.

HOSTELS AND BUNKHOUSES

Rates at the hostels (both independent and YHA) en route range from £16pp to £23pp, though you may pay as little as £10pp when there's a special offer on. Breakfast at hostels is about £5 and a two-course evening meal (where available) may cost £8-15. The only bunkhouse charges £30pp including breakfast and supper.

This means that, overall, it can cost around £30-35 per day, or £40-50 to live in a little more comfort and enjoy the odd beer or two.

B&Bs, GUESTHOUSES AND HOTELS

B&B rates start at £20pp (based on two sharing) per night but can be twice this, particularly if you are walking by yourself and are thus liable to pay single supplements. Add on the cost of lunch and dinner and you should reckon on about £40-45 minimum per day. Staying in a guesthouse or hotel would probably push the minimum up to £55-60.

Itineraries

Part 4 of this book has been written from west to east, though there is of course nothing to stop you from tackling it in the opposite direction, and there are advantages in doing so – see below.

To help you plan your walk there is a **planning map** (opposite the inside back cover) and a **table of village/town facilities** (pp38-9), which gives a run-down on the essential information you will need regarding accommodation possibilities and services.

You could follow one of the suggested itineraries (see opposite) which are based on preferred type of accommodation and walking speeds or, if tackling the entire walk seems a bit ambitious, you can tackle it a day or two at a time. To help you, we discuss the highlights of the Dorset & South Devon Coast Path on pp35-6 and you can use public transport to get to the start and end of the walk. The public transport map and service details are on pp55-60.

Once you have an idea of your approach turn to Part 4 for detailed information on accommodation, places to eat and other services in each village and town on the route. Also in Part 4 you will find summaries of the route to accompany the detailed trail maps.

WHICH DIRECTION?

It's more common for walkers attempting the entire SWCP to start from Minehead and finish at South Haven Point and this is the way the route is described in Part 4. Furthermore, the prevailing wind usually comes from the west, so by walking in this direction you'll find you have the weather behind you, pushing you on rather than driving in your face. That said, if this is your first taste of the coast path – and you think you're going to continue one day and complete the rest of the 630-mile trek – you may prefer to start at South Haven Point and finish at Plymouth. Those who prefer to swim against the tide of popular opinion and walk east to west should find it easy to use this book too.

SUGGESTED ITINERARIES

The itineraries in the boxes below and on p34 are based on different accommodation types (camping and B&B-style accommodation), with each one divided into three alternatives depending on your walking speed. They are only suggestions so feel free to adapt them. **Don't forget** to add your travelling time before and after the walk.

CAMPING

	Relaxed		Medium		Fast	
Night	**Place**	**Approx Distance** miles/km	**Place**	**Approx Distance** miles/km	**Place**	**Approx Distance** miles/km
0	Plymouth		Plymouth		Plymouth	
1	Wembury*	10.75/17.25	Wembury*	10.75/17.25	Wembury*	10.75/17.25
2	Bigbury	15.25/24.5	Bigbury	15.25/24.5	Bigbury	15.25/24.5
3	South Sands[1]	11.5/18.5	South Sands[1]	11.5/18.5	East Prawle*	18.5/29.75
4	East Prawle *	7/11.25	East Prawle*	7/11.25	Stoke Flm'g	13.25/21.25
5	Slapton*	8.75/14	Stoke Fleming	13.25/21.25	Brixham*	15.25/24.5
6	Stoke Fleming	4.5/7.25	Brixham *	15.25/24.5	Shaldon	19.75/31.75
7	Brixham *	15.25/24.5	Torquay[2]	8.5/13.5	Budleigh Sn	13.5/21.75
8	Torquay[2]	8.5/13.5	Shaldon	11.25/18	Seaton*	17.25/27.75
9	Shaldon	11.25/18	Exmouth*	8/13	Seatown	14.25/23.25
10	Exmouth *	8/13	Budleigh Sn*	5.5/9	East Fleet	19.25/31
11	Budleigh Sn*	5.5/9	Beer[1]*	16/25.75	Fortuneswell[1*3]	16/25.75
12	Sidmouth*	7/11.25	Charmouth*	11.5/18.5	Durdle Door	16/25.75
13	Beer[1]*	9/14.5	West Bay*	7/11.25	Kimmeridge*	7.25/11.75
14	Charmouth*	11.5/18.5	East Fleet Farm	16.25/26	Swanage[1]*	13.5/21.75
15	West Bay	7/11.25	Fortuneswell[1]*	6.25/10	South Haven	7.5/12
16	Abbotsbury*	9.5/15	Weymouth*[3]	14.75/23.75		
17	East Fleet Farm	6.75/11	Durdle Door	11/17.75		
18	Fortuneswell[1]*	6.25/10	Kimmeridge*	7.25/11.75		
19	Fortuneswell[1*3]	9.75/15.75	Swanage[1]*	13.5/21.75		
20	Osmington M	9.75/15.75	South Haven	7.5/12		
21	Durdle Door	6.25/10				
22	Kimmeridge*	7.25/11.75				
23	Swanage[1]*	13.5/21.75				
24	South Haven	7.5/12				
	TOTALS	**217.25/350**		**217.25/350**		**217.25/350**

* On this chart we have **not** included in the mile counts the distance from the path to the campsite, which can be a mile or more. The campsites/hostels that are off the path are marked with an asterisk. Consult the route guide for distances. Remember to factor these into your walk when calculating the distance you will walk for any one stage.

[1] No campsite but there is a hostel.

[2] No campsite or hostel – night must be spent in a B&B.

[3] After Isle of Portland circuit.

PLANNING YOUR WALK

STAYING IN B&B-STYLE ACCOMMODATION

Night	Relaxed Place	Approx Distance miles/km	Medium Place	Approx Distance miles/km	Fast Place	Approx Distance miles/km
0	Plymouth		Plymouth		Plymouth	
1	Wembury	10.75/17.25	Wembury	10.75/17.25	Wembury	10.75/17.25
2	Bigbury	15.25/24.5	Bigbury	15.25/24.5	Bigbury	15.25/24.5
3	Hope Cove	5/8	Salcombe	13/21	Salcombe	13/21
4	Salcombe	8/13	Torcross	12.75/20.5	Stoke Fleming	18.75/30
5	Torcross	12.75/20.5	Dartmouth	10.25/16.5	Brixham	15.25/24.5
6	Dartmouth	10.25/16.5	Brixham	11/17.5	Maidencombe	16.5/26.5
7	Brixham	11/17.75	Torquay	8.5/13.75	Exmouth	11.25/18.25
8	Torquay	8.5/13.75	Teignmouth	11.25/18.25	Sidmouth	12.5/20
9	Teignmouth	11.25/18.25	Exmouth	8/13	Seaton	10.25/16.5
10	Exmouth	8/13	Sidmouth	12.5/20	Seatown	14.25/23.25
11	Budleigh Sn	5.5/9	Seaton	10.25/16.5	Abbotsbury	12.5/20
12	Sidmouth	7/11.25	Lyme Regis	7.25/11.75	Fortuneswell	13/21
13	Beer	8.75/14	West Bay	10/16	Weymouth	14.75/23.75
14	Lyme Regis	8.5/13.75	Abbotsbury	9.5/15.25	Lulworth	11/17.75
15	Seatown	7.25/11.5	Fortuneswell	13/21	Kimmeridge	7.25/11.75
16	Abbotsbury	12.5/20	Weymouth	14.75/23.75	Swanage	13.5/21.75
17	Ferrybridge*	11/17.75	Lulworth Cove	11/17.75	South Haven	7.5/12
18	Fortuneswell[1]	11.75/19	Kimmeridge	7.25/11.75		
19	Weymouth	5/8	Swanage	13.5/21.75		
20	Lulworth	11/17.75	South Haven	7.5/12		
21	Kimmeridge	7.25/11.75				
22	Swanage	13.5/21.75				
23	South Haven	7.5/12				
TOTALS	**217.25/350**		**217.25/350**		**217.25/350**	

* For bus to Weymouth/Fortuneswell
[1] From Ferrybridge via Isle of Portland Circuit

❏ Crossing rivers

As you may expect from a coastal walk, the path from Plymouth to Poole (particularly Plymouth to Exmouth) is interrupted fairly frequently by rivers that bisect the path on their way down to the sea. In summer, this is not a problem: the coast path uses ferries to cross these waterways which actually provide a welcome relief (and a sit-down!) from all your exertions. But walk outside the high season and it's a different story: in places, particularly at the beginning of the walk, the ferries do not run all year. In these instances, trekkers must either resort to the (often infrequent) public transport, or take a lengthy diversion inland to a point where the river can be crossed, then return to the coastline to pick up the path again. In this book we describe these alternative walking routes at the appropriate places in the guide – as well as looking at the public transport options. Remember to add extra days to your trek should you need to take any of these alternative routes.

THE BEST DAY AND WEEKEND WALKS

We think that this leg of the South-West Coast Path is the most varied of the three and thus deserves to be walked in its entirety. But, if you don't have the time for that, the following will allow you to savour at least some of the joys of this walk.

All the routes below are designed to link up with public transport (see pp55-60) at both their start and finish. The only section of the path that doesn't is Kimmeridge, which is annoying as it sits at the end of possibly the most spectacular stage, over the Lulworth Ranges. But if you have a weekend free you can take one path through the ranges on one day – then walk back to Lulworth Cove on the wonderful alternative trail the next!).

Day walks

● **Bigbury-on-Sea to Salcombe** **13 miles/21km (see pp120-6)**
One of the remotest sections on the path, but just divine, beginning at pretty Bigbury and culminating in a saunter round Bolt Tail and Bolt Head, with Hope Cove a lovely place for lunch.

● **Brixham to Torquay** **8½ miles/13.6km (see pp163-70)**
Not everybody's idea of a pleasant promenade, but for those who fancy an easy, largely horizontal day strolling from one seaside resort to the next, with a camera in one hand and an ice-cream in the other, this is the heart of the English Riviera.

● **Exmouth to Sidmouth** **12½ miles/20km (see pp207-16)**
Not the easiest of walks, but one that takes in some spectacular scenery, refreshments at Budleigh Salterton – and the gateway to a World Heritage Coast.

● **Sidmouth to Seaton** **10¼ miles/16.5km (see pp221-8)**
A tough trek but the rewards are ample, with the settlements of Bramscombe Mouth and Beer lovely places to recover after some stiff strolling on undulating, natural terrain.

● **Seaton to Lyme Regis** **7 miles/11.5km (see pp231-6)**
One of the best – if not the best – walk on the path, taking in the sublime natural beauty of the phenomenon known as the Undercliffs.

● **Lyme Regis to Seatown (& Chideock)** **7¼ miles/11.75km (see pp243-8)**
A short (3hr) and relatively easy walk through some lovely coastal scenery, culminating in a conquest of the south coast's highest point, Golden Cap.

● **Portland Circuit** **14¾ miles/23.75km (see pp276-82)**
One of the oddest walks on the path, beginning and ending at Fortuneswell and taking in prisons and housing estates as well as some lovely walking on this idiosyncratic isle.

● **Weymouth to Lulworth Cove** **11 miles/17.75km (see pp287-94)**
A contender for the most photogenic walk in the book, with a straightforward stroll to Osmington Mills followed by the tough chalk rollercoaster leading to delightful Durdle Door and lovely Lulworth.

● **Lulworth Cove to Kimmeridge Bay** **7¼ miles/11.75km (see pp298-305)**
Cliff-top strolling doesn't get more awe-inspiring than this stiff hike through the

PLANNING YOUR WALK

ranges; just make sure you go when they're open! Transport from Kimmeridge Bay is limited but the walk can be combined with the first of the alternative routes around the ranges (13½ miles/21.75km) for one very long but immensely satisfying circular walk.

● **South Dorset Ridgeway**　　　　　　　　**17 miles/27.4km (see pp260-3)**
For those who are fed up with coastal walking but love burial barrows, hillforts, stone circles and other prehistoric constructions. A lovely, lovely walk.

Weekend walks
● **Salcombe to Dartmouth**　　　　　　　　**23 miles/37km (see pp131-48)**
One of the best couple of days on the South Devon coastline, very diverse with some fairly strenuous climbing in places, lots of easy flat walking too – and plenty of places for refreshments on the way.

● **Sidmouth to Lyme Regis**　　　　　　　　**17½ miles/28.2km (see pp221-36)**
Dreamy landscapes, pretty beaches, remote combes, lovely villages and the delightful Undercliffs to finish. This reasonably taxing but short walk is packed with interest.

● **Lyme Regis to Abbotsbury**　　　　　　　**19½ miles/31.4km (see pp243-66)**
Once past Charmouth this difficult-in-places stroll takes in some delicious Dorset countryside, with Golden Cap and Chesil Beach just two of the many highlights on the way. Abbotsbury is the perfect end to any walk, too.

● **Lulworth Cove to Swanage**　　　　　　　**20¾ miles/33.4km (see pp298-312)**
In these authors' opinion this is the best weekend walk on the path, especially if the ranges are open. Spectacular, wild, remote, delightful hiking through the Isle of Purbeck, bookended by two lovely settlements.

　　Your calf muscles may curse that you undertook such a testing trek – but your eyes, and your soul, will be forever grateful.

SIDE TRIPS

The SWCP isn't the only walking trail to meander through Devon and Dorset. Indeed, at times the coast path is bisected by another trail or even shares its route with another path.

　　A glance at an OS map will give you an idea of the many paths in the region but below is a brief description of the main ones you may encounter.

● **Erme-Plym Trail/The Two Moors Way** (⌨ www.devon.gov.uk/twomoors way.pdf) The Erme-Plym Trail begins in Wembury on the South Devon coast and travels as far north as Ivybridge (15 miles in all) where The Two Moors Way begins. Climbing onto Dartmoor can be strenuous but the effort is worth it.

　　The trail then heads north, traversing the length of Dartmoor to Drewsteignton before passing through Morchard Bishop and Witheridge, eventually entering Exmoor from the south before culminating in Lynmouth. Splendid scenery, and real solitude are just two of the joys of this trip.

● **Avon Estuary Walk** A pretty 7½-mile hike which circumvents the need to catch a ferry across the River Avon (see pp120-1).

● **John Musgrave Heritage Trail** A 35-mile inland trail that bypasses Torbay by linking Brixham with Maidencombe, crossing the River Dart twice and taking in Totnes and plenty of splendid Devonshire countryside as it does so. Established in 2005 in memory of John Musgrave, a local walking enthusiast and former chair of the South Devon Group of Ramblers.

● **Templer Way** (🖳 www.devon.gov.uk/templerwayleaflet.pdf) An 18-mile path that links Haytor on Dartmoor with the coast at Teignmouth, following the journey taken by the granite quarried there during the 19th century on its way to being exported; Templer, by the way, was the family name of those responsible for the canals and tramways that formed the granite's route.

● **Exe Estuary Trail** (🖳 www.exetrail.co.uk) As of 2012 this cycle path and walkway around the River Exe (Exmouth to Dawlish; see pp200-3) was still incomplete. Coastal walkers will find it useful when the ferry between Starcross and Exmouth is not operational – though it's a decent-enough stroll in its own right too.

● **Monarch's Way** (🖳 www.monarchsway.50megs.com) A whopping 615-mile route which follows in the footsteps of King Charles II who, having been defeated at the Battle of Worcester in 1651, was being pursued by Cromwell's Parliamentarians.

The Way passes through the Cotswolds and the Mendips before arriving on the south coast at Charmouth. It then follows the coast path around Bridport before going inland and finally traversing the South Downs to Shoreham – from where the monarch escaped to France.

● **Macmillan Way** (🖳 www.macmillanway.org) This 290-mile path links England's east coast and Boston in Lincolnshire with Chesil Beach and Abbotsbury in Dorset; the path also has tributaries leading off the main route to Banbury, Bath and Barnstaple. Set up in aid of Macmillan Cancer Support, so far over £350,000 has been raised from walkers' sponsorship!

● **The Jubilee Trail** (🖳 www.ramblers.org.uk/info/paths/name/j/jubileedorset) Launched in 1995, this 90-mile path connects the Somerset and Hampshire borders and in doing so slices through Dorset, purposefully following, wherever possible, what were previously little-known pathways. The jubilee of the title is the 60th anniversary of the founding of the Ramblers' Association (see box p47), now called Ramblers.

● **The Hardy Way** This 212-mile trail passes through the Dorset countryside that inspired Thomas Hardy's semi-fictional Wessex, the backdrop to his novels.

● **The Purbeck Way** (🖳 www.dorsetforyou.com/purbeckway) A Y-shaped pathway, this time passing through the stunning and varied scenery of the Isle of Purbeck, starting at Wareham Quay and ending either at Ballard Down (east of Swanage) or Chapman's Pool (near St Aldhelm's Head).

PLANNING YOUR WALK

VILLAGE AND

Place name (Places in brackets are a short walk off the South Devon/ Dorset coast path)	Distance from previous place approx miles/km (if in brackets the nearest point actually on the trail used)	Cash Machine (ATM)/Bank (£ = charge)	Post Office	Tourist Information Centre (TIC)/ Point (TIP)/ Visitor Centre (VC)
Plymouth		✔	✔	TIC
Wembury	10.75/17.25km	✔	✔	
(Noss Mayo/Newton Ferrers)	(2/3.25km)	✔		
Challaborough/Bigbury-on-Sea	15.25/24.5km	✔	✔	
Hope	5/8km	✔£	✔	
Salcombe	8/13km	✔	✔	TIC
(East Prawle)	(6/9.75km)		✔	
Beesands	12.25/19.75km		✔	
Torcross	0.5/.075km		✔	
(Slapton)	(2.5/4km)		✔	
Strete	3.5/5.75km	✔no HSBC cards!	✔	
Stoke Fleming	2.5/4km		✔	
Dartmouth	4.25/6.75km	✔	✔	TIC
Kingswear	FERRY	✔	✔	
Brixham	11/17.75km	✔	✔	TIC
Paignton	5.75/9.25km	✔	✔	TIC
Torquay	2.75/4.5km	✔	✔	TIC
(St Marychurch)	(6/9.75km)	✔	✔	
Maidencombe	8/13km			
Shaldon	3.25/5.25km		✔	TIC
Teignmouth	– / –	✔	✔	TIC
Dawlish	3.75/6km	✔	✔	TIC
Dawlish Warren	1.75/2.75km	✔£	✔	
Cockwood/Starcross	2.5/4km		✔	
Exmouth	FERRY	✔	✔	TIC
Budleigh Salterton	5.5/9km	✔	✔	TIC
Sidmouth	7/11.25km	✔	✔	TIC
Branscombe Mouth	6.5/10.5km			
Beer	2.25/3.5km	✔£	✔	
Seaton	1.5/2.5km	✔	✔	TIC
Lyme Regis	7/11.25km	✔	✔	TIC
Charmouth	3/4.75km	✔£	✔	VC
Seatown/(Chideock)	4.25/6.75km		✔	
Eype Mouth	2/3.25km			TIP
West Bay	1.25/2km	✔£	✔	
(Burton Bradstock)	(1.25/2km)	✔£	✔	
West Bexington	5.5/8.75km			
Abbotsbury	3.75/6km		✔	TIP
Fortuneswell	13/21km	✔	✔	VC
Weymouth	14.75/23.75km	✔	✔	TIC
Osmington Mills/Osmington	4.75/7.75km			
Lulworth Cove/(West Lulworth)	6.25/10km	✔£	✔	VC
(Kimmeridge)	(7.25/11.75km)			
(Worth Matravers)	(5.5/8.75km)			
Swanage/New Swanage	13.5/21.75km	✔	✔	TIC
South Haven	7.5/12km			
TOTAL DISTANCE	217.25 miles/350km			

TOWN FACILITIES

Eating Place ✔= one ✔✔= two ✔✔✔= three +	Food Store	Campsite (✔)= seasonal campsite	Hostels YHA/ H (IndHostel)/ B (Barn or Bunkhouse)	B&B-style accommodation ✔ = one; ✔✔ = two ✔✔✔= three+	Place name (Places in brackets are a short walk off South Devon/ Dorset coast path)
✔✔✔	✔		H	✔✔✔	Plymouth
✔	✔	✔ (Pilgrims Rest)		✔✔	Wembury
✔✔	✔			✔✔(Noss Mayo/Newton Ferrers)	
✔✔✔	✔	✔		✔✔✔ Challaborough/Bigbury-on-Sea	
✔✔✔	✔			✔✔	Hope
✔✔✔	✔		YHA	✔✔✔	Salcombe
✔✔	✔	(✔)		✔	East Prawle
✔✔	✔			✔	Beesands
✔✔✔	✔			✔✔	Torcross
✔✔	✔	✔ (Slapton Sands)		✔✔	(Slapton)
✔✔	✔	✔		✔✔	Strete
✔✔	✔	✔		✔✔✔	Stoke Fleming
✔✔✔	✔			✔✔✔	Dartmouth
✔✔✔	✔			✔	Kingswear
✔✔✔	✔	✔		✔✔✔	Brixham
✔✔✔	✔			✔✔✔	Paignton
✔✔✔	✔			✔✔✔	Torquay
✔✔✔	✔			✔	(St Marychurch)
✔				✔	Maidencombe
✔✔✔	✔	✔		✔✔✔	Shaldon
✔✔✔	✔			✔✔✔	Teignmouth
✔✔✔	✔			✔✔✔	Dawlish
✔✔	✔			✔✔	Dawlish Warren
✔✔✔	✔			✔✔✔	Cockwood/Starcross
✔✔✔	✔	✔ (Prattshayes)		✔✔✔	Exmouth
✔✔✔	✔	✔(Pooh Cottage)		✔✔✔	Budleigh Salterton
✔✔✔	✔			✔✔✔	Sidmouth
✔	✔			✔	Branscombe Mouth
✔✔✔	✔		YHA	✔✔✔	Beer
✔✔✔	✔	✔(Axe Farm)		✔✔✔	Seaton
✔✔✔	✔	✔(Wood Farm)		✔✔✔	Lyme Regis
✔✔✔	✔			✔✔✔	Charmouth
✔✔✔	✔	✔		✔✔✔	Seatown/(Chideock)
✔	✔	✔		✔	Eype Mouth
✔✔✔	✔	(✔)		✔✔✔	West Bay
✔✔	✔	✔(Freshwater)		✔✔✔	(Burton Bradstock)
✔✔				✔✔	West Bexington
✔✔✔	✔			✔✔✔	Abbotsbury
✔✔✔	✔		YHA/H	✔✔✔	Fortuneswell
✔✔✔	✔		H	✔✔✔	Weymouth
✔✔	✔	✔		✔✔ Osmington Mills/Osmington	
✔✔	✔	✔ (Durdle Door)	YHA	✔✔✔ Lulworth Cove /(West Lulworth)	
✔		✔(Steeple Leaze farm)		✔	(Kimmeridge)
✔		✔			(Worth Matravers)
✔✔✔	✔		YHA/H	✔✔✔ Swanage/New Swanage	
					South Haven

PLANNING YOUR WALK

What to take

'When you have worn out your shoes, the strength of the shoe leather has passed into the fiber of your body. I measure your health by the number of shoes and hats and clothes you have worn out.'
Ralph Waldo Emerson

Deciding how much to take can be difficult. Experienced walkers know that you should take only the bare essentials but at the same time you must ensure you have all the equipment necessary to make the trip safe and comfortable.

KEEP YOUR LUGGAGE LIGHT

Experienced backpackers know that there is some sort of complicated formula governing the success of a trek, in which the enjoyment of the walk is inversely proportional to the amount carried.

Carrying a heavy rucksack slows you down, tires you out and gives you aches and pains in parts of the body that you didn't even know existed. It is imperative, therefore, that you take a good deal of time packing and that you are ruthless when you do; if it's not essential, don't take it.

HOW TO CARRY IT

If you are using one of the baggage-carrier services, you must contact them beforehand to find out what their regulations are regarding the weight and size of the luggage you wish them to carry.

Even if you are using one of these services, you will still need to carry a small **daypack** with you, filled with those items that you will need during the day: water bottle or pouch, this book, map, sun-screen, sun hat, wet-weather gear, some food, camera, money and so on.

If you have decided to forego the services of the baggage carriers you will have to consider your **rucksack** even more carefully. Ultimately its size will depend on where you are planning to stay and how you are planning to eat. If you are camping and cooking for yourself you will probably need a 65- to 75-litre rucksack, which should be large enough to carry a small tent, sleeping bag, cooking equipment, crockery, cutlery and food. Those not carrying their home with them should find a 40- to 60-litre rucksack sufficient.

When choosing a rucksack, make sure it has a stiffened back and can be adjusted to fit your own back comfortably. Don't just try the rucksack out in the shop: take it home, fill it with things and then try it out around the house and take it out for a short walk. Only then can you be certain that it fits. Make sure the hip belt and chest strap (if there is one) are fastened tightly as this helps distribute the weight more comfortably with most of it being carried on your hips. Carry a small daypack inside the rucksack, as this will be useful to carry things in when leaving the main pack at the hostel or B&B.

PLANNING YOUR WALK

One reader has written in with the eminently sensible advice of taking a **waterproof rucksack cover**. Most rucksacks these days have them 'built in' to the sack, but you can also buy them separately for less than a tenner. Lining your bag with a **bin liner** is another sensible, cut-price idea. Finally, it's also a good idea to keep everything wrapped in plastic bags and put these in a bin-bag inside the rucksack. That way, even if it does pour with rain, everything should remain dry.

FOOTWEAR

Boots
Only a decent pair of strong, durable trekking boots are good enough to survive the rigours of the South-West Coast Path. Don't be tempted by a spell of hot weather into bringing something flimsier. Make sure, too, that your boots provide good ankle support, for the ground can occasionally be rough and stony and twisted ankles are commonplace. Make sure your boots are waterproof as well: these days most people opt for a synthetic waterproof lining (Gore-Tex or similar), though a good-quality leather boot with dubbin should prove just as reliable in keeping your feet dry.

In addition, many people bring an extra pair of shoes or trainers to wear off the trail. This is not essential but if you are using one of the luggage-carrying services and you've got room in your luggage, why not?

Socks
If you haven't got a pair of the modern hi-tech walking socks the old system of wearing a thin liner sock under a thicker wool sock is just as good. Bring a few pairs of each.

CLOTHES

In a country notorious for its unpredictable climate it is imperative that you pack enough clothes to cover every extreme of weather, from burning hot to bloomin' freezing. Modern hi-tech outdoor clothes come with a range of fancy names and brands but they all still follow the basic two- or three-layer principle, with an inner base layer to transport sweat away from your skin, a mid-layer for warmth and an outer layer to protect you from the wind and rain.

A thin lightweight **thermal top** of a synthetic material is ideal as the base layer as it draws moisture (ie sweat) away from your body. Cool in hot weather and warm when worn under other clothes in the cold, pack at least one thermal top. Over the top in cold weather a mid-weight **polyester fleece** should suffice. Fleeces are light, more water-resistant than the alternatives (such as a woolly jumper), remain warm even when wet and pack down small in rucksacks; they are thus ideal trekking gear.

Over the top of all this a **waterproof jacket** is essential. 'Breathable' jackets cost a small fortune (though prices are falling all the time) but they do prevent the build-up of condensation.

Leg wear

Many trekkers find trekking trousers an unnecessary investment. Any light, quick-drying trouser should suffice. Jeans are heavy and dry slowly and are thus not recommended. A pair of waterproof trousers *is* more than useful, however, while on really hot sunny days you'll be glad you brought your shorts. Thermal **long johns** take up little room in the rucksack and could be vital if the weather starts to close in.

Gaiters are not essential but, again, those who bring them are always glad they did, for they provide extra protection when walking through muddy ground and when the vegetation around the trail is dripping wet after bad weather.

Underwear

Three or four changes of underwear is fine. Any more is excessive, any less unhygienic. Because backpacks can cause bra straps to dig painfully into the skin, women may find a **sports bra** more comfortable.

Other clothes

You may like to consider a woolly **hat** and **gloves** – you'd be surprised how cold it can get up on the cliffs even in summer – and a **sun hat**.

TOILETRIES

Once again, take the minimum. **Soap**, **towel**, a **toothbrush** and **toothpaste** are pretty much essential (although those staying in B&Bs will find that most provide soap and towels anyway). Some **toilet paper** could also prove vital on the trail, particularly if using public toilets (which occasionally run out).

Other items: **razor**; **deodorant**; **tampons/sanitary towels** and a high factor **sun-screen** (see p69) should cover just about everything.

FIRST-AID KIT

A small first-aid kit could prove useful for those emergencies that occur along the trail. This kit should include **aspirin** or **paracetamol**; **plasters** for minor cuts; Compeed, **Second Skin** or some other treatment for blisters; a **bandage** or elasticated joint support for supporting a sprained ankle or a weak knee; **antiseptic wipes**; **antiseptic cream**; **safety pins**; **tweezers** and **scissors**.

❏ **Mobile phone reception and internet connections on the trail**
While many people view their trek in this remote corner of England as an escape from the modern world, for some people a decent connection with the outside world is vital. In our research we found Orange (together with its partner T-Mobile) provided the best coverage for mobile and internet connections (with Vodafone pretty good too); those who need to stay in touch online, and who are taking a laptop, may like to consider investing in an Orange dongle (a small device that plugs into a USB port and connects your computer to the internet) – though many B&Bs and pubs also offer wi-fi.

❏ **Tides**
Tides are the regular rise and fall of the ocean caused by the gravitational pull of the moon. They are actually very long waves which follow the path of the moon across the ocean. Twice a day there is a high tide and a low tide and there are approximately 6¼ hours between high and low water.

Spring tides (derived from the German word springen meaning to jump) are tides with a very large range that occur just after the full- and new-moon phases when the gravitational forces of the sun and the moon line up. High tides are higher and low tides lower than normal. Spring tides occur twice every month. Neap tides occur halfway between each spring tide and are tides with the smallest range, so you get comparatively high low tides and low high tides. They occur at the first and third quarters of the moon when the sun, moon and earth are all at right angles to each other, hence the gravitational forces of the sun and moon are weakened.

It is a good idea to carry a tide table with you; they can be purchased for about £1.30 from newsagents or TICs in coastal areas. Tide times are also available online at 🖥 www.tidetimes.org.uk (select your location) or from 🖥 easytide.ukho.gov.uk (click on Predict, choose area and then country/region ie England, then Show ports and choose the relevant port).

GENERAL ITEMS

Essential
Everybody should have a **map**, **torch**, **water bottle or pouch**, **spare batteries**, **penknife**, **whistle** (see p67 for details of the international distress signal), some emergency food and a **watch** (preferably with an alarm to help you make an early start each day). Those with weak knees will find a **walking pole** or **sticks** essential. Anyone who has walked in Scotland will recognise the importance of taking insect repellent to ward off midges, though they're not nearly so bad here.

A tide table (see box above) is also worth having and, if you know how to use it properly, you'll find a **compass** handy. A **mobile phone** (see box opposite) is invaluable too – and reception is usually pretty good – for arranging a lift from the path to the B&B, booking a table at a restaurant etc; just don't forget the charger!

Useful items and luxuries
Suggestions here include a **book** for days off or on train and bus journeys, a camera, a pair of **sunglasses**, **binoculars** and a **radio** or **iPod**.

CAMPING GEAR

Both campers and those intending to stay in the various bunkhouses en route will find a sleeping bag essential. A two- to three-season bag should suffice for summer.

In addition, campers will also need a decent bivvy bag or tent, a sleeping mat, fuel and stove, cutlery/pans, a cup and a scrubber for washing up.

PLANNING YOUR WALK

MONEY

Both banks and cash machines (ATMs) are fairly common along the Dorset & South Devon Coast Path and banks are fairly common too. Not everybody accepts **debit** or **credit cards** as payment – though some B&Bs and many restaurants now do. As a result, you should carry a fair amount of **cash** with you, just to be on the safe side. A **cheque book** from a British bank is useful in those places where credit cards are not accepted.

Crime on the trail is thankfully rare but it's always a good idea to carry your money safely in a **moneybelt**.

DOCUMENTS

National Trust and English Heritage memberships, as well as student cards and YHA hostel cards could all save you money on the trail. Some sort of ID, such as a driving licence, could also prove useful.

MAPS

It would be perfectly possible to walk long stretches of the coastal path unaided by map or compass. Just keep the sea to your right (or left, depending on which way you're heading) and you can't go too far off track. The hand-drawn maps in this book, too, which cover the trail at a scale of 1:20,000, will hopefully provide sufficient aid in areas where navigation is slightly more problematic.

Nevertheless, having other maps will paint a more fulfilling picture of your surroundings and will allow you to plan much more effectively for any accommodation or other facilities that lie off the trail. **Ordnance Survey** (🖳 www .ordnancesurveyleisure.co.uk) produce their maps to two scales: the 1:25,000 Explorer series in orange and the 1:50,000 Landranger in pink (which is less useful for trekking purposes). Alongside the paper versions they also produce an 'Active' edition of both which is 'weatherproof' (covered in a lightweight protective plastic coating). Those needed for the stretch of the SWCP covered by this book are Explorer: Outdoor Leisure OL20 South Devon; 110 Torquay & Dawlish; OL115 Exmouth & Sidmouth; OL116 Lyme Regis & Bridport; and OL15 Purbeck & South Dorset. If you don't feel that such precise cartography is needed the Landranger may be a more suitable choice; of the fourteen to cover the SWCP you will need the following six: OL21 Plymouth & Launceston; OL202 Torbay & South Dartmoor; OL192 Exeter & Sidmouth; OL193 Taunton & Lyme Regis; OL194 Dorchester & Weymouth; and OL195 Bournemouth & Purbeck.

Harvey Maps (🖳 www.harveymaps.co.uk) produce a series of maps that cover all of the designated National Trails to a scale of 1:40,000. For full coverage of the SWCP you will need six in all but if you are intending to walk the section covered by this book only Map Five (Plymouth to Sidmouth) and Map Six (Sidmouth to South Haven Point) alone will suffice. This, of course, will save on weight and cost compared to buying the four OS maps, though the OS has more detail and will show you what is further inland.

While it may be extravagant to buy all the OS maps, Ramblers (see box p47) allows members to borrow up to ten maps for up to six weeks at just 50p per map, or £1 for waterproof maps. Members of the Backpackers' Club (see box p47) can also purchase maps at a significant discount through the club.

Both OS and Harvey maps can also be obtained online from Mapkiosk (🖳 www.mapkiosk.com).

RECOMMENDED READING

Below is a by no means exhaustive but hopefully helpful introduction to some of the literature relating to the SWCP and, in particular, the Dorset & South Devon Coast Path.

Guidebooks

If you're willing to carry a separate map undoubtedly the most detailed guide to the accommodation, tide tables and other useful information on the entire SWCP is the South West Coast Path Association's companion to the path, called simply *The South West Coast Path* and currently priced at £9.95. Alongside this annual guide they also produce and sell pamphlets for each section which can be found in tourist information centres en route or ordered via post or online for £1 (see SWCPA's website for details, 🖳 www.southwestcoastpath.org.uk).

Flora, fauna and geology

For identifying obscure plants and peculiar-looking beasties as you walk, Collins and New Holland publish a pocket-sized range to Britain's natural riches. Both series contain a wealth of information.

The **Collins Gem** series are tough little books; current titles include guides to *Trees*, *Birds*, *Mushrooms*, *Wild Flowers*, *Wild Animals*, *Insects* and *Butterflies*. In addition, for any budding crustacean connoisseur there is a *Seashore* book, and there is also a handbook to the *Stars*, which could be of particular interest for those who are considering sleeping under them. Also in the Collins series, there's an adapted version of Richard Mabey's classic bestseller *Food for Free* – great for anyone intent on getting back to nature, saving the pennies, or just with an interest in what's edible outside of a supermarket. You could also consult *Wild Food: Foraging for Food in the Wild*, written by Jane Eastoe and published by the National Trust.

New Holland's Concise range covers many of the same topics as the Gem series, comes in a waterproof plastic jacket and also includes useful quick reference foldout charts.

For books that are more **specific to the walk**, *Wildlife of the Jurassic Coast* by Bryan Edwards is available in local tourist information offices, while *Where to Watch Wildlife in Devon* by Robert Hesketh is our favourite of the several books dealing with the nature in that county.

If you need help grappling with the complex **geology** you'll encounter, *The Official Guide to the Jurassic Coast: Dorset and East Devon's World Heritage Coast (Walk Through Time Guide)* by Denys Brunsden is available both locally and online, while *Dorset and East Devon: Landscape and Geology* by Malcolm

Hart is a more recent addition to the subject. You'll probably also be interested in *Discover Dorset Fossils* by Richard Edmonds, or the tiny but useful paperback *Finding Fossils in Lyme Bay* by Robert Coram.

Autobiography

With the Falklands War imminent Mark Wallington set off to walk the SWCP in an attempt to impress a girl that he had met at a party. Accompanied by the more-loathed-than-loved Boogie the dog, man and beast survive all that the path can throw at them on a diet of tinned soup and Kennomeat. *Travels with Boogie: 500 Mile Walkies* is Wallington's humorous account of his own time spent on the trail. If you have walked and camped or have ever walked a long distance with a dog many of the author's anecdotes will ring true – a light-hearted and thoroughly enjoyable read. Another dog goes walking in *Two feet, four paws*, Spud Talbot-Ponsonby's tale of her time circumnavigating Britain.

The Tarka Trail is a local path named after Henry Williamson's much-loved *Tarka the Otter*, just one of many books in which Williamson's extraordinary ability to evoke the Devonshire countryside gilds every page.

PLANNING YOUR WALK

❑ SOURCES OF FURTHER INFORMATION

Online information

● **www.southwestcoastpath.com** The official and most useful website to Britain's longest national trail. Good for background information on the trail. The site also has the latest news on the path, information on river crossings and army ranges, as well as lots of information on accommodation, suggested itineraries and distance and timing calculators.

● **www.southwestcoastpath.org.uk** The site for the South West Coast Path Association (SWCPA), a registered charity that exists to support users of the path. Many of the features on the official site are replicated here – distance calculators, river-crossing details etc – though there is much more information here too.

The Association is also very active politically, pressurising government bodies to ensure that the path is properly maintained along its length. Membership (£12.50/14/21 for single/joint/group for UK residents; £19 for both single and joint for non-UK residents) includes a free copy of their guidebook and twice-yearly newsletters.

● **www.southwestcoastalpath.co.uk** Unusual website that concentrates on day-walks along short stretches of the SWCP. Also includes information on accommodation, pubs and restaurants.

● **www.jurassiccoast.com** Website dedicated to Britain's first natural World Heritage Site with good explanations on the geology of the region and just why it is of such global importance.

● **www.worldheritagesouthwest.org.uk** Site dedicated to the World Heritage sites in the south-west of England. While Stonehenge and the city of Bath may not be of much relevance to coastal walkers, their section on the Jurassic coastline is certainly worth a look.

● **www.southdevonaonb.org.uk** Official website of the South Devon Areas of Outstanding Natural Beauty. Good for background information on the geology, flora and fauna of the region.

History

One thousand years of farming, quarrying and the Home Guard are crammed into Felicity Goodall's *Lost Devon*, which is good for those with an interest in the lost heritage of the county.

Derrick Warren's *Curious Devon* examines the quirkier side of the county, as does his *Curious Dorset*, while for something a little darker there's John Van Der Kiste's *Grim Almanac of Devon* that recounts 366 of the county's more macabre episodes.

A more general tome on Dorset is Cecil North Cullingford's *A History of Dorset*. *The South West Coast Path – An Illustrated History* recounts, in probably rather too much detail for the layman, the struggle to establish Britain's longest national trail.

Finally, we think the most entertaining read on one aspect of the history of this coastline is *The Dinosaur Hunters: A True Story of Scientific Rivalry and the Discovery of the Prehistoric World* by Deborah Cadbury, detailing the work of Mary Anning, Gideon Mantell et al and their rivalry in the 19th century.

Tourist information centres (TICs) and points (TIPs)

As one of the busiest tourist areas of the country, it is no surprise to find that the South-West is well served by tourist information offices: **Plymouth** (see p95); **Salcombe** (see p128); **Dartmouth** (see p149); **Brixham** (see p160); **Paignton** (see p167); **Torquay** (see p173); **Shaldon** (see p185); **Teignmouth** (see p187); **Dawlish** (see p194); **Exmouth** (see p203); **Budleigh Salterton** (see p212); **Sidmouth** (see p218); **Seaton** (see p228); **Lyme Regis** (see p237); **Weymouth** (see p283); **Swanage** (see p312); **Poole** (see p322).

There are also some **visitor centres** and **tourist information points** along the way where it is possible to pick up leaflets about local attractions. TIPs are often at caravan parks and may also be in libraries, where there isn't a tourist information centre.

Organisations for walkers

● **Backpackers' Club** (🖳 www.backpackersclub.co.uk) A club aimed at people who are involved or interested in lightweight camping through walking, cycling, skiing and canoeing. They produce a quarterly magazine, provide members with a comprehensive advisory and information service on all aspects of backpacking, organise weekend trips, offer discounts for maps and at outdoor stores, and also publish a farm-pitch directory. Membership is £12 a year (£15 for a family; £7 for under 18s).

● **The Long Distance Walkers' Association** (🖳 www.ldwa.org.uk) Membership (£13 a year; family and international membership £19.50) includes a copy of their journal *Strider* three times per year giving details of challenge events and local group walks as well as articles on the subject. Members also receive a discount on maps and also on the UK Trailwalker's Handbook which details 730 trails across the UK.

● **Ramblers** (formerly Ramblers' Association; 🖳 www.ramblers.org.uk) Looks after the interests of walkers throughout Britain. They publish a large amount of useful information including their quarterly *Walk* magazine (£5.99 to non-members). The website also has a discussion forum. Membership costs £31/41 individual/joint; concessionary rates are £19.50/25.50 individual/joint; £10 discount for individual/joint membership if paid by direct debit.

PLANNING YOUR WALK

Fiction

The two counties have been fairly blessed with bestselling authors. Thomas Hardy began the trend, his novels and short stories nearly always set in his fictional Wessex – which is essentially Dorset and the surrounding counties but with the names changed. Hardy's hometown of Dorchester, for example, became 'Casterbridge' in his novels, while Weymouth is 'Budmouth' in his novel *Far from the Madding Crowd*, and is also Eustacia Vye's hometown in *The Return of the Native*. Portland, by the way, is the 'Isle of Slingers'.

Hardy's book sales, however, are outstripped by those of another homegrown talent, Agatha Christie. Once again her homeland features prominently in her books; indeed, the Imperial Hotel at her home town of Torquay appears in three of her novels, *Peril at End House*, *The Body in the Library* and *Sleeping Murder*, while Burgh Island is the setting for two of her thrillers, *And Then There Were None* and *Evil Under the Sun*.

Thomas Hardy's practice of changing local place-names (while otherwise remaining true to the local geography) was emulated by his fellow Victorian, J Meade Falkner, in his most famous work, *Moonfleet*. Written at the end of the 19th century, this children's story is set in a small Dorset village (based on East Fleet behind Chesil Beach) and involves smuggling, kidnapping – and an awful lot of intrigue. Falkner stayed in Abbotsbury while he wrote the novel.

Set in the same location, though this time in 1962, before the sexual revolution really took off, *On Chesil Beach* is by one of Britain's most celebrated contemporary novelists, Ian McEwan, and concerns the wedding night of two twenty-somethings, their fears and dreams.

Further west, Lyme Regis is the home of Sarah Woodruff, better known as *The French Lieutenant's Woman* in the novel by John Fowles. She spends her days on the Cobb, staring out to sea, in disgrace because of her affair with the Frenchman Varguennes, who, unbeknown to her until later, was already married; it is while standing there that she is spied by Charles Smithson and his fiancée, Ernestina Freeman, and a close relationship between Charles and Sarah ensues. The novel is perhaps most remarkable in that the author offers three different endings. It was made into a film in 1981 starring Jeremy Irons and Meryl Streep.

For something much lighter, PG Wodehouse's *Thank you, Jeeves* is the first to feature the eponymous butler-cum-hero; indeed, the story begins with Jeeves leaving Bertie Wooster's service because of the latter's incessant playing of the banjolele, finding employment instead with Bertie's old chum Lord 'Chuffy' Chuffnell. Bertie retreats to one of Chuffy's cottages in Dorset – and the usual wonderfully entertaining chaos ensues.

TAKING DOGS ALONG THE PATH

The South-West Coast Path is a dog-friendly path and many are the rewards that await those prepared to make the extra effort required to bring their best friend along the trail. However, you shouldn't underestimate the amount of work involved in bringing your pooch to the path. Indeed, just about every decision you make will be influenced by the fact that you've got a dog: how you plan to travel to the start of the trail, where you're going to stay, how far you're going to walk each day, where you're going to rest and where you're going to eat in the evening etc etc.

The decision-making begins well before you've set foot on the trail. For starters, you have to ask – and be honest with – yourself: can your dog really cope with walking 10+ miles (16+km) a day, day after day, week after week? And just as importantly, will he or she actually enjoy it?!?

If you think the answer is yes to both, you need to start preparing accordingly. For one thing, extra thought needs to go into your itinerary. The best starting point is to study the Village & town facilities table on pp38-9 (and the advice below), and plan where to stop, where to eat, where to buy food for your mutt.

Looking after your dog

To begin with, you need to make sure that your dog is fully **inoculated** against the usual doggy illnesses, and also up-to-date with regard to **worm pills** (eg Drontal) and **flea preventatives** such as Frontline – they are, after all, following in the pawprints of many a dog before them, some of whom may well have left fleas or other parasites on the trail that now lie in wait for their next meal to arrive. **Pet insurance** is also a very good idea; if you've already got insurance do check that it will cover a trip such as this.

On the subject of looking after your dog's health, perhaps the most important implement you can take with you is the **plastic tick remover**, available from vets for a couple of quid. Ticks are a real problem on the SWCP, as they hide in the long grass waiting for unsuspecting victims to trot past. These removers, while fiddly, help you to remove the tick safely (ie without leaving its head behind buried under the dog's skin).

Being in unfamiliar territory also makes it more likely that you and your dog could become separated. For this reason, make sure your dog has a **tag with your contact details on it** (a mobile phone number would be best if you are carrying one with you); you could also consider having it **microchipped** for further security.

Dogs on beaches

There is no general rule regarding whether dogs are allowed on beaches or not. Some of the beaches on the SWCP are open to dogs all year; some allow them on the beach only outside the summer season (1st May to 30th Sep); while a few beaches don't allow dogs at all. (Guide dogs, by the way, are usually excluded from any bans.) If in doubt, look for the noticeboards that will tell you the exact rules. See also box p50.

Alternatively, South Devon's website (💻 www.visitdevon.co.uk/things-to-do/attractions/beaches/dog-friendly-beaches) says which beaches allow dogs and which don't, as does Visit Dorset (💻 www.visit-dorset.com/plan-your-visit/dog-friendly-dorset/dogs-on-beaches).

PLANNING YOUR WALK

❏ **Beaches with restrictions**

Unless otherwise stated, dogs are not allowed on the beaches listed below between May and September.

Devon: Bigbury-on-Sea; **Blackpool Sands** (1st Mar to 1st Nov); **Bovisand; Challaborough; Coryton's Cove; Hope Cove; Salcombe South Sands; Shaldon Beach; Teignmouth Town Beach; Wembury**.

Dorset: **Lyme Regis** No dogs on the area of beach from Cobb Gate Car Park west to the Lifeboat slipway between 1st April and 31st Oct, though dogs are allowed on East Cliff Beach and Monmouth Beach year-round; **Charmouth West Beach; Charmouth East Beach**: No dogs between 10am and 6pm during July & August; **Seatown** No dogs at any time; **West Bay** No dogs within the East Pier to East Cliffs and West Pier to West Cliffs areas between May & Sep; **Burton Bradstock; West Bexington** Dogs allowed at all times within a restricted area; **Weymouth** No dogs on main beach between May & Sep. Dogs permitted year-round within a restricted area; **Swanage; Studland** Dogs are not allowed on Middle and Knoll beaches (from Red-end point to training bank) between early July and early September.

Dogs are allowed on Shell Bay and South Beach all year provided they are on a lead and that owners clean up after them.

Where dogs are banned from a beach there will usually be an alternative path that you can take that avoids the sands. If there isn't an alternative, and you have no choice but to cross the beach even though dogs are officially banned, you are permitted to do so as long as you cross the beach as speedily as possible, follow the line of the path (which is usually well above the high-water mark) and keep your dog tightly under control **on a lead**.

Whatever the rules of access are for the beach, remember that your dog shouldn't disturb other beach-users – and you must always **clean up after your dog**.

Finally, remember that you need to bring drinking water with you on the beach as dogs can overheat with the lack of shade.

What to pack

You've probably already got a good idea of what to bring to keep your dog alive and happy, but the following is a checklist:

● **Food/water bowl** Foldable cloth bowls are popular with walkers as they are light and take up little room in the rucksack. It is also possible to get a

---

❏ **Packing for your dog**

When it comes to packing, I always leave an exterior pocket of my rucksack empty so I can put used poo bags in there (for deposit at the first bin I come to). I always like to keep all the dog's kit together and separate from the other luggage (usually inside a plastic bag inside my rucksack). I have also seen several dogs sporting their own 'doggy rucksack, so they can carry their own food, water, poo etc – which certainly reduces the burden on their owner! **Henry Stedman**

❏ **When to keep your dog on a lead**
● **On cliff tops** It's a sad fact that, every year, a few dogs lose their lives falling over the edge of the cliffs. It usually occurs when they are chasing rabbits (which know where the cliff-edge is and are able, unlike your poor pooch, to stop in time).
● **When crossing farmland**, particularly in the lambing season (around May) when your dog can scare the sheep, causing them to lose their young. Farmers are allowed by law to shoot at and kill any dogs that they consider are worrying their sheep. During lambing, most farmers would prefer it if you didn't bring your dog at all.

The exception is if your dog is being attacked by cows. A couple of years ago there were three deaths in the UK caused by walkers being trampled as they tried to rescue their dogs from the attentions of cattle. The advice in this instance is to let go of the lead, head speedily to a position of safety (usually the other side of the field gate or stile) and call your dog to you.
● **On National Trust land**, where it is compulsory to keep your dog on a lead.
● **Around ground-nesting birds** It's important to keep your dog under control when crossing an area where certain species of birds nest on the ground. Most dogs love foraging around in the woods but make sure you have permission to do so; some woods are used as 'nurseries' for game birds and dogs are only allowed through them if they are on a lead.

water-bottle-and-bowl combination, where the bottle folds into a 'trough' from which the dog can drink.
● **Lead and collar** An extendable one is probably preferable for this sort of trip. Make sure both lead and collar are in good condition – you don't want either to snap on the trail, or you may end up carrying your dog through sheep fields until a replacement can be found.
● **Medication** You'll know if you need to bring any lotions or potions.
● **Tick remover** See p49.
● **Bedding** A simple blanket may suffice, or you can opt for something more elaborate if you aren't carrying your own luggage.
● **Poo bags** Essential.
● **Hygiene wipes** For cleaning your dog after it's rolled in stuff.
● **A favourite toy** Helps prevent your dog from pining for the entire walk.
● **Food/water** Remember to bring treats as well as regular food to keep up the mutt's morale. That said, if your dog is anything like mine the chances are it will spend most of the walk dining on rabbit droppings and sheep poo anyway.
● **Corkscrew stake** Available from camping or pet shops, this will help you to keep your dog secure in one place while you set up camp/doze.
● **Raingear** It can rain a lot!
● **Old towels** For drying your dog after the deluge.

Cleaning up after your dog
It is extremely important that dog owners behave in a responsible way when walking the path and all excrement should be cleaned up. In towns, villages and fields where animals graze or which will be cut for silage, hay etc, you need to

pick up and bag the excrement. In other places you can possibly get away with merely flicking it with a nearby stick into the undergrowth, thus ensuring there is none left on the path to decorate the boots of others.

If your dog is anything like Daisy, it'll wait until you are 300m past the nearest bin – and about four miles from the next one – before relieving itself. Don't be tempted to leave it, but bag it up; this means you're likely to have to carry it for a couple of miles – just look on it as your own personalised little hand warmer.

Staying and eating with your dog

In this guide we have used the symbol 🐕 to denote where a hotel, pub or B&B welcomes dogs. However, this always needs to be arranged in advance and some places may charge extra. Hostels (both YHA and independent) do not permit them unless they are an assistance (guide) dog; smaller campsites tend to accept them, but some of the larger holiday parks do not. Before you turn up always double check whether the place you would like to stay accepts dogs and whether there is space for them; many places have only one or two rooms suitable for people with dogs.

When it comes to eating, most landlords allow dogs in at least a section of their pubs, though few restaurants do. Make sure you always ask first and ensure your dog doesn't run around the pub but is secured to your table or a radiator.

Getting to and from the Coast Path

All the major towns along the coast path are reasonably well served by rail and/or coach services from the rest of Britain. Travelling by train or coach is the most convenient way to get to the trail as you do not need to worry about where to leave your car, how safe it will be while you're walking, or how to get back to it at the end of your holiday.

Choosing to travel by public transport is also choosing to help the environment; a creative step in minimising your impact on the countryside. It can also be an enjoyable experience in itself. How many of us have fond memories of relaxing to the regular rattle of the train wheels while sleepily watching the scenery pass by?

NATIONAL TRANSPORT

By train

The main Devon line (operated by First Great Western, ☎ 0845-700 0125, 🖳 www.firstgreatwestern.co.uk) runs from London Paddington through Exeter to **Plymouth**, with branch lines connecting major towns on the coast path. There are several services every day as well as a night train (the Night Riviera, Sun-Fri).

❏ GETTING TO BRITAIN

● **By air** The best international gateway to Britain for the Dorset & South Devon Coast Path is London; its most convenient airports are Heathrow (🖳 www.heathrow airport.com), the main airport, and Gatwick (🖳 www.gatwickairport.com).

Exeter Airport (🖳 www.exeter-airport.co.uk), Southampton (🖳 www.southamp tonairport.com) and Bournemouth (🖳 www.bournemouthairport.com), near Poole, are closer to the walk and have international flights though mostly from Europe only.

● **Eurostar** (🖳 www.eurostar.com) operates a high-speed passenger service via the Channel Tunnel between Paris, Brussels and Lille and London. The Eurostar terminal in London is at St Pancras International with connections to the London Underground and to all other main railway stations in London. Trains to Dorset and Devon leave from Paddington station (Great Western services) and also from Waterloo (South-West Trains); see below for details.

There are also various rail services from mainland Europe to Britain; for more information contact your national rail provider or Railteam (🖳 www.railteam.eu).

● **From Europe by coach** Eurolines (🖳 www.eurolines.com) have a wide network of long-distance bus services connecting over 500 destinations in 25 European countries to London (Victoria Coach Station). Visit the Eurolines website for details of services from your country.

● **From Europe with a car Ferry services** operate between: Santander/Roscoff and Plymouth; Cherbourg/St Malo/Caen and Poole/Portsmouth; Le Havre and Portsmouth; Calais and Dover; Dunkirk and Dover; Rotterdam/Zeebrugge and Hull; Dublin and Liverpool.

Look at 🖳 www.ferrysavers.com or 🖳 www.directferries.com for a full list of companies and services.

Eurotunnel (🖳 www.eurotunnel.com) operates a **shuttle train service** for vehicles via the Channel Tunnel between Calais and Folkestone taking 35 minutes only.

PLANNING YOUR WALK

Cross Country (☎ 0844-811 0124, 🖳 www.crosscountrytrains.co.uk) operates services from Scotland, the North-East, Manchester and the Midlands to Bournemouth, Exeter and Plymouth.

To access Dorset, and **Poole** or **Weymouth** from London, South West Trains (☎ 0845-600 0650, 🖳 www.southwesttrains.co.uk) run regularly and direct from London Waterloo.

National rail enquiries (☎ 0845-748 4950, 24hrs, 🖳 www.nationalrail.co.uk) is the only number you need to find out all timetable and fare information.

Rail **tickets** are generally cheaper if you book them well in advance and also if you buy online. Most discounted tickets carry some restrictions so check what they are before you purchase them. It is best to buy tickets through the relevant companies or at any rail station. However, they can also be bought online at 🖳 www.thetrainline.com and 🖳 www.qjump.co.uk.

It is often possible to buy a train ticket that includes bus travel at your destination: for further information visit the **Plusbus** website (🖳 www.plusbus.info).

If you think you'll want a **taxi** when you arrive consult the town guides included in this book, many of which have taxi numbers in their transport sections. Alternatively, visit 🖳 www.traintaxi.co.uk or 🖳 www.mylocaltaxi.co.uk.

By coach

National Express (☎ 0871-781 8178, lines open 24 hrs daily; 🖥 www.national express.com) is the principal coach (ie long-distance bus) operator in Britain. Travel by coach is usually cheaper than by rail but does take longer. See box below for details of services to Devon and Dorset.

To get the cheapest fares you need to book in advance. You can purchase tickets from coach and bus station ticket offices, National Express agents, directly from the driver (though not always, so do check with locals in advance), by telephone, or online. An easier option is to print your ticket yourself at home. Known as an e-ticket, you should be able to do this direct from the National Express website.

By car

● **From the Midlands and the North** The easiest way to reach **Devon** is along the M5, remaining on the motorway until Exeter and then following the A38 to Plymouth, or the A380 to Torbay (Paignton, Torquay, Brixham).

For **Dorset** leave the M5 at Bristol and follow the A37 to Dorchester and then the A35 to Poole.

PLANNING YOUR WALK

❏ **Useful National Express services**
Note: not all stops are listed

SH035 London to Bournemouth: numerous daily (some are direct, some call at places en route, such as Southampton); some continue to **Poole** (10/day), **Swanage** (1-2/day), **Weymouth** (1/day)

FK205 Heathrow Airport to **Poole** via Bournemouth, 12/day

FK206 Gatwick Airport to **Poole** via Portsmouth, Southampton & Bournemouth, 10/day

NX304 Liverpool to **Weymouth** via Birmingham, Oxford, Southampton & Bournemouth, 1/day

NX315 Eastbourne to Helston via Brighton, Portsmouth, Southampton, Bournemouth, **Poole**, **Weymouth**, Dorchester, Bridport, Exeter, **Plymouth**, St Austell, Truro & Falmouth, 1/day

NX328 Bristol to **Plymouth** via Taunton, 1/day

NX330 Birmingham to **Plymouth** via Worcester & Bristol, 1/day

NX333 Blackpool to **Weymouth** via Manchester, Birmingham, Bristol & Dorchester, 1/day

NX336 Birmingham to **Plymouth** via Bristol & Exeter, 1/day

NX404 London Victoria to **Plymouth** via Heathrow Airport, Reading, Bath, Bristol Airport, Exeter, Newton Abbot, **Torquay**, **Paignton** & Totnes, 1/day

NX500 London Victoria to Penzance via Heathrow Airport, Reading & **Plymouth**, 2/day

NX501 London Victoria to **Torquay** via Heathrow, Reading, Exeter or Taunton, 6/day; some services stop at **Dawlish** (1/day) and **Teignmouth** (1/day) and some continue to **Paignton** (4/day), **Brixham** (1/day) & **Starcross** (1/day)

NX504 London Victoria to Penzance via Heathrow, Reading, **Plymouth**, Truro & Falmouth, 2/day

NX531 Leeds to **Plymouth** via Birmingham, Gloucester & Bristol, 1-2/day.

● **From London** For **Devon**, if you are a fan of driving on motorways take the M4 across to Bristol and then the M5 south before following the directions above. Far more scenic – if a little longer (30-45 mins) – you could also take the M3, then pass Southampton on the M27 before taking the A31 through the New Forest, the A35 as far as Honiton, the A30 to Exeter, the M5 south (briefly) and the A38 to Plymouth. This route will take you directly above a number of places that feature on the coastal path. For **Dorset**, follow the above, turning off the A31 to join the A348 into Poole.

A good road atlas will be required to navigate Devon and Dorset's country lanes. The following roads are particularly useful: B357: Weymouth–Abbotsbury–Swyre (for West Bexington)–Burton Bradstock–Bridport (for West Bay); A35 & A3052: Bridport–Chideock–Charmouth–Lyme Regis–Seaton–Sidmouth–Exeter (with relatively easy access to Seatown, Beer, Branscombe & Budleigh Salterton); A379: Exeter–Starcross–Dawlish Warren–Dawlish–Teignmouth–Shaldon–Torbay–Dartmouth–Slapton–Torcross–Salcombe–Plymouth (and relatively easy access to Bigbury-on-Sea and Wembury).

You can get detailed driving directions from the AA website (🖳 www.theaa.com/route-planner/index.jsp) by clicking on the route planner.

Parking There are a couple of long-stay car parks (☎ 01752-304021, 🖳 www.plymouth.gov.uk/homepage/transportandroads/parking) in **Plymouth** that are central and should be safe. The cheapest option is Western Approach Car Park (£25 per week). Simply take your ticket as if going shopping and wander off along the coastal path, paying on your return.

The best option for long-stay parking in **Poole** is to leave your car at the Greyhound Stadium (☎ 01202-677449, 🖳 www.stadiauk.com/poole), a five-minute walk from the centre, which charges £5.40 per day.

By air
Please bear in mind that air travel is by far the least environmentally sound option (see 🖳 www.chooseclimate.org for the true costs of flying). However, if you do prefer to fly see box p53.

LOCAL TRANSPORT
Bus services
Both Devon and Dorset have reasonable public transport networks linking most of the coastal villages. There are usually several buses per day in the summer, though fewer in winter. This is great news for the walker as it opens up the possibility of walking along the coast path from a fixed base. Note, however, that the stretch between Wembury, Bigbury-on-Sea and Salcombe has very limited public transport options, as does the stretch between Lulworth Cove and Swanage.

Timetables Three timetables cover southern Devon. If walking the whole path you will need all of them. Starting from Plymouth you will need: **South Hams** (pink), which covers Plymouth to Torquay; **Teignbridge** (blue), which covers Brixham to the Exe Estuary and Exeter; and **East Devon** (green), that covers Exeter and Exmouth to Lyme Regis. Once in Dorset you will need the Southern Dorset Area timetable only.

In both counties you can pick the timetables up for free from bus stations, train stations, and tourist information centres. The timetables can also be either ordered online or downloaded from Devon County Council (☎ 01392-382800, 🖳 www.devon.gov.uk) and Dorset County Council (🖳 www.dorsetforyou .com/bustimetables). The service numbers of the most useful buses are given in the table below and on p58 and p60 so you can flip straight to the page you need in the actual timetable.

Bus companies and customer helplines If the contact details in the box below, or above, prove unsatisfactory, you can contact traveline (☎ 0871-200 2233, 8am-8pm; 🖳 traveline.info which has public transport information for the whole of the UK or, just for the south-west, 🖳 www.travelinesw.com).

Tickets

If you are going to be using the bus frequently over several days, 3-day or weekly tickets can be great value. They allow 'unlimited' travel within either Devon

---

❏ **PUBLIC TRANSPORT SERVICES**
Note: not all stops are listed. Also that details about the various ferry services on this section of the SWCP are provided, where relevant, in Part 4.

Bus services
Axe Valley Mini Travel (☎ 01297-625959)
899 Sidmouth to Seaton via Sidford, Branscombe & Beer, Mon-Fri 3/day plus 2/day during term-time, Sat 2/day

Damory Coaches (☎ 01258-452545; see Wilts & Dorset website for information)
40 (Purbeck Breezer) Swanage Bus Station to Poole Bus Station via Langton Matravers, Corfe Castle & Wareham, Mon-Sat 2/hr, Sun 1/hr
X43 Weymouth to Swanage via Osmington, Durdle Door (Holiday Park), Lulworth Cove, West Lulworth, Wool, Wareham & Corfe Castle, late July to early Sep, daily 4/day
61 Wyke Regis to Dorchester via Chickerell, Langton Herring, Portesham, Winterborne Abbas & Abbotsbury, Wed only 1/day
103 Bovington to Dorchester via Wool, East Lulworth, Lulworth Camp, West Lulworth, Lulworth Cove & Durdle Door, Mon-Sat 1/day plus 1/day Wool to Dorchester
104 Wareham to Dorchester via Bovington, Wool, East Lulworth, Lulworth Camp, West Lulworth, Lulworth Cove & Durdle Door, Mon-Sat 1/day plus 1/day Wareham to Lulworth Cove
275 Swanage to Wareham via Corfe Castle & Kimmeridge, Thur only 1/day

First Devon and Cornwall (🖳 www.firstgroup.com/ukbus/devon_cornwall)
48 Plymouth to Wembury via Plymstock, Mon-Sat 6/day
X80 Plymouth to Torquay via Totnes, South Brent, Ivybridge & Paignton, Mon-Sat 1/hr, Sun 6/day
X81 Paignton to Dartmouth via Collaton, Totnes & Halwell, Mon-Sat 1/hr, Sun Dartmouth to Totnes only 4/day

or Dorset on the relevant company's services. Note that not all services are included in some of these deals so you should always check that the pass you are purchasing covers the route you need to take. Check the relevant bus operator's website for further details.

Public transport at a glance

The map on p59 and table below are designed to make it easy for you to plan your day using public transport. Use the map to see which towns are covered by each service and then turn to the table to check that service's frequency. Take time to read the table carefully: some services run only one day a week, while others don't run at weekends. The definition of a summer service depends on the company and the route; in some cases it is from Easter to October but in others it's May/July to September – again, always check before you plan to use a summer service.

Note that bus services do change from year to year. Use this information as a rough guide and confirm details with the bus operators before travelling.

For information about tide timetables, see box p43.

(cont'd overleaf)

First Devon and Cornwall *(cont'd)*
93   Plymouth to Dartmouth via Brixton, Yealmpton, Aveton Gifford, Kingsbridge, Torcross, Slapton Turn, Strete, Blackpool & Stoke Fleming, Mon-Sat 1/hr, summer Sun 4/day.

First Dorset & South Somerset (💻 www.firstgroup.com/ukbus/dorset)
1   Weymouth to Portland via Wyke Regis, Mon-Sat 6/hr, Sun 4/hr
6   Weymouth to Wyke Regis circular route, Mon-Sat 2/hr
8   Weymouth to Chickerell circular route, Mon-Fri 4/hr, Sat 3/hr, Sun1/hr
10   Dorchester to Portland via Weymouth & Wyke Regis, Mon-Sat 2-3/hr in the evening (in the morning Portland to Dorchester); during the day 2/hr Dorchester to Weymouth Mon-Sat and 1/hr Sun
31   Axminster to Weymouth via Lyme Regis, Charmouth, Chideock & Bridport, Mon-Sat approx 1/hr, Sun 6/day
X53 **(Coastlinx Jurassic Coast)** Exeter to Weymouth via Beer Cross, Seaton, Colyford, Lyme Regis, Charmouth, Morcombelake, Chideock, Bridport, West Bay, Burton Bradstock, Swyre, Abbotsbury, Portesham & Chickerell, late Apr to early Nov, 8/day
X53 **(Coastlinx Jurassic Coast)** Weymouth to Poole via Osmington, Wool, Wareham, Sandord & Upton Cross, daily approx 1/hr, with some extra services in summer. Note: X53 services from Exeter to Weymouth connect with those from Weymouth to Poole
X54 Exeter to Colyton via Seaton & Axmouth, late Apr to early Nov, 1/day
102 Dorchester to Lulworth Cove via Crossways, Warmwell, Overmoigne, Winfrith Newburgh & Durdle Door, Sun 4/day
501 Weymouth to Portland Bill via Wyke Regis, Portland & Easton, summer only open-top bus, daily 8/day

PLANNING YOUR WALK

PUBLIC TRANSPORT SERVICES

Buses *(cont'd from p57)*
Stagecoach South West (🖳 www.stagecoachbus.com)
2   Newton Abbot to Exeter Bus Station via Teignmouth, Dawlish, Dawlish
       Warren, Cockwood & Starcross, Mon-Sat 3/hr, Sun 1/hr plus in summer 1/hr
       Newton Abbot to Teignmouth
11 Torquay to Teignmouth via St Marychurch, Maidencombe & Shaldon, Mon-Sat
       2/hr, Sun 7/day
12 Newton Abbot to Brixham via Torquay, Preston, Paignton & Broad Sands,
       Mon-Sat 4-6/hr, Sun 3/hr
22 Kingswear to Brixham via Hill Head & St Mary's Square, daily 1/hr
24 Kingswear to Brixham via Hill Head, Summercourt Way & St Mary's Square,
       Mon-Sat 1/hr
52A Exeter Bus Station to Seaton via Clyst St Mary, Sidmouth & Sidford, Mon-Sat
       1/hr, Sun 5/day
52B Exeter Bus Station to Honiton via Clyst St Mary, Sidmouth, Sidford & Sidbury,
       Mon-Sat 1/hr, Sun Exeter to Sidbury approx 1/hr
56 Exeter St David's Station to Exmouth via Exeter Bus Station, Exeter Airport,
       Woodbury & Lympstone, Mon-Sat 1/hr
56B Exeter St David's Station to Exeter Airport via Exeter Bus Station, year-round
       Sun & public holidays 1/hr
       Exeter St David's Station to Sidmouth via Exeter Bus Station, Exeter Airport,
       Ottery St Mary, Honiton & Sidbury, June-Sep Sun & public holidays 3/day
57 Exeter Bus Station to Exmouth via Topsham & Lympstone, Mon-Sat 4/hr, Sun
       & public holidays 2/hr
120 Kingswear to Paignton Bus Station via Churston & Goodrington, Mon-Sat 1/hr
157 Exmouth to Sidmouth via Budleigh Salterton, Mon-Sat 1/hr, Sun summer 4/day
357 Exmouth to Budleigh Salterton, Mon-Sat 1/hr
X46 Exeter Bus Station to Torquay, Mon-Fri 11/day, Sat 8/day plus Exeter to
       Torquay via Paignton Bus Station, Mon-Fri 5/day, Sat 6/day, Sun 3/day
X64 Exeter Bus Station to Salcombe via Newton Abbot, Totnes & Kingsbridge, Sun
       2/day

South West Coaches (🖳 www.southwestcoaches.co.uk)
205 Weymouth (King's Statue) to Portland Bill via Wyke Regis, Fortuneswell,
       Portland & Easton, Mon-Sat 3-4/day
206 Weymouth circular route to Wyke Regis, Mon-Sat 2/hr
210 Portland to Dorchester via Easton, Fortuneswell, Wyke Regis & Weymouth,
       Mon-Fri 1-2/hr

Tally Ho Coaches (☎ 01548-853081, 🖳 www.tallyhocoaches.co.uk)
94 Plymouth Bus Station to Noss Mayo via Plymstock, Brixton, Yealmpton &
       Newton Ferrers, Mon-Sat 5/day
162 Kingsbridge Bus Station circular route via Thurlestone, Outer Hope & Inner
       Hope, Mon-Sat 3/day
164 Totnes to Kingsbridge Bus Station, Mon-Sat 8/day
606 Kingsbridge Bus Station to Salcombe, Mon-Sat approx 1/hr
612 Ivybridge to Mothecombe via Modbury, Tue only 1/day
875 Plymouth Bus Station to Bigbury-on-Sea via Yealmpton, Modbury &
       Challaborough, Fri only 1/day

(cont'd on p60)

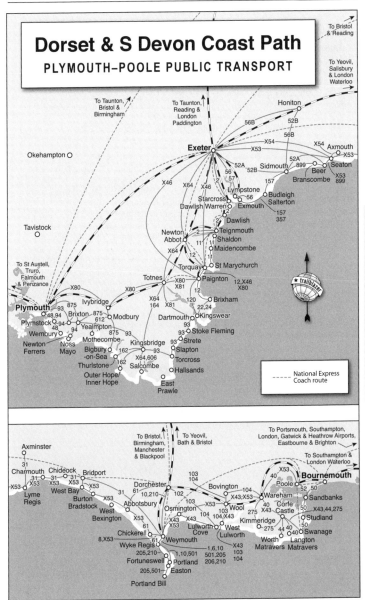

Dorset & S Devon Coast Path
PLYMOUTH–POOLE PUBLIC TRANSPORT

To Bristol & Reading

To Yeovil, Salisbury & London Waterloo

To Taunton, Bristol & Birmingham

To Taunton, Reading & London Paddington

Honiton

Okehampton

Exeter

56B   52B
56B
X54   X54   Axmouth
X53   X53
52A
X53
Sidmouth   899   Seaton
157   Beer   X53
Branscombe   899

X46   X64   X46
X64
52A   56
2   57   52B
Lympstone
Starcross   Budleigh
Dawlish Warren   Exmouth   Salterton
Newton   2   Dawlish   157
Abbot   2   Teignmouth   357
X64   11   Shaldon
12   11   Maidencombe
11   St Marychurch
Torquay
Totnes   X80   Paignton   12,X46
X80   X80   X80
X64   X81   12   X80
164   X81   120   Brixham
Dartmouth   Kingswear   22,24
93
93   Stoke Fleming
Kingsbridge   93   Strete
X64,606   93   Slapton
162   Salcombe   Torcross
162   Hallsands
Outer Hope/
Inner Hope   East
Prawle

Tavistock

To St Austell, Truro, Falmouth & Penzance

Plymouth
93   875
48,94   Brixton   875
Plymstock   94   Modbury
48   Yealmpton   612
Wembury   94
875   93
Newton   Noss   Mothecombe
Ferrers   Mayo   Bigbury
-on-Sea
Thurlstone
Ivybridge

trailblazer

National Express Coach route

Axminster

To Bristol, Birmingham, Manchester & Blackpool

To Yeovil, Bath & Bristol

To Portsmouth, Southampton, London, Gatwick & Heathrow Airports, Eastbourne & Brighton

To Southampton & London Waterloo

31
Charmouth   Chideock   Bridport
X53   31   31   31
Lyme   X53   X53   X53
Regis   West Bay   X53
31   Dorchester   Bovington
Burton   61   103
Bradstock   Abbotsbury   102   104
West   103   X43,X53
Bexington   Osmington   X53   Wareham
X43   103   Wool   275
X53   104   104,X43
Chickerell   Lulworth   West
8,X53   61   Cove   Lulworth   Kimmeridge
Wyke Regis   61
205,210   1,10,501   X43   Worth   Langton
Fortuneswell   501,205   103   Matravers   Matravers
205,501   206,210   104
Portland
Easton

103
104

Bournemouth
X53
40
52   50   Poole
Sandbanks
40
X43   Corfe   50   X43,44,275
Castle   Studland
150
44   40   Swanage
40

N

PLANNING YOUR WALK

PLANNING YOUR WALK

PUBLIC TRANSPORT SERVICES

Buses *(cont'd from p58)*

Wilts & Dorset Bus Company (🖥 www.morebus.co.uk); some of the services are operated in conjunction with Damory (see p56)

44 (Breezer) Swanage Bus Station to Worth Matravers via Harman's Cross, Corfe Castle & Kingston, Mon-Fri 2/day, Sat 3/day

50 (Purbeck Breezer Open Top) Swanage Bus Station to Bournemouth Station via Studland & Sandbanks, Apr-Sep daily 1-3/hr

52 Sandbanks to Poole via Canford Cliffs, daily 1-2/hr

Rail services

First Great Western (☎ 0845-700 0125, 🖥 www.firstgreatwestern.co.uk)

- London Paddington to Plymouth via Reading, Taunton, Tiverton Parkway & Exeter St David's (Timetable 30), daily approx 1/hr
- Exeter St David's to Plymouth via Newton Abbot, Totnes & Ivybridge (Timetable 31), daily 1-3/hr (1/hr stops at Ivybridge)
- Exmouth (The Riviera Line) to Paignton via Topsham, Digby & Sowton, Exeter Central, Exeter St David's, Exeter St Thomas, Starcross, Dawlish Warren, Dawlish, Teignmouth, Newton Abbot, Torre & Torquay, daily approx 1/hr (Timetable 33)
- Exeter St David's to Exmouth (The Avocet Line) via Exeter Central, St James's Park, Polsloe Bridge, Digby & Sowton, Topsham, Exton, Lympstone Commando & Lympstone Village, Mon-Sat 2/hr, Sun 1/hr (Timetable 32/34)
- Penzance to Plymouth via Redruth, Truro, Par & Bodmin Parkway, Mon-Sat 1-2/hr, Sun 1/hr (Timetable 35)
- Bristol Temple Meads to Weymouth via Bath Spa, Bradford-on-Avon, Frome, Bruton, Castle Clary, Yeovil, Dorchester West & Upwey (Timetable 27), Mon-Sat 7/day, Sun 4/day

South West Trains (☎ 0845-600 0650, 🖥 www.southwesttrains.co.uk)

- London Waterloo to Weymouth via Basingstoke, Southampton, Brockenhurst, Bournemouth, Poole, Wareham, Wool, Moreton, Dorchester South & Upwey, Mon-Sat 2/hr, Sun 1/hr (Timetable 28; not all services stop at every station)
- London Waterloo to Exeter St David's via Basingstoke, Andover, Salisbury, Yeovil Junction, Axminster, Honiton & Exeter Central (Timetable 20; not all services stop at every station), daily 1/hr

MINIMUM IMPACT & OUTDOOR SAFETY

2

Minimum impact walking

By visiting this rural corner of England you are having a positive impact, not just on your own well-being but on local communities as well. Your presence brings money and jobs into the local economy and also pride in and awareness of the region's environment and culture.

However, the environment should not just be considered in terms of its value as a tourist asset. Its long-term survival and enjoyment by future generations will only be possible if both visitors and local communities protect it now. The following points are made to help you reduce your impact on the environment, encourage conservation and promote sustainable tourism in the area.

ECONOMIC IMPACT

Rural businesses and communities in Britain have been hit hard in recent years by a seemingly endless series of crises. Most people are aware of the country code; not dropping litter and closing the gate behind you are still as pertinent as ever. But in light of the economic pressures that local countryside businesses are under, there is something else you can do: **buy local**.

Look and ask for local produce (see box p22) to buy and eat. Not only does this cut down on the amount of pollution and congestion that the transportation of food creates – so-called 'food miles' – but also ensures that you are supporting local farmers and producers, the very people who have moulded the countryside you have come to see and who are in the best position to protect it. If you can find local food which is also organic so much the better.

It's a fact of life that money spent at local level – perhaps in a market, or at the greengrocer, or in an independent pub – has a far greater impact for good on that community than the equivalent spent in a branch of a national chain store or restaurant. While no-one would advocate that walkers should boycott the larger supermarkets, which after all do provide local employment, it's worth remembering that businesses in rural communities rely heavily on visitors for their very existence. If we want to keep these shops and post offices, we need to use them.

ENVIRONMENTAL IMPACT

A walking holiday in itself is an environmentally friendly approach to tourism. The following are some ideas on how you can go a few steps further in helping to minimise your impact on the environment while walking the South-West Coast Path.

Use public transport whenever possible
While we recognise that public transport along this section of the South-West Coast Path is not great, using it is preferable to taking a car as it benefits everyone: visitors, locals and the environment.

Never leave litter
Leaving litter shows a total disrespect for the natural world and others coming after you. As well as being unsightly, litter kills wildlife, pollutes the environment and can be dangerous to farm animals. Please carry a plastic bag so you can dispose of your rubbish in a bin in the next village. It would be very helpful if you could pick up litter left by other people too.

● **Is it OK if it's biodegradable?** Not really. Apple cores, banana skins, orange peel and the like are unsightly, encourage flies, ants and wasps and ruin a picnic spot for others. Using the excuse that they are natural and biodegradable just doesn't cut any ice. When was the last time you saw a banana tree in England?

● **The lasting impact of litter** A piece of orange peel left on the ground takes six months to decompose; silver foil 18 months; a plastic bag 10 years; clothes 15 years; and an aluminium can 85 years.

Respect all wildlife
Care for all wildlife you come across along the path; it has as much right to be there as you. As tempting as it may be to pick wild flowers, leave them in place so the next people who pass can enjoy them too. Don't break branches off or damage trees in any way.

If you come across wildlife, keep your distance and don't watch for too long. Your presence can cause considerable stress, particularly if the adults are with young, or in winter when the weather is harsh and food is scarce. Young animals are rarely abandoned. If you come across young birds, keep away so that their mother can return.

Outdoor toiletry
As more and more people discover the joys of walking in the natural environment issues such as how to go to the loo outdoors rapidly gain importance. How many of us have shaken our heads at the sight of toilet paper strewn beside the path, or even worse, someone's dump left in full view? Human excrement is not only offensive to our senses but, more importantly, can infect water sources.

Where to go The coast path is a high-use area and many habitats will not benefit from your fertilisation. As far as 'number twos' are concerned try whenever possible to use public toilets. There is no shortage of public toilets along the coast path and they are all marked on the trail maps. However, there are those times when the only time is now. If you have to go outdoors help the environment to deal with your deposit in the best possible way by following a few simple guidelines:

● **Choose your site carefully** It should be at least 30 metres away from running water and out of reach of the high tide and not on any site of historical or archaeological interest. Carry a small trowel or use a sturdy stick to dig a small hole about 15cm (6") deep to bury your faeces in. Faeces decompose quicker when in contact with the top layer of soil or leaf mould; by using a stick to stir loose soil into your deposit you will speed decomposition up even more. Do not squash it under rocks as this slows down the decomposition process. If you have to use rocks as a cover make sure they are not in contact with your faeces.

● **Pack out toilet paper and tampons** Toilet paper takes a long time to decompose whether buried or not. It is easily dug up by animals and will then blow into water sources or onto the trail. The best method for dealing with used toilet paper is to pack it out. Put it in a paper bag placed inside a plastic bag and then dispose of it at the next toilet. Tampons and sanitary towels also need to be packed out in a similar way. They take years to decompose and may be dug up and scattered about by animals.

ACCESS

Britain is a crowded cluster of islands with few places where you can wander as you please. Most of the land is a patchwork of fields and agriculture and the environment through which the Dorset & South Devon Coast Path marches is no different. However, there are countless public rights of way, in addition to the main trail, that criss-cross the land.

This is fine, but what happens if you feel a little more adventurous and want to explore the moorland, woodland and hills that can also be found near the walk. Access to the countryside has always been a hot topic in Britain. In the 1940s soldiers coming back from the Second World War were horrified and disgruntled to find that landowners were denying them the right to walk across the moors; ironically the very country that they had been fighting to protect. Since then it has been an ongoing battle and it is a battle that has finally been won as new legislation came into force in 2005 granting public access to thousands of acres of Britain's wildest land.

All those who enjoy access to the countryside must respect the land, its wildlife, the interests of those who live and work there and other users; we all share a common interest in the countryside. Knowing your rights and responsibilities gives you the information you need to act with minimal impact.

Rights of way

As a designated National Trail the coast path is a public right of way. A public right of way is either a footpath, a bridleway or a byway. The Dorset & South Devon Coast Path is a footpath for almost all its length which means that anyone has the legal right to use it on foot only.

Rights of way are theoretically established because the owner has dedicated them to public use. However, very few paths are formally dedicated in this way.

If members of the public have been using a path without interference for 20 years or more the law assumes the owner has intended to dedicate it as a right of way. If a path has been unused for 20 years it does not cease to exist; the guiding principle is 'once a highway, always a highway'.

On a public right of way you have the right to 'pass and repass along the way' which includes stopping to rest or admire the view, or to consume refreshments. You can also take with you a 'natural accompaniment' (!) which includes a dog, but it must be kept under close control (see p51).

Farmers and land managers must ensure that paths are not blocked by crops or other vegetation, or otherwise obstructed, that the route is identifiable and the surface is restored soon after cultivation. If crops are growing over the path you have every right to walk through them, following the line of the right of way as closely as possible.

If you find a path blocked or impassable you should report it to the appropriate highway authority. Highway authorities are responsible for maintaining footpaths. In Devon and Dorset the highway authorities are the respective county councils. The council is also the surveying authority with responsibility for maintaining the official definitive map of public rights of way.

Wider access

The access situation to land around the coast path is a little more complicated. Trying to unravel and understand the seemingly thousands of different laws and acts is never easy in any legal system. Parliamentary Acts give a right to walk over certain areas of land such as some, but by no means all, common land and some specific places such as Dartmoor and the New Forest. However, in other places, such as Bodmin Moor and many British beaches, right of access is not written in law. It is merely tolerated by the landowner and could be terminated at any time.

Some landowners, such as the Forestry Commission, water companies and the National Trust, are obliged by law to allow some degree of access to their land. Land covered by schemes such as the Environmental Stewardship Scheme, formerly the Countryside Stewardship Scheme, gives landowners a financial incentive to manage their land for conservation and to provide limited public access. There are also a few truly altruistic landowners who have allowed access over their land and these include organisations such as the RSPB, the Woodland Trust, and some local authorities. Overall, however, access to most of Britain's countryside is forbidden to Britain's people, in marked contrast to the general rights of access that prevail in other European countries.

Right to roam

For many years groups such as Ramblers (see box p47) and the British Mountaineering Council (🖥 www.thebmc.co.uk) campaigned for new and wider access legislation. This finally bore fruit in the form of the Countryside and Rights of Way Act of November 2000, colloquially known as the CRoW Act, which granted access for 'recreation on foot' to mountain, moor, heath, down and registered common land in England and Wales. In essence it allows walkers the freedom to roam responsibly away from footpaths, without being accused of trespass, on about four million acres of open, uncultivated land.

On 28th August 2005 the South-West became the sixth region in England and Wales to be opened up under this act; however, restrictions may still be in place from time to time – check the situation on 🖳 www.open access.gov.uk.

The new agreed areas of open access are clearly marked on all the latest Ordnance Survey Explorer (1:25,000) maps. In the future it is hoped that the legislation can be extended to include other types of land such as cliff, foreshore, woodland, riverside and canal side.

Old milestone in miles, furlongs and poles. In case you've forgotten, 40 poles make one furlong and eight furlongs equal one mile.

The Countryside Code

The countryside is a fragile place which every visitor should respect. The Countryside Code seems common sense but sadly some people still seem to have no understanding of how to treat the countryside they walk in. Everyone visiting the countryside has a responsibility to minimise the impact of their visit so that other people can enjoy the same peaceful landscapes. It does not take much effort; it really is common sense.

Below is an expanded version of the Countryside Code, the logo of which is 'Respect, Protect and Enjoy':

● **Be safe** Walking on the SWCP is pretty much hazard free but you're responsible for your own safety so follow the simple guidelines outlined on pp66-9.

● **Leave all gates as you found them** Normally a farmer leaves gates closed to keep livestock in but may sometimes leave them open to allow livestock access to food or water. Leave them as you find them and if there is a sign, follow the instructions.

● **Leave livestock, crops and machinery alone** Help farmers by not interfering with their means of livelihood.

● **Take your litter home** 'Pack it in, pack it out'. Litter is not only ugly but can be harmful to wildlife. Small mammals often become trapped in discarded cans and bottles. Many walkers think that orange peel and banana skins do not count as litter. Even biodegradable foodstuffs attract common scavenging species such as crows and gulls to the detriment of less-dominant species. See p62.

● **Keep your dog under control** Across farmland dogs should be kept on a lead. During lambing time they should not be taken with you at all; see box p51.

● **Enjoy the countryside and respect its life and work** Access to the countryside depends on being sensitive to the needs and wishes of those who live and work there. Being courteous and friendly to those you meet will ensure a healthy future for all based on partnership and co-operation.

● **Keep to paths across farmland** Stick to the official path across arable or pasture land. Minimise erosion by not cutting corners or widening the path.

● **Use gates and stiles to cross fences, hedges and walls** The path is well supplied with stiles where it crosses field boundaries. If you have to climb over a gate because you can't open it always do so at the hinged end.

● **Help keep all water clean** Leaving litter and going to the toilet near a water source can pollute people's water supplies. See pp62-3 for more advice.

● **Take special care on country roads** Drivers often go dangerously fast on narrow winding lanes. To be safe, walk facing the oncoming traffic and carry a torch or wear highly visible clothing when it's getting dark. If you travel by car drive with care and reduce your speed on country roads. Park your car with consideration for others' needs; never block a gateway.

● **Protect wildlife, plants and trees** Care for and respect all wildlife you come across along the path. Don't pick plants, break trees or scare wild animals. If you come across young birds that appear to have been abandoned leave them alone.

● **Guard against all risk of fire** Accidental fire is a great fear for farmers and foresters. Never make a camp fire: the deep burn damages turf and destroys flora and fauna. Take cigarette butts with you to dispose of safely.

● **Make no unnecessary noise** Stay in small groups and act unobtrusively. Avoid noisy and disruptive behaviour which might annoy residents and other visitors and frighten farm animals and wildlife.

Outdoor safety

AVOIDANCE OF HAZARDS

Swimming

If you are not an experienced swimmer or familiar with the sea, plan ahead and swim at beaches where there is a lifeguard service, such as Exmouth, Teignmouth and Dawlish Warren. On such beaches you should swim between the red and yellow flags as this is the patrolled area. Don't swim between black

❏ **Landslides**
The geology of the Jurassic coast makes the cliffs and beaches along this stretch particularly susceptible to landslides, especially after periods of prolonged rainfall. Remember to tread carefully when walking on top of the cliffs and **always avoid walking and sitting directly below them where possible**. Remain aware of the edges, particularly in conditions that may leave you vulnerable to sudden gusts of wind and keep your dog on a lead if it has a tendency to chase rabbits.

Despite being relatively rare, landslides are occasionally responsible for fatalities, most recently in July 2012 when 400 tonnes of rock slid from the cliffs on to Hive Beach, near Burton Bradstock.

and white chequered flags as these areas are only for surfboards. A red flag flying indicates that it is dangerous to enter the water. If you are not sure about anything ask one of the lifeguards; after all they are there to help you.

If you are going to swim at unsupervised beaches never do so alone and always take care. Some beaches are prone to strong rips. Never swim off headlands or near river mouths as there may be strong currents. Always be aware of changing weather conditions and tidal movement. The South-West has a huge tidal range and it can be very easy to get cut off by the tide.

If you see someone in difficulty do not attempt a rescue until you have contacted the coastguard (see box p27). Once you know help is on the way try to assist the person by throwing something to help them stay afloat. Many beaches have rescue equipment located in red boxes; these are marked on the trail maps.

Walking alone

If you are walking alone you must appreciate and be prepared for the increased risk. It is always a good idea to leave word with somebody about where you are going; you can always ring ahead to book accommodation and let them know you are walking alone and what time you expect to arrive. Don't forget to contact whoever you have left word with to let them know you've arrived safely. Carrying a mobile phone can be useful though you cannot rely on getting good reception (see box p42).

Safety on the coast path

Sadly every year people are injured walking along the trail, though usually it's nothing more than a badly twisted ankle. Parts of the path can be pretty remote, however, and it certainly pays to take precautions when walking. Abiding by the following rules should minimise the risks.

● Avoid walking on your own if possible.
● Make sure that somebody knows your plans for every day you are on the trail. This could be a friend or relative whom you have promised to call every night or the B&B or hostel you plan to stay in at the end of each day's walk. That way, if you fail to turn up or call, they can raise the alarm.
● If the weather closes in suddenly and fog or mist descends while you are on the trail and you become uncertain of the correct trail, do not be tempted to continue. Just wait where you are and you'll find that mist often clears, at least for long enough to allow you to get your bearings.

If you are still uncertain and the weather does not look like improving, return the way you came to the nearest point of civilisation and try again another time when conditions have improved.
● Always fill your water bottle or pouch at every available opportunity and ensure you have some food such as high-energy snacks.

There may be a good reason why you shouldn't take a short cut.

MINIMUM IMPACT & OUTDOOR SAFETY

- Always carry a torch, compass, map, whistle and wet-weather gear with you.
- Wear strong sturdy boots with good ankle support and a good grip, not trainers.
- Be extra vigilant with children and dogs.

Dealing with an accident

- Use basic first aid to treat the injury to the best of your ability.
- Try to attract the attention of anybody else who may be in the area. The **international distress (emergency) signal** is six blasts on a whistle, or six flashes with a torch.
- If possible leave someone with the casualty while others go to get help. If there are only two people, you have a dilemma. If you decide to get help, leave all spare clothing and food with the casualty.
- In an emergency dial ☎ 999 and ask for the coastguard. They are responsible for dealing with any emergency that occurs on the coast or at sea. Make sure you know exactly where you are before you call.
- Report the exact position of the casualty and their condition.

WEATHER AND WEATHER FORECASTS

The trail suffers from extremes of weather so it's vital that you always try to find out what the weather is going to be like before you set off for the day. It is a good idea to pay attention to **wind and gale warnings**. The wind on any coastline can get very strong and if it is strong it is advisable not to walk, particularly if you are carrying a pack which can act as a sail. If you are on a steep incline or above high cliffs it is also dangerous. Even if the wind direction is inland it can literally blow you right over (unpleasant if there are gorse bushes around!), or if it suddenly stops or eddies (a common phenomenon when strong winds hit cliffs) it can cause you to lose your balance and stagger in the direction in which you have been leaning, ie towards the cliffs!

Another hazard on the coast is **sea mist or fog** which can dramatically decrease visibility. If a coastal fog blows over take extreme care where the path runs close to cliff edges.

Most hotels, some B&Bs and TICs will have pinned up somewhere a summary of the **weather forecast**. Alternatively you can get a forecast through 💻 www.bbc.co.uk/weather, or 💻 www.metoffice.gov.uk/weather.

Pay close attention to the weather forecast and alter your plans for the day accordingly. That said, even if the forecast is for a fine sunny day, always assume the worst and pack some wet-weather gear.

BLISTERS

It is important to break in new boots before embarking on a long trek. Make sure the boots are comfortable and try to avoid getting them wet on the inside. Air your feet at every opportunity, keep them clean and change your socks regularly; using talcum powder can help to keep them dry. If you feel any hot spots, stop immediately and apply a few strips of zinc oxide tape and leave it on until the 'hot spot' is pain free or the tape starts to come off.

MINIMUM IMPACT & OUTDOOR SAFETY

If you have left it too late and a blister has developed you should surround it with Compeed or any other blister kit to protect it from abrasion. Popping it can lead to infection. If the skin is broken keep the area clean with antiseptic and cover with a non-adhesive dressing material held in place with tape.

HYPOTHERMIA

Also known as exposure, this occurs when the body can't generate enough heat to maintain its normal temperature, usually as a result of being wet, cold, unprotected from the wind, tired and hungry. It is usually more of a problem in upland areas such as on the moors. Hypothermia is easily avoided by wearing suitable clothing, carrying and eating enough food and drink, being aware of the weather conditions and checking the morale of your companions.

Early signs to watch for are feeling cold and tired with involuntary shivering. Find some shelter as soon as possible and warm the victim up with a hot drink and some chocolate or other high-energy food. If possible give them another warm layer of clothing and allow them to rest until feeling better.

If allowed to worsen, strange behaviour, slurring of speech and poor coordination will become apparent and the victim can easily progress into unconsciousness, followed by coma and death. Quickly get the victim out of any wind and rain, improvising a shelter if necessary. Rapid restoration of bodily warmth is essential and best achieved by bare-skin contact: someone should get into the same sleeping bag as the patient, both having stripped to their underwear, putting any spare clothing under or over them to build up heat. Send urgently for help.

HYPERTHERMIA

Hyperthermia occurs when the body generates too much heat, eg heat exhaustion and heatstroke. Not ailments that you would normally associate with England, these are serious problems nonetheless.

Symptoms of **heat exhaustion** include thirst, fatigue, giddiness, a rapid pulse, raised body temperature, low urine output and, if not treated, delirium and finally a coma. The best cure is to drink plenty of water. The darker your urine the more you should drink.

Heatstroke is more serious. A high body temperature and an absence of sweating are early indications, followed by symptoms similar to hypothermia (see above) such as a lack of coordination, convulsions and coma. Death will follow if treatment is not given instantly. Sponge the victim down, wrap them in wet towels, fan them and get help immediately.

SUNBURN

The sun in the South-West can be very strong. The way to avoid sunburn is to stay wrapped up but that's not really an option. What you must do, therefore, is to wear a hat and smother yourself in sunscreen (with a minimum factor of 15); apply it regularly throughout the day.

Don't forget your lips, nose, the back of your neck, and even under your chin to protect you against rays reflected from the ground.

MINIMUM IMPACT & OUTDOOR SAFETY

3

THE ENVIRONMENT AND NATURE

Conserving the Dorset & South Devon Coast Path

Britain is an overcrowded island and England is the most densely populated part of it. As such, the English countryside has suffered a great deal of pressure from both over-population and the activities of an ever more industrialised world. Thankfully, there is some enlightened legislation to protect the surviving pockets of forest and heathland.

Beyond these fragments, it is interesting to note just how much man has altered the land he lives on. Whilst the aesthetic costs of such intrusions are open to debate, what is certain is the loss of biodiversity that has resulted. The last wild boar was shot a few centuries ago; add to its demise the extinction of bear and wolf as well as, far more recently, a number of other species lost or severely depleted and you get an idea of just how much an influence man has over the land, and how that influence is all too often used negatively.

There is good news, however. In these enlightened times when environmental issues are quite rightly given more precedence, many endangered species, such as the otter, have increased in number thanks to the active work of voluntary conservation bodies. There are other reasons to be optimistic; the environment is no longer the least important issue in party politics and this reflects the opinions of everyday people who are concerned about issues such as conservation on both a local and global scale.

CONSERVATION SCHEMES – WHAT'S AN AONB?

It is perhaps the chief joy of this walk that much of it is spent in either a national park or an Area of Outstanding Natural Beauty (AONB). But what exactly are these designations and what protection do they actually confer?

National parks

The highest level of landscape protection is the designation of land as a national park (💻 www.nationalparks.gov.uk). There are 15 in Britain of which nine are in England. This designation recognises the national importance of an area in terms of landscape, biodiversity and as a recreational resource. It does not signify national ownership and these are not uninhabited wildernesses, making conservation a knife-edged balance between protecting the environment and the rights and livelihoods of those living in the park. There are, alas, no national parks on this stretch of the coast path.

Areas of Outstanding Natural Beauty

The second level of protection is Area of Outstanding Natural Beauty (AONB; 🖥 www.aonb.org.uk), of which there are 38 in England and Wales. Much of the SWCP crosses land covered by either this designation or its close relative, **Heritage Coasts**. Around 33% of the English coastline has been designated a Heritage Coast and in this book South Devon, East Devon, West Dorset and Purbeck are all Heritage Coasts.

The primary objective of AONBs (and Heritage Coasts) is conservation of the natural beauty of a landscape. As there is no statutory administrative framework for their management, this is the responsibility of the local authority within whose boundaries they fall.

As well as many AONBs this section of coast is also blessed with its very own Geopark (see box p158), of which there are only eight in the UK.

National Nature Reserves and Sites of Special Scientific Interest

The next level of protection includes National Nature Reserves (NNRs) and Sites of Special Scientific Interest (SSSIs).

There are 224 **NNRs** in England, of which Axmouth–Lyme Regis Undercliffs, Berry Head to Sharkham Point, Dawlish Warren and Slapton Ley, Durlston and Studland are all covered by this book.

There are over 4100 **SSSIs** in England. SSSIs are a particularly important designation as they have some legal standing. They are managed in partnership with the owners and occupiers of the land who must give written notice before initiating any operations likely to damage the site and who cannot proceed without consent from **Natural England** (🖥 www.naturalengland.org.uk), the single body responsible for identifying, establishing and managing National Parks, AONBs, NNRs, SSSIs and Special Areas of Conservation (SAC), see below. There are plenty of SSSIs along this stretch of the SWCP, including 14 on the Jurassic Coast (such as Sidmouth to Beer SSSI and the South Dorset Coast SSSI that encompasses Kimmeridge Bay) and numerous SSSIs on the South Devon shore including Plymouth Sound, the Taw–Torridge, Yealm, Exe, Erme and Otter estuaries, the points at Wembury, Prawle and Start, the stretches of coastline from Bolt Head to Bolt Tail, Hallsands to Beesands, Roundham Head – and around Dawlish Warren.

Special Area of Conservation (SAC) is an international designation which came into being as a result of the 1992 Earth Summit in Rio de Janeiro, Brazil. This European-wide network of sites is designed to promote the conservation of habitats, wild animals and plants, both on land and at sea. At the time of writing 236 land sites in England had been designated as SACs including South Hams, Blackstone Point near Dartmouth, Beer Quarry Caves (see p226), Chesil and the Fleet, and St Alban's Head to Durlston Head and Sidmouth to West Bay.

Campaigning and conservation organisations

A number of voluntary organisations started the conservation movement in the mid 19th century and they are still at the forefront of developments. Independent of government but reliant on public support, they can concentrate their resources either on acquiring land which can then be managed purely for conservation purposes, or on influencing political decision-makers by lobbying and campaigning.

Managers and owners of land include well-known bodies such as the **National Trust** (NT; 🖥 www.nationaltrust.org.uk) that owns over 600 miles of coastline including Wembury, Noss Mayo, Salcombe to Hope Point, South Milton Sands in South Hams, Hallsands to Beesands, Bolberry Down, Branscombe, Overbecks in Salcombe, Orcombe Point, Studland Beach, Purbeck Countryside and, inland, the Hardy Monument (see p262); the **Royal Society for the Protection of Birds** (RSPB; 🖥 www.rspb.org.uk), and the **Council for the Protection of Rural England** (CPRE; 🖥 www.cpre.org.uk) and **Woodland Trust** (🖥 www.woodland-trust.org.uk).

The **Wildlife Trusts** (🖥 www.wildlifetrusts.org) are the umbrella organisa-tion for the 47 wildlife trusts in the UK that manage nature reserves and run marine conservation projects. The sole purpose of the **Marine Conservation Society** (🖥 www.mcsuk.org) is to protect the seas and shores as well as the wildlife in and around them so they also run marine conservation projects.

Geology

EONS, ERAS AND PERIODS

Give or take the odd thousand years, the Earth is four and a half billion years old. To make such a huge timespan more manageable, geologists have divided these four and a half billion years into four different **eons**, with each at least half a billion years or more in length; the **Phanerozoic eon** (from 570 million years to the present day) is the most relevant for this walk.

These eons are then further subdivided into **eras**, each spanning several hun-dred million years – and the cliffs, rocks and fossils found along this 217¼-mile stretch of coast date from three of these eras: the **Palaeozoic** (570-250 million years ago), the **Mesozoic** (250-65 million years ago), and the **Cenozoic** (65 mil-lion years ago to the present day).

Without wishing to complicate matters any further, these geological eras are further divided into **periods**. The length of each period varies because the divi-sions aren't arbitrary, but are defined by distinctive changes in the types of rocks and fossils that can be found in the layers. As you probably know, when you look at a cliff-face you'll notice that it has lines running horizontally through it. These lines are layers of sediment that have been laid down over time, with the oldest at the bottom and the newest at the top.

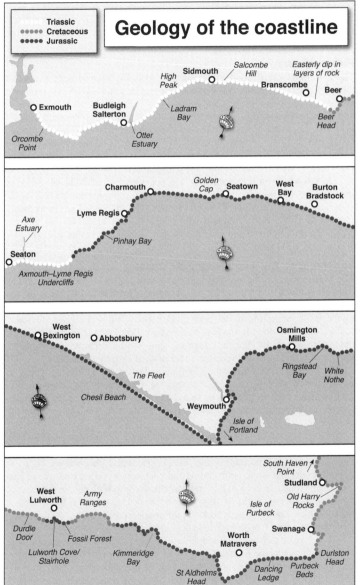

Geology of the coastline

Triassic
Cretaceous
Jurassic

Exmouth
Orcombe Point
Budleigh Salterton
Otter Estuary
High Peak
Ladram Bay
Sidmouth
Salcombe Hill
Branscombe
Easterly dip in layers of rock
Beer
Beer Head

Axe Estuary
Seaton
Axmouth–Lyme Regis Undercliffs
Lyme Regis
Pinhay Bay
Charmouth
Golden Cap
Seatown
West Bay
Burton Bradstock

West Bexington
Abbotsbury
The Fleet
Chesil Beach
Weymouth
Isle of Portland
Osmington Mills
Ringstead Bay
White Nothe

West Lulworth
Army Ranges
Durdle Door
Lulworth Cove/ Stairhole
Fossil Forest
Kimmeridge Bay
St Aldhelms Head
Worth Matravers
Dancing Ledge
Purbeck Beds
Isle of Purbeck
South Haven Point
Studland
Old Harry Rocks
Swanage
Durlston Head

THE ENVIRONMENT & NATURE

Geologists are able to identify how long ago each of those layers were formed, and from the type of rock and fossils found in each layer they can determine what the terrain and the climate were like – and what creatures roamed the Earth at that time.

Palaeozoic era

The Palaeozoic era is divided into six main periods. Starting from the oldest they are: the Cambrian, Ordovician, Silurian, Devonian, Carboniferous and Permian.

The Cambrian period stretched for 70 million years (570-500 million years ago) and was characterised by the first shellfish and, for the first time, fossils which can be found in great numbers. On the other hand the Permian period spans only 30 million years (280-250 million years ago) and is characterised by the widespread existence of reptiles and amphibians.

On this walk you'll come across significant geological evidence of two of these Palaeozoic periods: the **Devonian** (415-360 million years ago) is represented by the limestone sites between Plymouth and the River Exe (Berry Head, Daddyhole Cove, Hope's Nose); while the red cliffs near Dawlish Warren, which are actually fossilised sand dunes, date from the **Permian period** (290-250 million years ago).

The Mesozoic Era and the Jurassic Coast

The Mesozoic era is the one that will be of most interest to the walker on this route. It is divided into three periods, **Triassic**, **Jurassic** and **Cretaceous** and it's fair to say that these periods could be described – by the layman at least – as the most interesting of all geological periods, when the great dinosaurs roamed the Earth (the Mesozoic is commonly called the 'Age of the Reptiles'), the supercontinent of Pangaea began the split into the separate continents we know today, and birds and mammals also made their first appearance.

So what is it that makes the coastline of Devon and Dorset so special to geologists today? Well, there is, of course, the wealth of fossils and rocks from each of these periods that can be found along this stretch of southern British shoreline. Perhaps, more importantly, this evidence is both exposed and readily accessible.

The erosion so prevalent along most coastlines is partly responsible for this, the millennia of wind, weather and waves exposing the various strata of the three periods. But in part this is also due to a geological phenomenon called an **unconformity**. At some point during the Cretaceous period, rocks were first tilted then eroded, leading to the complete disappearance on certain stretches of the coast of Jurassic rock. As such, in certain places (such as at Sidmouth) on the coast there are Cretaceous rocks (ie the youngest rocks of the Mesozoic era) lying directly atop Triassic rocks (ie the oldest rocks).

Thus, while geology is impossible to escape and there are several sites between Plymouth and Exmouth that are of interest to rock-hounds, the subject becomes truly spectacular once you arrive at Orcombe Point (see Map 41, p208), just east of Exmouth, the official start of the Jurassic Coast that's

❏ **Where to see evidence of the Triassic Period**
● **Orcombe Point** The red mudstone and sandstone at Orcombe provide evidence of the harsh desert environment of the Triassic.
● **Budleigh Salterton** Here one finds Triassic pebble-beds overlain with red sandstone.
● **Otter Estuary** Formed of Triassic sandstone; a fossilised 'Devon rhynchosaur', a stocky dinosaur up to 2m in length with a powerful beak, was also found buried here.
● **Ladram Bay** The impressive red sea stacks here are made of Triassic sandstone, the result of erosion by the sea.
● **Sidmouth to Beer** This stretch provides a great example of the unconformity (see opposite), with the cliff's colours changing from orange Triassic rock to the white chalk of the Cretaceous period.
● **The Undercliffs** Beginning at the Axe estuary in the late Triassic period, 7 miles and 25 million years later you arrive near Pinhay Bay in the early Jurassic! Just to complete the Mesozoic set, landslips also expose Cretaceous chalk.

marked, as you will discover, by a geoneedle unveiled by Prince Charles. The following is a site-by-site guide to the coast, organised by geological period.

Triassic Period (250-200 million years ago) During this period Devon was located near to the centre of a super-continent: Pangaea. The county was part of a huge, hot and arid desert through which seasonal flash floods would sweep, depositing large amounts of sediment – mud and stone – as they carved their way through the landscape.

The red and orange rock that you see at the western end of the Jurassic Coast is indicative of the harsh, barren conditions in which they were formed. The few creatures that survived the mass extinction at the end of the Permian period began to dominate during the Triassic period; dinosaurs also began to evolve at this time. The period ended as it had begun, however, with a mass extinction – volcanic activity, an asteroid strike and climate change are all held up as possible culprits.

Jurassic Period (200-140 million years ago) As sea levels rose and tropical oceans flooded the deserts, Pangaea began to split, with the landmass that would become the modern-day Americas separated from that which would become Europe, while in between these continents the Atlantic Ocean formed. With an increase in the length and number of coastlines, the continental climate changed from desert to tropical, lush forests, allowing life to thrive. Birds first took to the wing at this time, dinosaurs stalked the land and mammals also first entered the fray.

This is also the period of the **ammonite**, one of the most common fossils found on beaches today. Luckily for all these creatures, there was no mass extinction at the end of the Jurassic period.

Ammonite

❏ **Where to see evidence of the Jurassic Period**
- **Beaches** At Lyme Regis, Charmouth and Seatown you can hunt the ancient fossilised remains of marine reptiles below the Jurassic Blue Lias cliffs.
- **Portland** One huge slab of Jurassic rock.
- **Weymouth to Ringstead Bay** The geological folds and faults en route consist of Jurassic clays, limestones and sandstones.
- **Osmington Mills** The fossilised burrows and markings of marine animals can be seen on the beach here.
- **Durdle Door/Stair Hole/Lulworth Cove** Jurassic limestone and Cretaceous chalk prove more resistant than the clays and sands that the sea have eroded away, leaving these impressive natural wonders.
- **Fossil Forest** Near Lulworth Cove, this is one of the most complete records of a fossil forest in the world.
- **Kimmeridge Bay** The clay found in these cliffs now gives its name to this type of rock the world over: Kimmeridgian. Meanwhile, the rocks found here were once the base of a tropical ocean.

Cretaceous Period (140-65 million years ago) The most important event in this period occurred midway through it: the South-West of England tilted eastwards, the Atlantic expanded and the whole area became covered by one vast ocean. Billions of algae living in the sea prospered before their skeletons sank to the sea floor to form chalk – the youngest rock of this period (the Latin for chalk is *creta*).

Hospitable conditions on land enabled the largest and most ferocious of dinosaurs to flourish; flowering plants also began to develop. Another mass extinction at the end of the period, however, led to the end of the reptiles' reign; the dawn of the Cenozoic era – and the reign of the mammals – was upon us.

Cenozoic era
The Cenozoic era is divided into two periods, the **Tertiary** (65-1.8 million years ago) and the **Quaternary** (1.8 million years ago to the present day). During the Tertiary period mammals began to dominate the Earth, and great shifts in the terrain led to the formation of some of the great mountain ranges, such as the

❏ **Where to see evidence of the Cretaceous Period**
- **High Peak, Salcombe Hill and Branscombe** Due to the unconformity, upper Greensand (ie Cretaceous sandstone) and chalk lie directly on top of distinctively red Triassic mudstone.
- **Beer Head** Here's an anomaly: chalk cliffs in the midst of red Triassic rocks.
- **Golden Cap** Upper Greensand lies directly on top of darker Jurassic clay on this, the south coast of England's highest peak; the greensand supposedly glowing at night.
- **White Nothe** Cretaceous chalk and sandstone on top of Jurassic clay.
- **The Purbeck Beds** Here you'll find a fossilised record of mammal evolution at the dawn of the Cretaceous period with the fossils of fish, amphibians, reptiles and even dinosaur footprints; mixture of Cretaceous and Jurassic rock.
- **Old Harry Rocks** Impressive chalk stacks.

Alps. The great folds in the terrain that run through the Isle of Purbeck at the end of the walk were also formed at this time.

The above is obviously a remarkably simplified description of the geology of the area. For those who wish to delve deeper there are several very good books (see Recommended reading, pp45-7).

Flora and fauna

With a varied topography that encompasses a full range of landscapes from windblasted moor to wetland marsh, hogback cliffs to wooded valleys, muddy estuaries to mobile sand dunes, you can begin to appreciate why the South-West can boast such a rich and varied countryside, with several unique species of flora and thriving populations of mammals and birds that, elsewhere in the UK, struggle to survive.

The following is not in any way a comprehensive guide – if it were, you would not have room for anything else in your rucksack – but merely a brief run-down of the more commonly seen flora and fauna on the trail, together with some of the rarer and more spectacular species.

TREES

Like most of Britain, Dorset and Devon would once have been covered in woodland and forest. Much of this woodland has of course long since vanished, having been cleared by our ancestors. Less than 10% of Dorset, for example, is covered in woodland today; and the figure is even lower – around 6% – in East Devon.

However, some of that cleared woodland grew back again several hundred years ago and is now known as ancient woodland. The presence of bluebells, wood anemones and other particular flowering plants are indicators that there has been tree cover for a very long time (the estimate we hear most frequently is 'over 400 years').

Despite man's interference, there are some surprisingly fine patches of woodland on the coast path. The most interesting species is the **oak** (family name *Quercus*), which was originally planted as coppice or scrub. Oak woodland is a diverse habitat and not

❏ **Oak leaves showing galls**
Oak trees support more kinds of insects than any other tree in Britain and some affect the oak in unusual ways. The eggs of gall-flies cause growths known as galls on the leaves. Each of these contains a single insect. Other kinds of gall-flies lay eggs in stalks or flowers, leading to flower galls, growths the size of currants.

THE ENVIRONMENT & NATURE

exclusively made up of oak. In Dorset the most prolific species of oak is **sessile oak** (*Quercus petraea*). Unfortunately, the two counties have been hit by sudden oak death and many of the trees have had to be felled to prevent further spread of the disease. Another tree currently affected by disease

BIRCH (WITH FLOWERS)

is the **ash** (*Fraxinus excelsior*). No doubt as ash dieback disease spreads across Britain over the next few years it will also kill many of the ash trees in Devon and Dorset. In Denmark, where the disease appears to have originated, up to 90% of the tree have been infected.

Other trees that flourish here include **downy birch** (*Betula pubescens*), its relative the **silver birch** (*Betula pendula*), **holly** (*Ilex aquifolium*) and **hazel** (*Corylus avellana*) which has traditionally been used for coppicing (the periodic cutting of small trees for harvesting).

HAZEL (WITH FLOWERS)

FLOWERS

The extraordinary geology of the area ensures that a wide diversity of plants is able to thrive too. Whatever ground a plant prefers, be it chalk, clay, shingle, woodland mulch or the acid soils below Golden Cap and the dunes of Studland Beach, there is something for them on this stretch of southern British coastline. Spring is the time to come and see the spectacular displays of colour on the South-West Coast Path, when most of the flowers are in bloom.

Alternatively, arrive in August and you'll see the heathers carpeting patches of the moors in a blaze of purple flowers, picked out with the brilliant yellow of the gorse bush; the latter will have been a feature of the landscape since spring.

Woodland and hedgerows

From March to May **bluebells** (*Hyacinthoides non-scripta*) proliferate in some of the woods along the trail, providing a wonderful spectacle.

The white **wood anemone** (*Anemone nemorosa*) – wide open flowers when sunny but closed and drooping when the weather's dull – and the yellow **primrose** (*Primula vulgaris*) also flower early in spring. **Red campion** (*Silene dioica*), which flowers from late April, can be found in hedgebanks along with rosebay willowherb (*Epilobium angustifolium*) which also has the name fire-weed due to its habit of colonising burnt areas.

In scrubland and on woodland edges you will find **bramble** (*Rubus fruticosus*), a common vigorous shrub responsible for many a ripped jacket thanks to its sharp thorns and prickles. **Blackberry** fruits ripen from late summer to autumn. Fairly common in scrubland and on woodland edges is the **dog rose** (*Rosa canina*) which has a large pink flower, the fruits of which are used to make rose-hip syrup.

Look out, too, on the water in streams or rivers for the white-flowered **water crow-foot** (*Ranunculus penicillatus pseudofluitans*) which, because it needs unpolluted, flowing water, is a good indicator of the cleanliness of the stream.

Other flowering plants to look for in wooded areas and in hedgerows include the tall **foxglove** (*Digitalis purpurea*) with its trumpet-like flowers, **forget-me-not** (*Myosotis arvensis*) with tiny, delicate blue flowers, and **cow parsley** (*Anthriscus sylvestris*), a tall member of the carrot family with a large globe of white flowers which often covers roadside verges and hedge banks.

Heathland and scrubland

There are three species of heather. The most dominant is **ling** (*Calluna vulgaris*) with tiny flowers on delicate upright stems. The other two species are **bell heather** (*Erica cinera*) with deep purple bell-shaped flowers and **cross-leaved heath** (*Erica tetralix*) with similarly shaped flowers of a lighter pink, almost white colour. Cross-leaved heath prefers wet and boggy ground. As a result, it usually grows away from bell heather which prefers well-drained soils.

Heather is an incredibly versatile plant which is put to many uses. It provides fodder for livestock, fuel for fires, an orange dye and material for bedding, thatching, basketwork and brooms. It is still sometimes used in place of hops to flavour beer and the flower heads can be brewed to make good tea. It is also incredibly hardy and thrives on the denuded hills, preventing other species from flourishing. Indeed, at times, highland cattle are brought to certain areas of the moors to graze on the heather, allowing other species a chance to grow.

On Portland there is also the **Portland sea lavender** (*Limonium recurvum*), a purple-flowered species first discovered in 1832, that flowers in abundance on the cliff edges on the eastern side of the island just north of the Bill between July and August – and which doesn't exist anywhere else in the world.

Grassland

There is much overlap between the hedge/woodland-edge habitat and that of pastures and meadows. You will come across **common birdsfoot-trefoil** (*Lotus corniculatus*), **Germander speedwell** (*Veronica chamaedrys*), **tufted** and **bush vetch** (*Vicia cracca* and *Vicia sepium*) and **meadow vetchling** (*Lathyrus pratensis*) in both. Often the only species you will see in heavily grazed pastures are the most resilient.

THE ENVIRONMENT & NATURE

Of the thistles, in late summer you should come across the **melancholy thistle** (*Cirsium helenoides*) drooping sadly on roadside verges and hay meadows. Unusually, it has no prickles on its stem. The **yellow rattle** is aptly named, for the dry seedpods rattle in the wind, a good indication for farmers that it is time to harvest the hay.

Other widespread grassland species include **harebell** (*Campanula rotundifolia*), delicate yellow **tormentil** (*Potentilla erecta*) and **devil's-bit scabious** (*Succisa pratensis*). Also keep an eye out for orchids such as the **fragrant orchid** (*Gymnaadenia conopsea*) and **early purple orchid** (*Orchis mascula*).

Dunes

Dunes are formed by wind action creating a fragile, unstable environment. Among the first colonisers is **marram grass** (*Ammophila arenaria*) which is able to withstand drought, exposure to wind and salt spray and has an ability to grow up through new layers of sand that cover it.

Other specialist plants are **sea holly** (*Eryngium maritimum*), **sea spurge** (*Euphorbia paralias*) and **sea bindweed** (*Calystegia soldanella*). The one thing that these seemingly indomitable plants can't tolerate is trampling by human feet; stay on the path which is nearly always well marked through dunes.

MAMMALS

The south-west is blessed with wildlife. The Lulworth Ranges play host to two of our largest mammal species, one native, one imported. The former is the **roe deer** (*Capreolus capreolus*), the most common of deer species in England. It is quite easy to distinguish from the other species, mainly due to its diminutive size (standing around 65cm to the shoulder), red-brown coat in summer and small antlers (around 25cm), white rump and short tail. Its nocturnal habits, however, mean that you will still be lucky to see one.

Britain's only other native deer, the **red deer** (*Cervus elaphus*), is also present in Devon and Dorset, mainly in Exmoor but also in patches throughout the two counties.

The exotic **sika deer** (*Cervus nippon*) also thrives in the Lulworth Ranges. They are believed to have come from herds that arrived in 1895 at Hyde House and the following year at Brownsea Island in Poole Harbour. Few people realised that the deer could swim to the mainland, and together with further escapees from Hyde House they were able to establish themselves on the ranges and nearby areas. Considered sacred in Japan – where they originally hail from – they find the conditions so benign on the ranges that they are now having to be culled before their numbers become unmanageable.

The South-West, in particular Exmoor, is also renowned as the spiritual home of the **otter** (*Lutra lutra*). The county was the home of the author Henry Williamson – creator of *Tarka the Otter* – and Devon today is proud to be associated with this most graceful of British carnivores. It wasn't always like this, however, and for much of the 20th century (and before) the otter was persecuted because it was (wrongly) believed to have an enormously detrimental effect on fish stocks.

Bell Heather
Erica cinerea

Heather (Ling)
Calluna vulgaris

Thrift (Sea Pink)
Armeria maritima

Rosebay Willowherb
Epilobium angustifolium

Common Vetch
Vicia sativa

Forget-me-not
Myosotis arvensis

Rowan (tree)
Sorbus aucuparia

Spear Thistle
Cirsium vulgare

Red Campion
Silene dioica

Early Purple Orchid
Orchis mascula

Foxglove
Digitalis purpurea

Sea Holly
Eryngium maritimum

Common Dog Violet
Viola riviniana

Common Centaury
Centaurium erythraea

Honeysuckle
Lonicera periclymemum

Ramsons (Wild Garlic)
Allium ursinum

Germander Speedwell
Veronica chamaedrys

Herb-Robert
Geranium robertianum

Lousewort
Pedicularis sylvatica

Self-heal
Prunella vulgaris

Scarlet Pimpernel
Anagallis arvensis

Sea Campion
Silene maritima

Bluebell
Hyacinthoides non-scripta

Hogweed
Heracleum sphondylium

Dog Rose
Rosa canina

Meadow Buttercup
Ranunculis acris

Gorse
Ulex europaeus

Tormentil
Potentilla erecta

Birdsfoot-trefoil
Lotus corniculatus

Ox-eye Daisy
Leucanthemum vulgare

Common Ragwort
Senecio jacobaea

Primrose
Primula vulgaris

Cowslip
Primula veris

Colour photos (following pages)

● **C4 Left, top**: Plymouth's art deco outdoor swimming pool, the Tinside Lido (see p93). **Bottom**: Looking over the River Yealm. **Right**: Strolling in the dappled morning sunlight, Kingswear (see p154), near Dartmouth.

● **C5 Left, top**: A colour co-ordinated beach hut owner in Paignton, on the English Riviera. **Bottom**: Sweet shop in Salcombe. **Right, top**: Walking past the beach huts on the way into Lyme Regis. **Bottom**: The Seaton Tramway (see p228) runs between Colyton and Seaton.

● **C6** You can't miss the replica of Sir Francis Drake's ship, *The Golden Hind*, in Brixham Harbour (see p160).

● **C7 Top**: Superb views west from near the summit of Flower's Barrow (see p300) in the Lulworth Ranges. **Bottom left**: The entrance to the Tout Quarry, Portland. **Centre**: The Radar Monument, St Aldhelm's Head (see p309), commemorates the pioneering work on radar undertaken at Worth Matravers during World War II. **Bottom, right**: The ruins of St Gabriel's Church (see p248), near Golden Cap.

78 C.T. & G. CRANCH 78

AWARD WINNING
WESTCOUNTRY
FUDGE
LOTS OF YUMMY
FLAVOURS!

20% OFF

C6

C7

SOUTH WEST
COAST PATH

MINEHEAD
581 MILES

POOLE
49 MILES

Today the otter is enjoying something of a renaissance thanks to concerted conservation efforts. At home both in salt water and fresh water, they are a good indicator of an unpolluted environment. It is unlikely that you'll spot one on your walk, although there are records of sightings all along the path. The Erme River, which you wade across on the path, is a particularly good spot to see one, according to records, and Devon is renowned as one of the otter's main strongholds.

Seeing any of the above requires patience and no little amount of luck. One creature that you will definitely see along the walk, however, is the **rabbit** (*Oryctolagus cuniculus*). Most of the time you'll get nothing more than a brief and distant glimpse of their white tails as they race for the nearest warren at the sound of your footfall since they're timid by nature. Because they are so numerous, however, the laws of probability dictate that you will at some stage during your walk get close enough to observe them without being spotted; trying to take a decent photo of one of them, however, is a different matter.

If you're lucky you may also come across **hares** (*Lepus europaeus*), often mistaken for rabbits but much larger, more elongated and with longer ears and back legs. There are populations of hares all over the arable parts of the South-West, and we saw several around the back of the Lulworth Ranges, near the start above West Lulworth, though nowhere are they common.

Like the otter, the **water vole** (*Arvicola terrestris*) has both been a major character in a well-known work of fiction (in this case 'Ratty' from Kenneth Grahame's classic children's story *Wind in the Willows*), and has suffered a devastating drop in its population. Their numbers had originally declined due to the arrival in the UK countryside of the mink from North America, which successfully adapted to living in the wild after escaping from local fur farms. Unfortunately, the mink not only hunts water voles but is small enough to slip inside their burrows. Thus, with the voles afforded no protection, the mink was able to wipe out an entire riverbank's population in a matter of months. (Incidentally, this is another reason why protecting the otter is important: they kill mink.) A programme is now in place in which the water vole and its habitat is not only protected but the mink are being trapped and killed.

Another native British species that has suffered at the hands of a foreign invader is the **red squirrel** (*Sciurus vulgaris*), a small, tufty-eared native that has been usurped by its larger cousin from North America, the **grey squirrel** (*Sciurus carolinensis*). The only place where it might be possible to see the red squirrel is on Brownsea Island in Poole Harbour – at the very end of the coast path.

The ubiquitous **fox** (*Vulpes vulpes*) is now just as at home in the city as it is in the country. While usually considered nocturnal, it's not unusual to encounter one during the day. Another creature of the night that you may occasionally see is the **badger** (*Meles meles*). Relatively common throughout the British Isles, these sociable mammals with their distinctive black-and-white striped muzzles live in large underground burrows called setts, appearing around sunset to root for worms and slugs.

(**Opposite**) The lighthouse at Portland Bill (see p279). Nearby, the old lower lighthouse is now a bird observatory.

The nocturnal **bat**, of which there are 17 species in Britain, is protected by law. Your best chance of spotting one is at dusk while there's still enough light in the sky to make out their flitting forms as they fly along hedgerows, over rivers and streams and around street lamps in their quest for moths and insects. The commonest species in Britain is the **pipistrelle** (*Pipistrellus pipistrellus*).

Keep a look out for other fairly common but little seen species such as the carnivorous **stoat** (*Mustela erminea*), its diminutive cousin the **weasel** (*Mustela nivalis*), the **hedgehog** (*Erinaceus europaeus*) – these days, alas, most commonly seen as roadkill – and any number of species of **voles**, **mice** and **shrews**.

Out at sea

The high cliffs are also a great place from which to look out over the sea. Searching for seals is an enjoyable and essential part of cliff walking. You'll spot lots of grey lobster-pot buoys before your first seal, but it's worth the effort. **Atlantic grey seals** (*Halichoerus grypus*) relax in the water, looking over their big Roman noses with doggy eyes, as interested in you as you are in them. Twice the weight of a red deer, a big bull can be over 200kg. On calm, sunny days it's possible to follow them down through the clear water as they dive, as elegant in their element as they are clumsy on land. Seals generally come ashore only to rest, moult their fur, or to breed. Devon is your best chance of seeing one, though there are small pockets of them as far east as Poole and beyond.

A cliff-top sighting of Britain's largest fish is also a real possibility, but is more chilling than endearing! **Basking sharks** (*Cetorhinus maximus*) can grow to a massive 36ft (11 metres) and weigh seven tonnes, and their two fins, a large shark-like dorsal fin followed by a notched tail fin, are so far apart it takes a second look to be convinced it's one fish. But these are gentle giants, cruising slowly with open jaws, filtering microscopic plankton from the sea. You are most likely to see one during late spring and summer when they feed at the surface during calm, warm weather. Though you are more likely to spy them in the waters off Cornwall, a beautiful specimen was spotted off Lyme Regis in 2011. Look out for coloured or numbered tags, put on for research into this sadly declining species, and report them to the web address given in the box above.

Taking a longer view and with some good luck, watch the sea for dolphins, porpoises or even a whale. **Harbour porpoises** (*Phocoena phocoena*) and

---

❏ **Reporting wildlife sightings**
Report basking shark or marine turtle sightings to the website of the Marine Conservation Society (🖳 www.mcsuk.org). Remember to note any tags you've spotted. Reports are greatly appreciated. If you see any of the other large marine creatures such as dolphins, whales or seals you can report them online through Seaquest Southwest, part of the Devon Biodiversity Records Centre (🖳 www.dbrc.org.uk). With any report give the location, number and the direction they were heading in.

If you come across a stranded marine animal like a dolphin or porpoise, don't approach it but contact either British Divers's Marine Life Rescue (☎ 01825-765546, 🖳 www.bdmlr.org.uk) or the RSPCA hotline (☎ 0300-123 4999, 🖳 www.rspca.org.uk).

bottlenose dolphins (*Tursiops truncatus*) both visit the offshore waters. One such dolphin, nicknamed George, has been turning up along the Dorset coast for years and even became something of a tabloid celebrity (see p226) when he settled in the waters off Beer one summer.

Other cetaceans you may catch a glimpse of are **Risso's dolphins** (*Grampus griseus*), **common dolphins** (*Delphinus delphis*), **striped dolphins** (*Stenella coeruleoalba*), **orcas** or **killer whales** (*Orcinus orca*) and **pilot whales** (*Globicephala melaena*) but, be warned, they are fiendishly difficult to tell apart: a brief glimpse of a fin is nothing like the 'whole animal' pictures shown in field guides.

REPTILES

Dorset and Devon both have populations of all six British reptile species: smooth snake, grass snake, adder, sand lizard, common lizard and slow worm. Of the above, by far the rarest is the **sand lizard**, though wonderfully Dorset is its stronghold. Unremarkable most of the time, during the mating season the male's sides become a vivid green. Confined largely to the heathlands of Dorset, there is a small population on Studland on the last day of the walk.

The **adder** (*Vipera berus*) is the only poisonous snake of the three mentioned above. They pose very little risk to walkers – indeed, you should consider yourself extremely fortunate to see one, providing you're a safe distance away. They bite only when provoked, preferring to hide instead. The venom is designed to kill small mammals such as mice, voles and shrews, so deaths in humans are very rare but a bite can be extremely unpleasant and occasionally dangerous to children or the elderly. You are most likely to encounter them in spring when they come out of hibernation and during the summer when pregnant females warm themselves in the sun. They are easily identified by the striking zigzag pattern on their back. Should you be lucky enough to encounter one (they enjoy basking on clifftops and on the moors), enjoy it but leave it undisturbed.

The **grass snake** (*Natrix natrix*) is the largest British species, growing up to over a metre in length. Olive-grey in colour with short black bars down each side and orange or yellow patches just below the head, they are harmless, relying not on venom or biting for defence but instead give off a foul odour if disturbed.

The **slow-worm** (*Anguis fragilis*) must be one of the more unusual creatures in the British Isles – a reptile that is called a worm, looks like a snake but is actually a legless lizard! Silver-grey with a dark line down the centre of the back and along each side, it is common in Devon and Dorset, where it feeds on slugs, worms and insects.

BIRDS

In and around the fishing villages

The wild laugh of the **herring gull** (*Larus argentatus*) is the wake-up call of the coast path. Perched on the rooftops of the stone villages, they are a reminder of

THE ENVIRONMENT & NATURE

the link between people and wildlife, the rocky coast and our stone and concrete towns and cities. Shoreline scavengers, they've adapted to the increasing waste thrown out by human society. Despite their bad reputation it's worth taking a closer look at these fascinating, ubiquitous birds. How do they keep their pale grey and white plumage so beautiful feeding on rubbish? Nobel-prize-winning animal behaviourist Nikko Tinbergen showed how the young pecking at the red dot on their bright yellow bills triggers the adults to regurgitate food. In August the newly fledged brown young follow their parents begging for food.

Over the next three years they'll go through a motley range of plumages, more grey and less brown each year till they reach adulthood. But please don't feed them and do watch your sandwiches and fish & chips – they are quite capable of grabbing food from your hand.

Village harbours are a good place for lunch or an evening drink after a hard day on the cliffs. Look out for the birds who are equally at home on a rocky shore or in villages, such as the beautiful little black-and-white **pied wagtail** (*Motacilla alba*) with its long, bobbing tail.

Also looking black from a distance as they strut the beach are **jackdaws** (*Corvus monedula*). Close up, however, they are beautiful with a grey nape giving them a hooded look and shining blue eyes. They are very sociable: you will often see them high up in the air in pairs or flocks playing tag or performing acrobatic tricks.

Small, dark brown and easy to miss, the **rock pipit** (*Anthus petrosus*) is one of our toughest birds, as it feeds whilst walking on the rocks between the land and the sea. They nest in crevices and caves along the rocky coastline.

Seen on or from the sea cliffs

Walking on the coastal path leads you into a world of rock and sea, high cliffs with bracken-clad slopes, exposed green pasture, dramatic drops and headlands, sweeping sandy beaches and softer country around the estuaries. Stunning **stonechats** (*Saxicola torquata*) with black, white and orange colouring are common on heath and grassy plains where you may hear their distinctive song, which is not dissimilar to two stones being clacked together.

STONECHAT
L: 135mm/5.25"

Twittering **linnets** (*Carduelis cannabina*) with their bright red breasts and grey heads fly ahead and perch on gorse and fences. The vertiginous swoops of the path mean it's often possible to be at eye level or even look down on birds and mammals.

Watch for **kestrels** (*Falco tinnunculus*), hovering on sharp brown wings, before plummeting onto their prey.

At eye level the black 'moustache' of the powerful slate-grey-backed **peregrine** (*Falco peregrinus*) is sometimes visible. At a glance it can be mistaken for a pigeon, its main prey. But the power and speed of this, the world's fastest bird, soon sets it apart. In the late summer whole families fly over the cliffs. In mid winter look for them over estuaries where they hunt ducks and waders.

Despite the remote fastness of the cliffs, peregrines have suffered terribly. Accidental poisoning by the pesticide DDT succeeded where WWII persecution for fear they would kill carrier pigeons failed, and they were almost extinct by the end of the 1960s. Their triumphant return means not only a thriving population on their traditional sea cliffs, but more and more nesting in our cities on man-made cliffs, such as tower blocks and cathedrals. We also saw one swooping around the Undercliffs near Lyme Regis.

Cliff ledges, a kind of multi-storey block of flats for birds, provide nesting places safe from marauding land predators such as foxes and rats. It's surprising just how close it's possible to get to **fulmars** (*Fulmarus glacialis*), which return to their nesting ledges in February for the start of the long breeding season that goes on into the autumn. Only in the depth of winter are the cliffs quiet. Fulmars are related to albatrosses and like them are masters of the air. You can distinguish them from gulls by their ridged, flat wings as they sail the wind close to the waves with the occasional burst of fast flapping. Fulmars are incredibly tenacious at holding their nesting sites and vomit a stinking oily secretion over any intruders, including rock-climbers! The elegant **kittiwake** (*Rissa tridactyla*), the one true seagull that never feeds on land, is another cliff nester, identified by its 'dipped in ink' black wingtips.

Black above, white below, **manx shearwaters** (*Puffinus puffinus*) make globe-encircling journeys as they sail effortlessly just above even the wildest sea.

Small and fast on hard-beating wings, black and white **guillemots** (*Uria troile*) and **razorbills** (*Alca torda*) shoot out from their nesting ledges hidden in the cliffs. Guillemots have a long thin bill and razorbills a heavy half circle bill.

Large colonies of guillemots, kittiwakes, razorbills, and a few puffins inhabit the cliff ledges near Durlston Head, just before Swanage. Purbeck also has several small colonies of puffins.

Less lovely in most people's eyes, though undeniably magnificent, the big, rapacious **great black-backed gulls** (*Larus marinus*) cruise the nesting colonies for prey. Star of the sea show, however, has to be the big, sharp-winged, Persil-white **gannets** (*Morus bassanus*) cruising slowly for fish, then suddenly plunging with folded wings into the sea. Their strengthened skulls protect them from the huge force of the impact with the water. Gannets, together with storm petrels, shearwaters and skuas are often seen from Portland Bill.

Two birds more familiar from the artificial cliffs of our cities can be seen here in their natural habitat – **house martins** (*Delichon urbica*), steely-blue backed like a **swallow** (*Hirundo rustica*), but with more V-shaped wings and a distinctive white rump, and **rock doves** (*Columba livia*). These are so mixed with

GUILLEMOT
L: 450MM/18"

GREAT BLACK-BACKED GULL
L: 750MM/30"

town pigeons (*Columba livia domestica*) it's hard to say if any 'pure' wild birds remain, but many individuals with the characteristic grey back, small white rump and two black wing bars can be seen.

Where the path drops steeply to a rocky bay, **oystercatchers** (*Haematopus ostralegus*), with their black and white plumage and spectacular carrot-coloured bill, pipe in panic when they fly off. This is also a good spot to get close to **shags** (*Phalacrocorax aristotelis*) and **cormorants** (*Phalacrocorax carbo*), common all round the coast, swimming low and black in the water. Shags are smaller and are always seen on the sea – cormorants are also on rivers and estuaries – and in the summer have a crest whilst cormorants have a white patch near their tail and a white face. Close up, these oily birds shine iridescently; shags are green, cormorants are purple. They are a primitive species and since their feathers are not completely waterproof both have to dry their bodies after time in the sea; their heraldic pose, standing upright with half-spread wings on drying rocks is one of the special sights of the coast path.

SHAG
L: 710MM/28"

In pastures, combes and woods

The one species that enjoys more publicity than any other on the coast path is the **cirl bunting** (*Emberiza cirlus*). Its rarity and declining numbers – by 1989 there were only 118 breeding pairs – led to the establishment of some large conservation efforts and you'll come across several cliff-top fields on the trail that have been entirely given over to their protection. Labrador Bay (four miles south of Teignmouth), Prawle Point, Maidencombe, Berry Head, Wembury, Jenny Cliff, and Stoke Point near Noss Mayo, are all good places to spot this smallish bird with a yellow-streaked head and green breast band – like a small

CORMORANT
L: 900MM/36"

yellowhammer. The programme is ongoing and there are now an estimated 862 pairs. There are also breeding pairs at Slapton Ley Nature Reserve.

On your walk you'll find that the path frequently rises up onto rich green pasture. **Skylarks** (*Alauda arvensis*) soar tunefully – almost disappearing into the spring sky, while in winter small green-brown **meadow pipits** (*Anthus pratensis*) flit weakly, giving a small high-pitched call.

Spring also brings migrant **wheatears** (*Oenanthe oenanthe*): they are beautiful with their grey and black feathers above, buff and white below, and unmistakable when they fly and show their distinctive white rump. **Buzzard** (*Buteo buteo*) soar up with their tilted, broad round wings, giving their high, wild Ke-oow cry.

Ravens (*Corvus corax*) cronk-cronk over the cliffs and are distinguished from more common **carrion crows** (*Corvus corone*) by their huge size and wedge-shaped tail.

In the woods you'll find all three native species of **woodpecker** – **green**, **great** and **lesser spotted** (*Picus viridis* and *Dendrocopos major* and *minor* respectively); the two latter are very much wedded to the woods, while the former, with its laughing call, can often be seen on the moors looking for insects.

In spring familiar birds such as **robins** (*Erithacus rubecula*), **blackbirds** (*Turdus merula*), **blue** and **great tits** (*Parus major* & *caeruleus*), **chaffinches** (*Fringila coelebs*) and **dunnocks** (*Prunella modularis*) are joined by the small green **chiffchaff** (*Phylloscopus collybita*); it's not much to look at but is one of the earliest returning migrants and unmistakably calls its own name in two repeated notes.

In and around estuaries

Descending to the long walk round the estuaries you move into a different, softer world of shelter and rich farmland. Best for birds in winter, they are a welcome refuge from the ferocity of the worst weather for wildlife and people.

There are large flocks of ducks – whistling **wigeon** (*Anas penelope*), a combination of grey and pinky brown, with big white wing patches in flight – and waders like the brown **curlew** (*Numenius arquata*) with its impossibly long, down-curved beak and beautiful sad fluting call, evocative of summer moors.

The **redshank** (*Tringa totanus*), **greenshank** (*Tringa nebularia*), golden and grey **plover** (*Pluvialis sp.*), and black-tailed and bar-tailed **godwit** (*Limosa sp.*) can also be seen in winter.

Look out for the big black, white and chestnut **shelduck** (*Tadorna tadorna*), and for the tall grey **heron** (*Ardea cinerea*), hunched at rest or extended to its full 175cm as it slowly, patiently stalks fish in the shallows.

A real rarity ten years ago, another species of heron, the stunning white **little egret** (*Egretta garzetta*) is now unmissable on estuaries. Here the more common gull is the nimble **black-headed gull** (*Larus ridibundus*), with its elegant cap, dark in summer but pale in winter. In summer, terns come: the big **sandwich tern** (*Sterna sandvicensis*) with its shaggy black cap and loud rasping call, and the smaller sleeker **aerobatic common tern** (*Sterna hirundo*).

THE ENVIRONMENT & NATURE

BUTTERFLIES AND MOTHS

Butterflies are an unexpected treat on the SWCP. Not only are they numerous, but there are several different varieties too. Portland alone plays host to two butterfly reserves, Broadcroft Quarry and the Perryfields Reserve (both, alas, off the path), home of the rare and fussy silver-studded blue and the island's very own **moth**, the Portland ribbon wave. Small blues, chalkhill blues and common blues are also present, and migrants such as clouded yellow and painted lady may also put in an appearance.

The most famous butterfly in the region is the orange and brown heath fritillary, which has declined rapidly over the last 30 years in the UK, but which is thriving in the combes of north Devon and around Thurlestone.

ROUTE GUIDE & MAPS

Using this guide

While this guide has been divided into stages, each of which approximates a day's walk, they are meant as a guide only. To plan an itinerary that better suits your pace, fitness and the time you have available, please see the 'Suggested itineraries' section on pp33-4.

The **route summaries** below describe the trail between significant places and are written as if walking the coast path from Plymouth to South Haven Point, near Poole. To enable you to plan your own itinerary, **practical information** is presented clearly on the trail maps. This includes walking times, all places to stay, camp and eat, as well as shops where you can buy supplies. Further service **details** are given in the text under the entry for each place.

For a condensed overview of this information see the town and village facilities table on pp38-9.

TRAIL MAPS
Scale and walking times
The trail maps are to a scale of 1:20,000 (1cm = 200m; $3^1/_8$ inches = one mile). Walking times are given along the side of each map and the arrow shows the direction to which the time refers. Black triangles indicate the points between which the times have been taken. **See the note on walking times in the box overleaf.**

The time-bars are a tool and are not there to judge your walking ability. There are so many variables that affect walking speed, from the weather conditions to how many beers you drank the previous evening. After the first hour or two of walking you will be able to see how your speed relates to the timings on the maps.

Up or down?
Other than when on a track or bridleway the trail is shown as a dotted line. An arrow across the trail indicates the slope; two arrows show that it is steep. Note that the arrow points towards the higher part of the trail. If, for example, you are walking from A (at 80m) to B (at 200m) and the trail between the two is short and steep it would be shown thus: A— — — >> — — – B. Reversed arrow heads indicate downward gradient.

GPS waypoints
The numbered GPS waypoints refer to the list on pp325-7.

> ❏ **Important note – walking times**
> Unless otherwise specified, **all times in this book refer only to the time spent walk-ing**. You will need to add 20-30% to allow for rests, photography, checking the map, drinking water etc. When planning the day's hike count on 5-7 hours of actual walking.

Accommodation

Apart from in large towns where some selection of places has been necessary, almost every place to stay that is within easy reach of the trail is marked. Details of each place are given in the accompanying text.

For **B&B-style accommodation** the number and **type of rooms** is given after each entry: S = single room, T = twin room, D = double room, Tr = triple, F = triple or family room (usually either three single beds, a double and bunk beds, or a double and two singles). Family rooms can therefore almost always also be used as a double or twin. Where a place has a lot of rooms that can be used as double, twin or family the text gives the number and says flexible rooms.

Rates quoted are **per person** (pp) based on two people sharing a room for a one-night stay; rates are almost always discounted for longer stays. Where a single room (sgl) is available the rate for that is quoted if different from the per person rate. The rate for single occupancy (sgl occ) of a double/twin may be higher, and the rate for three or more sharing a family room may be lower. Unless specified, rates are for B&B. At some places the only option is a room rate; this will be the same whether one or two people share.

Many places do not accept **advance bookings** for a single-night stay at peak times; the minimum is often two, or even, three nights. However, if you turn up on the day or even call the night before they may accept a booking.

Most B&Bs don't accept **credit/debit cards** but hotels usually do.

The text also mentions whether the premises have **wi-fi** (WI-FI); if a **bath** is available (☻) in at least one room; and whether **dogs** (🐾) are welcome. Most places will not take more than one dog in a room and also accept them subject to prior arrangement. Some make an additional charge (usually per night but occasionally per stay) while others may require a deposit which is refundable if the dog doesn't make a mess.

Prices for **camping** vary from site to site. For backpackers many sites charge for two people in a small tent although others charge per pitch and per

> ❏ **Food and drink planning**
> Remember, to plan ahead: certain stretches of the walk are virtually devoid of eating places (Kingswear to Brixham, Seaton to Lyme Regis, Abbotsbury to Wyke Regis, Lulworth Cove to Kimmeridge Bay and from there to Swanage, as well as the South Dorset Ridgeway) so read ahead about the next day's walk in Part 4 to make sure you never go hungry.

person. There is no single rule that applies everywhere. It is often the case that owners of large sites set aside a small field just for backpackers but their priority is families who book fixed tents or caravans for their annual holiday.

Booking is recommended for all campsites in summer school holidays but is usually not necessary at other times.

Other features
Features are marked on the map when pertinent to navigation. In order to avoid cluttering the maps and making them unusable not all features have been marked each time they occur.

The route guide

PLYMOUTH   [map p97]
'Plymouth is indeed a town of considera-tion, and of great importance to the public. The situation of it between two very large inlets of the sea, and in the bottom of a large bay [...] is very remarkable for the advantage of navigation.'
Daniel Defoe, *A Tour through the Whole Island of Great Britain*

Lying between the mouths of the rivers Plym and Tamar, Plymouth is a modern city with a rich and eventful past. The city's growth and prosperity are forever indebted to its proximity to – and relation-ship with – the sea. Not just as the famous departure point of the Pilgrim Fathers (see box p95) but also as a hub for trade (the commercial dockyards are amongst the largest in Europe) and, foremost, as a vital naval base: with a tradition that dates back to the very inception of the Royal Navy, there is much to see and do in this historic and thriving metropolis.

The first record of habitation in the area, Sudtone (Saxon for 'South Farm'), situated on the site of the present-day Barbican, can be found in the Domesday Book (1086). Initially just a small fishing village, its strategically important location soon brought prosperity and – despite bouts of plague, cholera and smallpox trimming the ever-burgeoning population as well as a concerted attempt at destruction by the

Luftwaffe during the Plymouth Blitz – the town has continued to swell in size.

Much of this success is down to its sit-uation at the mouths of two rivers, a crucial location that the nascent Royal Navy in the 17th century was quick to recognise. Her Majesty's Naval Base (HMNB) Devonport opened in 1690, with further docks being built in 1727, 1762 and 1795. Isambard Kingdom Brunel then designed the Great Western Docks (1844-50) and in 1854 the Keynham Steam Yard, built for the con-struction of steam ships, was also complet-ed. It's hardly surprising, then, that most of the town's defining moments are sea based, from the defeat of the Spanish Armada (1588; see box p92) to the sailing of the Mayflower (1620; see box p95) as well as the heroic resistance the city showed in WWII when, despite 59 German bombing sorties, it still played a full part in the Battle of the Atlantic and was a major embarka-tion point on D-Day.

Unfortunately, where the Luftwaffe flattened Plymouth some ugly buildings have sprouted and a large chunk of the town is actually fairly nondescript and pret-ty much devoid of charm. Thankfully, the **seafront** remains one of the more interest-ing and beautiful parts; and the area around the Mayflower Steps, known as **The Barbican**, is one of Plymouth's oldest, prettiest and most vibrant, with plenty of

ROUTE GUIDE AND MAPS

❏ **Francis Drake and the Spanish Armada**
The Elizabethan era was a time of turmoil. The major European powers were often at war, with religion frequently the cause. The two main protagonists at this time were Protestant England and Catholic Spain. The latter controlled the Netherlands where Protestant ideals were popular. England, as was their wont, aided the Dutch Protestants who were being hunted by the Spanish Inquisition, and it was this decision – as well as the beheading of the Catholic Mary Queen of Scots, ordered by the Protestant Queen Elizabeth I in 1587 – that led to King Philip II of Spain's decision to 'defend Catholicism' by invading England.

One of Queen Elizabeth I's most feared seamen was Sir Francis Drake. A buccaneering adventurer and hero to the English, the Spanish considered him a menace and he was a constant thorn in their side. Conducting his own personal Protestant crusade, by 1588 he had already harassed and harried many Spanish boats in the West Indies, occupied the ports of Cadiz and Corunna, destroying 37 Spanish ships as he did so, and plundered the treasures of Spain wherever he found them, describing his wish to 'singe the king of Spain's beard.'

King Philip II's Spanish Armada set sail from Lisbon in May 1588; their ships were attacked by English and Dutch boats throughout their journey. Struggling through, the Spanish were eventually spotted off The Lizard and the news of their arrival swiftly reached Plymouth, where the English navy was waiting. Famously, Drake purportedly scoffed on being told of the arrival of the Armada, and chose to finish his game of bowls, claiming he could do so and defeat the Spanish. A much debated incident, if it did actually happen it is possible that Drake would have known that the tide of the Tamar was against him – so preventing his boats from accessing the Channel until it turned – and thus recognised that he had ample time to complete his game.

History doesn't record whether Drake won his game of bowls. The outcome of the battle, however, is certain. Fighting between the Spanish and English navies went on for eight days before the Spaniards finally had to admit defeat, their navy beaten, burnt and scattered. To make matters worse, because of westerly winds many of the defeated boats couldn't return straight home, but instead had to sail around the tip of Scotland and down the coast of Ireland where they were further battered by storms – as well as being attacked by the English in Ireland. Drake meanwhile sailed home a hero, his legend forever cemented in English naval history for establishing England's dominance of the Atlantic – and refusing to end a game of bowls.

bars and restaurants in which to conduct any last-minute planning for your walk.

What to see and do
The Hoe The green expanse that separates the modern-day city centre from the sea, The Hoe is best known for playing host to Francis Drake's game of bowls in 1588 (see box above). It is also the place where, during the Plymouth Blitz of WWII, Nancy Astor, MP for the city and great friend of TE Lawrence (of Arabia) danced with servicemen, defiantly proclaiming that the city would go on despite the bombing.

Lighthouse lovers will be impressed by **Smeaton's Tower** (Mar-Oct Tue-Fri 10am-noon & 1-5.30pm, Sat 10am-noon & 1-5pm, Oct-Dec & Feb-Mar Tue-Sat 10am-noon & 1-3pm; Dec-Jan same hours but Sat only; £2.50).

Originally the third lighthouse to be put on Eddystone Rocks, which lie 14km south-west of Rame Head, it was dismantled in 1882 and the upper portions of the tower were rebuilt on The Hoe. John Smeaton, incidentally, after whom the tower is named, was the original builder of the tower way back in 1759.

Other notable sites on The Hoe include a three-tier **belvedere** (a structure that was deliberately designed to command a view) built in 1891, and the **Drake Statue** (1884), sculpted by one of the Victorian era's most pre-eminent producers of commemorative statues, Joseph Boehm. Many **war memorials** also adorn the area, fittingly so when one considers the number of servicemen and women to have departed from (and hopefully returned to) the city on various campaigns and missions over the years.

Finally, overlooked by the Smeaton Tower is **Tinside Lido** (☎ 01752-261915; end May to end Sep daily 10am-6pm; may close later in good weather), an Art Deco outdoor swimming pool that opened in 1935. Following years of neglect the pool became a Grade II-listed building before being renovated and reopened in 2005.

The Hoe is also the site of the **British Firework Championships** (🖳 www.britishfireworks.co.uk) in August. It is a competition between the country's professional firework companies that, for two nights, light up the skies above Devon.

The Citadel At The Hoe's eastern end is the **Royal Citadel**. A large and impressive limestone fort, it was built in the late 1660s on the orders of Charles II in response to the second Dutch War (1664-7). Encompassing a previous fort that Drake had requested to be built in the 16th century, its guns bear down on the town as well as out to sea, most likely as a reaction to Plymouth's Parliamentarian leanings during the English Civil War. Still militarily operational today, guided tours are available twice a week (May-Sep Tue & Thur, 2.30pm; £5). Note that as The Citadel is still a working fort, tours may be cancelled without notice and that photography is also prohibited.

The Barbican The Barbican is the old harbour area of the city and the heart of the old town. Fortuitously escaping much of the bombing inflicted on Plymouth during WWII, the mazes of narrow **cobbled streets** (the most extensive collection of cobbled thoroughfares in the UK, apparently) still exist in the originally medieval layout of what was then the town of Sutton. The former location of Plymouth's fish market, the area is now more of a draw to those seeking art, antiques and alcohol.

Speaking of the latter, if you feel that a celebratory tipple is in order the venerable **Plymouth Gin Distillery** (☎ 01752-665292, 🖳 www.plymouthgin.com), on Southside St, has been knocking out grade-A booze to discerning punters since 1793 and runs distillery tours (Mon-Sat 10.30am-4.30pm, Sun 11.30am-3.30pm; £6) round its building, which partly dates back to the mid 15th century. The building, incidentally, and more than a little ironically, was also where the Puritan Pilgrim Fathers supposedly spent their last night before embarking for America.

Only a couple of minutes away, **Elizabethan House** (☎ 01752-304774; Apr-Sep Tue-Fri 10am-noon & 1-5.30pm, Sat 10am-noon & 1-5pm; £2.50), 32 New St, retains much of its original structure and is kitted out in suitable period furniture.

Next to the pedestrian walkway which crosses Sutton Harbour, the **Mayflower Steps** commemorate the Pilgrim Fathers' departure for the New World in 1620. The steps consist of a portico that was built in 1934 and a platform hanging out over the water's edge. Nearby, above the tourist information office you will find the **Plymouth Mayflower Exhibition** (Apr-Oct Mon-Sat 9.30am-5pm, Sun 10.30am-4pm, Nov-Mar Mon-Fri 9.30am-5pm, Sat 10.30am-4pm; £2), covering three floors telling the story of the Pilgrim Fathers. It also has a balcony from which you can gaze out over the bustle below.

Not technically part of The Barbican but just across the walkway from the Mayflower Steps is the **National Marine Aquarium** (Map 1; ☎ 0844-893 7938, 🖳 www.national-aquarium.co.uk; daily Apr-Sep 10am-6pm, Oct-Mar to 5pm; £11.75, 10% off tickets bought online in advance). The UK's largest, it houses a tank that contains 2.5 million litres of water! Truly unmissable, the Atlantic Ocean display, as it is known, is home not only to tiger and ragged tooth sharks, stingrays and barracuda but also a full-sized replica of a WWII

ROUTE GUIDE AND MAPS

□ **The coast path through Plymouth**

While the route for this book starts at the Mayflower Steps, the South-West Coast Path begins way back in Minehead in Somerset, and thus on its way travels through the centre of Plymouth. Initially this 2¾-mile trail is a little confusing, the lack of coast path signs not helping. That said, the city has worked hard to add some quirky features to what is already a walk stuffed with points of interest.

The path begins at **Cremyll Ferry** by Admiral's Hard. Having wiped your feet on the welcome mat positioned there, you come to a fried breakfast expertly rendered in wool on the wall of **Elvira's Café**. Said to be the home of the fry-up, the café has also been immortalised in a Beryl Cook painting. Close by you come to the **Codeword Pavement**, where messages between sailors and their loved ones at home have been carved, in shorthand, into the pavement.

Taking a right onto Strand St and then a left onto Cremyll St leads you to **Royal William Yard**, passing **Ede Vinegar Works** on the way (owned by the same family for six generations). Named after King William IV (who stands overlooking the entrance), the yard was built, mostly from reclaimed land, to supply the navy with beef, biscuits and beer – with a brewery, bakery and slaughterhouse on site. The path doesn't actually go into the yard, following instead its eastern wall down Admiralty Rd to *Artillery Tower*, built to protect the harbour and yard but now a restaurant (see p100). The route then takes a hard left past the smart Georgian terraces of Durnford St, where Sir Arthur Conan-Doyle worked as a doctor – which explains the **Sherlock Holmes quotes** in the pavement. A hard right after Stonehouse Barracks leads you onto Millbay Rd, with Millbay Docks on the right; at the next roundabout is the **Wall of Stars** celebrating the famous figures – Bing Crosby and Judy Garland to name but two – who have arrived in the dock on the cruise ships that still call in here. Just past it there's the **Ingot Sculpture**, celebrating the flow of British bullion that used to pass through the docks almost daily. This sculpture, alas, is made of mere iron.

Moving to the next roundabout, to return to the waterfront you need to turn right onto West Hoe Rd (note the **Eddystone Pavement** to the east of Sippers Bar here, celebrating the groundbreaking design of John Smeaton for the lighthouse which used interlocking blocks to help resist the battering from sea and sky). The road leads you past the **Wall of Industrial Memories**, celebrating the heritage of the Millbay area.

Soon after, you join Hoe Rd, which you follow all the way to The Barbican, and pass a lovely lido – **Tinside Lido** (see p93) – on your right and **The Hoe** (see pp92-3) and **The Royal Citadel** (see p93) on the left. There are still some quirky little sights on the way, including a **cross** in the pavement to celebrate 1999's total eclipse of the sun and a marble **scallop shell** in the wall near the start of The Barbican, which celebrates the fact that Plymouth was one of only two English ports licensed by the king from which pilgrims were allowed to embark when heading to Santiago de Compostella on the Way of St James. St James is the patron saint of pilgrims and the shell is his symbol. Another patron saint is celebrated in the same wall a little further down: **Stella Maris, the Virgin, Star of the Sea**, patron saint of seafarers, was rescued from a lost cargo of marble and now sits illuminated by the pole star shining above.

Pilgrims would pray to these saints for protection during their journeys; although your journey is mostly land based, it can't hurt to ask for their help on your forthcoming expedition, just in case...

plane. There are regular talks and feedings as well as a 4D cinema.

Finally, **Plymouth Museum and Art Gallery** (☎ 01752-304774, 🖥 www.plymouth.gov.uk/museumpcmag.htm; Tue-Fri 10am-5.30pm, Sat & bank hol Mon 10am-5pm; free) is on Drake Circus, a few minutes north of The Barbican. Highlights include effects belonging to two of the city's heroes: a side drum (the oldest in the UK) that belonged to Francis Drake; and a pair of skis owned and used by Robert Falcon Scott in his 1902 Antarctic expedition.

Barbican International Jazz & Blues Festival (🖥 www.barbicanjazzandbluesfestival.com) is a four-day festival of music held at the end of July; concerts are held at various venues in the Barbican Area. It is held at the same time as Plymouth Classic Boat Rally and Port of Plymouth Regatta so book your accommodation in advance.

Services
As you'd expect, Plymouth has just about every amenity you need – though you may have to head into the new part of the city, on the other side of The Hoe, for some.

The **tourist information centre** (☎ 01752-306330, 🖥 www.visitplymouth.co.uk; Apr-Oct Mon-Sat 9am-5pm, Sun 10am-4pm, Nov-Mar Mon-Fri 9am-5pm,

---

❏ The Mayflower and the Pilgrim Fathers
Most visitors to Plymouth – and probably just about every American tourist in the city – are aware that amongst the first (and certainly the most famous) Europeans to settle in America (a group now celebrated as the Pilgrim Fathers) set sail from Plymouth in 1620. What is less well-known, perhaps, is the background to their emigration... and why they felt compelled to head for the New World in the first place.

The pilgrimage has its roots in Henry VIII's rejection of the Catholic Church back in 1534, an act that led to England becoming a Protestant country for the first time. Puritanism, the ideology followed by the Pilgrim fathers, emerged soon afterwards during the reign of Henry VIII's daughter, Elizabeth I. As the name suggests, the Puritans felt that Henry VIII's Church of England was neither strict nor pious enough for their rather fanatical tastes. This stance angered both Elizabeth and her successor, James I, and it wasn't long before the Puritans were being persecuted for their beliefs.

In 1609 a number of Puritans headed for Leiden in the Netherlands to seek a land where they could practise their faith in peace. Unfortunately, whilst the persecutions were less common, they were still unhappy with the tolerance and levity of their Dutch hosts; and more worrying still for the Puritans was the way their offspring were being assimilated into Dutch culture. There seemed to be only one solution: to build their own community, away from the persecution and profanity (as they saw it) of Europe, in the New World.

Plymouth's role in their story is actually both fortuitous and fairly minor. Setting sail from Southampton in *The Mayflower* and *The Speedwell* in August 1620, they only docked in Plymouth due to a storm that damaged the already old and leaking boats as they navigated The Channel. Fully stocked, and with the decision made to leave *The Speedwell* behind, a total of 102 passengers and crew (not all of whom were Puritans) finally left the city on 6th September 1620, reaching Cape Cod 66 days later to found the community they had dreamed of, in Massachusetts.

Alas, the Pilgrim Fathers' travails didn't end there. Weakened by their journey and unprepared for winter, half of them died within the first four months of landing. However, those who did survive owed their survival to the natives, a relationship cemented in the Pilgrims' first harvest of 1621 – a ceremony which would go on to become the basis for the American festival of Thanksgiving.

Sat 10am-4pm) is handily placed right by the Mayflower Steps on The Barbican and is one of the friendliest and most helpful on the entire walk. There are plenty of **banks** with **ATMs** in the city.

There's a Co-op **supermarket** (Mon-Thur 8am-10pm, Fri & Sat 8am-11pm, Sun 9am-10pm), which also contains a **sub post office** (Mon-Fri 9am-5.30pm, Sat 9am-12.30pm), nearby at 49-50 Southside St. The main branch is at 5 St Andrew's Cross Roundabout, about 10 minutes away. Nearby, but beyond Drake Circus Shopping Centre, the Central **library** (☎ 01752-305923, 🖳 www.plymouth.gov.uk/libraries; Mon & Fri 9am-7pm, Tue-Thur 9am-5.30pm, Sat 9am-5pm) has **internet** access (£1 for 15 mins plus two print-outs).

Those looking for **camping/trekking** supplies need to head this way to nearby New George St, north-west of St Andrew's

Cross Roundabout, where you'll find Millets at No 40, Trespass at No 34, and Blacks at No 71. There's also a Cotswolds round the corner at 25 Old Town St. All have approximately the same opening hours (Mon-Sat 9am-6pm, Sun 10.30am-4.30pm).

Back nearer the waterfront, the most convenient of Plymouth's **launderettes** is Hoegate Laundromat (☎ 01752-223031; Mon-Fri 8.30am-6pm, Sat 9am-1pm) at 55 Notte St.

Where to stay

There's a **hostel** in town: *Globe Backpackers* (☎ 01752-225158, 🖳 www .plymouthbackpackers.co.uk; 2D/32 dorm beds; WI-FI; from £16pp), 172 Citadel Rd, doesn't offer breakfast but does have a self-catering kitchen. It is in easy walking distance of both the path and train station.

PLYMOUTH MAP KEY

Where to stay
4 The Caraneal
5 The Firs
6 Duke of Cornwall Hotel
7 Globe Backpackers
8 Athenaeum Lodge
9 Caledonia Guesthouse
10 The Kynance
11 Invicta Hotel
12 The Bowling Green Hotel
13 The Yard Arm
14 George Guest House
15 Avalon Guesthouse
16 Acorns & Lawns
17 The Beeches
34 Casa Mia Guesthouse
35 Four Seasons Guesthouse
36 Mayflower Guesthouse
37 Seymour Guesthouse

Where to eat and drink
1 Elvira's Café
2 Artillery Tower
3 By the Park
11 Mariners Restaurant
18 Tanners
23 Buffet City
25 Yukisan
26 Favourite Foods
28 Eastern Eye

Where to eat and drink (cont'd)
29 Arribas
30 Barbican Steakhouse
31 Thai House
32 Hakka; Han's
33 Barbican Kitchen
39 Barbican Pasty
40 Mediterranean
41 Piermasters
42 Bites & Bar Rakuda
43 The Navy Inn
44 The Village
45 Rocky's Grill
46 Barbican Fish Bar
47 Harbourside
50 B-Bar

Other
19 Blacks
20 Millets
21 Trespass
22 Cotswold
24 Main Post Office
27 Hoegate Laundromat
33 Plymouth Gin Distillery
38 Co-op & Post Office
48 Elizabethan House
49 Tourist Office/Mayflower Exhb
50 Barbican Theatre

Plymouth 97

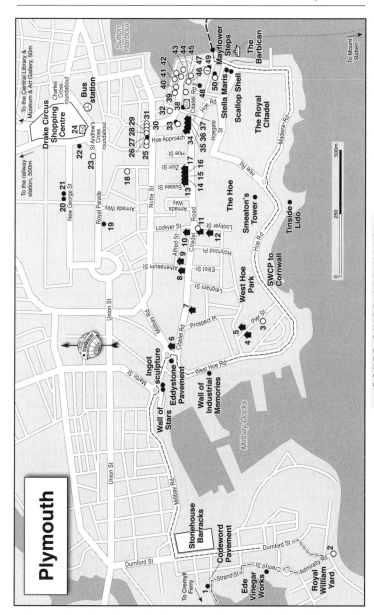

Plymouth

ROUTE GUIDE AND MAPS

There are **B&Bs** aplenty in Plymouth; a useful resource is 🖳 www.plymouthbed andbreakfast.co.uk. Many of them are well situated for both the path and the city centre.

Two near West Hoe Park are *The Firs* (☎ 01752-262870, 🖳 www.TheFirsinPly mouth.co.uk; 2S/4D/5T, some en suite; WI-FI; 🐕; £22.50-32.50pp, sgl £20-35), 13 Pier St; and *The Caraneal* (☎ 01752-663589, 🖳 www.caranealplymouth.co.uk; 8D/2T; WI-FI; 🐕; £25-30pp, sgl occ £35-40), 12-14 Pier St.

Those more central are generally based along **Citadel Rd**. Facing Hoe Park are *The Beeches* (☎ 01752-266475, 🖳 www.beech esplymouth.moonfruit.com; 2D or T/2F; WI-FI; 🐕; from £30pp), No 175; *Avalon Guesthouse* (☎ 01752-668127, 🖳 www .avalonguesthouse.moonfruit.com; 3S/2T/2F; WI-FI; 🐕; from £25pp) at No 167; and *Acorns & Lawns* (☎ 01752-229474, 🖳 www.plymouthhoeguesthouse.co.uk; 2D/1T; WI-FI; £30-37.50pp) at No 171. The latter has a 2-night minimum stay policy between May and September. *George Guesthouse* (☎ 01752-661517, 🖳 www .georgeguesthouse.com; 1S/3D or F/5T/1F; WI-FI; 🐕; £25-30pp) is at No 161.

Pubs that also offer accommodation include the co-owned public house *The Yard Arm* (☎ 01752-202405, 🖳 www.yard armplymouth.co.uk; 1T/2D or F; WI-FI; 🐕; from £25pp), at No 159. Morning munchies are dished up between 7 and 11am. Food is then served until 9.30pm.

Remaining on Citadel Rd, but on the other side of Armada Way from Hoe Park, there are more options such as *The Kynance* (☎ 01752-266821, 🖳 www.ky nancehouse.co.uk; 6S/18D or T/2F; 🛁; WI-FI; 🐕; £27-28pp, sgl £32-36), at 107-11.

Closer to the old town, but still on the same thoroughfare, on Citadel Road East there is a selection of guesthouses including *Seymour* (☎ 01752-667002, 🖳 www .seymourguesthouse.co.uk; 2S/2D/3T, some en suite; WI-FI; £29pp, sgl occ £38) at No 211; *Mayflower* (☎ 01752-667496, 🖳 www.mayflowerguesthouse.co.uk; 2S/7D or T; WI-FI; £30pp, sgl occ £37) at No 209; *Four Seasons* (☎ 01752-223591, 🖳 www .fourseasonsguesthouse.co.uk; 7D or T; WI-FI; 🐕; £27-31pp, sgl occ £32-48), at No 207, where there is a choice of breakfast including veggie or gluten-free; and *Casa Mia* (☎ 01752-265742, 🖳 www.casamia guesthouse.co.uk; 2S/2D or T/3D; WI-FI; £35-38pp, sgl occ £40-45), No 201, also a purveyor of the vegetarian breakfast.

Still central but on **Athenaeum St** are *The Caledonia Guesthouse* (☎ 01752-229052, 🖳 www.thecaledonia.co.uk; 1S/5D/4T; WI-FI; £30-65pp, sgl occ £40-65), at No 27; and *Athenaeum Lodge* (☎ 01752-665005, 🖳 www.athenaeumlodge .com; 3D/4T or T; WI-FI; £24-31pp, sgl occ £32-44), at No 4.

For **hotel** accommodation the plush *Duke of Cornwall Hotel* (☎ 01752-275850, 🖳 www.thedukeofcornwall.co.uk; 72 rooms; 🛁; WI-FI; £42.50-57.50pp, sgl £78) is on Millbay Rd, at the western end of Citadel Rd.

Closer to The Hoe are *The Bowling Green Hotel* (☎ 01752-209090, 🖳 www.thebowlinggreenplymouth.com; 1S/2T/8D/1D or F; 🛁; WI-FI; £37.50pp, sgl £50), 9-10 Osborne Place, which is used by a number of walking companies; and *Invicta Hotel* (☎ 01752-664997, 🖳 www.invictahotel.co.uk; 4S/8D/6D or T/4F; 🛁; WI-FI; 🐕; from £38.75pp, sgl £62.50), 11/12 Osborne Place, which also houses Mariners Restaurant (see Where to eat).

❏ **Where to stay: the details**

Unless specified, B&B-style accommodation is either en suite or has private facilities; 🛁 means at least one room has a bath; 🐕 signifies that dogs are welcome in at least one room but always by prior arrangement, an additional charge may also be payable; WI-FI means wi-fi is available in the property, though not always (reliably) in every room.

Where to eat and drink
The Barbican area This is the place to go for food; you can probably stay at least a fortnight without eating in the same place twice.

For **food-on-the-go** check out *Bites*, a sandwich bar squeezed in hard by the big establishments on The Quay; bespoke sarnies are £2.50/2.95 with extra fillings 25p. *Barbican Pasty* (☎ 01752-262462), on Southside St, does pasties from £1.95. Also on Southside St, at No 35, *Harbourside* (Mon 11am-10pm, Tue-Thur 11am-10.30pm, Fri & Sat to 11pm, Sun to 10pm) does haddock & chips for £5.30. A close rival, both geographically and commercially, is *Barbican Fish Bar* (☎ 01752-261432), at the eastern end of Southside St, offering cod, chips & a bottle of pop for £6.75.

Mediterranean (☎ 01752-665345, 🖥 mediterraneanplymouth.com; Mon-Fri 11.30am-2.30pm & 5.30-10.30pm, Sat & Sun 11.30am-10.30pm; 23 Southside St) offers 9" takeaway pizza for just £3.95 and pasta dishes from £7.95. *B-Bar* (☎ 01752-242021, 🖥 b-bar.co.uk; food served noon-9pm) is a Thai noodle bar in the Barbican Theatre on Castle St that has both in-house dining and a takeaway. Their scrumptious Thai noodle boxes start at £5.95 for the vegetarian option, £6.45 otherwise.

There are further takeaway options on Notte St. *Favourite Foods* (☎ 01752-222232; daily 4.30pm-1am) is a fast-food joint serving a rolled-up chicken kebab for £4.10. *The Eastern Eye* (☎ 01752-262948, 🖥 www.easterneyeplymouth.com; Sun-Thur 6pm to midnight, Fri & Sat 6pm-2am) is a recommended Indian restaurant offering 10% discount on its takeaway meals. *Thai House* (☎ 01752-661600; Tue-Sat 6-10.30pm, Sun 6-10pm) offers a 15% takeaway discount. *Arribas* (☎ 01752-603303, 🖥 www.arribasmexican.co.uk; Sun-Thur noon-2pm & 5.30-10pm, Fri & Sat noon-10pm) does all the Mexican favourites (chicken fajitas £12.95).

Also on Notte St, *Barbican Steakhouse* (☎ 01752-222214; Mon-Thur 5-10.30pm, Fri 5-11pm, Sat noon-11pm, Sun noon-10pm) does a mouthwatering 12oz rib-eye for £11.25.

The Barbican also plays host to several good Chinese places. *Hakka* (☎ 01752-224777; noon-3pm & 6-9.30pm) is an upmarket Cantonese joint with the only home-made dim sum in Devon. Upstairs, *Han's Chinatown* (☎ 01752-266677, 🖥 www.hanschinatown.co.uk; Sun-Thur noon-8pm, Fri & Sat noon-9pm) is the smartest Chinese in town but still reasonable with roast pork and noodles in soup for around a fiver.

On Notte St, *Yukisan* (☎ 01752-250240, 🖥 www.yukisan.co.uk; Mon-Wed 11.30am-2.30pm & 5-10pm, Thur 11.30am-10pm, Fri-Sat 11.30am-10.30pm, Sun noon-10pm) is the only Japanese restaurant in town. The sushi's good, of course, but try the *yakitori* (grilled meat/veg skewers in a Japanese barbecue sauce) from £3.60.

Also on Southside St, *Barbican Kitchen* (☎ 01752-604448, 🖥 www.barbicankitchen.com; daily noon-3pm & 5pm-late) is located in Plymouth Gin Distillery. The menu is eclectic, including dishes from Japan to Italy, though they also do a lovely sausages and mash with onion gravy (£9.95). *The Village* (☎ 01752-667688; 🖥 thevillagerestaurantplymouth.co.uk; Mon-Sat 11am-2pm & 5.30-10.30pm, Sun 11am-10.30pm) is at No 32, where seafood is a speciality though they also do a terrific roast beef on Sundays (£6.50). *Piermasters* (☎ 01752-229345, 🖥 www.piermastersrestaurant.com; Mon-Sat noon-2.30pm & 5-11pm), at No 33, is the city's oldest seafood restaurant. Mains start at £12 but include such delights as confit fillet of brill with a razor clam, mussel & potato stew served with baby spinach (£17.95). A little further along, *Rocky's Grill* (☎ 01752-227392, 🖥 www.rockysgrill.co.uk; Mon-Thur 8am-10pm, Fri & Sat 8am-11pm, Sun 9am-10pm), 41-42 Southside St, does a decent 8oz New York loin strip for £5.45.

Still on Southside St, *The Navy Inn* (☎ 01752-301812, 🖥 www.thenavyinn.co.uk) does a good roast and is always lively; its main draw, however, is the terrace on the first floor with views along the waterfront. Round the corner on The Quay, *Bar Rakuda* (☎ 01752-221155, 🖥 barbicanleisurebars.com; 9am-2am) is a glitzy tapas and cocktail bar with a set menu for £11.95. It has a pleasant outdoor seating area.

Elsewhere in Plymouth The small deli-café *By The Park* (daily 9.30am-5pm), at 26 Pier St, does wonderful cakes and cream teas as well as lunches and hot and cold drinks. For the ultimate in filling Oriental cuisine, *Buffet City* (☎ 01752-269888; food served Mon-Sat 11.45am-4.30pm & 5-11pm, Sun 11.45am-11pm) offers 'all-u-can-eat' buffets for £5.95-8.95. *Mariners Restaurant* (see Where to stay; Mon-Sat 7-9.30pm) is in Invicta Hotel on Osborne Place; all food is cooked to order and where possible locally sourced.

Artillery Tower (☎ 01752-257610, 🖳 www.artillerytower.co.uk; lunch Tue-Fri noon-2.30pm by reservation only, Tue-Sat 7-9.30pm), is one of the more discreet places in the city; however, you probably won't come this far unless you are walking towards the Cremyll ferry. Evening meals are set at £39.50 for three courses, but include mains such as roast duck with marinated cherries, or peppered loin of venison with quince & chestnuts. It's set in a 15th-century defensive tower on the sea wall and overlooking Plymouth Sound.

The eponymous *Tanners* (☎ 01752-252001, 🖳 www.tannersrestaurant.com; Tue-Sat noon-2.30pm & 6.30pm-late), at Prysten House on Finewell St, north of Notte St, has long been cited as the finest in town. Mains start at about £15 (and go up to £25), with sides an extra £5; expensive, but there are some delightful dishes including roast fillet of brill, buttered leeks, clams, chervil and vermouth (£23.95).

Transport
[See also pp55-60] First's 48 **bus** runs to Wembury regularly throughout the day whilst their 93 service journeys along the coast as far as Dartmouth via Kingsbridge, Torcross, Slapton & Strete. Note that getting public transport to most coastal destinations between Plymouth and Salcombe and then from there to Torcross is not easy. If you want to avoid an area so devoid in public transport then First's X80 will take you on to Torquay and the English Riviera.

Trains depart regularly for Exeter and London as well as west to Penzance and the rest of Cornwall.

For a **taxi**, try Excel Cabs (☎ 01752-666699) or Armada Cabs (☎ 01752-666222).

PLYMOUTH TO WEMBURY   [MAPS 1-6]

For such a lovely trek, this initial **10¾-mile (17.25km; 4¼hrs)** leg is a bit of an inauspicious start. True, there may be the occasional stroller who will swoon at this saunter through the city's unsung suburbs and praise the opportunity it provides to plod through Plymouth's less picturesque parts. But for most people the start of their 217¼-mile odyssey is little more than a fairly mundane trudge through an unappealing industrial estate followed by an only-slightly-more-interesting hike through the suburban sprawl that precedes Mount Batten Point.

You can, of course, opt to take the ferry (see box below) from The Barbican to Mount Batten, and if time is short this would be a good decision. It does, after all, completely cut out the dullest stretch of this stage (possibly, some may argue, of

❏ **The ferry to Mount Batten**
The ferry to Mount Batten Point (☎ 01752-408590, 🖳 www.mountbattenferry.com; £1.50, 🐾 free) is not actually part of the coast path – though many trekkers treat it as such to cut out the rather dull walking through Plymouth. Sailings are every 30 minutes (summer daily 7.15am-11pm, winter Mon-Thur 7.45am-6.15pm, Fri 7.45am-11pm, Sat 8.45am-11pm, Sun 8.45am-6.15pm).

the entire SWCP), and leaves you with just its more appetising latter half along the eastern edge of Plymouth Sound and on past Heybrook Bay to Wembury.

But if you do have the time – and you're serious about completing the walk described in this book – you should probably attempt the whole stage, from Mayflower Steps to Wembury: taking a short-cut before you've even begun walking is no way to begin a challenge such as this. And besides, the path is not entirely without interest. There's the signage, for one thing, which for some unknown reason is by far the best on the entire coast path. Why anyone designed such a variegated array of signposts and waymarks is anyone's guess – but the fact is the path is marked with signposts made from huge recycled navigation beacons, some Communist-style iron star plaques and even giant metal sycamore keys. It's all rather bizarre – but they do serve to provide much-needed distractions for this stage. The city authorities have also gone to some length to provide interest to this section and are to be applauded for their efforts. On the first half of this stage, for example, you'll come across a holy shrine, a wall of poetry and a rhino. There's also a 19th-century 'castle', situated between the neighbouring lakes of Hooe and Radford; with swans drifting lazily nearby this is, in most people's opinions, the prettiest part of this stage (though you'll have to compose your photos carefully if you want to exclude all the rude graffiti with which it's been embellished down the years).

At least after Mount Batten matters improve and the countryside for the first time starts to dominate. While the bucolic beauty of this stage's second half is still interrupted on occasion – most noticeably by the holiday park at Bovisand – it is, on the whole, a largely rustic, gentle ramble, and much more characteristic of the trek to come. So strap on those boots, tighten the shoulder straps and get going: you've got 217¼ miles to go, and these paths don't walk themselves...

However, before you set off make sure you have checked the ferry times for this section of the path.

ROUTE GUIDE AND MAPS

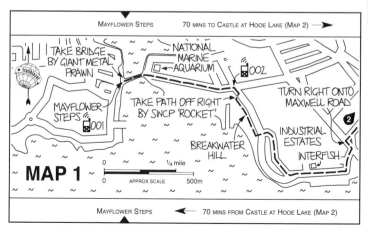

LAIRA BRIDGE-
BUSY ROAD
BRIDGE -STINKS!
TURN RIGHT
OFF ROAD BEFORE
ORESTON RHINO
POETRY 003
WALL
MORLEY
ARMS
BILLACOMBE
ROAD
THE
SWCP
BENCH!
RIVER PLYM
BREAKWATER RD
PATH RUNS TO
LEFT OF FENCE
PATH KINKS
RIGHT BY
BOAT TRAILERS
MARINE
ROAD
PARK
LANE
WEST DEVON
WAY
004
BOAT
GRAVEYARD
RADFORD CASTLE
RADFORD
LAKE
ROYAL
OAK PUB
(PLAQUE)
HOOE LAKE
WATER
WORKS
CONTINUE
HUGGING
WATERFRONT
HEXTON
HILL RD

0   1/4 mile
MAP 2
0   APPROX SCALE   500m

70 MINS FROM MAYFLOWER STEPS (MAP 1)
70 MINS TO MAYFLOWER STEPS (MAP 1)
CASTLE AT HOOE LAKE
CASTLE AT HOOE LAKE
50 MINS FROM SLIPWAY AT MOUNTBATTEN POINT (MAP 3)
50 MINS TO SLIPWAY AT MOUNTBATTEN POINT (MAP 3)

ROUTE GUIDE AND MAPS

The route

Beginning at the Mayflower Steps, the path leaves the busy delights of The Barbican behind by crossing the lock gates that secure Sutton Harbour, passing the huge **National Marine Aquarium** on the left on its way to the **Wallsend** and **Cattedown Wharf industrial estates**. (You may be surprised to find that the former is actually an SSSI (see p71), a disused quarry clearly showing the development of Devonian Plymouth limestone.) It's not the only surprise on this section of the trail: the **giant 'rocket' SWCP waypoint** leading you on to Breakwater Hill was once a navigational beacon for sailors and it now serves much the same purpose for land-lubbing trekkers, pointing the way to the **shrine to St Christopher** (which, given that he is the patron saint of travellers, is entirely appropriate for the start of your journey). A section of speeding through an industrial estate then separates you from **Laira Bridge** and a crossing of the Plym. A **poetry wall** lines busy Billacombe Rd, which brightens an otherwise unpleasant stretch.

You leave this thoroughfare at **Oreston Rhino** which celebrates the prehistoric fossils of lion, ox, elephant, hippo, camel and, yes, rhino, that have been found in the caves near the city. Heading down Breakwater Rd, it's not long before the banks of **Hooe Lake** are reached, which you then hug most of the way to the neat suburb of Turnchapel. On the way you pass the **Castle**, originally built for the 'keeper', a member of staff of nearby Radford House, who was responsible for looking after the estate's moorings and quays. Shortly after, by Hooe Green, a pub has a **plaque** on its wall facing the path – one of several such plaques that decorate the walls around here. It is a large-scale re-creation of a medallion issued by John Smeaton (see p92), builder of the Eddystone Lighthouse, which he gave to his highly skilled workers to prevent them being taken by press-gangs – hired thugs employed to force men into the military service.

Eventually, after passing through **Turnchapel**, you arrive at **Mount Batten** (see box below). You'll find several places to eat round here though we advise holding off until you're strolling on the **Jennycliffs** and reach *Jennycliff Café* (Map 3; ☎ 01752-402358, 💻 www.jennycliffcafe.com; daily 9am-6pm but if the weather is bad they may closer earlier), with the best views over the Sound and a decent menu encompassing omelettes (£3.90-4.40), burgers, breakfasts and baked potatoes.

After Mount Batten the path changes character and finally becomes the rustic ramble you were hoping for. True, Plymouth is still a huge looming presence over your right shoulder. The large naval contingent in the Sound and the helicopters swooping overhead further remind you that you aren't free of the city shackles just yet. But climbing away from Mount Batten the path is soon dodging amongst woods and meadows rather than warehouses and marinas.

This rural idyll is interrupted by naval defences near **Bovisand Point**, which is home to the seasonal *Cliffedge Café* and its neighbouring holiday park – which in turn plays host to *The Beachcomber Café* (☎ 01752-862679, 💻 www.thebeachcombercafe.co.uk; daily 10am-3pm, summer 9.30am-6pm depending on the weather) and a **shop** (Apr-Sep 9am-5pm). But it's not long before you are once again away from civilisation on a reasonably flat path heading via **Heybrook Bay** to round **Wembury Point**.

The island out to sea, by the way, is **Great Mew Stone**, now uninhabited but once occupied by one Sam Wakeman, who was exiled there for seven years

ROUTE GUIDE AND MAPS

❏ **Mount Batten Point**
Though today it seems little more than an unprepossessing pimple of grassy rock, Mount Batten Point actually has a lengthy history, as a few of its old buildings may suggest. Indeed, excavations indicate that this spot was the location for the very earliest trade the British had with Europe. From the late Bronze Age right through to the Roman era, archaeologists at Mount Batten Point have found evidence of a market that lead some to suggest that this spot could be the 'Tamaris' mentioned by Ptolemy in his *Geographica* (often cited as the world's earliest guidebook). The most obvious building here today, however, the austere **Mount Batten Tower**, is significantly younger, having been constructed in 1652 to protect the burgeoning new settlement around Plymouth Harbour.

Skip forward a few hundred years and the waters off Mount Batten Point were used to test the first sea-plane models, and an air station was subsequently established here. A **monument in the shape of a propellor** from a Sunderland flying boat, situated at the very end of the point, celebrates the RAF's tenure.

as punishment for some misdemeanour and paid his rent by supplying rabbits for the table of the local manor. There is a painting of the island by JMW Turner, dated 1816, which is now in the National Gallery of Ireland, Dublin.

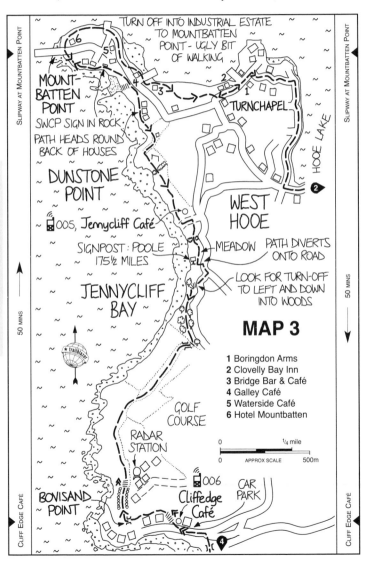

TURN OFF INTO INDUSTRIAL ESTATE
TO MOUNTBATTEN
POINT - UGLY BIT
OF WALKING

SLIPWAY AT MOUNTBATTEN POINT

MOUNT-
BATTEN
POINT

TURNCHAPEL

HOOE LAKE

SWCP SIGN IN ROCK
PATH HEADS ROUND
BACK OF HOUSES

DUNSTONE
POINT

WEST
HOOE

005, Jennycliff Café

MEADOW

PATH DIVERTS
ONTO ROAD

SIGNPOST: POOLE
175½ MILES

LOOK FOR TURN-OFF
TO LEFT AND DOWN
INTO WOODS

JENNYCLIFF
BAY

MAP 3

trailblaze

1 Boringdon Arms
2 Clovelly Bay Inn
3 Bridge Bar & Café
4 Galley Café
5 Waterside Café
6 Hotel Mountbatten

GOLF
COURSE

RADAR
STATION

0 ¼ mile
0 APPROX SCALE 500m

BOVISAND
POINT

006
Cliffedge
Café

CAR
PARK

ROUTE GUIDE AND MAPS

50 MINS

50 MINS

CLIFF EDGE CAFÉ

CLIFF EDGE CAFÉ

With Wembury Marine Conservation Area to the right, rising ground to the left and an easy flat path ahead, it's a pleasant final stretch to *The Old Mill Café* (☎ 01752-862314, 🖥 theoldmillwembury.co.uk; Apr-Oct daily 10am-5pm, rest of year weekends & hols 10am-4pm; all hours depend on the

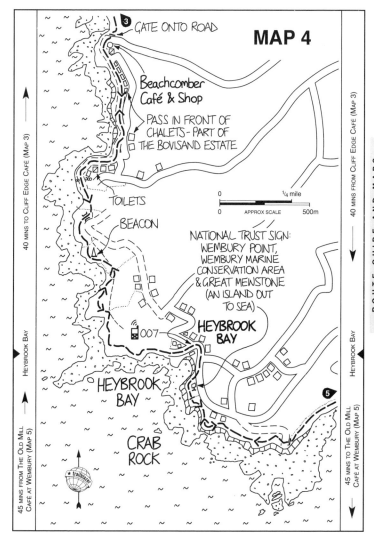

MAP 4

3 GATE ONTO ROAD

Beachcomber Café & Shop

PASS IN FRONT OF CHALETS - PART OF THE BOVISAND ESTATE

TOILETS

BEACON

NATIONAL TRUST SIGN: WEMBURY POINT, WEMBURY MARINE CONSERVATION AREA & GREAT MEWSTONE (AN ISLAND OUT TO SEA)

007

HEYBROOK BAY

HEYBROOK BAY

CRAB ROCK

0   ¼ mile
0   APPROX SCALE   500m

trailblazer

40 MINS TO CLIFF EDGE CAFÉ (MAP 3)

HEYBROOK BAY

45 MINS FROM THE OLD MILL CAFÉ AT WEMBURY (MAP 5)

40 MINS FROM CLIFF EDGE CAFÉ (MAP 3)

HEYBROOK BAY

45 MINS TO THE OLD MILL CAFÉ AT WEMBURY (MAP 5)

ROUTE GUIDE AND MAPS

5

weather), a 150-year-old watermill turned eatery. The road to Wembury runs steeply up the hill from here – or you can continue along the coast path to the mouth of the Yealm, from where a much flatter path heads inland to the village. Alternatively, you can carry on down to the ferry launch and the continuation of the trail.

WEMBURY   [opposite, top]

An unassuming little place nestling in the shadow of Plymouth and its suburbs, Wembury has been around for a long time – some flint tools have been found hereabouts which proves that man has been stomping around since at least the Mesolithic era (10,000-4000BC). (Mesolithic means 'middle stone age' and it was the period when the hunter-gatherer lifestyle changed to one based far more on agriculture.)

Little happened here in Wembury but it's a pleasant-enough place, if a little too uphill from the coast for most tired trekkers. There are just enough services, however, to make the trek worthwhile: **Wembury Stores** (Mon, Tue, Thur & Fri 8am-5.30pm, Sat 8am-1pm, Sun 9am-noon) is well stocked, has a free **ATM** and doubles up as the **post office** (Mon-Fri 9am-5.30pm, Sat 9am-12.30pm). There's also a Londis **store** (Mon-Fri 8am-6pm, Sat 7am-6pm, Sun 8am-1pm) on the way out of the village (on the walking route around the Yealm; see below).

Accommodation in the village will either be in a suburban house that doubles as a B&B or under canvas. The latter option is *Pilgrims Rest Camping & Caravan Site* (☎ 01752-863429, 🖥 www.pilgrimsrest.co

.uk; 🐾 OK if on lead) with pitches for just £3-4 per tent plus £2 per person; a shower costs 20p.

For **B&Bs**, *Wenbiria* (☎ 01752-862160; 2D, but not let out separately; 🛏; £25pp, sgl occ £30), 10 Hawthorn Drive, is unusual in that they have two rooms but because of their configuration they are not let separately. Still, it's a homely place and if you're continuing on the long remote stretch east from here a packed lunch costs £4.50.

Other options include *Seahorses* (☎ 01752-863038, 🖥 seahorsescurfhx.supanet .com; 1D/1T or F; 🛏; £30pp, sgl occ £25-30pp), at 10 Hawthorn Park Rd, *11 Valley Drive* (☎ 01752-862581; 1D or F; 🐾), charging £25-30pp, and *Knoll Cottage* (☎ 01752-862036; 1S/1T/1D; 🛏; £25-30pp) at 104 Church Rd.

Wembury Cars (see p105) also do B&B from *1 Barton Close* (☎ 01752-863710; 1T; 🛏; £30pp).

For **food** *The Odd Wheel* (☎ 01752-863052; food served Mon-Fri noon-2.30pm & 5-9pm Sat & Sun noon-9pm) does some great dishes including a mean Sunday roast for £8.95 and takeaways from £4.95.

First's 48 **bus** service (see pp55-60) travels between the village and Plymouth.

TACKLING THE YEALM

Ferry details
For the coast path you need the Warren Point to Noss Mayo service (the service from Warren Point to Newton Ferrers will still get you across the river, but further away from the coast path than the Noss Mayo service).

The ferry (☎ 07817-132757; £2.50; 🐾 50p, bikes £1) operates Easter to end September weekdays and bad weather 10am-noon & 3-4pm on demand, 10am-4pm in school summer holidays and good weather.

Walking around the Yealm   [Map 5, Map 6a, pp110-11]
The **nine-mile (14.5km; 4hrs)** diversion is not without its attractions including some pleasant walking on the **Erme-Plym Trail** (see p36). However,

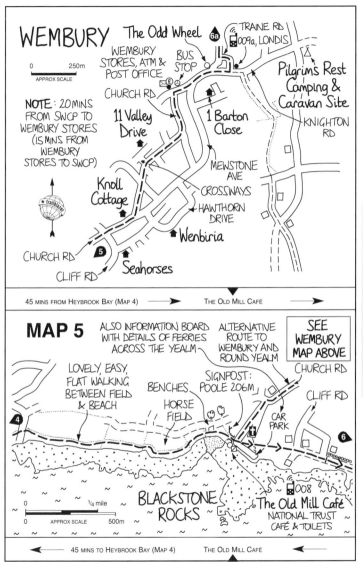

WEMBURY The Odd Wheel 6a TRAINE RD
009a, LONDIS

WEMBURY BUS
STORES, ATM & STOP
POST OFFICE

Pilgrim's Rest
Camping &
Caravan Site

CHURCH RD

0   250m
APPROX SCALE

NOTE: 20 MINS
FROM SWCP TO
WEMBURY STORES
(15 MINS FROM
WEMBURY
STORES TO SWCP)

11 Valley
Drive

1 Barton
Close

KNIGHTON
RD

MEWSTONE
AVE

CROSSWAYS

trailblazer

Knoll
Cottage

HAWTHORN
DRIVE

Wenbiria

CHURCH RD

5

CLIFF RD

Seahorses

45 MINS FROM HEYBROOK BAY (MAP 4) ⟶   THE OLD MILL CAFÉ   ⟶

MAP 5 ALSO INFORMATION BOARD ALTERNATIVE
WITH DETAILS OF FERRIES ROUTE TO
ACROSS THE YEALM WEMBURY AND
ROUND YEALM

SEE
WEMBURY
MAP ABOVE

CHURCH RD

LOVELY, EASY,
FLAT WALKING BENCHES
BETWEEN FIELD
& BEACH

SIGNPOST:
POOLE 206M

HORSE
FIELD

CLIFF RD

CAR
PARK

4

6

0   ¼ mile
0   APPROX SCALE   500m

BLACKSTONE
~ ROCKS ~

008

The Old Mill Café
NATIONAL TRUST
CAFÉ & TOILETS

⟵ 45 MINS TO HEYBROOK BAY (MAP 4)   THE OLD MILL CAFÉ   ⟵

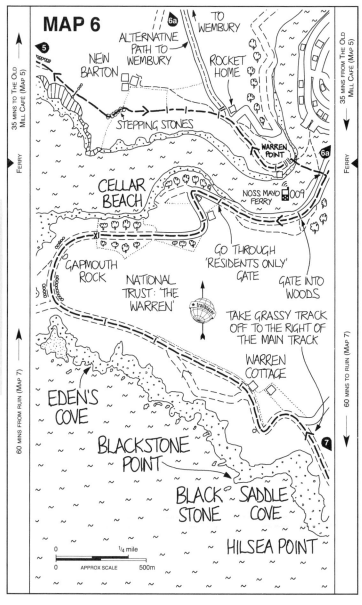

MAP 6

TO WEMBURY

ALTERNATIVE PATH TO WEMBURY

NEW BARTON

ROCKET HOME

STEPPING STONES

WARREN POINT

CELLAR BEACH

NOSS MAYO FERRY 009

GO THROUGH 'RESIDENTS ONLY' GATE

GAPMOUTH ROCK

NATIONAL TRUST: 'THE WARREN'

GATE INTO WOODS

TAKE GRASSY TRACK OFF TO THE RIGHT OF THE MAIN TRACK

WARREN COTTAGE

EDEN'S COVE

BLACKSTONE POINT

BLACK STONE

SADDLE COVE

HILSEA POINT

35 MINS TO THE OLD MILL CAFÉ (MAP 5)

FERRY

35 MINS FROM THE OLD MILL CAFÉ (MAP 5)

FERRY

60 MINS FROM RUIN (MAP 7)

60 MINS TO RUIN (MAP 7)

0   1/4 mile
0   APPROX SCALE   500m

overall there are times, particularly when you reach the Devonshire village of Brixton, that the coast path seems an awfully long way away and it won't be long before you'll be yearning for the sound of the sea again.

The trail begins by the Londis store at the eastern end of Wembury, where a small country lane, Traine Rd, runs north away from the village onto Wembury Rd. Opposite, the Erme-Plym Trail continues north-east on a wooded track to tiny **Spriddlestone**.

Continue across **Cofflete Creek** to the busy A379, which you should join to reach **Brixton**. Here you'll find a **post office** (Mon-Fri 8am-5.30pm, Sat 9am-12.30pm) and **shop** (Mon-Sat 8am-8pm, Sun 8am-noon) with a small **café** in the back; a pub, *The Foxhound Inn* (☎ 01752-880271, 💻 www.foxhoundinn.co.uk; food served Mon-Sat noon-2pm, Sun noon-2.30pm, Sun-Thur 6-9pm, Fri & Sat 6-9.30pm); and a lovely B&B, *Venn Farm* (☎ 01752-880378, 💻 www.vennfarm.co.uk; 4D; 🛏; wi-fi; £32.50-35pp, sgl occ £45), with accommodation either in the house or in a converted barn.

From Brixton the path continues along the Erme-Plym Trail which you rejoin by the post office, heading through fields of crops and pheasants on your way to a small country lane that you join at **Gorlofen**. This you leave via a steep climb up a field, rejoining the A379 at **Yealmpton**. Tally Ho Coaches' No 875 **bus** service calls here and also First's No 93 from Plymouth (see pp55-60).

A lovely stretch now follows as you say goodbye to the Erme-Plym for the last time, briefly heading west back along the A379 and down Stray Park to the end to reach a lovely wooded track on the right that heads, via some charmingly overgrown quarry works, to **Puslinch Bridge**, where you actually cross the Yealm.

Much of the next section is, alas, on roads as you climb steeply out of the valley, diverting off the road briefly to cross a couple of fields (via some plastic sheep!) before returning to the tarmac for the long straight stretch to the **Water Tower** at Butts Park and the B3186 leading down (right) to **Newton Ferrers** (see below).

Sticking to the road, you skirt the end of Newton Creek to reach the even tinier settlement of **Noss Mayo** (see below) – at the end of which, of course, lies the **ferry launch** and a reunion with the coast path.

NOSS MAYO & NEWTON FERRERS
[Map 6a, pp110-11]
Separated by a narrow tidal creek, these tidy twin villages lie on the estuary of the River Yealm. Newton Ferrers is the larger of the two. Originally called *Niwetone*, the town was given as a gift to the Norman Ferrers family – hence the name.

Noss Mayo is the nearer of the two to the coast path, with the ferry across the Yealm calling in at the edge of the village, about ten minutes away from the centre of Noss Mayo. However, those who take the diversion around the Yealm will walk through both villages on their way back to the coast path.

There are some facilities here including a Co-op **supermarket** (Mon-Sat 8am-8pm, Sun 9am-7pm) with a free **ATM** in Newton Ferrers – convenient for those walking around the Yealm though quite a walk from the coast path.

For **accommodation** in the two villages you can try *Revelstoke Coombe* (off Map 6a; ☎ 01752-872663, 💻 www.nossmayobandb.net; 2D private facilities/1D or T en suite; 🐾 charge negotiable; wi-fi; £40pp) in the fields above Noss Mayo.

Alternatively you can choose to stay in *The Swan Inn* (☎ 01752-872392, 💻 www.swaninnnossmayo.co.uk; 1D/1T;

ROUTE GUIDE AND MAPS

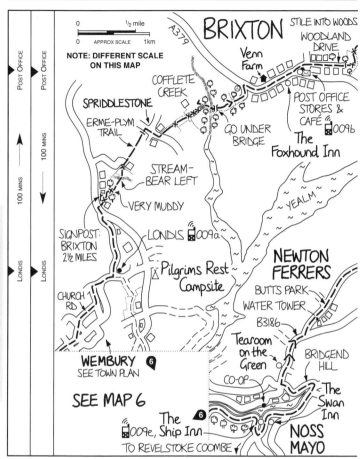

shared facilities; ♥; WI-FI; 🐾; ; £40pp), one of two great pubs in Noss Mayo. They provide simple accommodation with no televisions in the rooms; nevertheless, it's a lovely homely place in a great location. Their **food** (Mon-Sat noon-3pm & 6-9pm, school summer Sun noon-9pm, rest of year Sun noon-3pm & 6-9pm; mains around £8-12) is fairly standard pub fare though their homemade burgers – with toppings of cheddar cheese, bacon or stilton – for £9.45 are great. The other pub, *The Ship*

Inn (☎ 01752-872387, 🖳 nossmayo.com; food daily noon-9.30pm), has mains for £8.95-18.95, the menu containing the odd surprise including pan-fried duck breast served on a potato rosti with plum sauce and green vegetables (£14.50). Finally, *Tearoom on the Green* (☎ 01752-873368; Wed-Sun 10am-5pm) is a lovely place for a cup of tea.

Tally Ho Coaches No 94 **bus service** journeys between Plymouth, Newton Ferrers & Noss Mayo. You can also connect with the No 93 in Yealmpton; see pp55-60.

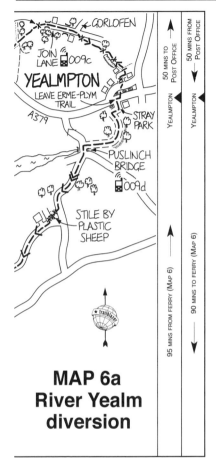

**MAP 6a
River Yealm
diversion**

WEMBURY TO BIGBURY-ON-SEA [MAPS 6-11]

This **15¼-mile (24.5km; 5hrs 25mins)** stage is fairly typical of the South Devon section of the SWCP. With a couple of river crossings (including one, uniquely for this stretch of the coast path, that you have to wade across), a reasonable café to stop at for lunch, a quiet village at the end of your hike with a very quirky pub... and mile after mile of lovely scenery to delight the eyes and lift the soul, this is very much in keeping with this county's ability to inspire and entertain.

There are some possible problems on the trail. The first is that this is actually one of the quietest stretches on the entire path and you need to make sure you reach the tearooms at Mothecombe when they're open (or bring a packed lunch) as it's the only place to eat at before the holiday camp at Challaborough, just before Bigbury.

The second problem is the crossing of the Erme: with no ferry, the only way to tackle it is to wade across – which, according to the noticeboards dotted about, **is possible only an hour either side of low tide**. It's important, therefore, that you find out when this will be and keep a close eye on your progress against the clock. Mistime your arrival and you'll have to arrange a taxi, or walk around – and given that this walk around the estuary is almost entirely on roads, this is one estuary diversion where we really do urge you to take a cab.

The route

Having crossed the Yealm, your next task on the trail is to follow an old carriage drive west round **Gapmouth Rock** then east past various old ruins (including an **old signal station**) to Stoke Beach. *(continued on p114)*

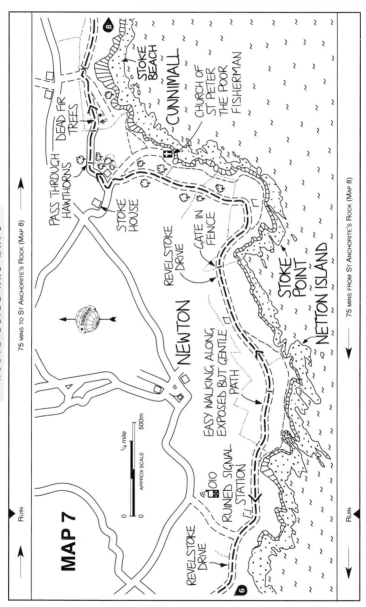

MAP 7

RUIN

REVELSTOKE DRIVE

75 MINS TO ST ANCHORITE'S ROCK (MAP 8)

PASS THROUGH HAWTHORNS

DEAD FIR TREES

STOKE BEACH

CUNNIMALL

CHURCH OF ST PETER THE POOR FISHERMAN

STOKE HOUSE

REVELSTOKE DRIVE

GATE IN FENCE

NEWTON

STOKE POINT

NETTON ISLAND

EASY WALKING ALONG, EXPOSED BUT GENTLE PATH

RUINED SIGNAL STATION

¼ mile
500m
APPROX SCALE
0
0

RUIN

75 MINS FROM ST ANCHORITE'S ROCK (MAP 8)

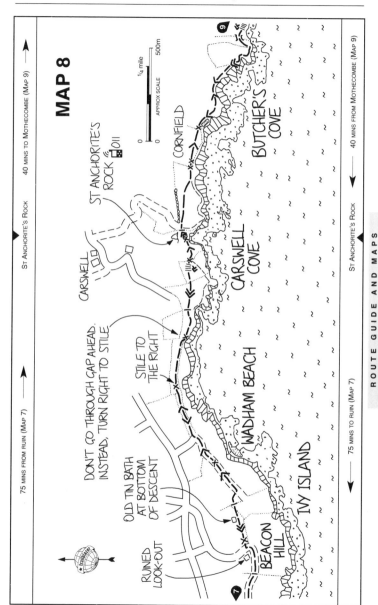

MAP 8

75 MINS FROM RUIN (MAP 7) → ◄ ST ANCHORITE'S ROCK → 40 MINS TO MOTHECOMBE (MAP 9) →

St Anchorite's Rock 011

CARSWELL

DON'T GO THROUGH GAP AHEAD. INSTEAD, TURN RIGHT TO STILE

STILE TO THE RIGHT

CORNFIELD

OLD TIN BATH AT BOTTOM OF DESCENT

RUINED LOOK-OUT

BEACON HILL

IVY ISLAND

WADHAM BEACH

CARSWELL COVE

BUTCHER'S COVE

¼ mile

500m

APPROX SCALE

9

7

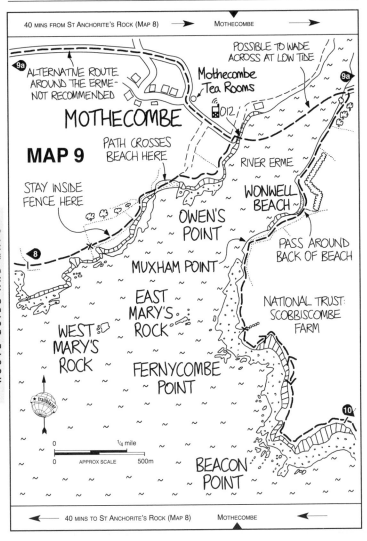

40 MINS FROM ST ANCHORITE'S ROCK (MAP 8) ⟶ MOTHECOMBE ⟶

POSSIBLE TO WADE ACROSS AT LOW TIDE

ALTERNATIVE ROUTE AROUND THE ERME - NOT RECOMMENDED

9a

Mothecombe Tea Rooms

☎ 012

MOTHECOMBE

9a

MAP 9

PATH CROSSES BEACH HERE

RIVER ERME

STAY INSIDE FENCE HERE

WONWELL BEACH

~ OWEN'S POINT ~

8

PASS AROUND BACK OF BEACH

MUXHAM POINT

~ EAST MARY'S ROCK ~

NATIONAL TRUST: SCOBBISCOMBE FARM

WEST MARY'S ROCK ~

FERNYCOMBE POINT

10

★ trailblazer

0   1/4 mile
0   APPROX SCALE   500m

BEACON POINT

(cont'd from p111) This really is a lovely stretch, fairly straightforward on gentle, grassy **Revelstoke Drive**, wooded in places, with delicious sea views every now and then on your right. Passing above the **St Peter the Poor Fisherman Church** – which dates back to the 12th century and is once again, following extensive

repairs in the 1970s, used for services twice a year – the path reaches the drive to **Stoke House** and, soon after, at **Beacon Hill** (note the ruined look-out by the path), becomes even more strenuous – though, if anything, more gorgeous too.

The main feature on this approach to the River Erme is undoubtedly **St Anchorite's Rock**, a huge tor gazing silently out over the sea. (An anchorite, by the way, is an old term for a hermit and it is probable that a hermitage was established near here at some point in the dim and distant past.)

Not long afterwards the mouth at **Mothecombe** is reached; head inland for *Mothecombe Tea Rooms* (Easter-Oct 11am-5pm) – though do bear in mind the time and tide – it would be a shame to miss your only chance of fording the Erme for the sake of a cuppa.

TACKLING THE ERME   [Map 9; Map 9a, p116]
Wading across
Assuming you are here an hour either side of low tide you can wade across the river; the best place is clearly signposted. The terrain underfoot is sandy and, on occasion, pebbly too – but it doesn't take more than a few minutes at most to cross.

By taxi
A taxi will cost £20-30. Since it's quite a way from any of the taxi offices to Mothecombe it is advisable to book a taxi in advance. Be aware that the taxi driver may not know where you are and also may not know the route.

Taxi firms worth trying include: Clarke Cars (☎ 07976-551532); Eco-Taxi (☎ 01548-856347 or 07811-385275); Ivy Cabs (☎ 01752-696969); John Edwards (☎ 07967-374502 or ☎ 01548-830859); Steve's Taxi (☎ 07811-150349); and Wembury Cars (☎ 01752-863710).

Walking around the Erme
This is the least pleasant of the riverside diversions in the book – so either of the above options is far more preferable.

The walk (**8¾ miles; 3 hrs 10 mins**) begins – and largely continues – along roads, both upriver and back down the other side again. Hopefully Maps 9 and 9a make the correct route clear. Don't be tempted by some attractive-looking footpaths leading off the roads in what seems to be the correct direction; trust us when we say that they don't lead to anywhere useful. It goes without saying that you need to be careful as most of these country lanes have no pavements. The OL20 Ordnance Survey map is useful to find your way, though it's not particularly difficult.

Follow the road west out of Mothecombe, turning right at Battisborough Cross, continue north for a couple of miles to **Holbeton** before following Vicarage Hill to the left of the Village Stores.

The even tinier village of **Ford** is your next destination, again signposted, north of which is **Hole Farm**. Continuing north, eventually you'll hit the Erme-Plym Trail which you should take right to join the A379. Thankfully, your stay on this road lasts for only a few hundred metres, where a road to the right is signed to Orcheton.

Follow this for another couple of miles down past **Orcheton Mill** and its nearby quay, then **Oldaport**, **Clyng Mill**, the **turn-off to Waster and**

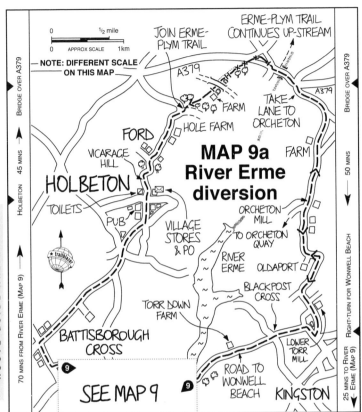

MAP 9a
River Erme
diversion

Shearlangstone, and so on to **Torr Rock** and **Lower Torr**. Finally a road to the right is signposted to **Wonwell Beach** (if you reach Kingston you've walked too far), your destination for this walk, and reachable after taking a left where the road forks past the row of pink cottages, passing Blackpost Cross and Torr Down Farm on your way down to the east bank of the Erme.

There's no let-up in the beauty of the walking after the Erme, though there are no major sites – just more miles of magnificence to meander through including **Muxham Point** and **Beacon Point**, both of which have wonderful panoramic views, and the cliffs of **Westcombe** and **Ayrmer Cove**.

Finally, you find yourself trudging, weary but happy, into **Challaborough** and its neighbour, **Bigbury-on-Sea**.

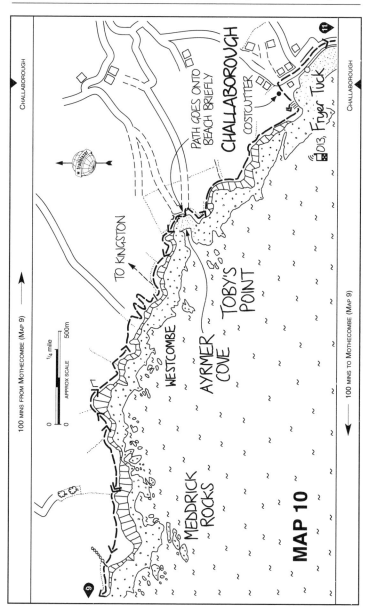

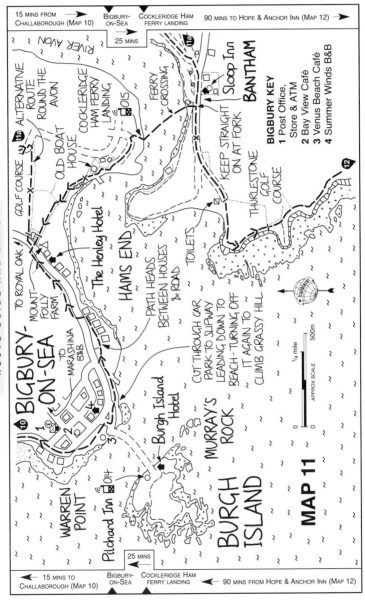

15 MINS FROM
CHALLABOROUGH (MAP 10)

BIGBURY-
ON-SEA

COCKLERIDGE HAM
FERRY LANDING

90 MINS TO HOPE & ANCHOR INN (MAP 12)

25 MINS

RIVER AVON

11a

SLOOP INN

BANTHAM

ALTERNATIVE
ROUTE
ROUND THE
AVON

COCKLERIDGE
HAM FERRY
LANDING

015

FERRY
CROSSING

KEEP STRAIGHT
ON AT FORK

BIGBURY KEY
1 Post Office,
  Store & ATM
2 Bay View Café
3 Venus Beach Café
4 Summer Winds B&B

11a

GOLF COURSE

OLD BOAT
HOUSE

THURLESTONE
GOLF
COURSE

12

The Henley Hotel

HAMS END

TO ROYAL OAK

MOUNT
FOLLY FARM

PATH HEADS
BETWEEN HOUSES
& ROAD

TOILETS

trailblazer

TO
MARASHINA B&B

CUT THROUGH CAR
PARK TO SLIPWAY
LEADING DOWN TO
BEACH – TURNING OFF
IT AGAIN TO
CLIMB GRASSY HILL

¼ mile

500m

APPROX SCALE

0

0

BIGBURY-
ON-SEA

10

1

2

3

Burgh Island
Hotel

MURRAY'S
ROCK

MAP 11

WARREN
POINT

Pitchard Inn 014

BURGH
ISLAND

15 MINS TO
CHALLABOROUGH (MAP 10)

BIGBURY-
ON-SEA

COCKLERIDGE HAM
FERRY LANDING

90 MINS FROM HOPE & ANCHOR INN (MAP 12)

25 MINS

CHALLABOROUGH & BIGBURY-ON-SEA [Map 10, p117 & Map 11]

These two conjoined settlements probably wouldn't linger in the memory for too long, were it not for the curious island that sits just offshore (see box below).

Challaborough, which is dominated by a couple of sprawling holiday parks, is home to *Fryer Tuck* (☎ 01548-810425; Easter/Apr to end Oct daily 10am-10pm), the local chippy. There is also a Costcutter **store** (Mon-Fri 8am-7pm, Sat & Sun to 6pm) here.

Facilities in **Bigbury** include a **post office** (Mon, Tue, Thur & Fri 9am-1pm) and **store** (Mon & Wed-Sat 9am-5.30pm, Tue 9am-1pm, Sun 9am-12.30pm) with free **ATM**. At **Mount Folly Farm** (☎ 01548-810267, ☐ bigburyholidays.co.uk), which is right on the coast path (it's where the path turns off down to the ferry crossing), you'll find a very basic **campsite** (£5pp; showers £1). They are also planning a **camping barn** in the village – given the paucity of accommodation in Bigbury, this could well be a hit; contact them for details.

B&Bs include *Summer Winds* (☎ 01548-810669, ☐ pritchard212@btinternet .com; 2D/1D, T or F; ☜; from £65pp, sgl occ £45) which is closest to both coast and coastal path; *Marashina* (off Map 11; ☎ 01548-810387, ☐ bigburyroom@btinternet .com; 1S shared facilities/1D or F en suite;

£25-30pp, sgl £30-40), at the top of Parker Rd; and smart Edwardian holiday cottage *The Henley Hotel* (☎ 01548-810240, ☐ www.thehenleyhotel.co.uk; 2D/3T; ☜; WI-FI; ♞ £5; from £60pp, sgl occ £85).

For **food**, *The Bay View Café* (☎ 01548-810796; Easter-Oct daily 10am-6pm, also a bistro on a Fri & Sat eve, one sitting between 7.30 & 8.30pm and must be booked in advance; opening days/hours for the rest of the year depend on the weather so ring to check) is a friendly relaxing place with good views out to sea. There is also a *Venus Beach Café* (☎ 01548-810141, ☐ www.lovingthebeach.co.uk; daily July-Aug 9am-6pm, rest of year 10am-5pm), down on the front facing the island, one of a chain of cafés that also includes establishments at Portlemouth and Blackpool Sands.

If the chippy in Challaborough doesn't appeal, your only other choice for food in the evenings is *The Royal Oak* (off Map 11; ☎ 01548-810313, ☐ www.theroyaloak bigbury.com; daily noon-2.30pm & 6-9pm but may be all day in the summer months), in Bigbury itself, about a mile uphill and inland. The menu changes daily but includes standard pub fare.

The only **bus service** is Tally Ho Coaches No 875, which travels between Bigbury and Plymouth via Yealmpton and Modbury on Friday only; see pp55-60.

❏ Burgh Island

Burgh Island is joined to the mainland at low tide by a lovely sand spit. However, if you wish to visit it when the tide's against you, you'll have to take the specially adapted sea tractor. There is good reason to visit, too, for not only does this small lump of grassy rock boast the remains of a chapel (possibly part of an ancient monastery) and an equally venerable pub but also, dominating the whole island, the exclusive and extortionate 1920s' Art Deco **Burgh Island Hotel** (☎ 01548-810514, ☐ www.burghisland.com; 10D/15 suites; ☜; WI-FI), which inspired the setting for Agatha Christie's *And Then There Were None*. Their more celebrated guests – Noel Coward, Josephine Baker, Amy Johnson and Gertie Lawrence – now each lend their names to one of the hotel's suites. With most rooms around the £500 mark, and none less than £400, it's out of reach for most trekkers – but that doesn't stop one from being able to admire it, if only from afar.

By the way, the *Pilchard Inn* on the island is actually rather disappointing when it comes to serving walkers; much of the bar is given over for the sole use of the island's hotel residents and the only food currently on offer are some overpriced baguettes at lunchtime. Such a shame.

BIGBURY-ON-SEA TO SALCOMBE [MAPS 11-16]

The coast path for this **13-mile (21km; 5hrs 5mins)** stage continues to be fairly remote and wild though there are, thankfully, more places on the way where you can get refreshments than on the previous stage.

The highlight – other than the scenery, of course, particularly during the latter half of the walk which is just unremittingly breathtaking – is the likeable village of **Hope** (or Outer Hope to give it its full title and to distinguish it from neighbouring Inner Hope, to the south). Overall, it's one of those stages where you should pray for fine weather; if your prayers are answered you can expect the memory card in your camera to be pretty full by the end of the day.

However, before you set off make sure you have checked the ferry times for this section of the path.

The route

As before, the day begins with a crossing of a river, in this case the **Avon** (no, not *that* one). Getting to the ferry launch is a little tricky: from the beach at Bigbury, the path meanders close to – or on – the road out of the village up to **Mount Folly Farm**, which it cuts through on its way, via a sheep field or two, down to the ferry at **Cockleridge Ham**.

TACKLING THE AVON [Map 11, p118; Map 11a]

Ferry

The short ferry trip (☎ 01548-561196) across the Avon from Cockleridge Ham in Bigbury to Bantham operates May to late September Monday to Saturday between 10 and 11am and 3 and 4pm only. The ferry runs by request and if the ferryman happens to be on the opposite bank to you, you have to signal to him by waving that you are waiting for a lift. If it's not running and you don't want to tackle the walk around the Avon, you can always call a **taxi** (Arrow Cabs ☎ 01548-856120; Eco-Taxi ☎ 01548-856347).

Avon Estuary Walk – walking around the Avon

This pleasant **8-mile (13km; 3hrs) diversion** is gentle on the eye without being stunning. The scenery is unsurprisingly verdant, there's a village at the halfway point where you can get a bite to eat, and it's very peaceful. Furthermore, though this trail has been officially designated as the Avon Estuary Walk, it's rare to find other people on the trail, giving you plenty of time to take in the lovely views and contemplate how much further along the coastal path you would be if only you had managed to catch the boat across the Avon.

The trail begins on the road just uphill from **Mount Folly Farm** where a path off right takes you into the fields and across a **golf course**. The climb up the western side of the Avon is a little meandering but never more than a field or two away from the river, the path picked out with the blue 'heron' waymarkers of the Avon Estuary Walk. Undulating at first, towards its northern end the path flattens to cross the mudflats and creeks on its way to the only settlement on the route.

Aveton Gifford is not the prettiest of places but there is a pub here, *The Fisherman's Rest* (☎ 01548-550284; food served daily mid July & Aug noon-9pm, rest of year Mon-Sat 11.30am-2pm & 7-9pm, Sun noon-2pm &

AVETON GIFFORD
TO SHOP, PO & CAFÉ
The Fisherman's Rest
CAR PARK

0   ½ mile
APPROX SCALE
0   1km
NOTE: DIFFERENT SCALE ON THIS MAP

AVETON GIFFORD

ROAD CROSSES CREEK

trailblazer

AVETON GIFFORD

HIGHER STADBURY

STIDDICOMBE CREEK

BEAR LEFT AT HIGHER STADBURY TO JOIN FOOTPATH

GOLF COURSE

STILE INTO WOODS

TAKE SMALLER PATH LEFT OFF TRACK

11

SEE MAP 11

GATE INTO VILLAGE **11**

MAP 11a River Avon diversion

3HRS FROM MOUNT FOLLY FARM (MAP 11)

3HRS TO MOUNT FOLLY FARM (MAP 11)

ROUTE GUIDE AND MAPS

7-8.30pm) and, approximately ten minutes along the road, a **shop** (Mon-Fri 8am-6pm, Sat 8.30am-3pm, Sun 8.30am-2.30pm) which also houses the **post office** (Mon, Tue, Thur & Fri 9am-6pm, Wed 9am-2.30pm, Sat 9am-3pm, Sun 9am-2.30pm) and a *café*. The café sells sandwiches and pasties and has limited indoor seating, however, its ambience is a pleasant alternative to the pub.

First's 93 **bus** (see pp55-60) passes though on its way to Dartmouth & Kingsbridge from Plymouth.

It's just outside the village that the path changes direction, crosses the Avon, and starts to head back south towards the coast again. A steep climb takes you away from the riverbank, before the path stumbles back down to cross **Stiddicombe Creek**. A lovely stretch follows through the woods and fields leading eventually to the village of **Bantham**, where you'll find accommodation at the 14th-century *Sloop Inn* (☎ 01548-560489, 🖥 www.thesloop .co.uk; 4D/1D or T/1F; 🛁; WI-FI; 🐾; £39.50-41.50pp, sgl occ £48; food served Mon-Sat noon-2pm, Sun noon-4pm, daily 6-9pm). A Sunday roast is served in the winter months for which booking is advised.

From the inn it's a few steps to the top of the road leading down to the ferry point – and a reunion with the coast path.

From the ferry point the path heads up to a car park, thereafter bending west then south and skirting the edge of **Thurlestone Golf Course**. The first eatery on this stage, the imaginatively monikered *Rocky's Chew, Lick & Suck Shop and Café* (Easter to late Oct 8.30am-8.30pm), has been in business for almost two decades and is almost as much of a local landmark as the holed **Thurlestone Rock** which stands, sea-battered but proud, nearby. From here, a relatively straightforward stroll on low cliffs brings you to **Outer Hope**.

OUTER & INNER HOPE
[Map 12 & Map 13, p124]

Given the remote location of these two con-joined villages, it won't surprise you to discover that Hope Cove was once a favourite haunt of smugglers. You perhaps also won't be too shocked to discover that the wild and rugged coast around here has also seen its fair share of shipwrecks; as a result, the village is something of a Mecca for divers.

The focus of interest on the cove for trekkers is Outer Hope. Facilities are minimal though there is a **post office** (Mon, Wed & Fri 9am-1pm) and **store** (daily 8am-6pm) as well as a **cash machine** (£1.50) in the Hope & Anchor pub.

For **accommodation**, *Cottage Hotel* (☎ 01548-561555, 🖳 www.hopecove.com; 34 flexible rooms; 🖵; WI-FI in public spaces; 🐾 £5.50; £38.50-80pp, sgl occ £38.50-100pp, B&B with dinner an additional £15; closed Jan to early Feb) is the main place in town, a smart old pile dating back to the 19th century, though the hotel only opened in the 1920s and its décor certainly harks back more to that era. They also run *Tanfield B&B* (book through Cottage Hotel; 2S/4D/2T; 🖵; 🐾 £5.50; £28-43pp, sgl occ £28-53; closed Jan to early Feb) a little way up the hill on the road leading out of town.

Below Cottage Hotel, *Hope & Anchor Inn* (☎ 01548-561294, 🖳 www.hopeand anchor.co.uk; 1T/7D/3F; 🖵; WI-FI; 🐾 £5 per dog; £40-50pp, £50-80 sgl occ) offers some of the best accommodation in the village though the prices reflect this. *Lantern Lodge Hotel* (☎ 01548-561280, 🖳 www .lantern-lodge.co.uk; 3T/10D/1F; 🖵; WI-FI; £40-60pp, sgl occ £60-90; mid Mar to mid Nov) is on the cliffs above town with some smart bedrooms – three with four-poster beds – that are designed to make the most of the far-reaching views (not all rooms have a view). DB&B rates are available. Evening meal served 7-8pm; booking required for non residents.

Sand Pebbles (☎ 01548-561673, 🖳 www.sandpebbles.co.uk; 8D/1T; 🖵; WI-FI; £30-55pp, sgl occ £60; Mar-Oct) is a large and recently refurbished place up above the beaches. They offer **food** in the new *Goody Rock Grill* (Tue-Sat 6-8.30pm) with a great selection of burgers including 'The Lamb One', a minted lamb burger topped with salad and mayo and fries (£10.95).

Nearer the beach, *Beachcomber Café* (☎ 01548-561974; Apr-Oct daily 10am-5pm, school summer hols 8.30am-6pm but may close early in bad weather) is the main daytime stop, offering coffees, snacks and burgers. Nearby, *Harbour Lights Restaurant* (☎ 01548-897579, 🖳 www .harbourlightshopecove.com; Apr-Oct Tue-Sun 12.30-3.30pm & Tue-Sat 7-9pm), where a rack of South Devon lamb is £16.95, is quieter. They also, unusually, offer a takeaway menu during the day; an evening takeaway must be booked the day before.

Finally, *Hope & Anchor* (see opposite; food served daily noon-2.30pm & 6-9.30pm) offers a large and imaginative menu with plenty of locally caught fish on the menu such as fillet of sea bass on crab and avocado mash (£13.50). It's the busiest in town and, although huge, arrive after 8pm and you may not get a place.

Tally Ho's 162 **bus service** travels between Outer Hope and Kingsbridge, where you can connect with other services. See pp55-60.

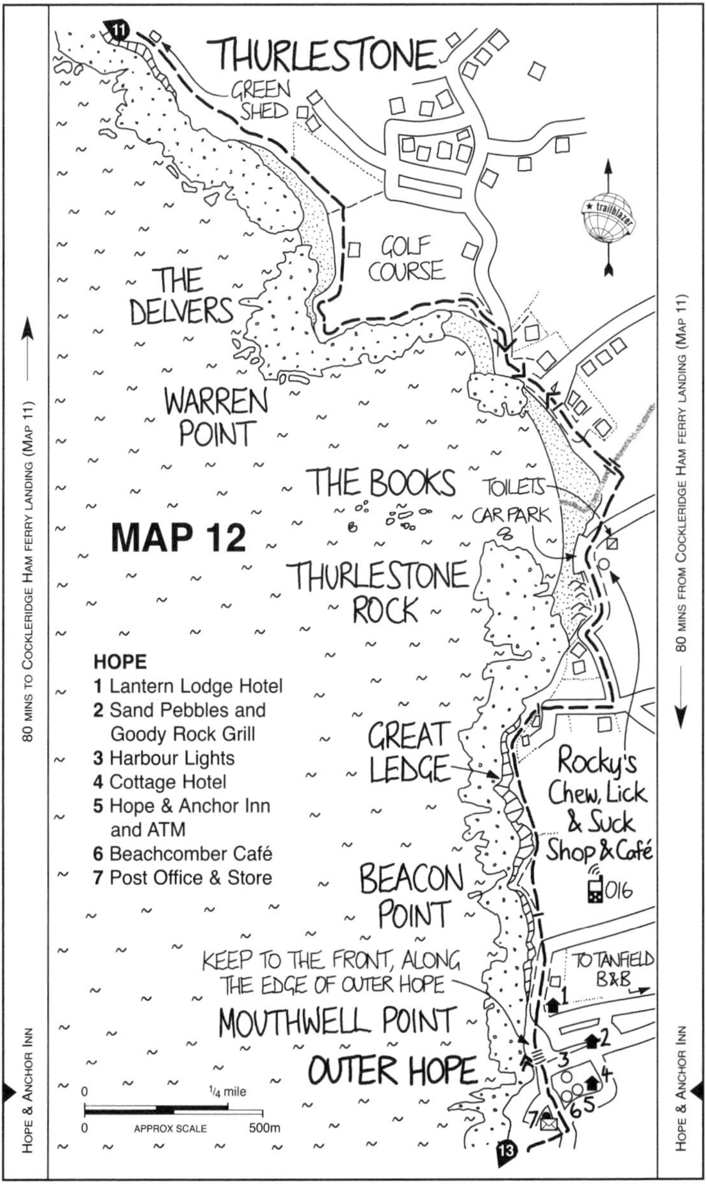
THURLESTONE
GREEN SHED
GOLF COURSE
THE DELVERS
WARREN POINT
THE BOOKS
TOILETS
CAR PARK
MAP 12
THURLESTONE ROCK
HOPE
1 Lantern Lodge Hotel
2 Sand Pebbles and Goody Rock Grill
3 Harbour Lights
4 Cottage Hotel
5 Hope & Anchor Inn and ATM
6 Beachcomber Café
7 Post Office & Store
GREAT LEDGE
Rocky's Chew, Lick & Suck Shop & Café
016
BEACON POINT
KEEP TO THE FRONT, ALONG THE EDGE OF OUTER HOPE
TO TANFIELD B&B
MOUTHWELL POINT
OUTER HOPE
0
1/4 mile
0
APPROX SCALE
500m
11
13
trailblazer
80 MINS TO COCKLERIDGE HAM FERRY LANDING (MAP 11)
80 MINS FROM COCKLERIDGE HAM FERRY LANDING (MAP 11)
HOPE & ANCHOR INN
HOPE & ANCHOR INN

From Outer Hope the path meanders past seafront residences to its Siamese twin, **Inner Hope**, from where a wooded path once again leads you away from civilisation. This stretch from Inner Hope to Salcombe is book-ended by two

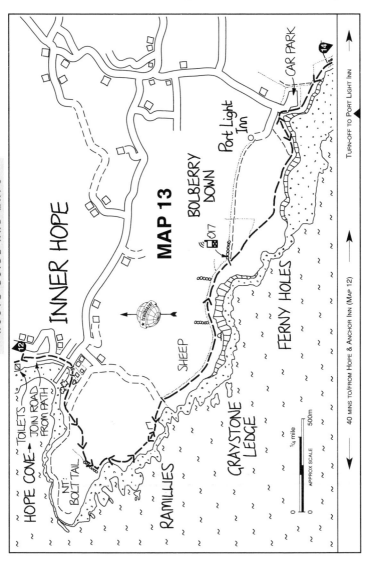

MAP 13

INNER HOPE

BOLBERRY DOWN

CAR PARK

Port Light Inn

FERNY HOLES

CRAYSTONE LEDGE

RAMILLIES

SHEEP

HOPE COVE — TOILETS
JOIN ROAD FROM PATH

NT: BOLT TAIL

TURN-OFF TO PORT LIGHT INN

40 MINS TO/FROM HOPE & ANCHOR INN (MAP 12)

APPROX SCALE
¼ mile
500m

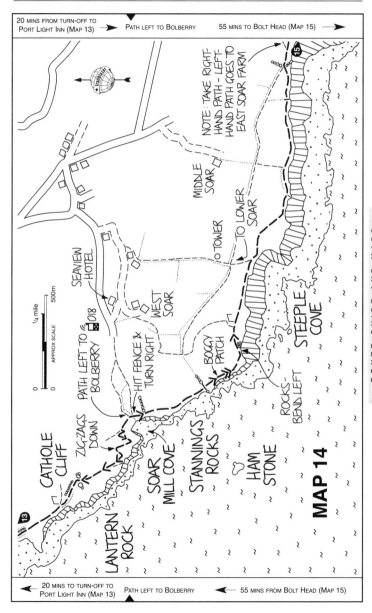

NOTE : TAKE RIGHT-HAND PATH – LEFT-HAND PATH GOES TO EAST SOAR FARM

15

MIDDLE SOAR

TO LOWER SOAR

o TOWER

WEST SOAR

SEAVIEW HOTEL

¼ mile

APPROX SCALE

500m

0

PATH LEFT TO BOLBERRY

018

HIT FENCE & TURN RIGHT

BOGGY PATCH

STEEPLE COVE

ROCKS- BEAR LEFT

ZIG-ZAGS DOWN

CATHOLE CLIFF

SOAR MILL COVE

STANNINGS ROCKS

HAM STONE

MAP 14

13

LANTERN ROCK

ROUTE GUIDE AND MAPS

promontories, **Bolt Tail** (Map 13) and **Bolt Head** (Map 15). Bolt Tail comes first, a lovely westerly-facing headland which the path contours round before describing a hairpin bend south-east through fields to **Bolberry Down**; the whole stretch, by the way, is owned by National Trust. Despite the car park here the path feels quite remote; though if you missed your chance for refreshments at Hope, there are a couple of picturesque alternatives near the path.

Port Light Inn (Map 13; ☎ 01548-561384, 🖳 www.portlight.co.uk; 3T/4D or T; ✆; 🐾; £38-57pp for B&B, £58-77pp for DB&B; sgl occ £76-102 B&B, £96-122 DB&B only; food served mid Feb to mid Nov noon-2pm & 7-8pm; school summer holidays 6.30-9pm) has accommodation but is probably of more use to trekkers as a place for lunch (sandwiches start at £4.95, rising to £7.25 for the Salcombe crab).

Further on (and about 1km off the trail), *East Soar Farm* (Map 15; ☎ 01548-561904, 🖳 www.eastsoaroutdoorexperience.co.uk; 🐾 £25 per stay) is an upmarket and innovative **camping service** where they supply a pre-pitched bell tent (there are six) with outdoor furniture, lanterns, and sleeping mats – and even bedding and half-board, if required, and all for £30pp (£25pp for breakfast only). They also offer indoor camping in the autumn/winter months. In addition, they have a **bunkhouse** (also £30pp) which sleeps up to eight people. Booking is essential for all accommodation and food cannot be prepared on site. They have also established a **Walker's Hut** (open to anyone; summer daily 10am-6pm, winter weekends only and depending on the weather) from where they offer hot drinks, snacks and shelter.

The approach to Bolt Head is marked by increasingly severe gradients, ensuring that by the time you reach civilisation again, at the twin millionaire hamlets of **South Sands** (home to YHA Salcombe; see p128) and **North Sands** you'll be ready for a drink again.

The very busy *Winking Prawn* (Map 15; ☎ 01548-842326, 🖳 www.winkingprawn.co.uk; in the summer they are usually open daily 9am-9pm and in the winter Mon-Fri 10am-4pm, Sat & Sun 9am-9pm) can help you in terms of a drink and the food is good if a little expensive, with sandwiches and baguettes £6-7. Most people, however, will probably want to continue to Salcombe, where further options await...

SALCOMBE [map p129]

Sophisticated, seafaring Salcombe sits at the mouth of Kingsbridge Estuary, its condos, penthouses, hotels and holiday homes stretching up the steep surrounding hills. Its written history harks back only as far as 1244, making it a positive youngster compared to some of the settlements around here and, in this respect, it very much sits in the shadow of neighbouring Dartmouth, whose past is indubitably both longer and richer. For Salcombe followed the well-trodden path of many villages around here,

eking out a living from the industries of fishing, smuggling and piracy. However, in 1764, the first holiday home, 'The Moult', was built by a Mr John Hawkins between Salcombe and North Sands (and still stands there); and Salcombe has been thriving on holidaymakers pretty much ever since.

A second income stream, from ship-building, started up at the same time and ensured the town's prosperity for much of the next century. In particular, Salcombe specialised in the building of fruit

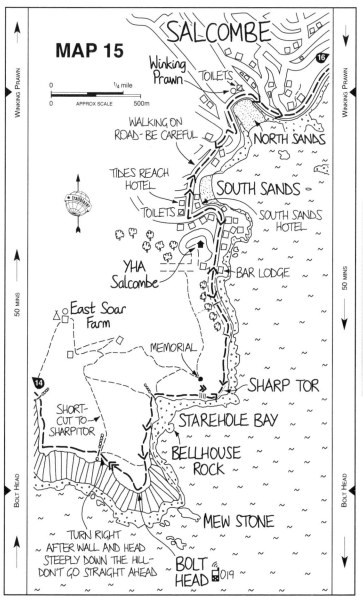

MAP 15

SALCOMBE

Winking Prawn

TOILETS

16

0   1/4 mile

0   APPROX SCALE   500m

WALKING ON
ROAD - BE CAREFUL

NORTH SANDS

TIDES REACH
HOTEL

SOUTH SANDS

TOILETS

SOUTH SANDS
HOTEL

★ trailblazer

YHA
Salcombe

BAR LODGE

East Soar
Farm

MEMORIAL

14

SHORT-
CUT TO
SHARPITOR

SHARP TOR

STAREHOLE BAY

BELLHOUSE
ROCK

MEW STONE

TURN RIGHT
AFTER WALL AND HEAD
STEEPLY DOWN THE HILL-
DON'T GO STRAIGHT AHEAD

BOLT
HEAD   019

WINKING PRAWN

50 MINS

BOLT HEAD

WINKING PRAWN

50 MINS

BOLT HEAD

ROUTE GUIDE AND MAPS

schooners – light and rapid craft required by traders to hurry their cargo of perishable fruit back from Spain and the Azores before it spoilt. The invention of ships made of iron and steel spelt the end of the industry in Salcombe and while its reputation as a seafaring centre remains to this day, these days the sailors tend to be the retired and wealthy rather than the ambitious and intrepid.

There's a lot to like about the town, not least **Salcombe Maritime Museum** (🖳 www.salcombemuseum.org.uk; Apr-Oct daily 10.30am-12.30pm & 2.30-4.30pm; £1.50) below the tourist office, which has a number of displays recounting the town's history; the friendly staff are also a good source of local knowledge. For coastal trekkers it also signals the end of the trail from Plymouth – one of the remotest stretches of the entire coast path. But while there's no doubting that swanky Salcombe's a very becoming place, for sweaty, scruffy and slightly grubby trekkers who drag themselves into the town after another hot day's hiking, such smartness can make one feel a little out of place.

Services
The **tourist information centre** (🕿 01548-843927, 🖳 www.salcombeinformation.co .uk; Easter to late July and Sep-Oct daily 10am-5pm, late July to Aug Mon-Sat 9am-6pm & Sun 10am-5pm, Nov to Easter Mon-Sat 10am-3pm) is at the Market St end of Fore St.

For **internet** try the café at Bluewater Marine on Island St or the library (🕿 01548-843423; Wed & Sat 10am-noon, Thur 3-5pm; ½hr free) at Cliff House, Cliff Rd. Adapting to the closure of so many, the **post office** (Mon-Fri 9am-5.30pm, Sat 9am-12.30pm) is now housed in Shipwrights of Salcombe, a lace shop. There are also some **banks** around the town. For a **pharmacy** there's a Boots (Mon-Fri 9am-6pm, Sat 9am-5pm) on Fore St, while for general **provisions** try Spar (Mon-Sat 7am-10pm, Sun 8am-10pm) on Loring Rd.

A decent **bookshop**, Salter's Bookshelf (Thur-Tue 10am-5pm, Wed

10am-1pm), is tucked away off Fore St on Russell Court.

Where to stay
Salcombe is one of the few places on this section of the coast path that has a YHA hostel. **YHA Salcombe** (Map 15; 🕿 0845-371 9341, 🖳 www.yha.org.uk/hostel/sal combe; 52 beds; dorm beds from £15, twin room (bunk beds) from £35.50, also some 4-bedded bunk rooms) – although the hostel's location is actually south of South Sands up a steep hill. It is also one of the few options around here that takes one-night bookings. The hostel shares the house and beautiful grounds and views with the National Trust. The building has an interesting past, having once been owned by the inventor Otto Christoph Joseph Gerhardt Ludwig Overbeck (1852-1937), who made his fortune with his 'Rejuvenator' – a device that supposedly promoted health and well-being via the administration of low-voltage electrical currents. You may feel like you need a go on one yourself once you crawl into the hostel – though you'll have to make do with a cup of tea from the on-site café instead. To reach the hostel, before the descent to South Sands take the track off to the left, following signs for 'Overbecks' or 'YHA'.

Finding a **B&B** in Salcombe that both allows walkers to stay and also allows them to stay for only one night, is not as easy as you may initially have hoped. Those that do also tend to be quite a way from the town centre up some of the steep slopes. One notable exception is *Victoria Inn* (🕿 01548-842604, 🖳 www.victoriainn-salcom be.co.uk; 1D/1T; WI-FI; room only £25-35pp, sgl occ negotiable), on Fore St, where two rooms have been built in the grounds of the pub and together have been christened 'The Hobbit House.' Watch your head as you enter through the particularly low front door and note that the tariff does not include breakfast.

Ria View (🕿 0776-766 5321, 🖳 www .salcombebandb.co.uk; 3D; WI-FI; £35-44pp; sgl occ £70-88; Easter to end Oct) on Devon Rd is another that is, by Salcombe standards, close to the water and comes

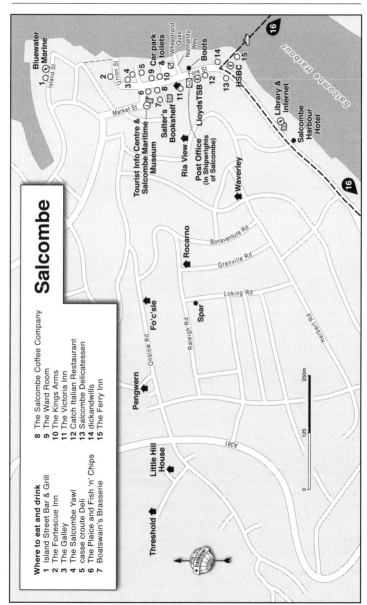

☐ **Where to stay: the details**

Unless specified, B&B-style accommodation is either en suite or has private facilities; ➥ means at least one room has a bath; 🐾 signifies that dogs are welcome in at least one room but always by prior arrangement, an additional charge may also be payable; WI-FI means wi-fi is available in the property, though not always (reliably) in every room.

---

highly recommended; however, they're another place for whom the minimum booking is two nights. Most of their rooms have harbour views.

Rocarno (☎ 01548-842732, 🖥 www.rocarno.co.uk; 1T/1D; WI-FI; £33pp, sgl occ from £50) isn't anything out of the ordinary but they are more central than some.

On the very edge of town, *Threshold B&B* (☎ 01548-842877, 🖥 www.threshold-online.co.uk; 2D/1T; ➥; WI-FI; £30-42.50pp; sgl occ £45; Apr-Oct) is right at the top of the hill, a good 10- to 15-minute walk from the centre on Longfield Drive. One of the doubles has a waterbed.

Also at this far-flung outpost of Salcombe, and with a two-night stay policy, is *Little Hill House* (☎ 01548-842530, 🖥 little.hill@virgin.net; 2D; shared facilities if both rooms booked; ➥; WI-FI; £32.50-35pp, sgl occ negotiable), on the road of the same name, which comes highly recommended by one trekker.

Another option to try is *Waverley* (☎ 01548-842633, 🖥 www.waverleybandb.co .uk; 2D/4D, T or F; WI-FI; 🐾; £32-38pp, sgl occ £50; Apr-Oct), one of the few that allows dogs to stay.

Finally, sharing a similar location on – or just off – Onslow Rd, and even the same website (🖥 www.bedandbreakfastsalcombe.co.uk), are two suburban houses offering both self-catering and B&B, namely *Fo'c'sle* (☎ 01548-843243; 2D or T/1D or F; ➥; 🐾; £35pp, sgl occ £45) and *Pengwern* (☎ 01548-844148; 2D or T; 🐾; £35pp, sgl occ £45).

Where to eat and drink

Salcombe has endless eateries. If a quick sandwich and a sit down on a bench is what

you're after *Salcombe Delicatessen* (☎ 01548-842332, 🖥 www.salcombedeli.co .uk; Feb-Oct daily 9am-5pm, possibly longer in the summer months), 52 Fore St, supplies gourmet sandwiches such as a baguette filled with handpicked Salcombe crab (£5.95).

Nearby, at 10a Fore St, you'll find *The Salcombe Yawl* (☎ 01548-842143, 🖥 www .salcombeyawl.co.uk; daily 8am-5pm, closed in Jan), with their Parma ham, breast of chicken and avocado sandwiches (£4.50), whilst practically opposite is the lower case *casse croute* (8am-5pm, limited hours in winter), who as well as serving typical deli produce also bake pizzas until 10pm during the school summer holidays.

Café lunches are available at *The Salcombe Coffee Company* (☎ 01548-842319; summer 9am-9.30pm, winter 9am-5pm; WI-FI), Fore St. They do a great bacon bap (£3.95) as well as crab sandwiches (£7.50). In summer, they also serve supper from 6pm: their jailhouse chilli served with rice, tortilla wraps and sour cream dip (£13.95) may seem too good to turn down.

At 19 Fore St, through Crew Clothing shop, is *The Ward Room* (☎ 01548-843333; Mon-Sat 9am-5pm, Sun 9am-4.30pm) where views over the harbour, drinks, cakes and cream teas are all on offer. *The Plaice* (☎ 01548-843693; Sun-Wed 11am-5pm, Thur-Sat 11am-8pm, hours may differ depending on demand), Fore St, has reasonably priced lunches, with main meals including pizzas (£5-8) costing an average price of £7. There is also an adjoining **chippy** (Mon-Sat noon-9pm, Sun noon-6pm).

For a pub lunch next to the ferry passenger terminal (and thus the path) *The Ferry Inn* (☎ 01548-844000; food daily noon-3pm & 6-9pm, Sun noon-9pm) is on Fore St; it's not cheap, though, with a crab sandwich costing £8.50. Other pubs include *Victoria Inn* (see Where to stay; food served daily noon-2.30pm & 6-9pm although snacks/cream teas are available between these hours; 🐾) welcomes dogs and has a great beer garden. Food offered includes rich vegetable goulash (£10.95) and half a pot-roasted pheasant (£12.95). A little further along Fore St, *The King's Arms* (☎ 01548-842202; food noon-2.30pm & 6.30-9.30pm) also offers sustenance, including pan-fried scallops (£14.50).

Live music and good food can be enjoyed at *The Fortescue Inn* (☎ 01548-842868, 🖳 www.thefortsalcombe.com; food noon-2.30pm & 7-9.30pm), Union St. Tap your feet along to the entertainment whilst gobbling down an 'Aune Valley' rump steak (£13.50) or a sea bream (£13.95).

Hidden away from the centre – and a great venue for watching sport – *Island Street Bar & Grill* (☎ 01548-844007, 🖳 www.islandstreet.co.uk; summer daily 9.30am to midnight, winter Sun-Thur 10am-11pm, Fri & Sat to midnight; food daily all year 10am-9pm) overlooks the estuary at Hannafords Landing. It's a decent and friendly sports bar which you could imagine becoming quite raucous in the evenings; food choices include a smoked duck salad (£6.50) and salmon burger (£9.50).

Restaurant-wise, Salcombe does not disappoint. At either end of Fore St are: *The Galley* (☎ 01548-842828, 🖳 www.thegal leyrestaurant.co.uk; generally Mar-Dec Mon-Sat from 7pm but may be shorter hours in the winter months, daily from 6pm in the school summer holidays) at No 5, whose dining room boasts great harbour views and where two courses cost £16.95 and three £20.95; and *dickandwills* (☎ 01548-843408, 🖳 www.dickandwills .co.uk; food noon-1.45pm & from 6pm), where you can have your fillets of local fish vodka battered (£15.95). They also serve coffee and snacks from 11am.

Finally on Fore St, seafood linguine (£14.95) is available at *Catch Italian Restaurant* (☎ 01548-842646; from 6.30pm) at No 55. Just off Fore St, if only just, *Boatswain's Brasserie* (☎ 01548-842189; summer daily 6.30-10pm, call to check their days/hours in winter), on Russell Court, is a fine and relaxed establishment where you can expect excellent service. Try their rack of ribs (£15.95).

Transport

[See also pp55-60] The town is connected to Kingsbridge via Tally Ho Coaches' regular 606 **bus** service and on a Sunday via Stagecoach's X64 .

For a **taxi**, try Salcombe and District Taxi Company (☎ 0771-451 2516, 🖳 www .salcombeanddistricttaxico.co.uk), or Clark Cars (☎ 01548-842914).

SALCOMBE TO SLAPTON CROSS   [MAPS 16-22]

Another stage, another lovely walk, on this occasion consisting of **14¼ reasonably untaxing miles (23km; 4hrs 35mins)**, a few of which are actually iron flat – though there are just enough sharp ascents, too, to keep you honest.

This stage also boasts several places to stop and get some refreshments on the way and some great places to bed down for the night should you come to the justifiable conclusion that the scenery along this stretch is just too good to be hurrying through. These settlements include the camping Mecca of East Prawle and the one-street seafront villages of Beesands and Torcross. These places are undoubtedly charming in their own way; but it's the countryside around here that truly makes the heart soar and stays in the memory long after you've finished this walk.

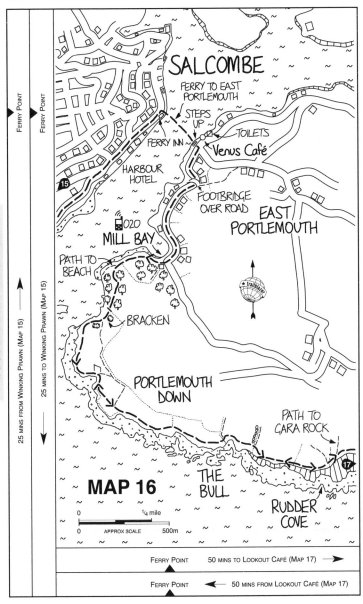

SALCOMBE

FERRY TO EAST
PORTLEMOUTH

STEPS
UP

TOILETS

Venus Café

FERRY INN

HARBOUR
HOTEL

FOOTBRIDGE
OVER ROAD

EAST
PORTLEMOUTH

15

020

MILL BAY

PATH TO
BEACH

★ trailblazer

BRACKEN

PORTLEMOUTH
DOWN

PATH TO
GARA ROCK

17

MAP 16

THE
BULL

RUDDER
COVE

0   ¼ mile

0   APPROX SCALE   500m

FERRY POINT   25 MINS FROM WINKING PRAWN (MAP 15)
FERRY POINT   25 MINS TO WINKING PRAWN (MAP 15)

FERRY POINT   50 MINS TO LOOKOUT CAFÉ (MAP 17) →

FERRY POINT   ← 50 MINS FROM LOOKOUT CAFÉ (MAP 17)

The route

As has become traditional on this trek, before you even begin walking you have to cross a stretch of water, in this case by catching the boat to **East Portlemouth**. The **ferry** (Easter-Oct Mon-Fri 8am-6pm, Sat, Sun & Bank Hols from 8.30am; approx 6/hr but depends on demand; £1.50; dogs free) leaves, appropriately, from behind Salcombe's Ferry Inn, taking just a couple of minutes to reach the other side. Between November and Easter you will have to catch the ferry from Whitestrand; call ☎ 01548-842061 for details.

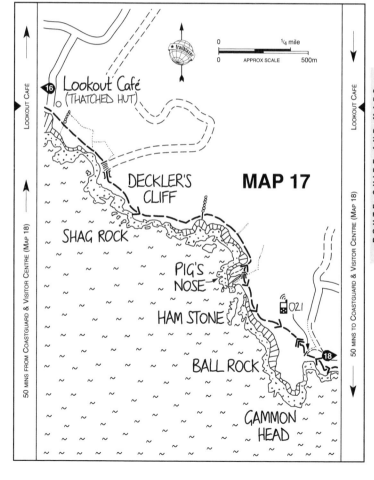

Back on *terra firma*, turn left and you'll come to **The Venus Café** (☎ 01548-843558, 🖳 www.lovingthebeach.co.uk; Apr-Oct daily 10am-5pm, July & Aug 10am-6pm), another in the chain of waterside cafés (you'll already have encountered one at Bigbury) where hot and cold drinks are available as well as sandwiches (£3-5); turn right, however, and you'll pick up the trail along the tree-shaded tarmac leading to **Mill Bay**.

The woods mark the start of a relatively easy, largely flat, very pleasant and pretty spectacular south-easterly amble. The path takes on a decidedly porcine theme, passing **Pig's Nose** and **Ham Stone** before reaching (after one of the larger climbs of the day) **Gammon Head**. On the way you'll pass, on the left, a conical thatched building – the edge of the Gara Rock complex where their *Lookout Café* (Easter to Sep daily 9am-5pm) serves lovely cakes baked on the premises (from £2).

More largely flat walking follows before a steady ascent leads to the Coastguard Hut at **Prawle Point**, complete with its own small **Visitor Centre**. Descending from here, there is now a very flat section that hugs the coast, contouring round fields, passing the turn-off to **East Prawle**.

EAST PRAWLE   [Map 18]

It's a steep climb up from the path to Devon's southernmost village – but for campers and those who take delight in ancient, isolated and offbeat pubs, the exertions are worth it. The centre of the village is the great **The Pigs Nose Inn** (☎ 01548-511209, 🖳 www.pigsnose.co.uk; daily noon-2pm, summer daily 6.30-9pm, winter Tue-Sat 7-9pm; 🐾), voted the best pub in Devon by CAMRA in 2011. Overlooking the green, the pub is over 500 years old and used to be a haunt of smugglers who would store their booty here. Complete with board games, live music, a pool room, a knitting corner and piggy paraphernalia galore, it's the kind of quirky place you'll be telling your friends about long after you've returned home. The menu offers pretty standard/basic pub grub (though they also have a separate menu for dogs!). Nearby is *Piglet Stores & Café* (daily 9am-4pm).

East Prawle is a Mecca for **campers**, at least during high summer. *Mollie Tucker*

(☎ 01548-511422, 🖳 www.eastprawlefarm holidays.co.uk; £5 for a tent and two people; 🐾 if tethered) gives one to two fields, 'Stephen's Field' and 'Little Hollaway', over to campers in July and August, but sometimes also in June. Stephen's Field is closer to the village, but Little Hollaway is probably of more interest to trekkers, with great views over Prawle Point and a location nearer to the coast path. Simply pitch your tent in either field and Mrs Tucker will come round in the morning to collect money. However, ringing in advance to check at least one field is open is recommended. There are no showers on either site but you can shower in the pub (£2).

For a **B&B**, *Welle House* (☎ 01548-511151, 🖳 www.wellehouse.co.uk; 1D/1D or T/1T/1D or F; ✒; WI-FI; 🐾; £30-33pp, sgl occ £50-55) is friendly and unfussy. Note, however, they don't take one-night bookings at weekends in high season unless there is some last-minute availability.

Those sticking to the path will continue past Maelcombe House before emerging at *Lannacombe Farm B&B* (☎ 01548-511158; 1T/1D, shared bathroom; ✒; 🐾; £30-35pp; Feb-Oct) and its lovely beach. They also have a **campsite** (£10 per pitch) but no toilet or shower facilities. Booking is essential in the summer months.

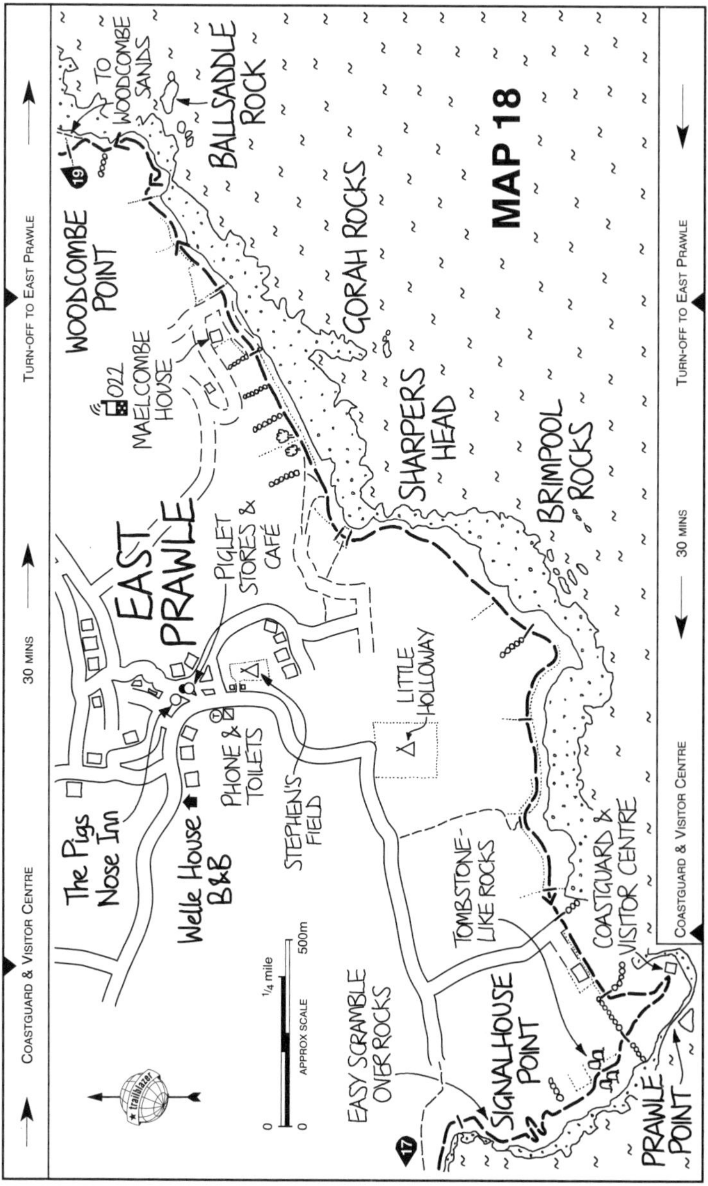

MAP 18

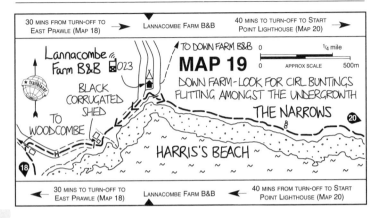

A steady ascent through the nature trail of 600-year-old ***Down Farm*** (☎ 01548-511234, 🖥 www.downfarm.co.uk; 1D/1D or T/1F; ☛; WI-FI; £35pp, sgl occ £45) follows, the trail passing through an area specifically preserved for the benefit of the declining population of **cirl buntings** (see p86).

The path climbs steadily now towards the lighthouse at **Start Point**, though walkers will probably be more interested in photographing the signpost at the top that states that there are 168 miles left to Poole (or, for those aiming to complete the whole trail and are heading in the other direction, the signpost also says there are 462 miles to Minehead in Somerset).

The path now heads towards and through a car park on its way to **Hallsands**; it's worth pausing here awhile to look over the devastated and abandoned village of Old Hallsands (see box p138), standing hard against the cliffs below.

It's a relatively easy stroll from here to Beesands – and its pub.

BEESANDS   [Map 21, p139]

Derived from 'Bay Sands', Beesands is a typically tiny Devonian settlement, consisting of around 50 houses, 100 people, a church, snack shack and a good pub.

The Cricket Inn (☎ 01548-580215, 🖥 www.thecricketinn.com; 2S/5D/1F; WI-FI; £45-55pp, sgl occ £80-100) is the social centre of the village, a fine place that dates back to the 19th century but is thoroughly up to date, with modern rooms named after English cricket grounds or famous English cricketers; they don't, however, take one-night bookings at weekends. The award-winning **food** (daily noon-2.30pm &

6-8.30pm; summer school holidays also 3-5pm) is reportedly great, with the focus firmly on fresh and local seafood; try a seafood pancake (£11).

Just a little way along the seafront is ***Britannia Shellfish Café*** (☎ 01548-581168; Mar-Oct daily 8.30am-9pm, Nov-Feb Thur-Sun approx 10am-4pm), a shop-cum-café-cum-fresh-shellfish-specialist. A seafood platter here will set you back £10.95 but if it's just a quick sugar hit you're after try their cream tea (£3.60). The **shop** sells essentials including batteries, toiletries and fruit.

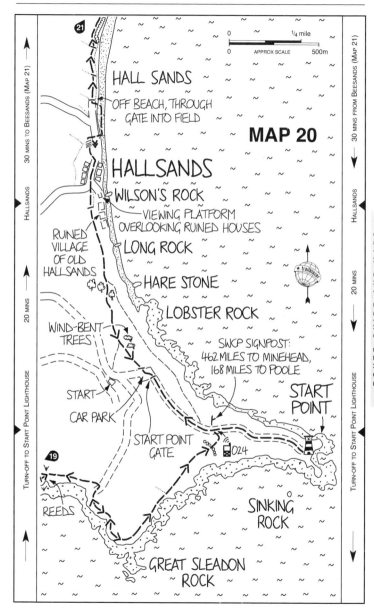

21

0 ¼ mile
0 APPROX SCALE 500m

HALL SANDS

OFF BEACH, THROUGH GATE INTO FIELD

MAP 20

HALLSANDS

WILSON'S ROCK

VIEWING PLATFORM OVERLOOKING RUINED HOUSES

RUINED VILLAGE OF OLD HALLSANDS

LONG ROCK

HARE STONE

★ trailblazer

LOBSTER ROCK

WIND-BENT TREES

SWCP SIGNPOST: 462 MILES TO MINEHEAD, 168 MILES TO POOLE

START

CAR PARK

START POINT

START POINT GATE

024

19

SINKING ROCK

REEDS

GREAT SLEADON ROCK

30 MINS TO BEESANDS (MAP 21)

HALLSANDS

20 MINS

TURN-OFF TO START POINT LIGHTHOUSE

30 MINS FROM BEESANDS (MAP 21)

HALLSANDS

20 MINS

TURN-OFF TO START POINT LIGHTHOUSE

❏ The Destruction of Old Hallsands

Set precariously between sea and cliff, the existence of Hallsands (or Old Hallsands as we must call now it to distinguish it from the clifftop village that still stands) was always a perilous one. Its eventual demise, however, became the subject of controversy and legal disputes that rumble on even to this day.

Originally founded sometime in the 18th century, by the time of its destruction there were 37 houses in Old Hallsands and, according to the 1891 census, 159 inhabitants living in them, most of whom made their living by fishing. The pebble beach was all that separated the village from the often tempestuous tides that pounded the shoreline of southern Devon.

That beach, however, was largely removed in the 1890s by Sir John Jackson Ltd, a huge engineering firm that had recently received permission to dredge for shingle along the shoreline between Hallsands and Beesands. The locals were very unhappy with the granting of this licence, complaining that the dredging would cause damage to their crab pots, disturb the fish and might also cause damage to their houses.

Little did they know the full extent of that damage. To ameliorate their tempers, Sir John Jackson Ltd agreed to pay the villagers £125 for every year the dredging continued. It wasn't until 1900, however, that it dawned on everyone how slight this reward was. By then, the sea wall had washed away and the locals were complaining to their MP about the damage being caused. By this time the beach had also fallen by an estimated 7-12ft because of the dredging work, and a report concluded that '*in the event of a heavy gale from the East...few houses will not be flooded, if not seriously damaged*'. The work was only stopped in 1902, however, when the villagers decided upon direct action and prevented the dredgers from landing.

Unfortunately, by then, the damage had been done and in 1903 the engineers were forced to compensate the owners of six houses that had been lost to the sea, since the newly lowered beach was no longer an effective barrier against time and tide. Further huge storms in 1917 washed the village away, leaving only one building standing. Miraculously, however, no-one in the village was killed during these storms – though the village itself never recovered.

A reasonably sharp up-and-downer brings you to the next settlement on the route, **Torcross**, with even more places at which to eat.

TORCROSS   [Map 21]

Like a movie set, Torcross consists of a busy bustling promenade lining the sea wall – and very little behind. Back from the seafront there is a **post office** (Mon-Tue & Thur-Fri 9am-4pm, Sat 9am-1pm) in Start Bay **Stores** (Mon-Sat 7am-5pm, Sun 7.30am-5pm), a **bus stop** and, incongruously, a WWII tank (see box p142) – but it's on the promenade that the action happens.

Here you'll find several places to eat including *Start Bay Inn* (☎ 01548-580553, 🖳 www.startbayinn.co.uk; food daily summer school holidays 11.30am-10pm, rest of

year 11.30am-2.15pm & 6-9.30pm) where you can scoff on Dartmouth smokehouse smoked mackerel with horseradish (£5.70) or a pint of prawns (£7.15); *Boat House* (☎ 01548-580747; daily noon-9pm, later in school summer holidays), a family-friendly place with spice-the-main-brace pizza (pepperoni and chorizo) for £9.30; and a regular family-run café, *Seabreeze* (☎ 01548-580697, 🖳 www.seabreezebreaks .com; school summer holidays daily 9.30am-5pm, rest of year Thur-Sun 9.30am-4.30; weekends only Dec/Jan). The

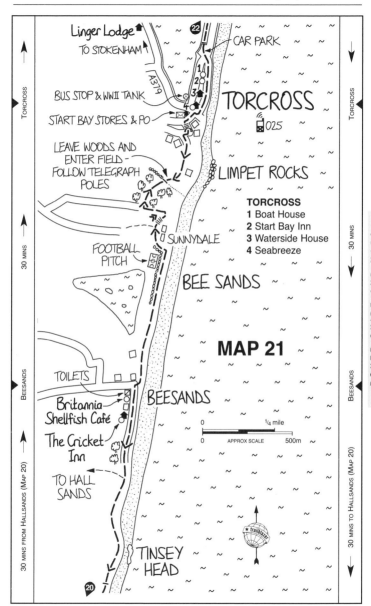

Linger Lodge
TO STOKENHAM
CAR PARK
A379
BUS STOP & WWII TANK
START BAY STORES & PO
TORCROSS
025
LEAVE WOODS AND
ENTER FIELD –
FOLLOW TELEGRAPH
POLES
LIMPET ROCKS

TORCROSS
1 Boat House
2 Start Bay Inn
3 Waterside House
4 Seabreeze

SUNNYDALE
FOOTBALL
PITCH
BEE SANDS
MAP 21
TOILETS
BEESANDS
Britania
Shellfish Café
0   1/4 mile
0   APPROX SCALE   500m
The Cricket
Inn
TO HALL
SANDS
trailblazer
TINSEY
HEAD

30 MINS FROM HALLSANDS (MAP 20)
30 MINS to HALLSANDS (MAP 20)

TORCROSS
30 MINS
BEESANDS

TORCROSS
30 MINS
BEESANDS

ROUTE GUIDE AND MAPS

last also offers **accommodation** (1T/1D; ❤; WI-FI; Apr-Sep £62.50-70pp, Oct-Mar £50-60pp, sgl occ negotiable) though not usually just for one night – but it's always worth calling in to see.

Other options away from the front include *Linger Lodge* (☎ 01548-580599, 🖥 www.lingerlodge.co.uk; 3D; ❤; £44pp, sgl occ £65-78), occupying an elevated position on the main A379 road that allows it to make the most of the views across Slapton Ley; and *Waterside House* (☎ 01548-580280, 🖥 www.torcrosshotel.co .uk; 1S/1T/1D/1F; ❤; access to WI-FI possible; £40-50pp) with a massive breakfast (however, advance bookings for single-

night stays are not accepted between May and September).

If you're still struggling to find accommodation, about 1½ miles (2km) inland in the village of **Stokenham** is the thatched 14th-century *Tradesman's Arms* (☎ 01548-580996, 🖥 www.thetradesmansarms.com; 3D; 🐾 £5; WI-FI in the pub; rooms £37.50-42.50pp, sgl occ £75-85) which also offers food (daily summer noon-2pm & 6-9pm, winter Wed-Sat noon-2pm & 6-9pm, Sun 11.30am-2pm & 6-8.30pm).

First's 93 **bus service** (see pp55-60) stops in Torcross and Stokenham on its journey between Plymouth and Dartmouth.

For those who want to push on still further, an entirely horizontal 1½-mile stroll leads you to **Slapton Cross**, the turn-off to pretty Slapton village, about three-quarters of a mile inland.

SLAPTON   [Map 22]

A quiet little huddle of often ancient buildings, Slapton lies about a mile off the coast path on the other side of the Ley from the beach which both share its name. The village is perhaps most famous for being evacuated to allow American GIs to stay (see box p142). Facilities-wise, there's not much to the place other than a **store** (Mon, Tue, Thur & Fri 8am-12.45pm & 2.15-5pm, Wed 8am-12.45pm, Sat 8am-12.45pm & 2.15-4pm, Sun 8-11.45am), a pub and inn, a good campsite and a couple of B&Bs.

On the way to the village from Slapton Turn is *Slapton Sands Camping & Caravanning Club Site* (☎ 01548-580538, 🖥 campingandcaravanningclub.co.uk; hiker and tent £5.85-8.65, members £4.20-6.75; WI-FI £2/day but unreliable at time of research; 🐾; Apr to early Nov), a well-run and clean site. There is a laundry and shop (open reception hours) which sells basics, although the amount of stock available depends on the time of year.

For **B&Bs**, right at the start of the village centre is *Ley Cottage* (☎ 01548-581376, 🖥 www.leycottage.co.uk; 1T; WI-FI; from £30pp, sgl occ £35), one of the newer houses in the village, set in a great location with views over the sheep. Just a

little way along the road, *Old Walls* (☎ 01548-580516, 🖥 www.slaptonbandb.co .uk; 1S/1T/2F; ❤; 🐾 £1 donated to a charity; WI-FI; £32-35pp) is a wonderful old house which is owned by a knowledgeable and friendly lady; indeed, more than one person has said that staying here feels a bit like visiting your gran.

There's also accommodation at the other end of the village at *The Tower Inn* (☎ 01548-580216, 🖥 www.thetowerinn .com; 3D; 🐾; WI-FI; £42.50pp, sgl occ £65), which sits in the shadow of the old church, the tower of which, like the inn itself, dates back to the 14th century. The **food** (daily noon-2.30pm & 6.30-9.30pm, winter hours more limited & closed on a Sunday eve) is said to be the finest in town with such delights as a trio of spring lamb for £16.95.

If this is out of your budget, don't despair, for some scintillating dishes (Devonshire devil curry for £8.95, for example) are also on offer at *The Queens Arms* (☎ 01548-580800, 🖥 www.queensarms slapton.co.uk; food served Easter to Nov Mon-Sat noon-2pm & 5.30-9pm, Sun noon-2pm & 6-9pm; Nov to Easter Mon-Sat noon-2pm, Mon-Fri 6-9pm, Sat & Sun 7-9pm;

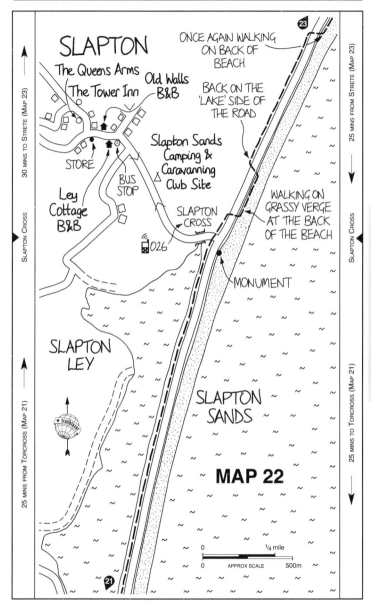

SLAPTON

The Queens Arms
The Tower Inn
Old Walls B&B

STORE

Ley Cottage B&B

BUS STOP

Slapton Sands Camping & Caravanning Club Site

SLAPTON CROSS

☎026

SLAPTON LEY

★ trailblazer

SLAPTON SANDS

MAP 22

ONCE AGAIN WALKING ON BACK OF BEACH

BACK ON THE 'LAKE' SIDE OF THE ROAD

WALKING ON GRASSY VERGE AT THE BACK OF THE BEACH

MONUMENT

30 MINS TO STRETE (MAP 23)

SLAPTON CROSS

25 MINS FROM TORCROSS (MAP 21)

25 MINS FROM STRETE (MAP 23)

SLAPTON CROSS

25 MINS TO TORCROSS (MAP 21)

ROUTE GUIDE AND MAPS

0   1/4 mile
0   APPROX SCALE   500m

🐾), a small, old (14th century) and exceptionally friendly pub – especially to (well-behaved) dogs, who often outnumber the human patrons. Its size, however, is a disadvantage – turn up early or you could be waiting a while for both a seat and your meal.

Transport-wise, First's 93 **bus service** is easily accessed from Slapton Turn and also less frequently from the village itself. See pp55-60 for details.

See pp55-60 for details.

❏ Operation Tiger

As tranquil and picturesque as Slapton Sands and its namesake village may appear today, during World War II this whole area was converted into a 'practice ground' for 30,000 American troops prior to the Normandy landings. The site was chosen because of its similarity to Utah Beach in Normandy – namely a gravel beach followed by a thin ribbon of land and a lake – where the troops were planning to land during D-Day. As a result of this likeness, the 3000 residents of Slapton and Torcross – some of whom had never left their village before – were forced to evacuate.

While the landings were, of course, ultimately successful, the rehearsal itself was marred by tragedy on a huge scale. Despite protection from the Royal Navy, a convoy of eight Allied ships heading to this 'rehearsal' was attacked by nine German E-Boats, leading to the loss of 638 servicemen. Worse was to follow: when the remaining boats reached land, a further 308 personnel were killed by – unbelievably – friendly fire, following an order by Dwight Eisenhower to use live ammunition to harden the troops!

As a result of the tragedy the landings were almost cancelled altogether. Ten men were unaccounted for following the Battle of Lyme Bay (as it became known) and with the generals afraid that they may have been picked up by the Germans and forced to reveal the plans, the invasion was close to being cancelled until the bodies of each of these 10 men were found.

Those who witnessed the tragic events of April 28th, 1943, were sworn to secrecy and indeed the incident was pretty well covered up by the authorities. Indeed, if it wasn't for local resident Ken Small, who used to find evidence of Operation Tiger while beachcombing in southern Devon in the '70s, it's uncertain whether there would be any memorial to the battle at all. Ken made it his ambition to find out exactly what had happened that day and, having done so, decided to try to commemorate the event. The Sherman DD tank at the eastern end of Torcross was bought by Ken and raised from the seabed in 1984, and now stands as a tribute to the 946 US servicemen who died that day. A second memorial, at Slapton Turn, was erected to thank the people of the local area for abandoning their homes whilst the American GIs moved in. In recent times people have placed stones at its base emblazoned with messages and memorials for those serving in contemporary wars.

SLAPTON CROSS TO DARTMOUTH   [MAPS 22-25]

This lovely **8¾-mile (14km; 3hrs 25mins)** stage is full of interest and, given the rugged nature of much of this coastline, surprisingly straightforward too. True, there are several climbs – but they are uniformly short and nearly always gentle. Indeed, the only difficulty with this stage is the stretch after the tourist beach at Blackpool Sands, much of which is undertaken on a busy and pavement-less main road. As with the previous stage, there are several places to stop and eat at including the villages of Strete and Stoke Fleming – as well as a beach or two where you can kick off your boots and feel the sand between your toes.

The route

This stage starts with a stroll along the road at Slapton Sands. With the nature reserve on one side and a lovely pebbled shore on the other, it's hard to know on which side of the road to walk; the SWCP seems similarly uncertain, criss-crossing the tarmac a few times here to flit between the two.

At the end, as the road bends left to climb up to **Strete**, the path begins its own gentle climb up to the village by the **Lime Coffee Company van** (🖥 www .limecoffeecompany.co.uk; Easter to end Oct). As with much of this day, some of the houses lining the path – whether olde-worlde thatch cottages or state-of-the-art glass-fronted chic – are, fittingly for such a lovely (and prosperous!) part of the world, simply gorgeous.

STRETE [Map 23, p145]

Strete was another settlement where the residents were evacuated for Operation Tiger (see box opposite) during WWII and if you walk through here in the low season, it can feel like they never came back. It's a sleepy place at the best of times, the only activity – save for the occasional inhabitant emerging to mow their lawns or tend to their begonias – focusing around the **Strete Post Office and Stores** (☎ 01803-770225; Mon-Sat 7am-5.30pm, Sun 8am-noon; post office open Mon & Wed-Sat 9am-5.30pm, Tue 9am-1pm); there's a free **ATM** here (note HSBC cards aren't accepted).

For **accommodation**, to the north of the village, past the Laughing Monk restaurant, *Manor Farm Campsite* (☎ 01548-511441, 🖥 www.manorfarmstrete.co.uk;

WI-FI; £10-14 per pitch and two people, £9-10 for one person; Mar-Oct/Nov) has a lovely six-acre slope of green fields running down in the direction of the sea. Facilities include a full kitchen and washing machine, a TV room and showers (50p-£1). Note that much of the site is given over to naturists – do not stay if the thought of 100% naked British beef roaming around the place doesn't appeal.

Nearby, *Strete Barton House* (☎ 01803-770364, 🖥 www.stretebarton.co.uk; 4D/2D or T/1D in a self-contained cottage; ▾; WI-FI; 🐾 allowed in cottage £7; £52.50-80pp, sgl occ £105-160) is definitely at the top end of the scale for **B&B** and has a splendid garden in which you could relax after a long day's slog. Unfortunately they

ROUTE GUIDE AND MAPS

❏ Slapton Ley Nature Reserve

Separated from the sea by only the narrowest sliver of beach and tarmac, Slapton Ley can boast of being the largest freshwater lake in the South-West. A national nature reserve, the area plays host to badgers, dormice, bats and otters; unsurprisingly, however, it's the birdlife for which the reserve is famous, with the lake a natural staging post for migrants.

One resident of Slapton Ley is **Cetti's warbler** (*Cettia cetti*), which can often be seen from the road at Slapton Bridge, where two males often nest (one on either side). As an insect-eating non-migrant, the warbler can suffer during very cold winters but at Slapton the population is stable at around 40 singing males. **Greater crested grebes** (*Podiceps cristatus*) and **cirl buntings** (*Emberiza cirlus*; around four pairs) also live near the lake. See also p86.

take one-night bookings in advance between November and March only. However, if you phone and they have a free room on the day you are welcome; their prices, though, may put many walkers off.

A little further along the road that leads from the middle of the village is *Frogwell B&B* (☎ 01803-770273, 🖥 www.frogwell.net; 3D; ✿; WI-FI; £45pp; sgl occ £75), set in a great location, one of the original houses (it dates back to the 1600s) of Strete that back on to fields which in turn back on to the sea. A two-night minimum stay is, however, required in summer.

You may be surprised that slumbering Strete has not one but two **places to eat**. At the time of research the village pub, *King's Arms* (☎ 01803-770377; food daily noon-4pm & 6-9pm), had just been taken over by new tenants and their menu focuses on standard pub food (£8-10).

Round the corner and up the hill, *The Laughing Monk* (☎ 01803-770639, 🖥 www.thelaughingmonk.co.uk; Apr-Oct Mon-Sat 5-9pm, Nov-Mar Mon-Sat 6.30-9pm) offers early evening specials (summer 5-7pm, winter 6.30-7.30pm) where *some* starters are £5 (normally £6.50-8.50), mains are £12 (normally £12-19) and desserts £5. Our favourite dish is their eight-hour braised shoulder of Aune Valley lamb Wellington with red cabbage and root vegetable purée, roast potatoes and a red wine and rosemary sauce, though this tends to be on their winter menu. In summer it is replaced by the just as scrumptious slow-roasted belly of pork.

First's 93 **bus service** (see pp55-60) passes through Strete en route between Plymouth and Dartmouth.

From Strete the path passes through several fields which may or may not be filled with cows when you visit, before traversing the vertiginous dip in the earth's surface separating you from the road; it's steep but it's also mercifully very short and, having rejoined the road, you cross it then hug it, strolling alongside the tarmac in lush fields of livestock.

The path leaves the line of the road briefly to cut down to **Blackpool Sands**, yet another gorgeous stretch of sand and home to *Venus Café* (☎ 01803-712648, 🖥 www.lovingthebeach.co.uk; daily 8.30am-5pm) where you will get hot and cold drinks and takeaway meals. Its accompanying **restaurant** (daily 5.30-9pm in summer; Thur, Fri & Sat only in winter) is a little smarter; you can feast on lobster or whole local crab (£16.95) here whilst contemplating the beauty of the beach and surrounding woodland.

From here the path continues along the road, diverting off to the left (currently unsigned) to follow a mercifully quieter lane, past the church into **Stoke Fleming** by The Green Dragon.

STOKE FLEMING   [Map 24, p147]

Recorded in the Domesday book as 'Stoc', Stoke Fleming is an ancient village dominated by a church, St Peter's, that's almost as old as the village itself, with written references dating back to 1272; George Parker Bidder, the famous engineer who worked with George Stephenson in the early days of steam railways, is buried in the graveyard.

Facilities include a **village shop and post office** (shop Mon, Tue, Thur & Fri 8am-1pm & 2-5.30pm, Wed 8am-1pm, Sat 8.30am-12.30pm, Sun 9-11am) and, round the corner and right on the path, a great pub. *The Green Dragon* (☎ 01803-770238, 🖥 www.green-dragon-pub.co.uk; food daily noon-2pm & 6.30-8.30pm) is a lovely old snug with a stone floor, big fireplace and comfy old sofas to fling your tired frame onto at the end of the day. **Main courses** cost £6-12 and there is a specials board that changes regularly.

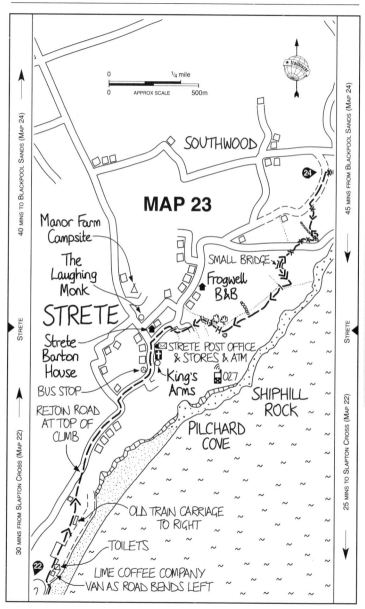

The only real alternative for sustenance is *The Brill Plaice* (☎ 01803-770007, 🖳 www.thebrillplaice.co.uk; food served summer Tue-Sat 6.30-9pm, for other hours check their website or social media), where you can get pan-cooked fillet of brill for £12.90. They also have a takeaway service (summer daily 5.30-9pm, winter Wed-Sat).

Accommodation includes a place for **campers** behind The Brill Plaice: *Leonard's Cove Holiday Park* (☎ 01803-770206, 🖳 www.leonardscoveholiday camping.co.uk; wi-fi; May-Sep), charges £15.50-23 for a tent for up to two persons.

B&Bs include *Channel View* (☎ 01803-770389, 🖳 www.channelviewguest house.com; 2D/2D or T/1F; 🛥; 🐾; wi-fi; £45pp, sgl occ £65), a dog-friendly establishment (they have two labradors themselves) standing opposite the entrance to the campsite. Note that advance one-night bookings may not be accepted here between April and October.

There is also the smart *Ford's House* (☎ 01803-770105, 🖳 www.stoktefleming .com; 2D; 🛥; wi-fi; £35-37.50pp; sgl occ £50), on Dartmouth Rd, while *Fairholme* (☎ 01803-770356, 🖳 www.fairholmedart mouth.co.uk; 2D/1T; wi-fi; £30-32.50pp, sgl occ £40-45) has salmon and scrambled eggs on the breakfast menu.

Near Ford's House, but a fair way up the price scale, stands *Stoke Lodge Hotel* (☎ 01803-770523, 🖳 www.stokelodge.co .uk; 3S/21D or T; 🛥; wi-fi in lounge and bar; 🐾; £49.50-74.50pp, sgl £71-75.50), a smart place set in three acres of gardens, with tennis courts, a pond, putting green and chess set. They have a restaurant (daily 7-9pm) and bar snacks are available in the bar (daily noon-11pm).

The only **bus service** to call here is First's 93 (Plymouth to Dartmouth); see also pp55-60.

The path continues past the pub to an alleyway. Follow the signposts carefully and you'll eventually leave the village by Windward Nursing Home. The route now follows a very quiet country lane to the National Trust owned **Little Dartmouth** (look out for hares), where you finally get to enjoy a little bit of clifftop walking – once again very gentle – as you stroll round **Blackstone Point** before heading up the Dart via **Dartmouth Castle** and **Warfleet** and on to the lovely town itself.

❑ Dartmouth Castle

Built in 1388 to protect the town from invasion from the sea, Dartmouth Castle was in use right up to the Second World War. Features include the gun tower – the first, so it is believed, purpose built to carry heavy cannon big enough to sink ships – a Victorian gun battery and, unusually, a church, St Petrox. Doubtless the one aspect of the castle that will linger longest in the memory, however, is the beautiful view it provides of the Dart and the wooded slopes beyond.

The castle (Apr-June & Sep daily 10am-5pm, Jul-Aug daily 10am-6pm, Oct daily 10am-4pm, Nov-Mar Sat & Sun only 10am-4pm; £4.70, free for EH members) is today owned by English Heritage, which means it's in a fine state of preservation, the displays are interesting and well presented, and the story of the castle is clearly and imaginatively presented.

Outside the castle are the *Dartmouth Castle Tearooms* (☎ 01803-833897, 🖳 www .castletearoomsdartmouth.co.uk; daily 8.30am-5.30pm but may close earlier if it is quiet) serving breakfast until noon, with three items for £3.95 – rising to six for £5.95. The tearooms were known as the Castle Light in the mid-19th century when they were built and acted as a form of lighthouse, providing light to ships sailing up the Dart.

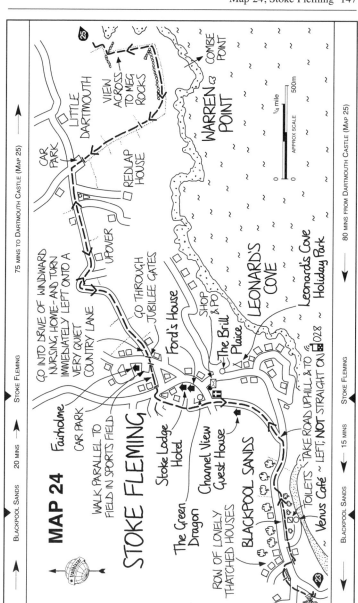

MAP 24

STOKE FLEMING

- Fairholme CAR PARK
- WALK PARALLEL TO FIELD IN SPORTS FIELD
- GO INTO DRIVE OF WINDWARD NURSING HOME - AND TURN IMMEDIATELY LEFT ONTO A VERY QUIET COUNTRY LANE
- GO THROUGH JUBILEE GATES
- 25
- CAR PARK
- LITTLE DARTMOUTH
- VIEW ACROSS TO MEG ROCKS
- COMBE POINT
- REDLAP HOUSE
- UPDOVER
- WARREN POINT
- Ford's House
- SHOP & PO
- The Brill
- Plaice
- LEONARD'S COVE
- Leonard's Cove Holiday Park
- 028
- Stoke Lodge Hotel
- Channel View Guest House
- The Green Dragon
- ROW OF LONELY THATCHED HOUSES
- BLACKPOOL SANDS
- TOILETS ~ TAKE ROAD UPHILL & TO Venus Café ~ LEFT; NOT STRAIGHT ON
- 23
- ¼ mile
- 500m
- 0 APPROX SCALE 0

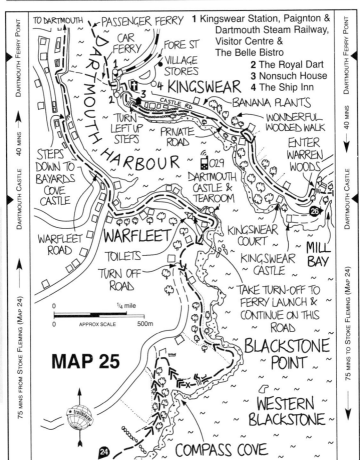

MAP 25

ROUTE GUIDE AND MAPS

Labels on map:

TO DARTMOUTH
PASSENGER FERRY
CAR FERRY
FORE ST
VILLAGE STORES
DARTMOUTH HARBOUR
KINGSWEAR
CASTLE RD
BANANA PLANTS
WONDERFUL WOODED WALK
ENTER WARREN WOODS
TURN LEFT UP STEPS
PRIVATE ROAD
STEPS DOWN TO BAYARDS COVE CASTLE
DARTMOUTH CASTLE & TEAROOM
WARFLEET ROAD
WARFLEET
TOILETS
TURN OFF ROAD
KINGSWEAR COURT
KINGSWEAR CASTLE
MILL BAY
TAKE TURN-OFF TO FERRY LAUNCH & CONTINUE ON THIS ROAD
BLACKSTONE POINT
WESTERN BLACKSTONE
COMPASS COVE
trailblazer
0   ¼ mile
0   APPROX SCALE   500m

1 Kingswear Station, Paignton &
Dartmouth Steam Railway,
Visitor Centre &
The Belle Bistro
2 The Royal Dart
3 Nonsuch House
4 The Ship Inn

Side margin labels:
DARTMOUTH FERRY POINT
40 MINS
DARTMOUTH CASTLE
75 MINS FROM STOKE FLEMING (MAP 24)
DARTMOUTH FERRY POINT
40 MINS
DARTMOUTH CASTLE
75 MINS TO STOKE FLEMING (MAP 24)

DARTMOUTH   [map p151]

Dartmouth – or Clifton-Dartmouth-Hardnesso to give it its full name – is a pleasant town, friendly, fascinating, with some lovely medieval streets and a rich history. Dartmouth's prosperity was founded on the natural deep-water harbour and its accompanying port, the latter having originally been developed by the Normans almost a thousand years ago.

By 1147 that harbour was being used as a muster point for the 164 ships leaving for the Second Crusade – a role it reprised in 1190 during the Third Crusade under King John. (The suburb of Warfleet is said to be so named because of the numerous times fleets have assembled here before heading off to battle.) Home to the Royal Navy since Edward III's reign (1327-77), unsurprisingly the town has often been the target of attacks by foreign foes, a problem exacerbated by the town's secondary reputation as a centre for privateers (officially sanctioned pirates). The twin castles of Dartmouth and Kingswear were built at the end of the 14th century to defend against such assaults, and a chain once stretched across the narrow river mouth to prevent invaders sailing straight up to the port.

With such a rich maritime heritage, it's no surprise that the town is home to the only naval college in Britain. **Britannia Royal Naval College** occupies a glorious hilltop building that dates back to the turn of the 19th century; prior to this, the college was based on two large hulks moored in the Dart itself. The college is famous for its royal links. Kings George V and VI and the current princes of Wales and York all trained here, as did their father the Duke of Edinburgh; indeed, it is said that Philip first met his wife, Queen (at that time Princess) Elizabeth here while still a student.

Given its long history and worldwide fame, it comes as something of a surprise to discover just how small the town actually is, with a permanent population of fewer than 6000. Nevertheless, there's enough here, including some great old buildings, to warrant a rest day should time and inclination allow.

Dart Music Festival (🖳 www.dart musicfestival.co.uk) is held here in May and **Dartmouth Food Festival** (🖳 www .dartmouthfoodfestival.com) in October.

Services

Dartmouth's centre is a compact place and it doesn't take long to get your bearings. Facilities in the centre include a **tourist information centre** (☎ 01803-834224, 🖳 www.discoverdartmouth.com; summer Mon-Sat 9.30am-5pm, Sun 10am-4pm, winter Mon-Sat 9.30am-4pm, may close at 1pm on Wed; they have a screen in the window where people can see available accommodation when they are closed) in the Engine House on Mayor's Ave, and a **post office** (Mon-Fri 8.30am-5.30pm, Sat 9am-12.30pm) inside a Spar **supermarket** (daily 7am-10pm) on Victoria Rd. There's

also a larger Co-op supermarket (daily 8am-8pm) on Fairfax, the **chemist** Boots (Mon-Sat 9am-5.30pm, Sun 11am-3pm), a **launderette** (daily 8am-8pm, service wash 9am-1pm only), on Market St, and **internet** at Dartmouth Library (Mon & Sat 9am-1pm, Tue & Fri 9am-5pm, Thur 9am-6pm; £2.20 for 30 mins; WI-FI free) in the swish Flavel Arts Centre, which doubles as the local **cinema**. There are also plenty of **banks** with **ATMs**.

Where to stay

There's a massive choice of accommodation in Dartmouth. Unfortunately, by the time you've weeded out those that don't take single-night bookings or are at the upper end of town (and thus too far for weary walkers), the selection is more manageable.

Centrally, *Anzac Street Bistro* (☎ 01803-835515, 🖳 www.anzacstreetbistro .co.uk; 2D; ✆; WI-FI; £40pp, sgl occ £55), 2 Anzac St, is a tempting option with the sweet aromas wafting in the air from the café below.

Nearby is the longstanding and remarkably pretty *Charity House* (☎ 01803-832176, 🖳 www.dartmouth.org.uk/ Details/Charity-House-Dartmouth.html; 2D/1D or T; ✆; WI-FI; £40pp, sgl occ £60) on Collaford Lane. It is known for the breakfast that begins with strawberries and blueberries before moving through a plethora of locally sourced comestibles including rare-breed sausages and bread.

The town's B&Bs are centred on Victoria Rd. Closest to the amenities are *The Maitland* (☎ 01803-835854, 🖳 www .themaitland.co.uk; 3D; ✆; 🐾 £10; WI-FI; £30-35pp, sgl occ £45-50) at No 28; *Camelot* (☎ 01803-833805, ☎ 07870-665863, 🖳 jjwright@talktalk.net; 2D/1T; WI-FI; £30-35pp, sgl occ £40-45) at No 61; and *Capritia* (☎ 01803-833419, 🖳 www .capritia.com; 3D/1T; WI-FI; £37.50-40pp, sgl occ negotiable) at No 69. They don't accept one-night advance bookings in the main season.

As you wander further along Victoria Rd you will also come across *Valley House* (☎ 01803-834045, 🖳 www.valleyhousedart mouth.com; 2D/1T; WI-FI; £30-45pp, sgl occ £50-70), at No 46, which has drying facilities; *Hill View House* (☎ 01803-839372, 🖳 www.hillviewdartmouth.co.uk; 1S/3D/1T; ☛; WI-FI; £35pp, sgl £47, sgl occ £70) at No 76 – whose breakfast includes muffins and banana smoothies; and the dog-friendly *Paper Moon* (☎ 01803-833943, 🖳 www.papermoon-bed-and-breakfast.co.uk; 2D; ☛; WI-FI; £40pp, sgl occ £60) at No 107.

Also on Victoria Rd and highly recommended is the delightful and award-winning *Cladda* (☎ 01803-835957, 🖳 www.cladda-dartmouth.co.uk; 2D/4D or T; ☛; 🐾 £5; WI-FI; £40-62.50pp, sgl occ £70-113), at No 90, who welcome four-legged companions and will happily provide packed lunches.

Finally, back near the market at No 51, some lovely rooms can be found at *Angélique Rooms* (☎ 01803-839425, 🖳 www.theangeldartmouth.co.uk; 5D/1T/1F; ☛; WI-FI; rooms from £99), which is owned by The Angel (see Where to eat); and virtually opposite is the unpretentious *Seale Arms* (☎ 01803-832719, 🖳 www.sealearms .co.uk; 2D/2F; WI-FI; £35pp, sgl occ £40).

A little away from the bustle of Victoria Rd is another excellent option. *Avondale* (☎ 07968-026449, 🖳 www .AvondaleDartmouth.co.uk; 1D/1D, T or F/ 1F; ☛; WI-FI and free internet access; £30-45pp, sgl occ £50-55), 5 Vicarage Hill, is a lovely house full of books; peruse one as you enjoy the views across the river from one of the more than sufficiently sized rooms.

The Captain's House (☎ 01803-832133, 🖳 www.captainshouse.co.uk; 2D or T/2D; ☛; WI-FI; £37.50-46pp, sgl occ £60-90) is a Grade II listed townhouse just to the north of the centre.

Even more central, *Just B* (☎ 01803-834311, 🖳 www.justbdartmouth.co.uk; 4D/1D or T/4D, T or F; ☛; 🐾 £5; £26-32.50, sgl occ from £40, £65-90 for one of the family studio rooms which have some self-catering facilities), at 17 Foss St, is an unusual place, an establishment that offers room-only accommodation with no breakfast. It feels a little like a hostel, though with some very smart rooms that are very

good value. It's good – the only problem being the fact that they don't allow one-night bookings in advance for Saturday nights.

Where to eat and drink

For food on the go, we were rather taken with the friendliness and imaginative fillings on offer at the *Crabshell Sandwich Bar* (☎ 01803-839036; Mon-Sat 10.30am-2.30pm, Sun from 11am) on Raleigh St; particularly delicious was the smoked mackerel and horseradish mayo (£2.80).

Café-wise you won't be short of choices. *Singing Kettle* (☎ 01803-832624; daily Mar-Sep 10am-6pm, Sep-Mar Tue-Sun 10am-5pm) is what one imagines a proper 'tea shoppe' to look like – quaint, old, garlanded with flowers and with a fine selection of cakes and teas. *No 8* (☎ 01803-832999; Mon-Sat 10am-9.30pm in summer, 10am-4.30pm in winter, Sun from 11am), on Foss St, claims to serve the best coffee in town. It also has an eclectic menu of dishes (lasagne, salmon pasta bake and butternut squash risotto to name but three – all from £9.95) as well as high tea with two scones for £8.95.

There are some great **cafés** in the Market area. *Old Market Café* (Mon, Wed, Thur & Sat 8am-4pm, Tue & Fri from 7.30am) does good old fashioned builders' breakfasts for £7.75, or a more refined homemade soup and crusty bread (£4.45). *Dart to Mouth Deli* (☎ 01803-839377; Mon-Fri 9am-4pm, Sat 9am-2pm) is a family-run place and a lovely option both for snacks and consumable souvenirs (chutneys etc).

There are also some good **pubs** close to the market too. The green-tiled *Dolphin Inn* (☎ 01803-833698; bar daily noon-11pm, food Tue-Sat noon-3pm & 6-9pm, Sun & Mon noon-3pm) is a 19th-century pub now serving beers from their own brewery. It can get very busy on Saturday nights, possibly because of their reputation for good food served in huge portions; arrive early if you want a table. Dishes include the regatta platter for £13.95, a plate that includes calamari, octopus and crab.

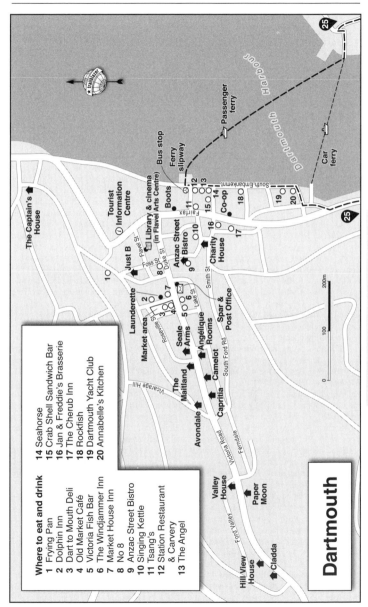

Where to eat and drink
1 Frying Pan
2 Dolphin Inn
3 Dart to Mouth Deli
4 Old Market Café
5 Victoria Fish Bar
6 The Windjammer Inn
7 Market House Inn
8 No 8
9 Anzac Street Bistro
10 Singing Kettle
11 Tsang's
12 Station Restaurant & Carvery
13 The Angel
14 Seahorse
15 Crab Shell Sandwich Bar
16 Jan & Freddie's Brasserie
17 The Cherub Inn
18 Rockfish
19 Dartmouth Yacht Club
20 Annabelle's Kitchen

Dartmouth

ROUTE GUIDE AND MAPS

Nearby, *Market House Inn* (☎ 01803-832128; Mon-Fri noon-3pm & 6-9pm, Fri & Sat to 8pm) also offers a pizza takeaway service (£7.95-9.95), the upper limit being for their fishy pizza that's topped with scallops, prawns and smoked salmon.

Just south of the market, *The Windjammer Inn* (☎ 01803 832228, 🖥 www.thewindjammer.co.uk; Mon-Sat noon-2pm & 6-9pm, Sun 12.30-2.30pm) is a lovely flower-festooned place on Victoria Rd, with mains for £8.95 (vegetarian five-bean casserole) to £15.95 (steak). Best of all, however, the pub has its own boat with which it catches its own fish for the table. If it is available, try their delicious smoked haddock, mussel and crab chowder (£10.45).

Of all the venerable buildings in town, *The Cherub Inn* (☎ 01803-832571, 🖥 thecherub.co.uk; Mon-Sat 11am-11pm, Sun noon-11pm, food served restaurant noon-2pm & 6.30-9pm, bar noon-2.30pm & 6.30-9.30pm) is the oldest and it retains many of the original features such as old ship timbers. They do a good lunch menu including the renowned Cherub smokey (smoked haddock in a creamy sauce topped with bubbling cheese for £7.95).

For finer dining, there are several lovely places on the waterfront at the southern end of the Embankment. *Annabelle's Kitchen* (☎ 01803-833540, 🖥 www.annabelleskitchen.co.uk; Wed-Sat from 7pm) is the most southerly of these and comes recommended by more than one walker. The menu changes with the seasons but often does a lovely megrim sole with brown shrimps, caper butter & samphire, served with new potatoes (£17.50).

A little further north, *Dartmouth Yacht Club* (☎ 01803-839281, 🖥 dyc.org.uk; May-Sep daily noon-2pm, Mon-Sat 7-9pm) is open to non-members and does a fair crab linguine with sautéed chillis and flavoured with garlic and ginger for £12.

A little further north, *Rockfish* (☎ 01803-832800, 🖥 www.rockfishdevon.co.uk) is a smart fish restaurant with takeaway (daily noon-9.30pm) attached. More than just a chippy (though they perform that role very well too), they have some

unusual items including oysters (£1.50), whole South Devon crab (£15.95) and grilled royal bream fillet (£16.95).

At the South Embankment's northern end, *The Angel* (see Angélique Rooms, Where to stay; food Tue-Sat 11am-9pm, Sun 11am-4pm, no food on Tue in winter) is another smart eatery with large windows to take advantage of the views over the estuary. The all-day à la carte menu has starters from £7.95 and mains from £12.95.

Perhaps the smartest place on the waterfront is *Seahorse* (☎ 01803-835147, 🖥 www.seahorserestaurant.co.uk; Tue 6-10pm, Wed-Sat noon-3pm & 6-10pm, Sun 12.30-2.30pm), with some lovely fish dishes – try their skate with black butter and capers (£17). North of this and right on the front, *Station Restaurant & Carvery* (☎ 01803-832125; Apr-Oct daily 8.30am-9pm; winter daily 8.30am-5pm) is conveniently situated next to the bus stop and Kingswear ferry slipway; it also has splendid views down the Dart. It's a pleasant place to while away some time drinking tea and scoffing scones; if something more substantial is required a Dartmouth lamb shank costs £12.65 or you could take advantage of their carvery (£8.95).

There are a couple more restaurants with reputations for good, quality food. *Jan & Freddie's Brasserie* (☎ 01803-832491, 🖥 www.janandfreddiesbrasserie.co.uk; Mon-Sat from 6.30pm; booking is advised) sits on Fairfax Place and is building a solid reputation for sophisticated but unpretentious food (mains £15.95-18.95). Try the cheekily named 'a pair of tarts', one filled with a confit of white onion, the other with a chestnut mushroom sauté and both topped with a hen's egg and finished in a light cream sauce (£15.95).

Anzac Street Bistro (see Where to stay; daily 11am-2pm & Thur-Mon 6-9.30pm) boasts a central location; starters, such as garlic mushrooms in a cream and white wine sauce, are around £4.50 and beef meatballs in an aromatic tomato sauce with mashed potato costs £7.95.

At the other end of the price scale, takeaways include *Tsang's* (☎ 01803-832025; Mon-Sat 5.30-11pm, Sun 5.30-

10pm), on Fairfax Place – the local Chinese; *Frying Pan* (☎ 01803-832546; Wed-Mon noon-2pm & 5-9pm) on Broadstone, a local, traditional chippy; and there's another, *Victoria Fish Bar* (Mon-Sat noon-2pm & 5-10pm, Sun 4.30-8.30pm), near the market.

Transport
[See also pp55-60)] First's 93 **bus** service connects the town with Kingsbridge and Plymouth as well as a number of the smaller coastal locations along the way. Their X81 service goes to Paignton.

For destinations to the east it is usually necessary to cross to Kingswear. See below.

Greenway Ferries operate services from here to Greenway (see box p173) hourly and the journey is shorter than going from Torquay.

DARTMOUTH TO BRIXHAM [MAPS 25-29]

Once you've crossed the river, this **11-mile (17.5km; 4hrs)** stage starts and ends with some flat and easy walking which book-end a rather strenuous middle section.

After the simple stroll to Inner Froward Point, a particularly enjoyable wooded amble leads you to Pudcombe Cove and the marvellous views it offers out to sea. The shaded pathways here offer a splendid contrast to the long cliff-top walk that follows, a walk that's interrupted only by the need to descend to two gloriously quiet beaches. Your eventual arrival at Berry Head is an important point on your coastal journey as you now enter the area called the English Riviera (see box below) and also the English Riviera Global Geopark (see box p158), an area of international geological importance, as well as – unfortunately for the walker – a powerful magnet for tourists.

Note that refreshment options are limited to the towns that sandwich your walk; carrying plenty of water and a picnic to enjoy at one of the many beauty spots en route is thus recommended.

However, before you set off make sure you have checked the ferry times for this section of the path.

The route
To cross the river Dart take **Dartmouth to Kingswear Passenger Ferry** (☎ 01803-555872, 🖳 www.dartmouthrailriver.co.uk; Mon-Sat 7.30am-11.10pm, Sun 9am-11.10pm; £1.50, 🐾 50p), a shuttle service that departs regularly year-round from outside the Station Restaurant (see opposite) on the South Embankment.

❏ **The English Riviera/Torbay**
'Torbay is an area which endears itself to the patriot, the naturalist and the artist'
Charles Kingsley
The 'English Riviera' is the Victorian nickname given to the Torbay area of South Devon that encompasses the three main towns of Brixham, Paignton and Torquay, the title deriving from the area's plentiful beaches and mild climate. Torbay is the council's name for the area; the actual bay is called Tor Bay.

ROUTE GUIDE AND MAPS

Sandpiper of Dartmouth (☎ 07907-528201; during the day £2pp, after 11pm £4pp) operate a **water taxi** for up to five people which runs late into the night – useful for when you've missed the last public ferry.

Kingswear then causes a brief distraction...

KINGSWEAR   [Map 25, p148]

Lying on the eastern bank of the River Dart, the peaceful little settlement of Kingswear (🖥 www.kingswear-devon.co.uk) has historically been – and remains today – a transport hub.

The earliest mention of a ferry crossing the Dart was in 1365, and prior to that it had been used as a landing point for pilgrims heading to Canterbury following the death in 1170 of Thomas à Becket (for whom the village church was built and dedicated).

The arrival of the railway in 1864 further boosted Kingswear's reputation as a transport centre, and it became part of the Great Western Railway in 1876. Though the line was closed in 1968, the tracks were purchased privately and you can still access the national rail network in Paignton and Torquay today courtesy of the **Paignton and Dartmouth Steam Railway** (Apr-Oct daily 11.15am-5pm, slightly extended hours at peak times; Paignton return ticket £10). The railway's **visitor centre** is also in Kingswear (Apr-Oct 10am-5pm; free), though for walkers the nearby **post office and store** (Mon-Sat 8am-6pm, Sun 8am-5pm) may be of more interest.

Bed and breakfast-wise, *Nonsuch House* (☎ 01803-752829, 🖥 www.nonsuch-house.co.uk; 1D/3D or T; ✖; WI-FI; £60-75pp, sgl occ £95-125), Church Hill, is your only option. Far from cheap but exemplary in every way, if you've been camping so far but were planning on treating yourself once this may be the place to do it. On four nights a week three-course dinners are provided, although by the time you've added on the cost (£37.50) you will possibly have blown a whole week's camping budget. However, you can bring your own bottle.

As soon as you disembark the ferry there are a couple of **food** options, and both are reasonably priced. To your left, *The Belle Bistro* (Apr-Oct daily 10am-5pm; ✖ OK for outside seating) at the steam railway station serves up plenty of hot food including sausage rolls and breakfasts (£4.95) as well as having a specials board that changes daily; when we were there fish pie (£4.95) was scribbled in chalk on the board.

On the right of the slipway is *The Royal Dart* (☎ 01803-752213, 🖥 www.theroyaldart.co.uk; food Mon-Sat 9am-10pm, Sun 9am-9.30pm; ✖) which has a balcony with river views; they do a breakfast special (for an amazing £1.99!), while the lunch menu includes fresh crab sandwich (£6.95) and steak pasties (£6.95). They also offer an à la carte menu from noon that includes a huge variety of burgers (£6.95-10.95) with kangaroo, bison and ostrich burgers all advertised (£10.95 each).

Dishing up more standard fare, *The Ship Inn* (☎ 01803-752348, 🖥 shipinnforecast.com; summer daily noon-2.30pm & 6-9.30pm, winter Mon-Sat noon-2.30 & 7-9.30pm, Sun noon-4.30pm; WI-FI) is nicely tucked away on Higher St. There are two open log fires and the owners point out that their seafood has travelled less than 200 yards from sea to plate; try an oven-roasted cod or breaded Brixham plaice fillet (£10). If you've eaten more seafood than Moby Dick in the past few weeks then they also offer The Ship's cow pie with new potatoes (£10).

Transport

[See also pp55-60] Stagecoach's 22, 24 and 120 **bus services** connect Kingwear with Brixham and the rest of the Riviera.

Taxi-wise, Kingswear Taxis (☎ 01803-752626) serve landlubbers, while Sandpiper of Dartmouth (see above) operates a late-night water taxi service to Dartmouth.

If continuing straight on after the ferry crossing, turn immediately right after The Royal Dart public house to go underneath an archway (with the post

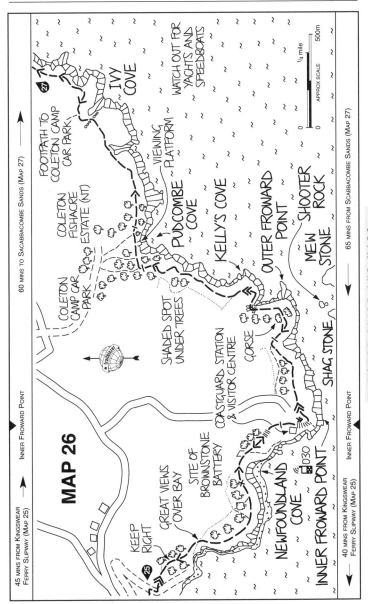

office to your right) before turning left up Alma Steps. A brief jaunt along a wooded road follows before the houses are left behind and you are once again left with just nature for company – banana plants and date palms turn to pine and other coniferous trees, while (hopefully!) sun-rays scatter sporadically through the branches. A right turn off the path will take you to **Kingswear Castle** (☎ 01628-825925, 🖥 www.landmarktrust.org.uk), built in 1502 to complement Dartmouth Castle (see box p146) on the other side of the river. It's now owned by The Landmark Trust and used as a holiday let (1D/1T; 🛥; 🐾; minimum stay three nights).

As you leave the minor road a sign welcomes you into Warren Woods, whilst below you shelter **Mill Bay** and **Newfoundland coves**.

Eventually, after a strenuous climb or two (looking back there are great views over Dartmouth Castle and the bay), you arrive at the Coastguard station at **Inner Froward Point**, from where both Start Point and Stoke Fleming Church can still be seen. During WWII this point was the site of **Brownstone Battery**, a WWII coastal defence position that now hosts a **visitor centre** and lighthouse. The path now zig-zags steeply down, its route etched along the cliff and hillsides in front of you. There is the occasional tree amongst the gorse but little else for cover should the weather turn against you. The larger of the rocks you see out at sea is **Mew Stone** and smaller companions **Shag Stone** and **Shooter Rock**: seals may occasionally be seen resting on these lonely outcrops.

Arriving at picturesque **Pudcombe Cove**, behind you in the woods is the **Coleton Fishacre Estate** (☎ 01803-752466, 🖥 www.nationaltrust.org.uk/coleton-fishacre; Mar-Oct Sat-Thur 10.30am-5pm, Nov & Dec Sat & Sun 11am-4pm; £8.75, £9.75 with Gift Aid, NT members free), the 1920s 'Arts and Crafts' holiday home of the D'Oyly Carte family with a lovely 30-acre garden.

The path again becomes exposed as it tacks its way along the hillside to **Scabbacombe Sands**, a pretty pebble beach worthy of a stop – the crystal-clear water certainly appears inviting on a hot summer's day. However, the beach may be used by naturists.

The trail now begins on the first of two substantial ascents in this stage, the initial descent presenting a large **lime kiln** on the right at **Man Sands**. The views back over the valley as you clamber away from the beach are wonderful.

Following the edge of **Southdown Cliff** you arrive at **Sharkham Point National Nature Reserve** which, along with the nearby 100-acre Berry Head National Nature Reserve (see below) plays host to a colony of guillemots, greater horseshoe bats and eight species of orchid.

There are more wildlife treats at nearby **St Mary's Bay** where, out at sea, dolphins and porpoises can sometimes be spotted. The path passes close to Centry Touring Park (see p160).

The walking is now easy. Reaching a road, the entrance to **Berry Head** – home to two Napoleonic-era forts – appears to your right. **Berry Head National Nature Reserve** (Map 29; ☎ 01803-882619, 🖥 www.berryhead.org.uk; visitor centre Easter-Oct summer daily 10am-4pm, winter Sun 10am-4pm) is open year-round. *Guardhouse Café* (☎ 01803-855778, 🖥 www.guardhousecafe.com)

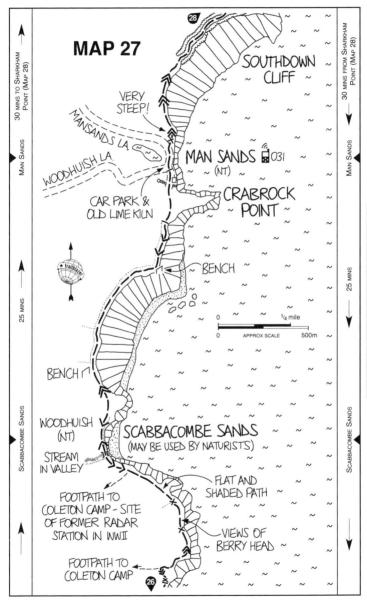

MAP 27

30 MINS TO SHARKHAM POINT (MAP 28)

30 MINS FROM SHARKHAM POINT (MAP 28)

SOUTHDOWN CLIFF

VERY STEEP!

MANSANDS LA.

WOODHUISH LA.

MAN SANDS (NT) 031

CRABROCK POINT

CAR PARK & OLD LIME KILN

trailblazer

BENCH

0   ¼ mile
0   APPROX SCALE   500m

BENCH

WOODHUISH (NT)

STREAM IN VALLEY

SCABBACOMBE SANDS
(MAY BE USED BY NATURISTS)

FOOTPATH TO COLETON CAMP - SITE OF FORMER RADAR STATION IN WWII

FLAT AND SHADED PATH

VIEWS OF BERRY HEAD

FOOTPATH TO COLETON CAMP

26

MAN SANDS

SCABBACOMBE SANDS

25 MINS

MAN SANDS

25 MINS

SCABBACOMBE SANDS

ROUTE GUIDE AND MAPS

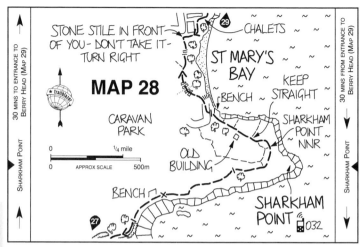

is open summer Tue-Sun 9am-4pm depending on the weather; the winter days/hours also depend on the weather so contact them to check they are open.

The **lighthouse** on Berry Head is, at 58m above sea level, located at the highest altitude of any British lighthouse. Probably as a result of its lofty location, it is also the smallest lighthouse in Britain, being just 5m high. Gentle walking continues as you amble to **Berry Head Hotel** (see p161), where the

❏ **The English Riviera Global Geopark**
The English Riviera Global Geopark straddles the area called The English Riviera (see box p153), its coastal borders being at Sharkham Point (just south of St Mary's Bay) and just north of Maidencombe Beach (see Map 36, p182).

A geopark is a site recognised and protected by UNESCO because of its unique geological significance. There are currently only 87 of these in the entire world, eight of which are in the UK, though the English Riviera is unique in being the only one that is largely urban. In addition to the Riviera's diverse geology, covering a number of periods, and its contribution to our understanding of geology, the area is also a rich source of fossils, wonderful examples being those of a **woolly rhinoceros** and a **cave lion** that were both discovered at Kent's Cavern near Torquay. The **oldest human fossil** (a jawbone) yet to be found in the UK was also discovered in this cavern.

The park includes 32 geosites (geological sites of international importance) in total, though not all are open to the public. However, **Berry Head National Nature Reserve**, guarding the southern entry to Tor Bay, **Petit Tor** and **Hope's Nose Site of Special Scientific Interest**, the latter at the geopark's northern extremity, are all visitable and on the path. Look out for the information boards that give further details on their geological importance.

The park also has three **visitor centres**, at Berry Head NNR (see p156); Kent's Cavern (see p178), near Torquay, and The Seashore Centre (see p164) on Tanner's Rd, next door to Inn on the Quay at Goodrington Sands.

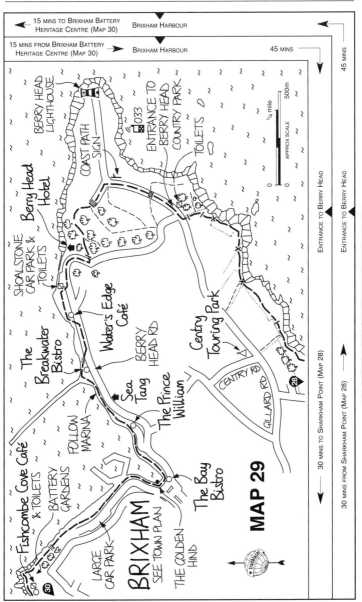

← 15 MINS TO BRIXHAM BATTERY HERITAGE CENTRE (MAP 30)

BRIXHAM HARBOUR

15 MINS FROM BRIXHAM BATTERY HERITAGE CENTRE (MAP 30) →

BRIXHAM HARBOUR

45 MINS

45 MINS

BERRY HEAD LIGHTHOUSE

COAST PATH SIGN

033

ENTRANCE TO BERRY HEAD COUNTRY PARK

TOILETS

Berry Head Hotel

500m

¼ mile

APPROX SCALE

SHOALSTONE CAR PARK & TOILETS

Water's Edge Café

BERRY HEAD RD

Centry Touring Park

ENTRANCE TO BERRY HEAD

ENTRANCE TO BERRY HEAD

The Breakwater Bistro

Sea Tang

The Prince William

CENTRY RD

GILLARD RD

28

ROUTE GUIDE AND MAPS

FOLLOW MARINA

Fishcombe Cove Café & TOILETS

BATTERY GARDENS

The Bay Bistro

MAP 29

LARGE CAR PARK

BRIXHAM SEE TOWN PLAN

THE GOLDEN HIND

30

30 MINS TO SHARKHAM POINT (MAP 28)

30 MINS FROM SHARKHAM POINT (MAP 28) →

trail leads right into **Shoalstone car park** and on, eventually, to *Water's Edge Café* (seasonal; opens from 10am, closes whenever climate or customers dictate) halfway between the hotel and the harbour-arm.

The path as you enter Brixham is not wonderfully signed: look out for the steps shortly before the harbour-arm for an easy walk along the marina. Eventually you pass *The Breakwater Bistro* (☎ 01803-856738, 🖳 www.the breakwater.co.uk; summer daily 9am-9.30pm, winter Sun-Thur 10am-4pm, Fri & Sat 10am-9pm) to arrive at Brixham Harbour.

BRIXHAM

Sitting at the southern end of Tor Bay, Brixham, or *Briseham* as it is recorded in the Domesday Book (when it had a population of 39!) is the first of the three main towns of the English Riviera (the other two being Paignton and Torquay). Not quite as noisy or bustling as either of those, the old harbour area will nevertheless still probably be a little too busy for the average trekker, particularly after the peace of the previous stage.

Synonymous with fishing, Brixham was the largest fishing port in South-West England during the Middle Ages. By the early 19th century there were over 200 trawlers operating out of the town and by 1850 it had become the largest fishery in England. Even today it remains the nation's foremost fishing port, landing over a staggering £20 million worth of fish every year.

The harbour is dominated by an impressive replica of *The Golden Hind* (☎ 01803-856223, 🖳 www.goldenhind.co.uk; daily 10am-4pm; £4), the ship with which Francis Drake became the first Englishman (and the second person in the world) to circumnavigate the globe. Behind the replica is the **statue** of William, Prince of Orange. Invited by Protestant English politicians concerned by King James II's Catholicism, William landed his 20,000-strong Dutch army at Fishcombe Cove, just outside Brixham, in 1688. From there he went on to overthrow James – in what became known as the Glorious Revolution – and become William III of England.

The social and maritime history of the town is celebrated at **Brixham Heritage Museum** (☎ 01803-856267, 🖳 www.brix hammuseum.org.uk; Apr-Oct Tue-Sat & Bank Hol Mons 10am-4pm, Nov-Mar Tue-Sat 10am-1pm; £2) in the Old Police Station at Bolton Cross, where there are two floors of galleries and displays including one on life at the Berry Head Barracks in Napoleonic times.

Brixham Pirate & Shanty Festival (🖳 www.brixhampiratefestival.co.uk), held here in May, features a variety of events including 'record attempts' for the 'Biggest gathering of pirates' (2010 saw the town gain – briefly – the world record).

Services

Quirkily, **Brixham Visitor Information Centre** (☎ 01803-858183, 🖳 www.brix ham.com; July-Sep Mon-Sat 9.30am-5pm, Sun 10am-3pm, Easter-July & Sep-Oct Mon-Sat 9.30am-4pm; closed Nov-Easter), 20 The Quay, is in Hobb Nobs Gift Shop!

Internet's availability is somewhat more orthodox and can be found at Brixham Library (Mon & Thur 9.30am-5pm, Tue & Fri 9.30am-7pm, Wed & Sat 9.30am-1pm; £1 per half-hour). Other services include a Co-op **supermarket** (daily 8am-8pm) near the harbour on Fore St, with both an **ATM** and Brixham's **post office** (Mon-Sat 9am-5.30pm) within it, and a branch of Tesco (daily 6am-11pm) near the top of the same street where you'll also find Boots the **chemist** (Mon-Sat 9am-5.30pm).

Where to stay

As you follow the path into Brixham you'll find **camping** is available at *Centry Touring Park* (see Map 29; ☎ 01803-856389, 🖳 www.centrytouring.co.uk; single hiker with PUP tent £10, pitch inc two people £13-15; 🐾 one free, if two 50p; Apr-Oct) where Centry Rd meets Gillard Rd. Booking is recommended for August.

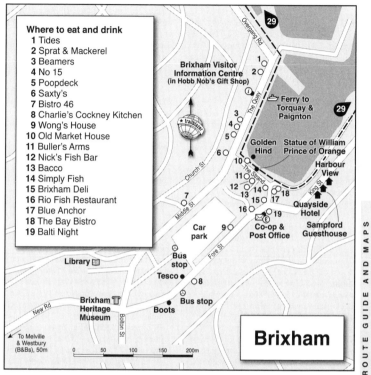

Where to eat and drink
1 Tides
2 Sprat & Mackerel
3 Beamers
4 No 15
5 Poopdeck
6 Saxty's
7 Bistro 46
8 Charlie's Cockney Kitchen
9 Wong's House
10 Old Market House
11 Buller's Arms
12 Nick's Fish Bar
13 Bacco
14 Simply Fish
15 Brixham Deli
16 Rio Fish Restaurant
17 Blue Anchor
18 The Bay Bistro
19 Balti Night

Brixham

ROUTE GUIDE AND MAPS

The first **B&B** you'll see as you enter town along Berry Head Rd is *Sea Tang* (Map 29; ☎ 01803-854651, 🖳 www.sea tang-guesthouse.com; 2S/2D/1T/1F; WI-FI; £30-35pp), No 67, from where there are tremendous views over the bay and marina. Overlooking the harbour from King St is *Harbour View* (☎ 01803-853052, 🖳 har bourviewbrixhambandb.co.uk; 6D/1T/1F; ➴; WI-FI; £34-37.50pp, sgl occ £55-65; Feb-Nov), No 65, which was previously the residence of the harbourmaster and is grade II listed. Further down King St there is dog-friendly *Sampford Guesthouse* (☎ 01803-857761, 🖳 www.sampfordhouse.com; 5D/1T; ➴; WI-FI; 🐾; £29-36pp, sgl occ £45-65), No 57-59, which unfortunately does not accept bookings for one-night stays in August.

At the back end of town on New Rd there are other decent options such as *Westbury Guesthouse* (☎ 01803-851684, 🖳 www.westburyguesthouse.co.uk; 4D/ 2D, T or F; ➴; WI-FI; £30pp, sgl occ £35), at No 51, where breakfast includes fresh fish caught by the owners and items grown on their allotment; and the licensed *Melville Guesthouse* (☎ 01803-852033, 🖳 www.mel villeguesthousebrixham.co.uk; 2T/6D; WI-FI; £25-30pp, sgl occ £35 or less) at No 45.

Hotel-wise, *Berry Head Hotel* (Map 29; ☎ 01803-853225, 🖳 www.berryhead hotel.com; 3S/29D, some can be T; ➴; WI-FI; 🐾 £5-15; £56-104pp) is a splendid – though not cheap – option to consider. Dinner can be provided but beware they do not accept bookings for one-night stays at weekends in summer.

Otherwise, **Quayside Hotel** (☎ 01803-855751, 🖥 www.quaysidehotel.co.uk; 27D or T; 🐾; WI-FI; 🍴 £12.50; £43-71pp, sgl occ £60-70), overlooking the harbour from King St, is a slightly more economical option – although not for your dog. Many of the higher-priced rooms have sea views.

Where to eat and drink

It comes as no surprise, given the fact that the town can boast of one of the largest and newest fish markets in the UK, that Brixham is enjoying a burgeoning reputation as a centre for foodies, with seafood something of a speciality. You don't have to stray too far from the path to sample it, either, with restaurants standing cheek by gill on the western side of the harbour making this a true paradise for piscivores.

All tastes and budgets are catered for here, from a simple good quality chippy such as **Nick's Fish Bar** (☎ 01803-853357; 11am-8.30pm, to 9.30pm for takeaway & 10pm on Fri & Sat) up to some real fine-dining establishments. Of the latter, **Poopdeck** (☎ 01803-858681, 🖥 www.poopdeckrestaurant.com; Mon-Fri 6.30pm to late, Sat & Sun noon-2.30pm & 6.30pm to late) describes itself as 'the mother of all fish restaurants' and has some lovely meals including a smoked haddock carbonara for £13.25. They also offer a taster menu, with six dishes for £15 at lunch (£25 in the evening).

Nearby, the menu at **No 15 Restaurant** (☎ 01803-853418, 🖥 www.no15restaurant.co.uk; Mon-Sat 6.30pm to late) changes constantly according to what has been caught; though if it's available, you can't go wrong with their monkfish medallions with king prawns in garlic butter (£17). On this same side, **Beamers** (☎ 01803-854777, 🖥 www.beamersrestaurant.co.uk; Wed-Mon from 6.30pm) is another fish-centric establishment, with mains from £15.95 for the fillet of pollock with clams, mussels and saffron, rising to £39.95 for the shellfish platter for two to share, with Brixham scallops, organic Elberry Cove mussels, clams and crevettes just some of the ingredients. **Tides Restaurant** (☎ 01803-852195, 🖥 www.tides-brixham.co.uk; daily 8am-4pm,

Easter-Oct Fri & Sat 7-10.30pm) is an unfussy place though there are some items on the menu that are unusual (a starter of deep-fried sardines with a parmesan crust served on a bed of lettuce for £4.50, for example). It's most popular, however, at breakfast (fry-ups for £5.50).

The new squid in the tank is **Simply Fish** (☎ 01803-883858; daily 11am-9pm, winter noon-3pm & 5-9pm), which has been opened by one of the merchants operating at the market. The restaurant does exactly what it says on the tin, serving such delights as monkfish curry (£17.95) as well as a takeaway service offering dishes not normally seen on your average chippy's menu, for example a large fillet of lemon sole (£8.50). Close by, you may like to try a whole grilled sea-bass (£13.95) at **The Bay Bistro** (☎ 01803-854469; summer 10am-8pm, winter 10am-3pm, closed Jan) at the end of New Quay Lane.

The marina can also boast some pretty good **pubs** including **The Prince William** (Map 29; ☎ 01803-854468, 🖥 www.theprincewilliam.co.uk; breakfast 10-11.30am, lunch noon-2.30pm, dinner 6-9pm) which is renowned for its carvery (£7.95) but also sells pizzas (£8.95) and many other mouth-watering meals; and **Blue Anchor** (☎ 01803-859373, food served Mon-Sat noon-2.30pm & 6.30-9.15pm, Sun noon-3pm) which offers that classic combination of live music, real ales and hearty food, with a 10oz rump steak for £12.95.

A little way along, **Old Market House** (☎ 01803-856891, 🖥 www.oldmarkethousebrixham.co.uk; food served daily noon-10pm) is, despite its description as a restaurant, more of a pub than anything else (though it's a smart one). The food is pretty standard fare though it's nice to sit in the sun and gorge on a bowl of their Brixham mussels with fries as an accompaniment (£12.95).

Back on The Quay's western side, **Sprat & Mackerel** (☎ 01803-882649; food served noon-3pm & 6.30-9pm) is a busy place that serves a decent Devon crab sandwich for £8. There's also **Bullers Arms** (☎ 01803-855622; daily noon-3pm & 6-9pm), at 4 The Strand, which will willingly dish you up their seafood platter for £8.95. There are other dishes available for those who'd rather not feast on the flesh of fish. Just off the front, on Fore St, *Brixham Deli* (☎ 01803-859585, 💻 www.thebrixhamdeli .co.uk; Easter to Oct Mon-Sat 9am-5pm, Sun 10am-4pm; Oct to Easter Mon-Thur 9am-4.30pm, Fri & Sat to 5.30pm) is a lovely place, with good food – locally sourced, where possible – to take away or eat in their small café. Their lengthy sandwich menu is the stuff of legends, including such delights as rare roast beef, blackcurrant jam and stilton for £3.95.

Indeed, Fore St is a happy hunting ground for foodies with eateries including *Charlie's Cockney Kitchen* (☎ 01803-858279; daily June-Sep 8.30am-8pm, Oct-May 8.30am-6pm), offering such East End delights as pie, mash and liquor for £4.95; *Rio Fish Restaurant* (Mon-Thur 11.30am-3pm & 5-8pm, Fri & Sat 11.30am-8.30pm, Sun noon-8pm), the oldest chippy in town (which is actually just off Fore St on Pump St); and both the local Indian, *Balti Night* (☎ 01803-882040, 💻 www.thebaltinight.com; Sun-Thur 5.30pm to midnight, Fri & Sat 5.30pm-12.30am) and a Chinese, *Wong's House* (☎ 01803-856314; Mon-Sat 5-11pm, Sun 5.30-11pm, closed Tue Oct-Mar) too.

Across Brixham's large and very central car park from Fore St lie further options. *Saxty's* (☎ 01803-858519; daily summer 10am-9pm, winter 10.30am-4pm, Fri & Sat 6-9pm) is a real anachronism, the oldest restaurant in town and one that feels like it hasn't been updated since its inception. In keeping with the timewarp theme, mobile phones are also banned – one of a long list of rules you are presented with. That said, the food can sometimes be great, with good sandwiches from £3.50, and cream teas for £4.80. Ignore the unsmiling service and you may grow to like this place.

Bistro 46 (☎ 01803-858936, 💻 www .bistro46.com; late May to mid July Wed-Sat 6.30-9.30pm, Sat 10.30am-3.30pm, mid July-Aug also open Tue 6.30-9.30pm; Feb-Dec Wed-Sat 6.30-9.30pm), squirrelled away at 46 Middle St, specialises in 'world' cuisine (which, one would have thought, is quite a big subject to specialise in!). Nevertheless, there are some rave reviews about this place and you can't fault the inventiveness of the menu. It changes regularly (check the website) but may include such delights as Madagascan-style lightly spiced Romazava lamb stew with fresh ginger, garlic, spinach, tomato & pumpkin, finished with sautéed new potatoes; or Mexican-style slow-roasted pork belly served on jalapeno, coriander and sour cream mash with a corn and plum sauce (both £13.95).

Finally, *Bacco* (☎ 01803-858266, 💻 www.bacco-brixham.co.uk; Tue-Thur 6.30-9.30pm, Fri & Sat 6-9.30pm) is the best Italian in town, hidden away down Beach Approach and with a reasonably priced (mains £10-15) menu: it has the usual Italian dishes such as wild mushroom risotto (£9.25) but, being Brixham, you're never far away from seafood too – their linguine with a sauce of fresh Brixham crab, chilli, garlic, fresh parsley & olive oil (£12.50) sounds particularly appetising.

Transport

[See also pp55-60] The town is well connected to the rest of the Riviera (and Kingswear) via Stagecoach's 12, 22 and 24 **bus** services. Assuming the weather and tides are OK Paignton Pleasure Cruises (☎ 01803-529147, or ☎ 0776-762 2727, boat ☎ 0776-801 4174, 💻 www.paigntonpleasurecruises .co.uk; Apr-Oct hourly 10.30am-4.30pm, about £3 single and £5-6 return) operate a **ferry** to Torquay and Paignton; see p169.

BRIXHAM TO TORQUAY   [MAPS 29-33]

For many, this is a stage to endure rather than enjoy. Involving vast stretches where you'll be plodding on pedestrian promenades, this easy (though hard-on-the-ankles) **8½-mile (13.6km; 3hrs 10 mins)** stretch starts with an interesting section of sylvan walking that passes by pretty coves and through ancient woodland. After **Broad Sands**, however, the walk has little to excite unless **beach huts** and **Brunellian railway lines** are your thing.

That said, and in spite of this stage's shortcomings, there are plenty of options for refreshment on the English Riviera. So we advise you not to hurry through. Instead, take your time, spoil yourself with snacks, have your fill of fish & chips and conduct some in-depth research into what flavour ice-cream is your favourite. In doing this, you'll be saving your legs for tomorrow's stage – a stretch which does not allow for such frivolities.

The route

Having left Brixham via the large car-park to the east of the harbour, you follow a set of steps that disappear into woodland. Continue on the path through **Battery Gardens** (see below) ready to defend England since the 16th century and one of the best-preserved WW2 Emergency coastal defence batteries.

At **Fishcombe Cove** there is a seasonal **café** (Easter-Oct daily 10am-6pm, weather permitting), after which you come to the **Battery Heritage Education Centre and Museum** (☎ 01803-852449, 🖳 www.brixhambattery.org; Mon, Fri & Sun 2-4pm also Thur late July-Aug; guided tours available on request; free). Note the fierce snout of the 1950s Humver 'pig' and twelve-pounder gun that guard the centre.

Following the battery you leave the road by **Brixham Holiday Park** and enter **Elberry** and **Marridge** ancient woods (aka **The Grove**). The walk is wonderful and the woods friendly as you pass by the peaceful little **Elberry Cove** (look out for wild campers) before climbing over **Churston Point** to arrive by the multicoloured beach huts at **Broad Sands**. Note the rich red colour of the earth (an indication of iron-rich soil) and watch the trains as they chug along the railway line on the approaching cliffs. It is that railway line you now follow, passing at one point **Saltern Cove** – an SSSI and nature reserve that's unique in Britain as its boundaries extend underwater for 376 metres further than the low-water mark due to its unusual geology.

Goodrington Sands is the next stop, essentially a larger version of the previous beach and the home of *South Sands Café* (Mar-Sep daily 10am-4pm weather permitting). The beach at Goodrington Sands is partitioned by the rocky spit of **Middle Stone** where, nearby, you'll find the popular *Inn on the Quay* (☎ 01803-559754; breakfast served Mon-Fri 6.30am-10.30am, Sat & Sun 7-11am, Mon-Sat noon-10pm; WI-FI), part of the Brewers Fayre chain. Dogs are not allowed in the restaurant but there is an area where they can be left.

A left-turn here will bring you to **The Seashore Centre** (☎ 01803-528841, 🖳 www.countryside-trust.org.uk; daily Apr-Sep 10am-4pm; free), which includes a life-size rockpool room with marine tanks and fun interactive displays; the coast path, however, passes in front of the pub and more beach huts to another **seasonal café**. It then climbs away from the beach to skirt the edge of **Roundham Head** where, as well as the possibility of spotting peregrine falcons and bottlenose dolphins, there is also the opportunity to play pitch 'n' putt.

From here it's a road walk into **Paignton** via the harbour, where there are various eateries.

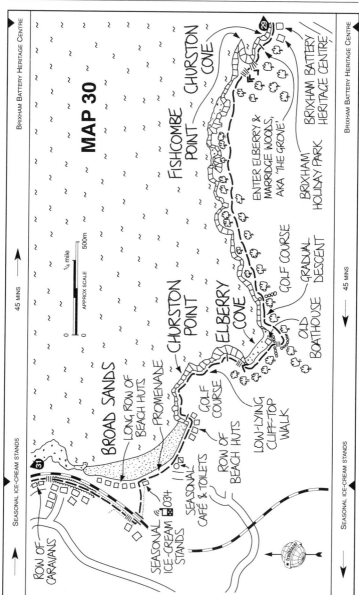

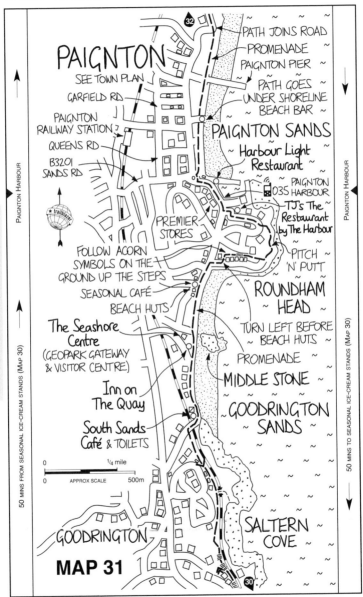

PAIGNTON [map p169]

Few people's favourite place on the path, Paignton is, it must be said, a rather run-down seaside town. It is not entirely without its charms, boasting a fine pier, pleasant harbour area and massive promenade where the pavement is separated from the traffic by a large empty sward of grass. What's more, the bed and breakfasts nearer the centre offer some of the cheapest accommodation along the whole of the South-West Coast Path, so if thrift is your byword Paignton may yet be your place. But for most people, this is a place to storm through rather than stay.

Originally a Celtic settlement and first mentioned in the Domesday Book of 1086, 'Peynton' or 'Paington' (note the spelling) was a small fishing village until the Paington Harbour Act of 1837 initiated the construction of a safe haven for craft in the village; the modern-day spelling, 'Paignton', arrived simultaneously. The town boomed with the construction of the railway in 1859 that linked the Riviera with London (the national rail network no longer goes as far as Brixham or Kingswear, though the Paignton & Dartmouth Steam Railway (see p154) provides some form of substitute).

Should you end up in the town for a while, you could take a relaxed amble amongst the gorillas and crocodiles at **Paignton Zoo** (☎ 0844-474 2222, 🖳 www.paigntonzoo.org.uk; daily 10am-6pm, last entry 5pm, closes earlier out of season; £14.45 inc Gift Aid). Passing the time of day on **Paignton Pier** (☎ 01803-522139, 🖳 www.paigntonpier.co.uk; pier free, charges for the attractions), from where you can admire the sun dancing off the gentle waves of Torbay, may be more appealing.

Torbay Carnival Paignton (🖳 www.torbaycarnival.com) is held here in July.

Services

Paignton Visitor Information Centre (☎ 0844-474 2233, 🖳 www.englishriviera.co.uk; July-Sep Mon-Sat 9.30am-5pm, Sun 10am-3pm, Easter-July & Sep-Oct Mon-Sat 9.30am-4pm; closed Nov-Easter) is in the cinema complex right on the front. Near the railway station on Great Western Rd is the Library and Information Centre (☎ 01803-208321; Mon-Fri 9am-5pm, Sat 9am-4pm, Tue & Thur open until 7pm) where **internet** is available (75p for 30 mins). There are **banks** with **ATMs** around town and there is also a post office here.

For **provisions** there is a Premier Stores (Sun-Thur 7am-9pm, Fri & Sat 7am-10pm), by the harbour; a Spar (daily 8am-10pm) on Torbay Rd, and a Lidl (Mon-Sat 8am-9pm, Sun 11am-5pm) a little further into town on Parkside Rd. A **chemist**, Superdrug (Mon-Sat 8.30am-5.30pm, Sun 10am-5pm) is on Victoria St while there's a fairly decent **bookshop**, Parkside Books (Mon-Sat 10am-5pm, Sun 10.30am-4.30pm), on the road of the same name.

Where to stay

Paignton is almost overrun with bed and breakfast accommodation; however, as with most places on the Riviera (and beyond) the main issue facing walkers will be proprietors' reluctance to take one-night bookings in advance.

Near to the harbour on Sands Rd there are a few decent options. *Seaways* (☎ 01803-551093, 🖳 www.seawayshotel.com; 1S/6D/2T/1F; 🐾 £2; WI-FI; £30-34pp, sgl £30), No 30, has a licensed bar and if requested in advance they will provide a two/four-course dinner (£10/16) at 6pm; they are happy to cater for special diets.

Both *The Sands* (☎ 01803-551282, 🖳 www.hotelsands.co.uk; 2S/7D or T/2F; WI-FI; £29-33pp, sgl £30-35; Mar-Nov), No 32, and *The Briars* (☎ 01803-557729, 🖳 www.briarshotel.co.uk; 1S/10D/1T or F; 🖤; WI-FI; £26-37.50pp, sgl £26-35, sgl occ £40; Feb-Nov), No 26, have a licensed bar although neither serves an evening meal.

The town centre is surrounded by swinging 'vacancy' boards. To the north of Torbay Rd along Garfield Rd you'll find *Blueberry Guesthouse* (☎ 01803-552211, 🖳 www.blueberryhouse.co.uk; 1S/7D; 🖤; WI-FI; £28-34pp, sgl occ £34-40) at No 34.

Also on this road and all just as reasonable are: *Kingswinford* (☎ 01803-558358, www.kingswinfordhotel.com; 7D or F; WI-FI; £24-28pp), No 32; *Beach House* (☎ 01803-525742, karen-l@btconnect.com; 5D/1F; £25-27pp, sgl occ £30) at No 39; and *Rosemead* (☎ 01803-557944, www .rosemeadpaignton.co.uk; 3S/3D/1T/2F; ; WI-FI; £22-30pp) at No 22, which has four-poster beds and a TV lounge for guests. There's also *Belle Dene* (☎ 01803-559645, www.belledeneguesthouse.co .uk; 1S/1T/3D; WI-FI; £25-30pp) at No 25, which has a great sun-trap front garden.

Further good-value places are available on Beach Rd, where you'll find: *Bay Cottage* (☎ 01803-525729, www.baycot tagepaignton.co.uk; 5D/3D or F; WI-FI; £22-25pp, sgl occ £44-50) at No 4; *Barbican Hotel* (☎ 01803-551332, www.barbicanhotelpaignton.co.uk; 5D/2T/ 2T or F; WI-FI; £25pp, sgl occ £30) at No 5; and *Brampton Guest House* (☎ 01803-665389, www.thebrampton.co.uk; 1S/ 1T/4D/3D or F; some en suite and some share facilities; WI-FI; £23-27pp), but they have a minimum three-night stay in July and August plus some bank holidays, at No 11. Nearby there's also *Dalehurst Guest House* (☎ 01803-557628, www.dalehur stguesthousepaignton.co.uk;1S/1T/4D; the single and 2D share facilities, other rooms are en suite; WI-FI; £22.50-30pp; sgl £30-35), 4 Berry Square, which has a couple of rooms that have what they'll honestly describe as a sea 'peep'.

Where to eat and drink

Paignton's residents are nicknamed 'Puddin' Eaters', a moniker that comes from the huge Paignton Pudding, which originated in the 13th century and is historically baked to celebrate local events. Thousands turning up for a piece of the one baked in celebration of the railway's arrival almost caused a riot, such was the desire for a chunk! You'll struggle to find any on a Paignton menu today, at least when there aren't any special occasions being celebrated; but if you do find some for sale somewhere, you'd be foolish to miss the chance!

The best place to eat in our opinion is also one of the first you come to on the path. *TJ's The Restaurant by The Harbour*

(☎ 01803-527389, tjsrestaurant.co.uk; May-Sep food served daily 5.30-9pm, Sat 9.30am-3pm, Sun noon-3pm, Oct-Dec & Mar-May Wed-Sun 5.30-9pm, Sat 9.30am-3pm, Sun noon-3pm – however, it is best to check as the hours depend on the weather/ demand etc; WI-FI) offers the best view of Paignton (though this could be because it's a distant one!) from its fairly lofty vantage point at the southern end of the promenade. They serve a full tapas menu (£2.95-7.95) and have a specials board; mains cost from £9.95 to about £15.95. Occasionally they have music nights. Recommended.

Nearby, the menu at *The Harbour Light Restaurant* (☎ 01803-666500, www.theharbourlight.co.uk; May-Oct daily from 6pm, Oct-Dec & Mar-May Fri, Sat & Sun noon-1.15pm), North Quay, may include a rainbow trout or seafood salad; main courses £12.50-22.

Moving into the centre of town, on Torbay Rd and Victoria St there are plenty of cafés and bars/diners serving up a variety of food. *Maison's Coffee House* (☎ 01803-551097; daily 9am-5pm, Sun 10am-4pm), at 52 Victoria St, is a decent-enough café. A simple pasty or custard doughnut can be purchased at *Hallett's Bakery* (summer Mon-Sat 8am-6pm, winter 8.30am-5pm, Sun 9am-5pm) at 3 Torbay Rd. There is also the usual Wetherspoons bar, *The Talk of the Town* (☎ 01803-668070; food daily 7am-10pm) at 46-52 Torbay Rd, and a couple of pseudo-American establishments nearby: *Grand Central Sports Bar* (☎ 01803-555151; food served daily 8am-9pm), at No 51, where you can tuck into a New York deli bruschetta (£4.50); and, at No 75, *Ocean's Las Vegas Diner* (☎ 01803-526353; summer 8.30am-11pm, winter 10am-8pm), which serves up a reasonable buffalo chicken burger (£7.95).

For takeaways, *Rooses Corner House* (☎ 01803-55812; summer 7am-11pm, winter 8am-8pm), at 49 Torbay Rd, will happily supply the tired walker with fish 'n' chips, while Chinese food can be had at *Thaiisaan Chinese* (☎ 01803-559938, www.thaiisaan.co.uk; daily 11.30am-2.30pm & 6-10.30pm), at No 1, where you'll get a *gaeng baa neua* (jungle curry

with a choice of meat or vegetables in a chilli paste) for £5.85.

There's a second Chinese back near the harbour area, *Rickshaw Boy* (☎ 01803-559901; daily 5-11pm), 55 Roundham Rd, where you can either get a set dinner for one (£8.90) or for two (£17.20).

Transport

[See also pp55-60] Stagecoach's 120 **bus** connects the town to Kingswear; Kingswear and Dartmouth are connected by ferry. To access Brixham or Torquay you will need to catch Stagecoach's No 12

service. First's X80 service goes to Plymouth and the X81 to Dartmouth. Regular **train services** connect the town with Dawlish and Exeter.

Paignton Pleasure Cruises (☎ 01803-529147, or ☎ 0776-762 2727, boat ☎ 0776-801 4174, 🖥 www.paigntonpleasurecruises .co.uk; Apr-Oct hourly 10.30am-4.30pm, about £3 single, £5-6 return) operate a **ferry** service to Torquay and Brixham though this is dependent on the weather, the sea and the tides. It is best to call the boat to check if the service is operating.

The path through Paignton pursues the promenade, passing the pier and the pretty huts at **Preston Sands**.

A brief dalliance with tranquil **Hollicombe Park** – a refreshing respite from the roads and promenades – leads, eventually, to **Corbyn's Head**, where (if

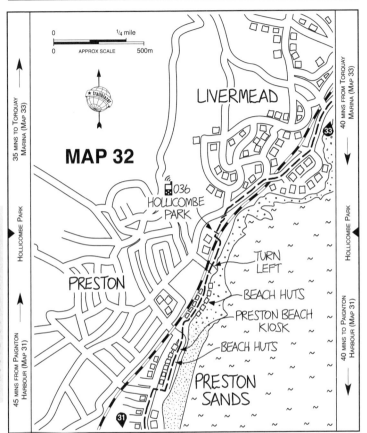

local folklore is to be believed) the pirate Samuel Corbyn was hanged for his swashbuckling crimes.

The beach at **Torre Abbey Sands** was at one time overshadowed by the huge air balloon, HiFlyer in **Abbey Park**. Passing the **Princess Theatre** (🖥 www.princesstheatre.org.uk), you soon arrive at Torquay Marina.

TORQUAY   [map p175]

The largest and most central of the three Riviera towns, Torquay's population swells from somewhere around the 65,000 mark to nearer 200,000 at the height of summer. At these times you'll either have to embrace it or continue to the far more peaceful suburb of St Marychurch – or even, if stamina allows, the blink-and-you'll-miss-it village of Maidencombe.

As with Brixham, Torquay has its origins as a fishing village (though one with an important abbey – see p172) but secured

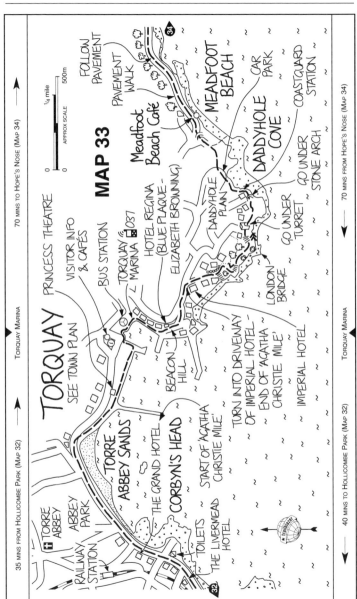

35 MINS FROM HOLLICOMBE PARK (MAP 32)

70 MINS TO HOPE'S NOSE (MAP 34)

TORQUAY MARINA

¼ mile

500m

APPROX SCALE

MAP 33

FOLLOW PAVEMENT

PAVEMENT WALK

Meadfoot Beach Café

MEADFOOT BEACH

CAR PARK

DADDYHOLE COVE

COASTGUARD STATION

GO UNDER STONE ARCH

DADDYHOLE PLAIN

GO UNDER TURRET

LONDON BRIDGE

HOTEL REGINA (BLUE PLAQUE - Elizabeth Browning)

TORQUAY MARINA

BUS STATION

VISITOR INFO & CAFÉS

PRINCESS THEATRE

TORQUAY

SEE TOWN PLAN

BEACON HILL

TURN INTO DRIVEWAY OF IMPERIAL HOTEL - END OF 'AGATHA CHRISTIE MILE'

IMPERIAL HOTEL

THE GRAND HOTEL

TORRE ABBEY SANDS

CORBYN'S HEAD

START OF AGATHA CHRISTIE MILE

TORRE ABBEY

ABBEY PARK

RAILWAY STATION

TOILETS

THE LIVERMEAD HOTEL

TORQUAY MARINA

70 MINS TO HOPE'S NOSE (MAP 34)

40 MINS TO HOLLICOMBE PARK (MAP 32)

an important advantage in the tourism stakes during the Napoleonic Wars. With the Royal Navy spending a lot of time anchored in Tor Bay, it became a chic (if rather exclusive) seaside resort, where the relatives of the boats' officers would visit. It was during the Victorian era that Torquay and its environs earned the nickname of the English Riviera, its mild and healthy climate being part of the attraction for holidaymakers as well as those wishing to convalesce. The opening of the town's railway stations (in 1848 and 1859) further accelerated Torquay's popularity.

Torre Abbey (☎ 01803-293593, 💻 www.torre-abbey.org.uk), the first building of note in the town, was a Premonstratensian (a Catholic order of canons founded at Premontre) monastery founded in 1196. Today it houses an art collection, runs tours and invites you to explore its exotic gardens. Under restoration at the time of research, the abbey should be reopening in July 2013 and can be found on the corner of Avenue Rd and Chestnut Ave, at the rear of Abbey Park. **Living Coasts** (☎ 0844-474 3366, 💻 www.livingcoasts.org.uk; daily 10am-5pm, to 6pm in summer months; £10) is Torquay's very own coastal zoo where penguins play and fur seals frolic. As you leave town, look for the nets on the right as you head up Beacon Hill and you can't miss it.

The area's most famous discovery, a prehistoric jawbone found at Kent's Cavern (see box p158), can currently be seen in **Torquay Museum** (☎ 01803-293975, 💻 www.torquaymuseum.org; Mon-Sat 10am-5pm, Sun mid-July to Sep 1.30-5pm; £4.90), which also tells the story of the caves and houses an Agatha Christie gallery (see box below).

Agatha Christie Festival (💻 www.englishriviera.co.uk/agathachristie/agatha-christie-festival) is held in and around the

---

❑ Torquay's most famous daughter: Agatha Christie

No-one can accuse Torquay of under-exploiting the legacy of its most famous daughter. In addition to **The Agatha Christie Literary Trail** and the **Agatha Christie Mile** (see opposite), the town also hosts an annual **Agatha Christie Festival** (see above) every September. But who exactly was Agatha Christie, anyway – and what precisely was her connection with the town?

Ms Christie's biography is, of course, fairly well documented. Born on 15th September, 1890, during her spectacularly successful career Agatha Christie tried her hand at a variety of formats and genres, from short stories to plays and even romances (under the pseudonym Mary Westmacott). But it is, of course, her crime fiction, particularly those stories involving the detectives Miss Marple and Hercule Poirot, that gave her worldwide fame and even earned her the sobriquet the 'Queen of Crime'. Her novels have sold over a staggering four billion copies, a figure that puts her third on the bestsellers list behind only Shakespeare and The Bible. What's more, her play *The Mousetrap*, having opened in November 1952, is still running in London's West End to this day, having ratcheted up over an incredible 24,500 performances (still the record for the longest initial run of any play).

There is no doubt that Agatha's Christie's links with Torquay are numerous. Born in the town in 1890, she also honeymooned here in 1914, worked as a nurse in the local hospital during the First World War and – though she travelled widely between the wars – in 1938 she and her second husband, the archaeologist Max Mallowan, purchased a holiday home on the nearby River Dart. Perhaps more importantly, however, Christie was greatly inspired by the rugged moors, cliffs, beaches, villages and islands of South Devon, many of which are recognisable (albeit under different names) in much of her work. Indeed the best-selling mystery novel of all time, *And Then There Were None* (1939), takes place on fictional Soldier Island which Agatha Christie based on Burgh Island (see box p119) in Bigbury Bay.

town during September. Some of the events in Torbay's **Festival of Poetry** (🖳 www .torbaypoetryfestival.co.uk) are held here in October.

Services

The **English Riviera Visitor Information Centre** (☎ 01803-211211, 🖳 www.english riviera.co.uk; July-Sep Mon-Sat 9.30am-5pm, Sun 10am-3pm, Easter-July & Sep-Oct Mon-Sat 9.30am-4pm; Nov-Easter Mon-Sat 10am-4pm) is conveniently placed on the front. For **internet**, once again the library (Mon, Wed & Fri 9.30am-7pm, Tue 9.30am-5pm, Thur 9.30am-1pm, Sat 9.30am-4pm) is the place to head to though it is a fair distance away from the path. Head up the main shopping thoroughfare, Union St, taking a right at Castle Circus to Lymington Rd; and it's on the left. There are plenty of **banks** with **ATMs** around town.

For **trekking gear and supplies**, Mountain Warehouse (Mon-Sat 9am-5.30pm, Sun 10.30am-4.30pm) and Trespass (Mon-Sat 9am-5.30pm, Sun 10.30am-4.30pm) sit next to each other. Above them is a branch of Jessops the **camera** people (Mon-Sat 9am-5.30pm, Sun 10.30am-4.30pm), opposite is the **chemist**, Boots (Mon-Sat 9am-5.30pm, Sun 10.30am-4.30pm) and further down the road on the same side is the **post office** (Mon-Sat 9am-5.30pm), hidden away in the local branch of WH Smith, and the **supermarket** Tesco (Mon-Sat 7am-10pm, Sun 11am-5pm); there is also a **convenience store**, McColl's (Mon-Sat 7am-11pm, Sun to 10pm), nearer the Marina.

Where to stay

It will be no surprise that Torquay is full of accommodation aimed at the holidaying masses. Behind Abbey Park and along

The island also features (though this time it's called Smugglers' Island) as Poirot's holiday destination in *Evil Under the Sun* (1941), the super sleuth's vacation being rather rudely interrupted by the discovery of an actress's strangled body in a nearby cove.

Today, Christie-philes – of which, to judge by the crowds that swarm in summer around all things Agatha, there are many – have plenty of ways of indulging their passion in her hometown. The holiday home she bought with her second husband, **The Greenway Estate** (☎ 01803-842382, 🖳 www.nationaltrust.org.uk/greenway; Feb-Oct Wed-Sun 10.30am-5pm, Tue-Sun in summer hols; £9.75 inc Gift Aid, £8.75 without, NT members free), is open to the public and can be reached by either bus or boat. The vintage **Greenway House Bus** (🖳 greenwayferry.co.uk/bus-trips; Feb-Oct 10am & 2pm; £10 return) is a classic green 1947 charabanc that you'll probably see driving along the esplanade of Paignton. If getting on the bus at Belgrave Rd ensure you get on the AC1 as it goes door to door whereas some other bus services deposit passengers about 1½ miles from Greenway.

Greenway Ferries also operate the large heritage ship, the *Fairmile* (☎ 01803-882811, 🖳 www.greenwayferry.co.uk; Feb-Oct Wed-Sun 10.45am; £14 return) to Greenway but since it takes two hours each way if wanting to go by boat it is better to go from Dartmouth (see p153) as the service operates hourly and takes less time.

There's also the **Agatha Christie Literary Trail**, stretching from Greenway on the River Dart to Babbacombe (north of Torquay), that links 20 of the writer's novels with locations that are believed to have influenced or inspired them. And the **Agatha Christie Mile** (see Map 33, p171) which begins at The Grand Hotel – where she honeymooned – and continues along Torquay seafront to The Imperial Hotel, which features in a number of her novels. For more details, the English Riviera Tourist Board produces a leaflet on both trails.

ROUTE GUIDE AND MAPS

Belgrave and Avenue roads there are numerous B&Bs and hotels; once again, however, finding one willing to do a one-night stop can be problematic.

Those that will accept a one-night booking along Belgrave Rd include the remarkably cheap *The Wayfarer* (☎ 01803-299138, 🖥 www.wayfarertorquay.co.uk; 1S/4D/2D or T; WI-FI; £22-32.50pp, sgl/sgl occ £32-50), No 37, where dinner can also be provided (£15 for three courses); *Kethla* (☎ 01803-294995, 🖥 www.kethlahouse.co.uk; 4D/3D, T or F; WI-FI; £27.50-31pp, sgl occ £35-48), No 33, who willingly cater for any special dietary requirements; and *Cranborne* (☎ 01803-211660, 🖥 www.cranbornetorquay.co.uk; 1S/7D/2T; ♥; WI-FI; £30-40pp) at No 58, which has a cocktail bar.

On Scarborough Rd, just off Belgrave Rd, you'll come across *South View* (☎ 01803-296029, 🖥 www.thesouthview.com; 4D/2D or T; ♥; internet access; £27.50-30pp, sgl occ £30-45), at No 12, another place where evening meals are available (£14), and *The Southbank* (☎ 01803-296701, 🖥 www.southbankhotel.co.uk; 2S/2D or T/5D/5F; ♥; WI-FI; £30-32.50pp, sgl 30-35, sgl occ by negotiation), Nos 15-17; neither, unfortunately, take one-night bookings in July and August. The Southbank is licensed and a bar meal (à la carte) is available 6-8pm.

It's a similar story along Chestnut Ave at Avenue Rd and *Avenue Park* (☎ 01803-293902, 🖥 www.avenuepark.co.uk; 6D/2D or T; WI-FI; £36-48pp, sgl occ £50; mid Mar to mid Nov) at No 3.

Nearer to the town centre on Babbacombe Rd and willing to take one-night bookings year-round are *Tusker Lodge* (☎ 01803-292668, 🖥 www.tuskerlodge.co.uk; 4S/5D/2T, shared facilities for single rooms; ♥; WI-FI; £25-31pp; Feb to mid Dec), at No 533, and *Ravenswood* (☎ 01803-292900, 🖥 www.ravenswoodhotel.co.uk;

1S/5D/1T/1F, all en suite though the single shares the bathroom with anyone wanting a bath; ♥; WI-FI; £27-30pp), at No 535.

Others worth considering on this stretch of road are the dog-friendly *Torwood Gardens Hotel* (☎ 01803-298408, 🖥 www.torwoodgardenshotel.co.uk; 1S/8D; ♥; 🐾; WI-FI; £30-35pp, sgl £25-30pp; Easter to end Oct only), at No 531, who will accept one-night stays if they have space on the day, and *The Palms Hotel* (☎ 01803-293970, 🖥 www.palmshoteltorquay.co.uk; 1S/5D/2T/1F; 🐾 £10; WI-FI; £25-40pp, sgl £25-30), No 537, who also welcome dogs. They have a bar which serves snacks such as jacket potatoes (£3.99) and also provide card and board games to help you while away any wet evenings spent in their bar. One-night bookings are welcomed year-round although they try to avoid them at the weekends where possible.

Still on Babbacombe, is *Kingsholm* (☎ 01803-297794, 🖥 www.kingsholmhotel.co.uk; 1S/5D/3T; ♥; WI-FI; £30-32.50pp, sgl £30-35, sgl occ £50-55) at No 539; again, they do not accept one-night bookings in advance in July and August but will happily put you up on the day if they have space.

Also on Babbacombe Rd are *Hotel Peppers* (☎ 01803-293856, 🖥 www.hotel-peppers.co.uk; 2S/8D or T; WI-FI; £28-36pp, sgl occ £46-62), at No 551, which has a licensed bar and is more than willing to put walkers up for a solitary night; and *Hotel Hudson* (☎ 01803-203407, 🖥 www.hotel hudson.co.uk; 2S/6D/2D or T; WI-FI; £27.50-39.50pp, sgl £37.50-40), No 545, which does not take one-night bookings at the weekends between April and September.

At the top of the hill (74 Braddons Hill Rd East) is the dog-friendly *Robin Hill International Hotel* (☎ 01803-214518, 🖥 robinhillhotel.co.uk; 5D/5T; WI-FI; 🐾;

❏ **Where to stay: the details**
Unless specified, B&B-style accommodation is either en suite or has private facilities; ♥ means at least one room has a bath; 🐾 signifies that dogs are welcome in at least one room but always by prior arrangement, an additional charge may also be payable; WI-FI means wi-fi is available in the property, though not always (reliably) in every room.

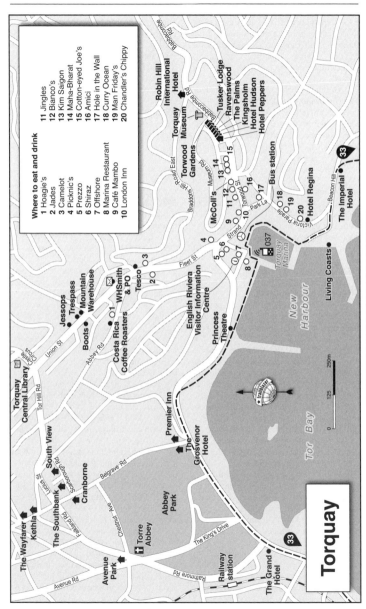

£35-60pp, sgl occ £50-65). It's a great place to stop although it's a fair old march from the path itself (however, Stagecoach's No 32 bus service stops near the top of Babbacombe Rd and leaves from The Strand).

Hotels available in Torquay include *The Grosvenor* (☎ 01803-294373, 🖥 www .grosvenorhoteltorquay.co.uk; 46 flexible rooms; ☛; 🐾; WI-FI; £39-67pp, sgl £39-57pp, sgl occ £78-114), also on Belgrave Rd, which has featured in the Channel 4 series *The Hotel*.

There is a branch of the *Premier Inn* (☎ 0871-527 9102, 🖥 www.premierinn .com/en/hotel/TORBEL/torquay; 143 flexible rooms; ☛; WI-FI, in room first half-hour free then £3 per 24hrs, free in bar/restaurant; from £65 per room but rates change daily; breakfast cooked £8.25 continental £5.25) chain just a short distance from the seafront and path at the bottom of Belgrave Rd. Check their website for any special deals.

Where to eat and drink
For a lunchtime feed-up the most popular destination in town is *Picknics* (aka *Big Baguette*; ☎ 01803-200444, 🖥 www.pick nics.co.uk; Mon-Fri 9.30am-3.30pm, Sat 9.30am-4.30pm) at the bottom of Fleet St. The size of their menu is almost over-whelming, as are the sometimes lovely combinations of fillings for their sarnies. Particularly popular are the hot cheese bombers (filled baguettes with hot cheese from £4.40) and their line of 'hot roast in a roll' (eg pork, stuffing and apple sauce for £3.50). They also sell local preserves and chutneys that make great souvenirs for any gourmands you happen to know.

Just a few steps down from here, across the busy Strand, the marina area on Torquay seafront is knee-deep in restau-rants. Some of them look quite sophisticat-ed but, thanks to the large amounts of com-petition, prices remain reasonable. The variety of food on offer here includes such traditional staples as cod & chips (£5.25) from *Chandler's Chippy* (☎ 01803-215213; daily Apr-Sep 10am-10pm, Oct to 6pm, to 3pm in winter) on Victoria Parade, who've been serving the good people of

Torquay for over 50 years now, to more imaginative fare at *Offshore* (☎ 01803-292108; food served daily 9am-9pm), with such unusual delights as squid and chorizo risotto (£10.95). They also make the most of the late licence they've been granted, with live music from 10pm to midnight. Despite its exotic name *Shiraz* (☎ 01803-200201; summer daily 9am-midnight, win-ter to 6pm on weekdays) does some pretty standard English fare such as fish & chips and some good special offers (eg two meals for £9.95 including roast chicken, chips, peas & gravy). At the end of the strip, *Prezzo* is a branch of an upmarket nation-wide pizza chain, with pizzas from just £5.95. At the other end of this strip, *Marina Restaurant* (☎ 01803-292255, 🖥 www .marinarestaurant.co.uk; Easter to Oct daily noon-2pm & 6-9.30pm, to 10pm on Sat; Oct to Easter Tue-Sat noon-2pm & 6-9.30pm, Sun noon-2.30pm only) is a big glass-sided affair with some of the best views of the harbour in the town: get a seat on the eastern wing if you can. They have a set two-/three-course menu (£14.95/18.95) in the evening; their à la carte options include pan-seared fillet of sea bass with new potatoes, prawns, capers & parsley butter for £15.95. They boast that, where possible, the fish they use in their meals has been bought from the trawlers that dock just 100 yards away – so it should be fresh!

Across the other side of the Marina on Victoria Parade are more interesting options: *Man Friday's* (☎ 01803-296416, 🖥 www.manfridays.co.uk; summer daily 7pm to late, closed Mon & Tue in winter) is a lovely, intriguing little fish restaurant with a very appetising menu including a selection of ocean kebabs – swordfish, blue-fin tuna, salmon and king prawns speared with pep-pers and shallots – at £15.95, a half lobster thermidor for £29.95, and monkfish wrapped in parma ham is £17.95.

Perhaps even more intriguing, howev-er, *Curry Ocean* (☎ 01803-292851; daily 12.30-2pm & 5.30pm to midnight) is a con-temporary Indian restaurant; try their *masi naga* – fish cooked in chilli pickle and sliced potatoes in spices. They do take-aways too.

Facing the marina from its location on The Strand, *Café Mambo* (☎ 01803-291112, 🖳 www.cafemambo.co.uk/torquay/; food daily 11.30am-9pm) is possibly the only Thai-English-Caribbean restaurant in the country! It's a big place, with WI-FI, and overlooks the front, though it's fair to say it won't be to everyone's taste, catering more for parties. Still, the food's not bad, with jerk steak (£10.25) and pad thai (£6.95).

Moving away from the front, one of the loveliest aspects of a stay in Torquay is the smell of coffee that wafts across parts of the town from the **Costa Rica coffee roasters** (🖳 www.costa-rica.co.uk), a family firm at 49 Abbey Rd that's been going for over 50 years now. If the smell on Friday morning is too much to resist, you can buy a cup made from the fruits of their labours at nearby *Hoagie's* (Mon-Fri 7.30am-2.30pm, Sat 8am-2pm), nearby, which does gammon, eggs & chips for £4, or an all-u-can-eat breakfast for £5. A good coffee shop, one that doesn't sell the local roasters' coffee but does have WI-FI and friendly staff, is *Jades* (Mon-Fri 8.30am-5.30pm, Sat 8.30am-6pm, Sun 9.30am-4pm), upstairs on Fleet Walk.

There is another pocket of great cosmopolitan options at the foot of Torwood St, where cuisines from all over the world stand together in (fairly) friendly rivalry. Amongst their number is *Bianco's* (☎ 01803-293430; daily 6-11pm), possibly the best Italian in town (try their *cappelletti ai porcini* – pasta filled with wild mushrooms in a creamy sauce of porcini mushrooms and truffles for £14.95); while across the way is *Amici* (☎ 01803-201770, 🖳 www.amicitorquay.co.uk; daily noon-11pm), another Italian with an outside eating area – though it can be a little noisy next to the busy road. *Jingles* (☎ 01803-293340, 🖳 www.jinglesrestaurant.com; Mon-Sat 6pm to late, Sun 7pm to late) is a typically exuberant Mexican restaurant, where you can eat enchilladas to your heart's content (or your wallet's limit: two beef, veg or chicken enchilladas are £12.95).

Moving north of the busy junction with The Terrace, there are three more places to consider: *Maha-Bharat* (☎

01803-215541, 🖳 www.maha-bharat-torquay.co.uk; daily 5pm to midnight) is an Indian restaurant with an emphasis on Bengali cuisine and some excellent Balti dishes (£5.95-10.95); while *Kim Saigon* (☎ 01803-213344, 🖳 kimsaigon.co.uk; summer noon-2.30pm & 5.30-11.30pm; winter eves only), is a Vietnamese that also offers Chinese and Cantonese dishes. *Cotton-eyed Joe's* (☎ 01803-214444, 🖳 www.cotton eyedjoes.co.uk; daily 5-10pm) is an American bar and grill with starters for £4.25 and steaks £10.95-18.50.

Fleet St, the main shopping street in Torquay, is not the best hunting ground for food but there are some possibilities.

For a feast, the Medieval-themed *Camelot* (☎ 01803-215399; 🖳 camelot-tq .com; daily 11am-10pm) dishes up a modern banquet. As you'd expect, the ale comes in pitchers, the wine in goblets and the food in massive portions, with such gut-busting grub as Guinevere's Platter (complete with lamb cutlets, steak, belly pork and a rack of ribs) at £29.95 for two people to share.

For **pubs**, the best in town is the discreet *Hole in the Wall* (☎ 01803-200755, 🖳 www.holeinthewalltorquay.co.uk; food daily noon-2.30 & 5.30-10pm, from 6pm on a Sat), 6 Park Lane, Torquay's oldest inn (c1540) with traditional hand-pumped beers, live music some nights, and fresh fish including Brixham local cod (£12.95).

Wetherspoons have their usual representative, too, in this case *London Inn* (☎ 01803-380003, 🖳 www.jdwetherspoon.co .uk/home/pubs/the-london-inn; food served daily 8am-10pm) where they operate a Curry Club on Thursday, with curries £5.75 including a free drink! Great value, of course – though as is usual for Wetherspoons, they don't allow dogs.

Transport
[See also pp55-60] Stagecoach's 11 and 12 **buses** travel as far west as Brixham and east as Shaldon and Teignmouth.

Regular **trains** connect the town with Paignton, Dawlish and Exeter.

For a **taxi** try 1st Class Cars (☎ 01803-299305).

TORQUAY TO TEIGNMOUTH   [MAPS 33-37]

This is a strenuous **11¼-mile (18km; 4hrs 35mins plus 10 mins for the ferry crossing to Teignmouth)** walk: after the concrete monotony of the previous stage it's time to open the lungs again and get back out into the wilds. Having passed Hope's Nose, Torbay is finally left behind and although you'll be sucked back into civilisation briefly at St Marychurch, for most of this stage you'll find yourself enjoying some beautiful walking and mesmerising views interrupted only by the occasional and pleasantly isolated public house or seasonal café.

With a ferry crossing (before you set off make sure you have checked the ferry times) from Shaldon to Teignmouth at the end of the day and numerous twists and turns, ascents and descents along the way, this stage should not be underestimated. Planning for rest-stops would be wise as well as carrying ample food and water.

The route

Leaving Torquay can take a little concentration: look for acorns on the ground and stickers on lamp posts – as well as more orthodox signage – and you should be fine. Eventually, after turning right at **The Imperial Hotel**, the path finally finds some space and freedom from humanity through a stone archway leading to **Daddyhole Plain**; due to its Devonian limestone, its accompanying cove is one of the Riviera's geosites (see box p158).

The path now passes through woodland overlooking **Meadfoot Beach** where there is *Meadfoot Beach Café* (☎ 01803-213988, 🖳 www.meadfoot beachcafe.co.uk; Mar/Apr-Oct/Nov daily 9am-5pm depending on the weather), before rounding **Thatcher Point**. More road-rambling brings you to a junction where, officially at least, the coast path turns right down to **Hope's Nose** (🖳 www.hopesnose.ukfossils.co.uk) – an SSSI (note that because it is an SSSI you can't hammer the rock in search of fossils or take specimens; you can only photograph any fossils you see) and the northern promontory of Tor Bay – before following a path above the road to continue. Wonderful woodland walking now follows as you continue along **Black Head** past **Anstey's Cove**.

Kent's Cavern (☎ 01803-215136, 🖳 www.kents-cavern.co.uk; off Map 34; Apr-Oct daily 9.30am-5pm, Nov-Mar 10am-4.30pm, café 9.30am-4.30pm, guided tours 11am, 12.30pm, 2pm, 3.30pm & 4/4.30pm in summer; £8.95), a prehistoric cave system where in 1927 the oldest human fossil – an upper jawbone – yet to be discovered in the UK was unearthed, can be accessed by turning left and heading inland here; it is about a 10-minute walk.

The coast path, however, continues above **Redgate Beach** to **Long Quarry Point**. The signage is particularly poor here but look out for a wooden signpost leading off into the trees shortly after the mock-Roman shelter. Descending steep wooded steps you eventually arrive at the charming *Cary Arms* (☎ 01803-327110, 🖳 www.caryarms.co.uk; 7D/1F; 🐾; 🐕 £15, will also provide a doggy meal £5; WI-FI; £85-135pp, sgl occ £120-220; food served daily noon-3pm & 6.30-9pm), where, if starving, their Devon Steak and Otter Ale pie (£13.95) may well prove too tempting to resist on a chilly day.

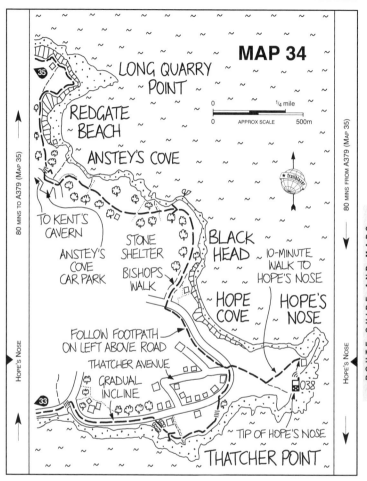

From the pub you can see where, in 2010, a 5000-tonne rockfall occurred at the northern end of **Oddicombe Beach** near **Petit Tor Point**. The path avoids this by climbing steeply beside **Babbacombe Cliff Railway** (☎ 01803-328750, 🖥 www.babbacombecliffrailway.co.uk; Jun-Sep daily 9.30am-6pm, Feb-May & Oct 9.30am-5pm, Nov & Dec weekends only; £1.60, £1.90 return) and so on, eventually, to the A379. Here you can either turn right to continue along the coastal path, or left to St Marychurch.

ST MARYCHURCH [Map 35]

An outer suburb of Torquay, St Marychurch plays host to the **Bygones Museum** (☎ 01803-326108, 🖥 www.bygones.co.uk; daily Nov-Mar 10am-3pm, Apr-Sep 10am-5pm, Oct 10am-4pm; £7.95), where there are numerous displays relating to the Victorian era as well as a life-size Victorian street.

Services here include a Co-op **supermarket** (daily 7am-10pm) with **ATM**, a Boots the **Chemist** (Mon-Fri 9am-5.30pm, Sat 9am-1pm) and, opposite, a **post office** (Mon-Fri 9am-5.30pm, Sat 9am-1pm).

Food-wise, at the top of the railway is *Cliff Railway Café* (☎ 01803-324025; daily 9.30am-4.30pm, to 5pm in summer, food served till 4pm). On Fore St, *Babbs Café & Restaurant* (☎ 01803-312619; Mon-Sat 9am-5pm, Sun 10am-4pm) serves all-day breakfasts (£4.50) and lasagne (£5.25), as well as cream teas (£3.45) and cake and coffee (£2.75). At No 55, *Driftwood Café* (☎ 01803-314057, 🖥 www.driftwood-torquay .co.uk; Mon-Sat 9am-5pm) also supplies 'a cake and a cuppa' deal (£3.50) as well as producing vegetarian soup (£3.50) and daily

specials (£4.95). For a pre-9am breakfast, *AJ's* (Mon-Fri 7.30am-3pm, Sat 7.30am-2pm), just off Fore St at 8 Foxlands Walk, is your best bet. You can get a great bacon bap (£2.60) or a breakfast special which includes a bap and a hot drink (£3). Back on Fore St, *Halletts Bakery* (Mon-Fri 9am-6pm, Sat 9am-1pm) will happily supply a lunch-time pasty (£1.70).

There are two pubs on Fore St too: *Molloys* (☎ 01803-311825; food Mon-Thur 11am-3pm, Fri-Sun 11.30am-4pm), where you'll get a Sunday roast for £6.95; and *The Dolphin Inn* (☎ 01803-328462; food Tue-Sat noon-9pm, Sun 1-8pm, school summer hols Mon noon-8pm; WI-FI) where a 10oz rump steak costs £10.95.

For a **B&B**, *Blue Conifer* (☎ 01803-327637, 🖥 www.blueconifer.co.uk; 3D/1T/3F; ➷; 🐾 £2; WI-FI; £30-36pp, sgl occ £40-46; Mar-Oct) has wonderful sea views over Oddicombe Beach.

Stagecoach's No 11 **bus** (see pp55-60) connects St Marychurch with both Torquay and Teignmouth.

You stay with the A379 only until the next roundabout, where Petitor Rd takes you to the back of the tor. Passing through the woods that decorate **Shag Cliff** you cross the track leading to **Watcombe Beach** where you'll find a **seasonal café** and **toilet**. More woodland wandering brings you to Maidencombe via a beautiful little glade called **Valley of Rocks** and a junction with the John Musgrave Heritage Trail

MAIDENCOMBE [Map 36, p182]

A quiet and remote cluster of houses, the centre of focus being the delightful *Thatched Tavern* (☎ 01803-329155, 🖥 www.thethatchedtaverndevon.co.uk; 2D; ➷; 🐾 in the pub area only; WI-FI; £50pp, sgl occ £80). This is the only place near the trail between Torquay and Shaldon that offers B&B. They also sell excellent **food** (served Mon-Sat noon-2.30pm & 6-9pm,

Sun noon-7.30pm). Brixham crab sandwiches are £6.95 and cream teas (Easter to Sep only) are £5.50. Mains start from £8 but they also have a specials board which may include venison casserole (£11.95). All of these can be enjoyed in their delightful garden.

You need to walk up to Maidencombe Cross to catch Stagecoach's 11 **bus** (Torquay to Teignmouth), see pp55-60.

❏ **Important note – walking times**
Unless otherwise specified, **all times in this book refer only to the time spent walking**. You will need to add 20-30% to allow for rests, photography, checking the map, drinking water etc. When planning the day's hike count on 5-7 hours of actual walking.

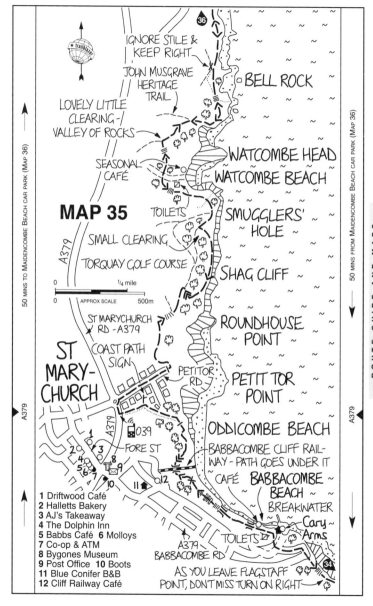

IGNORE STILE &
KEEP RIGHT

JOHN MUSGRAVE
HERITAGE
TRAIL

BELL ROCK

LOVELY LITTLE
CLEARING -
VALLEY OF ROCKS

SEASONAL
CAFÉ

WATCOMBE HEAD
WATCOMBE BEACH

MAP 35

TOILETS

SMUGGLERS'
HOLE

SMALL CLEARING

TORQUAY GOLF COURSE

SHAG CLIFF

A379

ST MARYCHURCH
RD - A379

ROUNDHOUSE
POINT

COAST PATH
SIGN

PETITOR
RD

PETIT TOR
POINT

ST
MARY-
CHURCH

A379

039

FORE ST

ODDICOMBE BEACH

BABBACOMBE CLIFF RAIL-
WAY - PATH GOES UNDER IT

CAFÉ BABBACOMBE
BEACH

BREAKWATER

Cary
Arms

1 Driftwood Café
2 Halletts Bakery
3 AJ's Takeaway
4 The Dolphin Inn
5 Babbs Café 6 Molloys
7 Co-op & ATM
8 Bygones Museum
9 Post Office 10 Boots
11 Blue Conifer B&B
12 Cliff Railway Café

TOILETS

A379
BABBACOMBE RD

AS YOU LEAVE FLAGSTAFF
POINT, DON'T MISS TURN ON RIGHT

0   1/4 mile
0   APPROX SCALE   500m

50 MINS TO MAIDENCOMBE BEACH CAR PARK (MAP 36)

50 MINS FROM MAIDENCOMBE BEACH CAR PARK (MAP 36)

A379

A379

ROUTE GUIDE AND MAPS

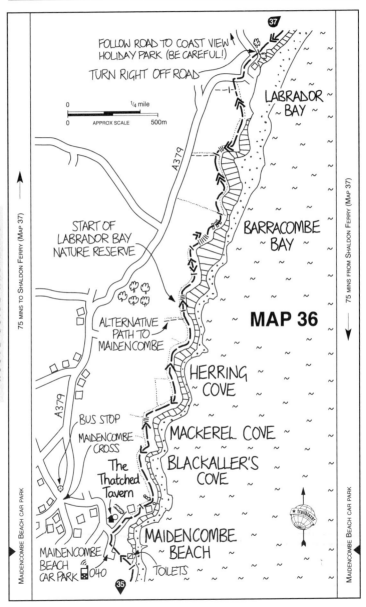

FOLLOW ROAD TO COAST VIEW
HOLIDAY PARK (BE CAREFUL!)

TURN RIGHT OFF ROAD

LABRADOR
~ BAY ~

0   ¼ mile
0   APPROX SCALE   500m

A379

START OF
LABRADOR BAY
NATURE RESERVE

BARRACOMBE
~ BAY ~

MAP 36

ALTERNATIVE
PATH TO
MAIDENCOMBE

HERRING
~ COVE ~

A379

BUS STOP

MAIDENCOMBE
CROSS

MACKEREL COVE ~

The
Thatched
Tavern

BLACKALLER'S
~ COVE ~

MAIDENCOMBE
~ BEACH ~

MAIDENCOMBE
BEACH
CAR PARK

☎040

35

★ trailblazer

TOILETS ~

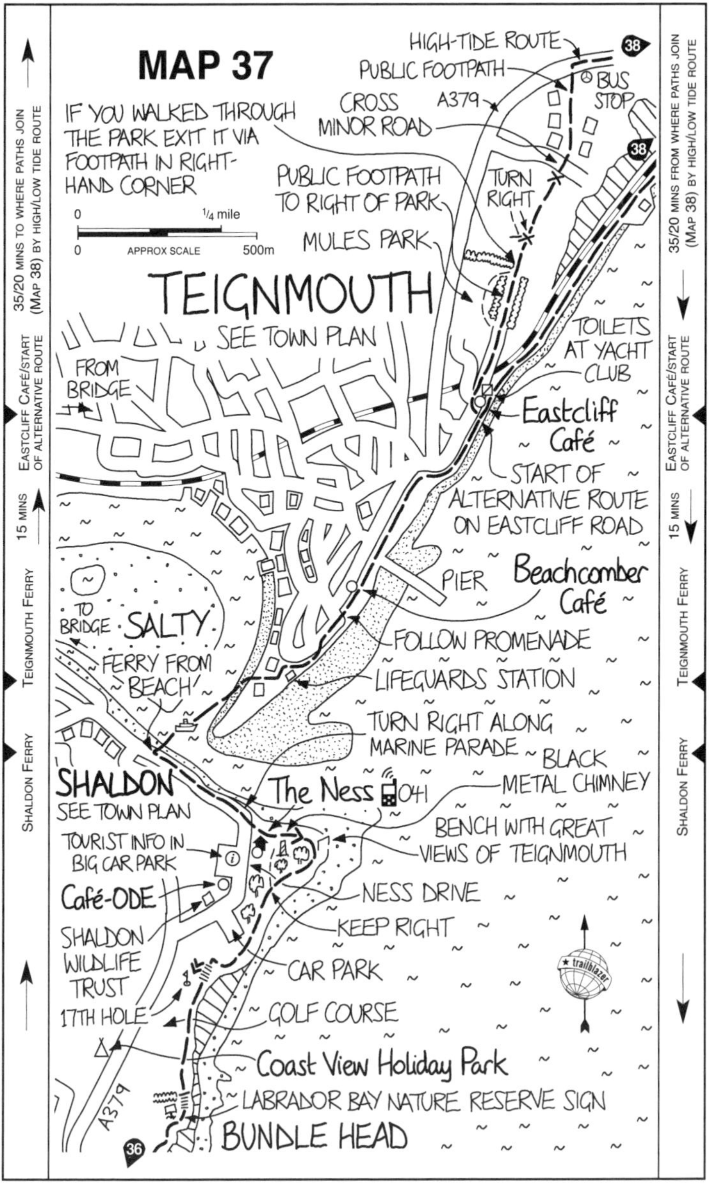
MAP 37
IF YOU WALKED THROUGH THE PARK EXIT IT VIA FOOTPATH IN RIGHT-HAND CORNER
HIGH-TIDE ROUTE
PUBLIC FOOTPATH
CROSS MINOR ROAD
A379
BUS STOP
38
PUBLIC FOOTPATH TO RIGHT OF PARK
TURN RIGHT
0
1/4 mile
0
APPROX SCALE
500m
MULES PARK
TEIGNMOUTH
SEE TOWN PLAN
FROM BRIDGE
TOILETS AT YACHT CLUB
Eastcliff Café
START OF ALTERNATIVE ROUTE ON EASTCLIFF ROAD
PIER
Beachcomber Café
TO BRIDGE
SALTY
FERRY FROM BEACH
FOLLOW PROMENADE
LIFEGUARDS STATION
TURN RIGHT ALONG MARINE PARADE
BLACK METAL CHIMNEY
SHALDON
SEE TOWN PLAN
The Ness
041
TOURIST INFO IN BIG CAR PARK
BENCH WITH GREAT VIEWS OF TEIGNMOUTH
Café-ODE
NESS DRIVE
KEEP RIGHT
SHALDON WILDLIFE TRUST
CAR PARK
17TH HOLE
GOLF COURSE
Coast View Holiday Park
A379
LABRADOR BAY NATURE RESERVE SIGN
BUNDLE HEAD
36
35/20 MINS TO WHERE PATHS JOIN (MAP 38) BY HIGH/LOW TIDE ROUTE
EASTCLIFF CAFÉ/START OF ALTERNATIVE ROUTE
15 MINS
TEIGNMOUTH FERRY
SHALDON FERRY
35/20 MINS FROM WHERE PATHS JOIN (MAP 38) BY HIGH/LOW TIDE ROUTE
EASTCLIFF CAFÉ/START OF ALTERNATIVE ROUTE
15 MINS
TEIGNMOUTH FERRY
SHALDON FERRY
trailblazer

A gravel path takes you away from Maidencombe; following the copper-coloured cliffs it careens its way past **Blackaller's** and **Mackerel coves**, never seeming to find a straight (or horizontal) line until arriving at **Labrador Bay Nature Reserve** (🖥 www.rspb.org.uk/reserves/guide/l/labradorbay). Purchased by the RSPB in 2008 the reserve's aim is to help protect the **cirl bunting**, a rare bird which is almost unique to South Devon. Other species regularly spotted include buzzards, peregrines and yellowhammers.

The path continues to dip and rise steeply via several combes, rejoining the A379 briefly before heading back into the fields. As you climb over **Bundle Head**, Teignmouth comes into full view – as does Shaldon Golf Course below you. Exmouth can also be seen – just – in the distance. A flat amble by the golf course brings you to a pleasant walk through woods. A bench offers a tremendous view across Teignmouth Pier as well as the delights that await you over the next few days.

Dropping down through the woods you arrive at a pub, The Ness (see opposite), on the outskirts of smart Shaldon.

SHALDON

The quiet Georgian village of Shaldon offers a peaceful alternative to staying over the water in Teignmouth (not that it's especially boisterous there either!). It's a pity that most people hurry over the Teign as Shaldon is much more than just a commuter village. For a start, it has a few decent accommodation options as well as a couple of very likeable boozers serving hearty food in an amiable atmosphere. It also boasts a **botanical garden** (Homeyards, built by the founder of Liqufruta cough medicine and with its own ruined castle!; open all year, free), **limekiln** (behind The Ness pub) and even a small **zoo**: **Shaldon Wildlife Trust** (☎ 01626-872234, 🖥 www .shaldonwildlifetrust.org.uk; summer daily 10am-6pm, winter daily 11am-4pm; £6.75/6.10 with/without Gift Aid) is set in one acre of woodland on Ness Drive and plays host to several endangered animals including the smallest monkey in the world, the South American pygmy marmoset.

The town also has its own **music festival** (🖥 www.shaldonfestival.co.uk) in June and a **water carnival** (🖥 www.shaldonwa tercarnival.co.uk) in August. Furthermore, when visiting in summer do not be surprised to see local people dressed in Georgian costume: Wednesdays between early June and mid September are known as

1785 day with celebrations including a farmer's market and craft fair (10am-4pm), as well as maypole dancing and Punch 'n' Judy shows in the evenings.

Services

The **tourist information centre** (☎ 01626-873723, 🖥 www.shaldon-village.co.uk; end of May to early Sep daily 10.30am-4.30pm) stands in its own building in the car park opposite The Ness pub. Everything else is down by the water in the village centre, including Londis, the local **store** (Mon-Sat 8am-6pm, Sun 9am-3pm), a **post office** (Mon-Fri 9am-5.30pm, Sat 9am-12.30pm) and a **pharmacy** (Mon-Wed & Fri 9am-1pm, 2-6pm, Tue & Sat 9am-1pm).

Where to stay

Camping-wise, as well as pitches, *Coast View Holiday Park* (Map 37; ☎ 01626-818350, 🖥 coastview.co.uk; 🐾£3; WI-FI; £16-26 per pitch; Apr-Sep), Torquay Rd, has a restaurant, bar, laundry and shop. The facilities are of a high quality; its only disadvantages being the steep schlep up to it from the village (so if planning to stay here it is best to walk along the A379; see Map 36) – and that in high season the bar area is packed with kids and is usually dominated by activities for them.

Right on the path and the first place you come to in Shaldon, **B&B** in a pub is a possibility at super-smart *The Ness* (Map 37; ☎ 01626-873480, ☐ theness.co.uk; 1S/8D; ♥; WI-FI; £42.50-55pp, sgl occ £70), on Ness Drive. All the rooms have balconies, only two of which do not look out over the estuary.

On The Strand by the Teignmouth ferry there are a couple of decent places: *Eastcliff House* (☎ 01626-872796, ☐ gwynethpengelly@googlemail.com; 1D or F; ☞; WI-FI; £30pp, sgl occ £60), at No 3, doesn't include breakfast but *Teign Crest* (☎ 01626-873212, ☐ www.teigncrest.co.uk; 1D/1T/1D, T or F; ♥; WI-FI; £42.50pp, sgl occ £50), at No 13, does and it also benefits from panoramic views over the estuary.

Meanwhile, away from the shoreline and facing onto The Green is the dog-friendly *Potters Mooring* (☎ 01626-873225, ☐ www.pottersmooring.co.uk; 4D/1T/1F plus two cottages (one with D & T, the other with 1T); ♥; ☞; WI-FI; £42.50-47.50pp, sgl occ £65), at No 30. Unfortunately, they are unlikely to be able to accept bookings for one-night stays at weekends in July and August.

Maybe, instead, you'd like to rent a **beach hut**! *Shaldon Beach Huts* (☎ 01626-873212, ☐ www.shaldonbeachhuts.co.uk; WI-FI; £90-120 per hut per night) have two self-catered cabins, two of which sleep two people and two of which can sleep up to four people. There is underground heating and they all have terraces which lead out on to the beach, as well as showers and their own little kitchens. Featured on BBC TV's *Countryfile* programme and available year-round, the fact they willingly take one-night bookings is an absolute bonus and even the cost seems fair. The huts are marketed by Teign Crest (see above and Teign Crest will also deliver breakfast (£8.50pp) or you can go to Teign Creast to eat it.

Where to eat and drink

For food on the go, *Shaldon Bakery* (☎ 01626-872401, ☐ www.shaldonbakery.com; summer Mon-Fri 8am-5.30pm, Sat 8am-5pm, winter closing an hour earlier)

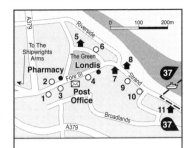

Shaldon

1 Coffee Rush
2 Clifford Arms
3 ODE-dining
4 Shaldon Bakery
5 Potters Mooring
6 The London Inn
7 Teign Crest
8 Shaldon Beach Huts
9 The Ferry Boat Inn
10 Beachcomber Bistro
11 Eastcliff House

sells breads and cakes as well as local preserves for souvenirs and hot drinks to take away. *Coffee Rush* (☎ 01626-873922, ☐ www.thecoffeerush.co.uk; Mon-Sat 8am-5pm, Sun & bank hols 9am-5pm) offers a good cake selection as well as a decent cream tea (£4.75).

Though the bakery and café enjoy a certain degree of renown in South Devon, Shaldon's speciality is undoubtedly its pubs. The largest and swishest of these is *The Ness* (see Where to stay; food served daily noon-2.45pm & 6-9.30pm, summer weekends until 10pm), another Hall & Woodhouse property – so you probably know what to expect by now: less a pub than a relaxed restaurant, the food is good value and sometimes borders on the brilliant, with mains from £9.75 up to £22.

A close rival to The Ness, *Ferry Boat Inn* (☎ 01626-872340; food served daily noon-3pm, Mon-Sat 6-9pm; ☞; WI-FI) is an atmospheric place which hosts a curry and quiz night on Wednesday, with curries a reasonable £6.95, and a barbecue in summer on their lovely patio across the road overlooking the water.

There are three more pubs for your consideration. On The Green, *The London Inn* (☎ 01626-872453; food served Easter to Sep Mon-Sat noon-2pm & 6-9pm, Sun noon-3.30pm & 6-7.30pm, Sep to Easter same but no food on Sun evening) serves real ales and plenty of decent walker-sized meals such as fresh plaice (£12.95) and fillet steaks (£17.95).

Along Fore St, *Clifford Arms* (☎ 01626-872311; Mon-Sat noon-2pm & 6.30-9.30pm, Sun noon-2.30pm & 7-9pm), converts into a jazz café on Mondays, where customers can enjoy a fixed-menu two-course dinner for £13.50 (including a trio of fresh fish in a lemon sauce), or three courses for £16, including a glass of house wine, while a band honks out some jazz tunes. They've got a nice beer garden out the back too.

A little further from Shaldon's centre and on Ringmore Rd, *The Shipwrights Arms* (☎ 01626-873232, 🖳 www.theshipwrights.co.uk; food Fri & Sat 9-11am, Tue-Fri noon-2pm & 6-9pm, Sat noon-9pm & Sun noon-3pm) serves pretty standard fare but does have a couple of interesting-sounding dishes including lamb's liver with bacon and onions (£5.75).

Away from the pubs, *ODE-dining* (☎ 01626-873977, 🖳 odetruefood.com; Wed-Sat 7-9.30pm; closed Oct) was recently voted one of the top 100 restaurants in the UK. It's certainly a treat, with such joys as a fillet of gurnard with tomato and basil, speckled lentils and courgettes costing £18.50. A more recent addition is *Café-ODE* (see ODE-dining; Wed-Mon 10am-7pm; 🐕) in Ness Cove; it serves locally sourced food.

Back by the ferry boat landing, *Beachcomber Bistro* (☎ 01626-872824; summer 8am-6pm, Feb, Mar, Sep & Oct Wed-Sun 9am-4.30pm, closed Nov-Jan) is another place with a great little patio overlooking the water and it serves food with an Italian influence.

Transport
[See also pp55-60] Stagecoach's 11 **bus** connects Shaldon with both Torquay and Teignmouth.

For a **taxi** try Riverside of Shaldon Taxis (☎ 01626-873378).

See below for details about the ferry to Teignmouth.

The cute **ferry to Teignmouth** (☎ 07896-711822, 🖳 www.teignmouthshaldonferry.co.uk; Apr to mid July, Sep & Oct 8am-6pm, mid July to end Aug 8am to about 9pm, Nov-Jan 8am-4.30pm, Feb & Mar 8am-5pm, no ferries on a Mon or a Tue in Dec & Jan; operate on demand and up to 6/hr in peak periods; £1.50, 🐕 free) leaves from the beach itself. If you happen to arrive when there's no ferry, the only alternative is to walk up to the bridge and cross there (about 40 mins) or take Stagecoach's No 11 bus (5-10 mins).

Note that, having arrived in Teignmouth, the coast path is far less well signed: to follow it, turn left by the lifeguards, then right to walk along Teignmouth's promenade.

TEIGNMOUTH   [map p189]
The last place in mainland England to have been successfully invaded by a foreign foe (in this instance the French in 1690), Teignmouth (pronounced 'Tinmouth') is a fun, friendly and compact place and one that's mercifully less hectic than its cousins down the coast. Lively cafés and proper pubs abound and there is also a decent amount of accommodation near to the centre – which, conveniently, is only a stone's throw away from the path. Should you decide against a night in Shaldon, this colourful and vibrant town will not disappoint.

Visitors started to frequent the town in great numbers during the Georgian era

(1714-1837) and many of the streets are adorned with architecture from this time. To be honest, there isn't actually that much to do in the town, though the **Victorian pier** is charming enough. There is also an **Orangery** (May-Sep, Tue, Thur, Sun and bank holiday Mons 2-4pm) at Bitton House, boasting an exotic plant collection. The octagonal **St James Parish Church**, at the junction of Exeter St and Bitton Park Rd, has a 13th-century sandstone tower.

Finally, **Teignmouth & Shaldon Museum** (☎ 01626-777041, 💻 www.teignheritage.org.uk; Apr-Sep Tue-Sat 10am-5pm, Sun & Bank Hol Mons 2-5pm, Mar & Oct-Nov to 4.30pm; £2.50), at 29 French St, has recently reopened following relocation and refurbishment; the new building houses a number of collections celebrating the area's maritime links.

Teignmouth Folk Festival (💻 www.teignmouthfolk.co.uk) is held here in June and the **Jazz Festival** (💻 www.teignmouthjazz.org) in November.

Services

The **tourist information office** (☎ 01626-215666, 💻 www.visitsouthdevon.co.uk; Apr-Sep Mon-Sat 10am-5pm, plus Sun 10am-2pm in school summer holidays, Oct-Mar Wed-Sat 10am-4pm) is near the front on Den Crescent – the road that runs parallel to the front.

On nearby Den Rd is the **post office** (Mon-Fri 9am-5.30pm, Sat 9am-12.30pm), with the Co-op **supermarket** (daily 8am-10pm) also close by on Bank St, though it also has an entrance on George St. There are **banks** with **ATMs** around town.

For camera gear, **PhotoShop** (☎ 01626-774197; Mon-Sat 9am-5pm), very nearby, has a few items for sale though it's mainly a printer's.

Internet access (Mon & Wed 9am-6pm, Tue & Fri 9am-5pm, Sat 9am-1pm) is available at the library on the A379, just outside the town centre. Quayside **Bookshop** (Mon-Sat 10am-5pm, Sun 11.30am-3pm) is in the old part of town on Northumberland Place, as is the local **chemist**, Maunder (Mon-Fri 9am-5.30pm, Sat 9am-1pm), at 4 Somerset Place. Finally, there's a **launderette** (daily 7am-6pm) next to Nautilus Restaurant.

Where to stay

The town has a decent amount of bed and breakfast accommodation. No more than a few hundred metres from the path and great value for money are: the dog-friendly ***Seaway*** (☎ 01626-879024, 💻 www.seawayteignmouth.co.uk; 2S/3D/1T/1F; ☕; 🐕 £5; WI-FI; £30-35pp, sgl £35; sgl occ £45 in summer, open to negotiation in winter), 27 Northumberland Place; and ***Old Salty House*** (☎ 01626-879574, 💻 www.oldsaltyhouse.co.uk; 2D/1D or T; WI-FI; £27.50pp, sgl occ £40), at No 21.

Slightly more expensive but offering evening meals is the licensed ***Lynton House*** (☎ 01626-774349, 💻 www.lyntonhouseteignmouth.com; 2S/3D/3T/4F; ☕; 🐕; WI-FI; B&B £35-37pp, DB&B £45-47pp) at 7 Powderham Terrace. Most of the rooms have great views over either the sea or river but they do not take one-night bookings in advance between June and August.

Centrally, on Brunswick St, the dog-friendly ***Brunswick House*** (☎ 01626-774102, 💻 www.brunswick-house.com; 1S/4D/3T or Tr; 🐕 £5; WI-FI; £29-34pp, sgl occ £45-58), No 5, and ***Devonia House*** (☎ 01626-775129, 💻 www.devoniaguesthouse.co.uk; 3D/2T/3F; £27.50-32.50pp, sgl occ £40), No 12, are both reasonably priced, whilst at the back end of town, on Teign St, is the luxurious but more expensive ***Thomas Luny House*** (☎ 01626-772976, 💻 www.thomas-luny-house.co.uk; 4D; ☕; WI-FI; £45-51pp, sgl occ £68-75). The extra cost is well worth it as the rates include not only afternoon tea but also homemade cake!

Further away from town there are two other decent options for walkers. Approximately 15 minutes from the centre, on Landscore Rd, ***Coombe Bank Hotel*** (☎ 01626-772369, 💻 www.coombebankhotel.net; 6D/3T/1F; ☕; WI-FI; £25-30pp, sgl occ £35-38) and ***The Craigs*** (☎ 01626-778003, 💻 val.grant2@virgin.net; 3D; ☕; 🐕 £5; WI-FI; £32pp, sgl occ £42); both offer rooms at competitive rates.

Finally, convenient for the path, **Bay Hotel** (☎ 01626-774123, 🖳 www.bayhotel teignmouth.co.uk; 2S/12D or T/3T/one penthouse; ✆; WI-FI £2.50/30 mins; £40-46pp, sgl £46, sgl occ £65-92) serves food (daily noon-2pm & 6.30-9pm) in their dining room and bar; £10-15 for main courses.

Where to eat and drink
The oldest part of town near the mouth of the river is undoubtedly the best place to search for food, with some idiosyncratic cafés as well as several characterful old pubs that have watched over the comings and goings on the Teign for centuries. Of the former, our favourite café is **Oystercatchers** (☎ 01626-774652; daily 8am-3pm), 12 Northumberland Place, a fully licensed place with WI-FI, a mellow vibe and some terrific food, with breakfasts or paninis for around £5. I urge you to try their homemade chilli which you can have in three levels of heat. Just along the way, **Relish** (☎ 01626-938204; Mon-Fri 9.30am-4pm, Sat 10am-3pm) is an unassuming burger place with some whopping great burgers at very reasonable prices: try their relish monster (£5) that includes two burgers, cheese and bacon.

The small but delightful **Crab Shack** (☎ 01626-777956, 🖳 www.crabshackon thebeach.co.uk; Wed-Sat noon-2.30pm & 6-8.30pm, Sun noon-2.30pm) is tucked away on the waterfront by the Ship Inn and has its own fishing boats. The menu, of course, changes according to the catch, though you can usually rely on there being some delicious crab sandwiches (£7.50). The views towards Shaldon are lovely too.

The Hobbit Café (☎ 01626-778170; Mon-Sat 10am-4pm, Sun 12.30-3pm), on Teign St, is another quirky little place, pleasant enough and with toast for just 45p.

It is the **pubs**, however, that really bring the crowds to this corner of Teignmouth. **Ship Inn** (☎ 01626-772674, 🖳 www.shipteignmouth.co.uk; food served Mon-Sat 12.30-2.30pm & 6-9.30pm, Sun noon-4pm, no food Mon & Tue in winter) is typical, a historical establishment (it was built in the 1830s – note the list of 14 men who served in the Battle of Trafalgar on the

exterior wall facing the sea). The food is just what you want from pub grub, being hearty and tasty, such as their 8oz Totnes 28-day hung ribeye steak (£16.95). Virtually next-door is **New Quay Inn** (☎ 01626-774145). However, at the time of research it was being refurbished and the new manager hadn't finalised the opening hours or what food, if any, would be served.

Back on Northumberland Place, **Endeavour** (☎ 01626-778899; food served Mon-Fri noon-4pm & 6-8pm, Sat 10am-4pm, Sun 10am-2pm) is renowned for its huge breakfasts of three rashers of bacon, three sausages, three eggs, fried bread, toast, black pudding – all for just £4.95. Its neighbour, **Drakes** (☎ 01626-772777; food served Fri-Wed 11.30am-9pm) also provides welcomingly filling fare, with an 8oz sirloin with tomatoes, onion rings, mushrooms & chips for £13, or cream teas for £3.25. Opposite, **F&Rs** (☎ 07767-333549, 🖳 www.fnrsbar.co.uk; Mon 11am-3pm, Tue-Sat 11am-8pm, Sun noon-5pm) boasts WI-FI and Sky TV; it's another place for those on a budget, with steaks from just £6.95 and pub favourites such as lasagne only £4.95. A few steps away, **The Queensbury Arms** (☎ 01626-778648; food daily from 5.30pm) is known for its large omelettes containing cheese, ham, mushrooms onions and tomatoes, all served with chips and salad (£4.95).

For restaurants, there are several recommended choices: **Nautilus** (☎ 01626-776999; Tue-Sat noon-2.30pm & 6-9.30pm), tucked away on Brunswick St, has some great mains (£12.95-22.95). Try their Moroccan-spiced shellfish stew of fresh crab meat in a rich Moroccan crab bisque (£18.95). On Tuesday to Thursday it's tapas in the evenings (£12.95pp).

Back in the old quarter on Northumberland Place, **Frescos** (☎ 01626-777181, 🖳 www.frescorestaurant.co.uk; July & Aug Wed-Mon 6pm to late, Sep-June Wed-Sun from 6pm) is a fine Italian with mains £9.50-19.50, including *tagliatelle con pesto rosso* (with mushrooms, spinach and red pesto) for £11. **The Owl and the Pussycat** (☎ 01626-775321, 🖳 www.the owlandpussycat.co.uk; daily Mon-Fri

Teignmouth

Where to eat and drink
1 Eastcliff Café
2 Colosseum
3 twentysix café
4 Jane's Ice Cream
5 Sea View Café
6 Lloyd Maunder
7 The Owl and the Pussycat
8 Bombay Delights
9 Hung Le
10 Hobbit Café
11 Ali's
12 Amanda's
13 Harbour Fish Bar
14 Relish
15 Nautilus Restaurant
16 Oystercatchers
17 Frescos
18 Queensbury Arms
19 New Quay Inn
20 Ship Inn
21 Drakes
22 F&Rs
23 Crab Shack
24 Endeavour

10am-2.30pm & 6-9.30pm, Sat 10am-2.30pm & 6-10pm, Sun noon-3pm & 6-9.30pm), at 3 Teign St, is a great little place, sophisticated and yet still willing to serve decent-sized portions of lovely food. Mains are priced up to £19.95 though can be as low as £15.50 for their fricassée of forest mushrooms and Dauphinoise potatoes with a poached egg and herb dressing.

There are some decent places on the other side of the town centre on Regent St. One such is *twentysix café* (☎ 01626-879000, 🖥 www.twentysixcafe.co.uk; daily 9am to 5.30pm plus Fri & Sat 6-9pm) which feels a bit too smart for this corner of town, and has equally sophisticated dishes such as coq au vin for £11 and *tartine crabe* (open crab sandwich; £7.25). Opposite, *Colosseum* (☎ 01626-870000, 🖥 www.col osseumitalian.co.uk; Mon-Sat 6.30-9.30pm) is another fine Italian with mains for £8.50-20; try the *pollo all cacciatore* (chicken breast, grilled peppers, onion and wild mushroom in a red wine sauce) for £14.

Takeaways include the Cantonese *Hung Le* (☎ 01626-773495; daily noon-2pm & 5pm to midnight) on Teign St; an Indian, *Bombay Delights* (☎ 01626-773824; daily 5.30pm to midnight) at No 38; and a kebab house, *Ali's* (☎ 01626-777911; Sun-Thur 4pm to midnight, Fri-Sat 4pm-2am) at 11 Somerset Place.

For quick snacks on-the-go, try *Lloyd Maunder* for a carvery baguette (£2.75, or £3.50 with crisps and a drink) or, back on Northumberland Place, *Amanda's Bakery* (☎ 01626-775068; Mon-Sat 8am-5pm, Sun 10am-5pm) where chicken and mushroom pasties are £2.45.

Harbour Fish Bar (☎ 01626-775906; Mon-Sat noon-2pm & 5-9.30pm) is Teignmouth's best chippy; and there's an ice-cream parlour, *Jane's Ice Cream* (daily 10am-6pm in summer, Mon-Sat 9.30am-5pm, Sun 10am-4.30pm in winter). Opposite Jane's is a café that's good if you're waiting for a bus, many of which leave from outside: *Sea View* (☎ 01626-777888; daily 8am-6.30pm) has cheap eats, such as spag bol (£3.95) and is friendly and central – all in all it has everything....except a sea view. At the far eastern end of the seafront, *Eastcliff Café* (☎ 01626-777621, 🖥 www.eastcliffcafe.co .uk; daily 10am-4.30pm) has lots of hot and cold drinks and snacks.

Transport
[See also pp55-60] Stagecoach's 2 **bus** (Newton Abbot to Exeter) calls here and their No 11 service goes to Torquay stopping at Shaldon en route. **Trains** call here regularly en route between Exeter and Paignton. For a **cab** try Alpha Taxis (☎ 01626-773030).

TEIGNMOUTH TO EXMOUTH   [MAPS 37-41]

This short and easy **8-mile (13km; low-tide route 3hrs, high-tide route 3¼hrs; times include the ferry journey)** section will likely be welcome following yesterday's exertions. For this stage you need to consult a **tide-timetable** as there is the possibility of having to follow two high-tide routes. You will also need to get to Starcross in time for the last ferry (before you set off make sure you have checked the ferry times) across to Exmouth; in other words, the success of this stage depends greatly on your organisational skills – and the mercy of the sea.

The terrain on this section is generally flat as you follow Brunel's railway along the sea-walls. Refreshments are also in ample supply, both in Dawlish and Dawlish Warren, and there are a couple of really cracking pubs in Cockwood. Once at Starcross, if the ferry's not running you need to consider your options: Exmouth can be reached by public transport from Starcross (see public transport pp55-60), though ambling addicts will probably prefer to tighten their bootlaces and stroll along the attractive Exe Estuary Trail (see pp200-3). Doing so will add another eight miles to your walk but it's an easy horizontal trail so, if you rise early enough, reaching Exmouth from Teignmouth is very possible in one day, even with the diversion.

The route

There are two alternative trails leaving Teignmouth which divide near Eastcliff Café (see Map 37, p183) at the eastern end of the seafront. If the tide is in your favour you can walk straight along the sea wall with the railway to your left, towards the two giant rock stacks that loom in front of you. These are the **Parson** and **Clerk**, said to have once been human until the devil turned them into stone (see box below). Just out to sea another rock formation, the finger-

---

❏ **The legend of the Parson and the Clerk**

East of Teignmouth stand two huge rock stacks – and as you probably would expect from such prominent features, there are various legends surrounding the formation of these outcrops. The best known is this gothic morality tale:

Once upon a time the Bishop of Exeter was lying in bed in Dawlish, severely ill and close to death. An ambitious local parson, spying an opportunity to succeed the bishop, contrived to visit him on a regular basis to try to persuade him of his suitability for the promotion. Accompanying him on these visits was his clerk, who was tasked with guiding the parson across the local moor to Dawlish.

One evening, having received news that the bishop's health had rapidly declined, the parson decided to leave for Dawlish immediately despite the lateness of the hour. The two men galloped as fast as they were able, whipping their horses and stabbing them with their spurred heels in their attempt to get to the bishop's deathbed. The weather, however, turned against them, and a huge storm rose as the sun descended. The rain lashed down so heavily that the two men became lost in the gloom. The parson, furious that he could miss the bishop's demise, turned on his clerk and sneered the ominous words: 'May Satan take us to Dawlish for we shall never get there ourselves.'

Strangely enough (or maybe not, for those who are familiar with such legends), it was shortly after this that the two men were surprised by the sound of galloping hooves and a peasant on a moor pony approached and offered to be the two men's guide. In desperation, the two men paid little attention to the fact that both pony and rider were as black as the darkest night and followed the man to Dawlish. On the way they came to a well-lit mansion that neither the parson or the clerk had noticed before. With the weather still against them, their guide, claiming to be the mansion's owner, invited them in, promising that he would guide them to Dawlish first thing in the morning instead.

Once inside, the pair were greeted by the sight of a large group of wild-looking folk indulging in an orgy of gorging and drinking and partying – a scene of unfettered hedonism to which the parson and the clerk were soon willing participants.

The next morning it was reported that the bishop had died, news that caused the two men to dash out of the mansion and mount their horses with the intention of continuing on their journey, realising that the parson's chances of promotion were slipping away. Their horses, however, would not move. To the backdrop of peals of laughter coming from the party within, the parson cursed 'Devil take the brutes'. It was at this point that their peasant guide appeared and thanked them – before ordering the horses to gallop into the sea, their cruel masters rooted in the saddles.

The following morning, when the god-fearing population of Dawlish left their homes to survey the damage caused by the storm, they saw that the red cliffs had been broken into two halves; and that on one half lay the lifeless body of the parson – while on the other lay that of his faithful clerk.

like rock that appears like Neptune's digit poking out of the waves, is **Shag Rock**. At the end, and having dipped underneath the railway line to ascend Smugglers Lane, the path meets up with the high tide route on the busy A379.

High-tide route: Teignmouth–Smugglers Lane (35 minutes)

Just before Eastcliff Café take the road on the left – Eastcliff Rd – to **Mules Park** (which you can either walk through or follow the public footpath that runs to the right). At the top of the park you cross a field and minor road, continuing down the footpath until you reach the A379.

The official path continues on this busy A-road, passing *The Moorings* (☎ 01626-770400, 🖥 www.themooringsteignmouth.co.uk; 2D; ✆; WI-FI; £35-40pp, sgl occ £50-60; Apr-Oct), at 33 Teignmouth Rd, and so on down the hill.

For a more pleasant walking experience, however, turn left at the **Holcombe** sign and head down Holcombe Rd, with the pink, crenallated and thatched *Minadab Cottage* (☎ 01626-772044, 🖥 www.minadab.co.uk; 2D/1D or T; ✆; 🐾 £20 per stay; WI-FI; £37.50-39.50pp, sgl occ £65-69), on your right. They don't accept a single-night booking in July and August.

Follow Holcombe Rd, a quiet country lane surrounded by hedgerows, until you walk down into a dip, coming to a minor crossroads. Take Hall Lane on your right and this will reacquaint you with the A-road, the official high-tide route – and indeed the low-tide route too.

With all the paths reunited, a short walk up a hill brings you to **Windward Lane**, from where a path leads you back to the railway, though it's not long before you're back on the A379 again. Don't follow this but instead take Old Teignmouth Rd on the right that leads past *The Beeches* (☎ 01626-866345, 🖥 www.thebeechesbandb.co.uk; 2D/1T; ✆; WI-FI; £36.50-42pp, sgl occ from £55), at No 15A.

Another encounter with the A379 follows before the path heads through **Lea Mount Park**, sandwiched between the noisy A-road and **Coryton's Cove**, with its wonderful little beach (off the path). The path descends sharply now, zig-zagging its way down to the railway and Dawlish.

DAWLISH [map p195]

Dawlish is a pleasant-enough place though the crowds in summer can be suffocating. Originally a little fishing community, Dawlish's name is thought to come from the Celtic 'Deawlisc', meaning 'Devil Water' – possibly because torrential rains are thought to have saturated the area's red cliffs, turning Dawlish Water – the stream which runs through the town's centre – a satanic red. Another hypothesis suggests that it comes from the Welsh 'du(g)lais', meaning 'black stream' and today the brook is known for its black swans that paddle happily in the very heart of the town.

Famous in fiction as the birthplace of Charles Dickens' *Nicholas Nickleby*, if you're interested in the town's history you may wish to visit **Dawlish Museum** (☎ 01626-888557; late Apr to Oct Wed-Fri 10.30am-5pm, Sat & Sun 2-5pm; £2); to get there follow Dawlish Water inland along Brunswick Place, passing the Waterfowl Enclosure before turning left on Barton Hill and then right along Barton Terrace.

There's little of essential appeal to the trekker in Dawlish but the town has a good selection of services and a scattering of eateries and accommodation.

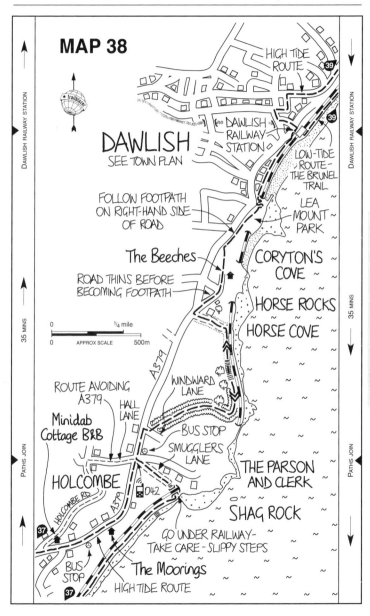

MAP 38

★ trailblazer

HIGH TIDE ROUTE

39

DAWLISH RAILWAY STATION

DAWLISH
SEE TOWN PLAN

LOW-TIDE ROUTE – THE BRUNEL TRAIL

FOLLOW FOOTPATH ON RIGHT-HAND SIDE OF ROAD

LEA MOUNT PARK

The Beeches

CORYTON'S COVE

ROAD THINS BEFORE BECOMING FOOTPATH

HORSE ROCKS

HORSE COVE

0   1/4 mile
0   APPROX SCALE   500m

A379

WINDWARD LANE

ROUTE AVOIDING A379

HALL LANE

Minidab Cottage B&B

BUS STOP

SMUGGLERS LANE

THE PARSON AND CLERK

HOLCOMBE

D042

SHAG ROCK

HOLCOMBE RD

A379

GO UNDER RAILWAY – TAKE CARE – SLIPPY STEPS

BUS STOP

37

The Moorings

HIGH TIDE ROUTE

35 MINS

35 MINS

PATHS JOIN

PATHS JOIN

35 MINS

Dawlish Arts Festival (🖳 www.daw
lish.com/event/details?eventdateid=2528)
is held here in June. It started in 1953 and is
thought to be the longest-running arts festival in the South-West.

Services

The **tourist information office** (☎ 01626-
215665; summer Mon-Sat 10am-5pm Sun
and Bank Hol Mons 10am-2pm, winter
Thur-Sat 10am-1.30pm & 2-4pm) is right
in the heart of the action by Dawlish Water,
overlooking the ducks. Also check out 🖳
www.dawlish.com.

Most of the other services lie along
The Strand that runs parallel and east of the
stream. They include a Co-op **supermarket** (Mon-Sat 8am-8pm, Sun 10am-4pm) at
No 4, the **post office** (Mon-Fri 9am-
5.30pm, Sat 9am-1pm) at No 26 and a
branch of Boots the **Chemists** (Mon-Fri
9am-6pm, Sat 1-5pm) between them. There
are also **banks** with **ATMs**.

Where to stay

On the walk into Dawlish, **B&B** is available at *The Marine Tavern* (☎ 01626-
865245, 🖳 www.marinetaverndawlish
.com; 2D/2D or Tr; ✔; WI-FI; 🐾 in the bar
only; £22.50-27.50pp, sgl occ £45-55), 2
Marine Parade; some food will always be
made available for residents – even if you
do turn up a little late.

The recently renovated *Gresham
House Inn* (☎ 01626-864061, 🖳 www.gre
shamhouseinn.co.uk; 2D/1T; ✔; 🐾; WI-FI;
£30-35pp, sgl occ from £50), 1 Commercial
Rd, also caters for walkers; the rate
includes breakfast and snacks are available
during the day.

Pretty much right on the path as you
head towards the railway station, on the
corner of Marine Parade and Teignmouth
Hill, is *The Blenheim* (☎ 01626-862372,
🖳 www.theblenheim.uk.net; 2S/8D or T/
3F; 🐾 £5; WI-FI; £34-44pp, sgl £46), 1
Marine Parade, from which there are great
views out to sea and along the immediate
stretch of coastline.

On West Cliff, the dog-friendly (but
expensive), *Lyme Bay House* (☎ 01626-
864211, 🖳 www.lymebaydawlish.co.uk;

5D/3T/1F; ✔; 🐾 £20; WI-FI; £43-47.50pp,
sgl occ £72), No 34, is a short walk up the
hill from the centre of town. Meanwhile, not
taking one-night bookings but willing to
help any stranded walker should they have a
vacancy on the night, the elegant *Dunluce
House* (☎ 01626-888633, 🖳 www.dunluce
house.co.uk; 2D/1T; ✔; WI-FI; £35-40pp, sgl
occ £70-80), 2 Priory Rd, has large and
splendid rooms with great sea views.

Where to eat and drink

On the way into Dawlish, *The Marine
Tavern* (see Where to stay; food summer
daily noon-9pm, limited hours in winter)
provides fairly standard pub grub (jacket
potatoes etc).

Old Mill Tearoom (☎ 07852-314708,
🖳 www.oldmilltearoom.co.uk; summer
10am-5pm, limited hours in winter dependent on weather; closed mid/late Dec to mid
Feb) dates back to 1717 when it used to be
a flour mill. Cream teas are a speciality here
as is their savoury tea – homemade cheese
scones and butter with mature cheddar
cheese. Just up the road is *Gay's Creamery*
(🖳 www.gayscreamery.co.uk; summer
Mon-Sat 8am-6.30pm or later, Sun from
9am; winter Mon-Sat 8am-5pm, Sun from
9am), a gift shop but one that also does
takeaway coffee and tea, as well as cream
teas for £3.50 and a vegetable pasty for £1.
Still on this strip, *Hoi Shing* (☎ 01626-
865351; daily 5.30-11pm, Sat lunch noon-
2pm) is a Cantonese restaurant that serves
food daily; mains are around £4.95-5.95.

Geronimo's Diner, at the railway station, is an unpretentious and cheap eatery
where cream teas are just £2.75 and a bacon
sarnie £2.25. On pedestrianised Beach St
just north of here, *The Railway Inn* (☎
01626-863226, 🖳 www.therailwayinn.ec
lipse.co.uk; food served Mon-Sat noon-
2.30pm & 5-7.15pm, Sun noon-2.30pm) is
a very cheap option with a decent ploughman's for £6.30 and even an 8oz rump steak
only £6.80.

At the end of Beach St on Piermont
Place is *Home Kitchen* (☎ 01626-895192,
🖳 www.thehomekitchen.co.uk; July to end
Sep daily 8am-4pm; rest of year Thur-Tue);
this is the first place that's open in the

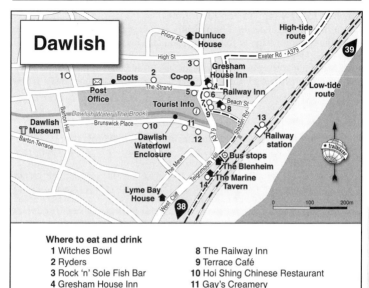

Where to eat and drink

1 Witches Bowl	8 The Railway Inn
2 Ryders	9 Terrace Café
3 Rock 'n' Sole Fish Bar	10 Hoi Shing Chinese Restaurant
4 Gresham House Inn	11 Gay's Creamery
5 Ugly Duckling	12 Old Mill Tearoom
6 Home Kitchen	13 Geronimo's Diner
7 Bombay Delights	14 The Marine Tavern

morning and specialises in gluten-free products. *The Terrace Café* (☎ 01626-867390; summer daily 9am-4pm, winter Thur-Tue 9am-3pm) specialises in the simple stuff, with a basic chip butty for £2.15; roast dinners and fish & chips are also available. There's also an Indian takeaway, *Bombay Delights* (☎ 01626-863316; daily noon-2pm & 5-11pm), while up the hill to the north *Rock 'n' Sole Fish Bar* (Mon-Wed 5-8pm, Thur noon-2pm & 5-8pm, Fri-Sat noon-2pm & 5-9pm) is the local chippy.

Back on The Strand and near the tourist office, *Ugly Duckling* (☎ 01626-863374; daily 11am-2.30pm, summer school holidays 5-9pm) is another eatery that offers simple British fare, with steak & kidney pies for £5.95 and a carvery available noon-3pm (adults £5.95).

Ryders (☎ 01626-86281; Mon-Sat 8am-5pm) is a pleasant bakery where a hog roast roll is £2.50 – delicious.

Towards the upper end of The Strand the turn-off to the right is Queen St where you'll find *Witches Bowl* (☎ 01626-863641; Tue 9.30am-3pm, Wed-Fri 9.30am-3pm & 6-9.30pm; Sat 9.30am-2pm & 6-9.30pm, Sun 11.30am-3pm), an unusual place with an unusual theme (yes, it really is all about witches) but it does do reasonable food, serving Teign mussels in bacon, thyme and cider for £12.99 for example.

Transport

[See also pp55-60] Stagecoach's 2 **bus** connects the village with Teignmouth, Dawlish Warren, Starcross and Exeter. **Trains** call here regularly en route between Exeter and Paignton.

For a **taxi** try Jim's Taxis (☎ 01626-779079, ☎ 0775-930 5093) and Dawlish Taxi (☎ 01626-888111).

Dawlish to Dawlish Warren (35 mins)

If you're sure that the tide is sufficiently low, begin this stretch by heading under the railway bridge to follow the path, also known as **The Brunel Trail** (Map 38), alongside the railway.

It's a straightforward stroll that leads you, eventually, to **Langstone Rock** and the quirky ***Red Rock Café*** (summer daily 8am-5pm, winter daily 10am-4pm) where you can get a chip butty for £2.20, a bucket for £1.20 and a spade for 70p. Cross the next pedestrian railway bridge and follow the path towards the road and into Dawlish Warren (see below).

High-tide route: Dawlish to Dawlish Warren (35 mins)

At Dawlish Railway Station turn left to follow the A379 – Exeter Rd – as it winds its way out of town. The road has a pavement but it regularly switches sides – take care. Rather tediously, you remain on the road for half a mile, passing ***Sea Lawn Lodge*** (☎ 01626-865998, 🖳 www.sealawnlodge.com; 1T en suite, 1D/1F share a bathroom; ☛; WI-FI; 🐕; £35-41pp, sgl occ £47), before turning right and entering a grassy area called **Rockstone Flats** (if you reach the Texaco petrol station you have gone too far). Keep to the left and follow what is signed as a bridleway. Passing some bungalows on your left you join a tarmac path that seems to roll out endlessly in front of you.

The path gradually descends past ***Langstone Cliff Hotel*** (☎ 01626-868000, 🖳 www.langstone-hotel.co.uk; 64 flexible rooms; ☛; WI-FI; 🐕 charge possible; £63-117pp B&B up to £133 with dinner; sgl £81-95 B&B, £97-111 with dinner) before eventually arriving in Dawlish Warren.

DAWLISH WARREN [Map 39]

Essentially a railway station – with a few amenities dotted here and there to service the area's numerous holiday parks – Dawlish Warren has little to warrant a lengthy stop.

Dawlish Warren National Nature Reserve is absorbing and sometimes plays host to rare vagrant birds including the greater sand plover, elegant tern and great spotted cuckoo. However, it's located on the sand-spit on the opposite side of the railway tracks and thus a walk away from the trail, which will deter all but the most determined twitcher.

Refreshments are available in the village, as is limited accommodation, but we would advise that you continue to Starcross and from there cross over the River Exe to Exmouth. There is, however, a Londis (daily 8am-7pm), the biggest **grocery shop** until Exmouth, and another supermarket, Gerald's (daily 8am-10pm), with an **ATM** (£1.50).

Unfortunately ***Sandays*** (☎ 01626-888973; 2D/1T; £30-32.50pp, sgl occ negotiable), on Warren Rd, operates a two-night minimum-stay policy year-round; the twin room is nice, however, and has its own sitting room overlooking the garden.

Mount Pleasant Inn (☎ 01626-863151, 🖳 www.mountpleasantinn.com; 2D/1T; ☛; £35pp, sgl occ £45) is a short walk up the hill which allows it to enjoy great views overlooking the bay. It's the best spot in town (though that's not saying too much). The inn also does **food** (served daily noon-2pm & 6-9.30pm, in the summer meals are served till 3.30pm and sandwiches/snacks from then till 6pm), with mains starting at £7.45 for the cod & chips rising to £19.95 for a fillet steak. Alternatives include a Chinese takeaway, ***Hakaryu*** (☎ 01626-888388, 🖳 www.hakaryu.co.uk; daily 5-11pm), at 3 Warren Rd, and a chippy, ***Penaligon's Plaice*** (summer daily noon-10pm, winter daily 5-8pm) at No 2.

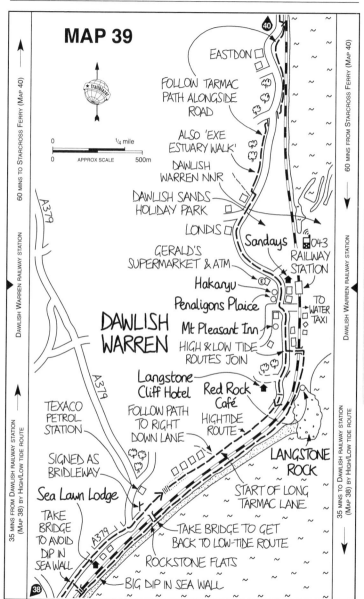

MAP 39

40

EASTDON

FOLLOW TARMAC
PATH ALONGSIDE
ROAD

★ trailblazer

0   1/4 mile
APPROX SCALE   500m
0

ALSO 'EXE
ESTUARY WALK'

DAWLISH
WARREN NNR

DAWLISH SANDS
HOLIDAY PARK

LONDIS

GERALD'S
SUPERMARKET & ATM

Sandays

043
RAILWAY
STATION

Hakaryu

Penaligons Plaice

DAWLISH
WARREN

Mt Pleasant Inn

HIGH & LOW TIDE
ROUTES JOIN

TO
WATER
TAXI

Langstone
Cliff Hotel

Red Rock
Café

TEXACO
PETROL
STATION

FOLLOW PATH
TO RIGHT
DOWN LANE

HIGHTIDE
ROUTE

LANGSTONE
~ ROCK

SIGNED AS
BRIDLEWAY

Sea Lawn Lodge

START OF LONG
~ TARMAC LANE

TAKE
BRIDGE
TO AVOID
DIP IN
SEA WALL

TAKE BRIDGE TO GET
BACK TO LOW-TIDE ROUTE ~

38

~ ROCKSTONE FLATS ~

~ BIG DIP IN SEA WALL ~

60 MINS TO STARCROSS FERRY (MAP 40)

60 MINS FROM STARCROSS FERRY (MAP 40)

DAWLISH WARREN RAILWAY STATION

DAWLISH WARREN RAILWAY STATION

ROUTE GUIDE AND MAPS

35 MINS FROM DAWLISH RAILWAY STATION
(MAP 38) BY HIGH/LOW TIDE ROUTE

35 MINS TO DAWLISH RAILWAY STATION
(MAP 38) BY HIGH/LOW TIDE ROUTE

Note that there is the option of a **water taxi** between Dawlish Warren and Exmouth Docks: ExePlorer Water Taxis Ltd (☎ 07970-918418, 💻 www.exexplorer.co.uk; Apr-Oct daily on the hour 8am-5pm, later in peak periods and also at other times by arrangement, latest return from Dawlish Warren at 6pm; £2 single, £4 return, no dogs as they are not allowed on the beach!) will come and collect you from the beach. The taxi leaves from near the end of the sand spit that juts out from Dawlish Warren. From the train station, walk to the end of the amusements past the Visitor Centre; keeping on the left-hand side (ie on the opposite side to the sea), continue past the golf course and through the dunes until you see the sign stating: 'Pick Up Point'. The walk will take approximately half an hour.

Stagecoach's 2 **bus** connects the village with Teignmouth, Dawlish, Starcross and Exeter. **Trains** call here regularly en route between Exeter and Paignton. See pp55-60.

The path leaves Dawlish Warren along the road, bypassing holiday parks and chippies. Joining the Exe Estuary Walk, aka Cycle Track 2, you soon arrive in Cockwood.

COCKWOOD [Map 40]

This small harbour village is blessed with two great pubs. The warm and friendly *Ship Inn* (☎ 01626-890373, 💻 www.ship inncockwood.co.uk; Mon-Sat noon-2.30pm & 6-9pm, Sun noon-9pm), on Church Rd, serves up a wonderful chicken stuffed with black pudding with a cider sauce (£10.25); they also always have a specials board with dishes featuring fish.

Meanwhile, right on the harbour-front on Dawlish Warren Rd, *The Anchor Inn* (☎ 01626-890203; Mon-Sat noon-10pm, Sun to 9.30pm) is over 450 years old and specialises in seafood. It's busier, noisier and the clientele seem 'younger' than at The Ship.

For **bed and breakfast** there is just *The Croft* (☎ 01626-890282, 💻 www.the croftcockwood.com; 6D/3T; WI-FI; 🐾 £5; £37.50-42.50pp, sgl occ £51), Exeter Rd, is a large house set in an acre of secluded gardens. The owner offers massage and reflexology, will dry clothes, supply packed lunches, and residents get a 10% discount in the two local pubs.

Follow the road over the bridge and out of the village. A brief interlude in a park follows before, in short order, you arrive in Starcross, from where you can board the Starcross to Exmouth **ferry**; for details, see p200.

STARCROSS
[Map 40; Map 40a, p201]

This is the main departure point for the ferry across the Exe, but there are a few amenities in the village. On The Strand you will find a Spar **supermarket** (7am-10pm daily) and Boots the **Chemist** (Map 40a; Mon-Fri 9am-6pm, Sat 9am-1pm).

Post office services are available in *The Galleon Inn* (☎ 01626-890412; food daily noon-2.30pm & 6.30-9pm) which also offers **accommodation** (2S/3D/2F; 🐾; £27.50pp, sgl from £35).

A quarter of a mile further along The Strand, *Chimneys* (☎ 01626-890813, 💻 www.chimneys-bandb.co.uk; 3D/2F; WI-FI; from £32.50pp, sgl occ £45) can provide food if requested in advance. High teas and cream teas are served May-September Sundays 2.30-5.30pm.

Pub food is also available opposite the railway station at *The Atmospheric Railway Inn* (☎ 01626-890335; summer noon-2pm & 6-8pm, winter Tue-Wed & Fri-Sun noon-2pm, not on Mon or Thur),

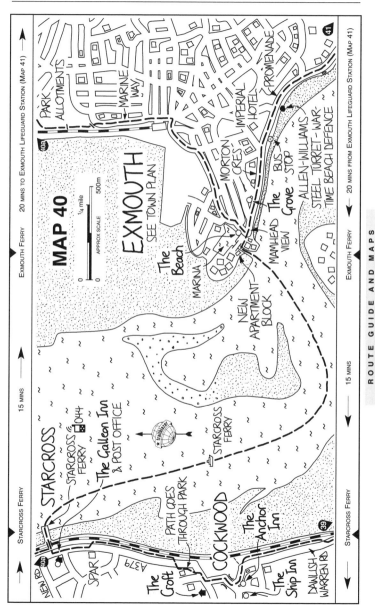

where you can enjoy one of their jacket potatoes (from £4.50) whilst supping an ale in their beer garden.

Stagecoach's 2 **bus** connects the village with Teignmouth, Dawlish, Dawlish Warren and Exeter. **Trains** call here regularly en route between Exeter and Paignton. See pp55-60 for more details.

Tackling the Exe   [Map 40, p199]

● **The Starcross to Exmouth Ferry** For a river that is crossed by no fewer than three ferry services, it can be surprisingly difficult crossing the Exe sometimes. The easiest way – and which is on the official coast path route – is the main **Starcross to Exmouth Ferry** (☎ 01626-774770, ☎ 07974-022536, 💻 www.exe2sea.co.uk; Apr-Oct daily, leaves Starcross hourly from 10.10am to 4.10pm & Exmouth 10.40am to 3.40pm, plus until 5.10pm & 5.40pm mid May-July & Sep-mid Sep, August only also at 6pm Starcross and 6.15pm Exmouth; 15-20 mins; single £4.50, day return £5; well-behaved 🐾).

As you cross the Exe look for out for avocets and ospreys in the skies above and grey seals from the waves below you.

For Exmouth and the continuation of the route see p203.

● **Water taxi** If the ferry isn't operating – and you don't fancy heading inland up the Exe to one of the other crossings – you can get the water taxi from Dawlish Warren. However, it also operates only between April and October but for longer hours. For Exmouth and the continuation of the route see p203.

● **Ferries further upstream** If neither of the above suits you'll have to head inland to get across the Exe. There are **two further ferry services** that operate upstream of Starcross and Exmouth. The first leaves from **Turf Lock** (2½ miles from Starcross), the second from **Topsham Lock** (4 miles from Starcross), with both heading to the launch at **Topsham**. Details of these ferry services can be found on p202. Taking either of these will save you having to walk all the way up to Exeter and back again. **Note with either service it is recommended that you phone beforehand to make sure they're operating.**

To get to either, you need to follow the **Exe Estuary Trail**, which heads north inland from Starcross round the pretty estuary, an SSSI with an abundance of wildlife including avocets and curlew. This is the route described below.

● **Public transport** Should there not be any ferries running when you plan to cross the Exe, there is a strong case to be made for taking public transport rather than walking all the way to Exeter and back. Stagecoach's No 2 **bus** service (see pp55-60) heads to Exeter from Starcross, from where you can get Stagecoach's No 56 back south to Exmouth.

Exe Estuary Trail
The way (**8 miles, 12.8km; 3½ hours plus 10 mins for Topsham ferry crossing**) is well-signed from Starcross Railway Station, the path following the edge of the estuary, initially with the road (A379) to your left and the railway tracks ever-present to your right. Leaving Starcross behind it's not long before you say a welcome farewell to the A379 as you follow a very quiet lane along

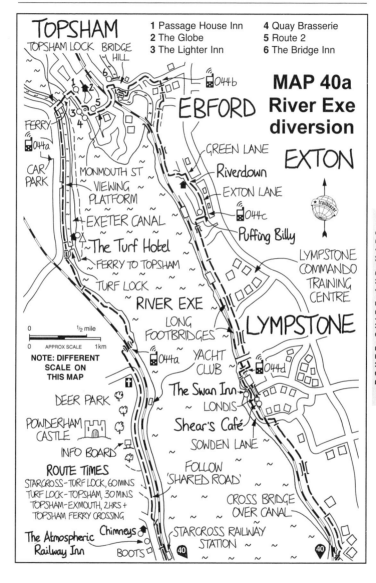

TOPSHAM

TOPSHAM LOCK BRIDGE
HILL

1 Passage House Inn   4 Quay Brasserie
2 The Globe   5 Route 2
3 The Lighter Inn   6 The Bridge Inn

044b

MAP 40a
River Exe
diversion

EBFORD

EXTON

FERRY

044a

GREEN LANE

Riverdown

EXTON LANE

044c

CAR
PARK

MONMOUTH ST

VIEWING
PLATFORM

EXETER CANAL

~The Turf Hotel

FERRY TO TOPSHAM

TURF LOCK

~ RIVER EXE ~

Puffing Billy

LYMPSTONE
COMMANDO
TRAINING
CENTRE

LYMPSTONE

LONG
FOOTBRIDGES

0   ½ mile
0   APPROX SCALE   1km

**NOTE: DIFFERENT
SCALE ON
THIS MAP**

044a

YACHT
CLUB

044d

The Swan Inn

DEER PARK

POWDERHAM
CASTLE

INFO BOARD

LONDIS

Shear's Café

SOWDEN LANE

ROUTE TIMES
STARCROSS-TURF LOCK, 60MINS
TURF LOCK-TOPSHAM, 30 MINS
TOPSHAM-EXMOUTH, 2HRS +
TOPSHAM FERRY CROSSING

FOLLOW
'SHARED ROAD'

CROSS BRIDGE
OVER CANAL

The Atmospheric
Railway Inn

Chimneys

BOOTS

STARCROSS RAILWAY
STATION

40

40

ROUTE GUIDE AND MAPS

the river and railway, your attention soon being diverted away from the water by the estimated 600 fallow deer residing in the grounds of impressive **Powderham Castle** – the historic home of the Earl of Devon – on your left.

Passing **Starcross Yacht Club** to your right and a church on your left, you cross the railway line to follow the edge of the estuary to **Turf Lock** and *The Turf Hotel* (☎ 01392-833128, 🖥 www.turfpub.net; 1D/1T, shared bathroom; 🐾; £40pp; food served Mon-Fri noon-2.30pm, Sat-Sun noon-3pm, daily 6.30-9pm; mid Feb to Dec). Note you can also **camp** (£5pp or £10pp with breakfast) here, though facilities for campers are limited to an outside toilet. This is also the launch of the first of the ferries.

Running from the back of the establishment, the **Turf Lock Ferry** (☎ 07778-370582, 🖥 www.topshamtoturfferry.co.uk; single £3, return £5, 🐾 50p) runs daily over Easter and from late May to mid September, as well as over weekends in April and until the end of September. Departs Turf Lock between 11.45am & 4pm and Topsham between 11.30am & 3.15pm. Note that times are subject to tides and weather conditions.

If you wish to (or have to) continue to the next ferry, keep to the left-hand side of the canal for just over a mile to **Topsham Lock** where a reasonably reliable service operates. The **Topsham Lock to Topsham ferry** (☎ 07801-203338; Apr-Sep Wed-Mon 9.30am-5.30pm; Oct-Mar weekends only 10am-5pm or dusk; £1, 🐾 20p) takes about two minutes. Note that the ferry doesn't operate at low tide so check the tide times (🖥 easytide.ukho.gov.uk).

Remember that you need to phone either ferry beforehand to make sure it's running.

Topsham has some good eateries. Shortly after the ferry slipway you will come to *Passage House Inn* (☎ 01392-873653, 🖥 www.passagehouseinntopsham.co.uk; food served weekdays noon-3pm & 6-9.30pm, weekends noon-9.30pm).

Also doing pub meals are *The Lighter Inn* (☎ 01392-875439, 🖥 www.lighterinn.co.uk; food daily noon-9pm; fish 'n' chips only on a Sun eve), and on the outskirts of town – but just selling snack-style food – is *The Bridge Inn* (☎ 01392-873862, 🖥 www.cheffers.co.uk/bridge.html; food served daily noon-2pm & Mon-Sat 6-8.30pm, Sun 7-8.30pm). In the evening they only serve pork pies with salad (£3.50) but at lunch they also serve pasties, sandwiches, ploughman's and in the winter soups.

There is also a café-bar: *Route 2* (☎ 01392-875085, 🖥 www.route2topsham.co.uk; daily 8am-8pm), on the corner of Monmouth Hill, whilst on the other side of the road to this cyclist's haunt is *The Quay Brasserie* (☎ 01392-876123, ☎ 07585-967765, 🖥 www.thequaybrasserie.com; food Mon-Sat 10-11.30am, noon-2.30pm & 6.30-9.30pm, Sun noon-4pm; winter closed on a Mon), from where you can get a quiche of the day (£5.95), or a steak baguette with red onion compote & chips (£8.95).

Should Topsham's considerable charms compel you to stay longer, hotel-style accommodation can be found at *The Globe* (☎ 01392-873471, 🖥 www.theglobetopsham.co.uk; 1D or T; ☎; WI-FI; room only £34.50-55pp; sgl occ full room rate), at 34 Fore St. Breakfast is available (£6.95-8); food is also served daily noon-5pm & 6-9pm; however, booking is recommended.

Stagecoach's 57 **bus** service (see pp55-60) calls here as does the train between Exmouth and Exeter.

Having disembarked from either ferry in Topsham, turn right and walk along Ferry Rd until you meet Fore St where you turn right. Crossing a mini roundabout, follow the thin lane up Monmouth Hill and after just over 100 metres turn left along **Monmouth St**; having followed this for approximately a quarter-of-a-mile you arrive on Bowling Green Rd. Turning left, cross a railway line and follow Elm Grove Rd – a residential street – as far as the junction with Bridge Hill where you turn right. Passing The Bridge Inn (see opposite) on your left, you follow the road for just over half a mile before turning off to the right to stick to a convoluted but well-signed footpath which leads you back to the railway line and on as far as **Exton**.

Diverting away from the railway track, you now turn right along Green Lane. Follow this and then Exton Lane as far as the junction with Station Rd where, turning right, you pass *The Puffing Billy* (☎ 01392-877888, 🖳 www .thepuffingbilly.co.uk; daily noon-2pm & 6-9pm) which serves up some hearty walking food, including Aberdeen Angus rump steaks (£15.95) and the Puffing Billy sustainable local fish pie (£10.95). Snacks may be available in the afternoon during the summer months.

For **B&B** on the eastern side of the Exe, *Riverdown* (☎ 01392-873852, 🖳 www.riverdownbedandbreakfast.co.uk; 1D/1T; 🛁; WI-FI; £35-37.50pp, sgl occ £50) is on Green Lane.

Having followed Station Rd for approximately 200 metres you pass through a gate on your left and arrive at the railway line. Gigantic wooden boardwalks now become your pathway and you follow them to **Lympstone** where, having crossed the railway line, you arrive opposite the Londis **shop** (Mon-Sat 8am-8pm, Sun 9am-4pm). There is also a **café** here, *Shear's* (Thur-Tue 8.30am-5pm), and a **pub**: *The Swan Inn* (☎ 01395-270403, 🖳 www .theswaninn-lympstone.co.uk; food served daily noon-3pm & 6-9.30pm). The lunch menu includes soup (£4.95), sandwiches (£5.95-7.25) and hot meals such as steak & kidney suet pudding (£10.95).

Turn right here and take the road to the outskirts of the village, with Exmouth finally appearing on the horizon. Follow **Sowden Lane**, turning sharp left to pass under the railway line before taking a footpath on your right, which is then followed for a further two miles into **Exmouth**.

EXMOUTH [map p205]

Exmouth is a decent sized town with all of the amenities required and a good supply of accommodation, all within easy walking distance of the ferry terminal and coastal path (the exception being the campsite). Called Lydwicnaesse, or 'The point of the Bretons' in the 11th century, the town's name today is somewhat more self-explanatory, with 'Exe' a Celtic word for 'fish'. The town grew with the construction of permanent docks in the 19th century, its popularity as a destination for holidaymakers increasing exponentially as a result.

If you are interested in the town's history and social development **Exmouth**

Museum (☎ 07768-184127, 🖳 www.de vonmuseums.net/Exmouth; Apr-Oct Mon, Fri, Sat 10.30am-12.30pm, Tue & Thur 10.30am-4.30pm, Wed 10.30am-4pm; £1.50) is on Sheppards Row.

Exmouth Festival (🖳 www.exmouth festival.org.uk) is held here in June.

Services

The helpful **tourist information centre** (☎ 01395-222299, 🖳 www.exmouth-guide.co .uk; Apr/May to Nov Mon-Fri 10am-5pm, Sat 10am-4pm, Nov-Apr/May Mon-Sat 10am-3pm) is in the Travelworld office on Rolle St. For **internet access** the library

(Mon, Tue, Thur & Fri 9am-6pm, Sat 9am-4pm) on Exeter Rd is, as always, a safe bet.

The pedestrianised centre is not the most becoming of places but just about everything you need can be found within it. There's a **post office** (Mon-Fri 9am-5.30pm, Sat 9am-12.30pm) in Magnolia Walk (the 'road' that runs through Magnolia Centre, a shopping precinct), as well as a **chemist,** Boots (Mon-Sat 8.30am-5.30pm, Sun 10am-4pm), the **trekking/camping shop** Millets (Mon-Sat 9am-5.30pm, Sun 10am-4pm) and a Co-op **supermarket** (Mon-Sat 7am-9pm, Sun 10am-4pm). There's also a Tesco (daily 6am-11pm) on Rolle St as well as a **launderette**, Wessex Cleaners (Mon-Fri 9am-5pm, Sat 9am-4pm).

There are also some **banks** with **ATMs** around town.

Where to stay

Camping is an option near Exmouth but, as with most of the towns along this stretch, the nearest site, *Prattshayes National Trust Campsite* (Map 41; ☎ 01395-276626, 🖳 www.nationaltrust.org.uk; click on Holidays and Camping; 🐾; £5 per hiker and tent; Apr-Oct) is a fair distance from the town itself. You can't get a bus there so you can either turn off the path at Maer Lane, just as you leave Exmouth, or you can continue on the coastal trail past Orcombe Point to a small path heading off left to Gore Lane, which in turn leads to Maer Lane. Sadly their bunkhouse is for groups only.

There are numerous **bed and breakfasts** in Exmouth that are well located for both the trail and town centre. The breakfast at *Alexandrahayes* (☎ 01395-273376; 1S/2D or T/2T/1F, all share facilities; 🛋; 🐾; WI-FI; £25pp), 100 Victoria Rd, is DIY: the ingredients are left upstairs in the guest

kitchen – which is also available for you to cook your own evening meal should you wish to – and you are left to prepare it. It's a novel but popular approach.

Closest to the centre on this road is *High Tide* (☎ 01395-272292, 🖳 www.bedandbreakfastexmouth.co.uk; 1D/1T/1F; 🛋; WI-FI; £30-35pp, sgl occ from £40), at No 30, from which the landlady will happily organise taxis for you to transfer your luggage.

At 1 Morton Rd – where it meets Victoria Rd – *New Moorings* (☎ 01395-223073, 🖳 www.newmoorings.co.uk; 1S/3D/2T; WI-FI; £30pp, sgl £30, sgl occ £40) offers kippers to start your day as well as the normal breakfast choices; whilst directly opposite is *Dolphin Hotel* (☎ 01395-263832, 🖳 www.dolphinhotelexmouth.co.uk; 6S/5T/10D/4F, most en suite but some rooms share facilities; 🛋; 🐾; WI-FI; £32-40pp, sgl £50-65 but also negotiable), which has its own bar (Mon-Sat 6-11.30pm, Sun 6-10.30pm) but they don't serve food.

Further along Morton Rd and close to the seafront, *Clinton House* (☎ 01395-271969, 🖳 www.clinton-house.com; 1S/3D or T/2F; 🛋; WI-FI; £30pp, sgl/sgl occ £30-40), No 41, offers mackerel and other fish options for breakfast. Meanwhile, opposite, *Seaforth Hotel* (☎ 01395-275252, 🖳 www.seaforthexmouth.co.uk; 2D/2T/2F, shared facilities; 🐾; WI-FI; room £25pp, sgl occ £35), at No 45, seems reasonably priced though breakfast costs an extra £5.

St Andrews Rd is also home to several good establishments. Both *Anchoring* (☎ 01395-268849, 🖳 www.anchoringbandb.com; 1S/1D/1T/1F; 🛋; WI-FI; £25-35pp, sgl/sgl occ £35-45), No 106, and *Aslema* (☎ 01395-270737, 🖳 www.aslemaguesthouse

---

❏ **Where to stay: the details**
Unless specified, B&B-style accommodation is either en suite or has private facilities; 🛋 means at least one room has a bath; 🐾 signifies that dogs are welcome in at least one room but always by prior arrangement, an additional charge may also be payable; WI-FI means wi-fi is available in the property, though not always (reliably) in every room.

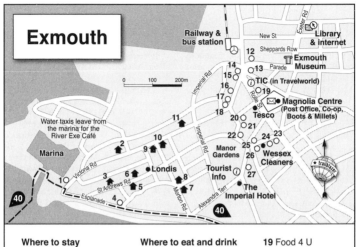

Where to stay
2 Alexandrahayes
3 Anchoring
5 Aslema
6 Beachend Guesthouse
7 Seaforth Hotel
8 Clinton House
9 Dolphin Hotel
10 New Moorings
11 High Tide

Where to eat and drink
1 The Beach
4 The Grove
12 The Mexican
13 Powder Monkey
14 Exmouth Indoor Market
15 Deli on the Strand
16 Crusty Cob
17 The Bamboo
18 The Clipper
19 Food 4 U
20 Franklin's
21 The Strand
22 The Chronicle
23 Avanti
24 Lemongrass
25 The Heavitree
26 Ganges
27 Golden Dragon

.co.uk; 1S/1D/1T/1F; WI-FI; 🐾 about £10; £27-30pp, sgl £35), No 61.

Meanwhile, ***Beach End Guest House*** (☎ 01395-222732, 🖥 www.beachend.co .uk; 2D/1T; ☞; WI-FI; £27.50-40pp, sgl occ negotiable) at No 68, whilst not taking one-night bookings over the summer months unless they fit in with their diary, is a popular stop for walkers. One of their double rooms has a roll-top bath and the bathroom itself is almost the same size as the bedroom!

Where to eat and drink
For most of Exmouth's eating options, of which there are plenty, you have to walk five minutes from the path into the town centre. This is dominated by a large plaza, around which are dotted numerous eateries.

Of the places on the main square the favourite among trekkers and also one of the newest is ***Deli On The Strand*** (☎ 01395-279977; Mon-Fri 9am-5pm, Sat 9.30am-5pm). It does well-made and delicious sandwiches and baguettes (including a crayfish, salad and lemon mayo for £4.25). Nearby, and cheaper, ***The Crusty Cob*** (☎ 01395-267634; Mon-Fri 7am-5pm, Sat 7.30am-4pm) is a cheap bakers with some good-value sandwiches (pork roll £3.10). Across the plaza, ***Franklins*** (☎ 01395-263086; Tue-Sat 7.30am-11.30pm, Sun-Mon 8am-5pm) does breakfast all day, lunch from 11am, tapas from 4pm (£3.95-4.50 per dish); they also have a restaurant (Fri & Sat 6-9.30pm) upstairs when they offer a small but eclectic menu, including chicken breast with barbecue sauce served with dauphinoise potatoes and veg (£10.95). Next door, *The Strand* (Wed-Sat & Mon 9.30am-4.30pm, Sun 9am-3pm) sells lovely homemade cakes from £1.60, which they also sell on a stall at **Exmouth Market**. Nearby, and offering the cheapest food of all, *Food4U* (☎ 01395-223332; Mon-Thur & Sat 8.30am-5pm, Sat 9am-5pm) has quiches for £1.50 and sandwiches from £1.79.

Also on the square, *Clipper* (9am-10pm; WI-FI) is a huge, Wetherspoon-esque place with similar good deals on food and also, like Wetherspoon's, bans dogs), with sandwiches from £2.95. Wetherspoon's actually has its own representative just off the square, *Powder Monkey* (☎ 01395-280090; Sun-Thur 8am-midnight, Fri and Sat to 1am) offering their usual unsurprising but very cheap menu; though, as with all of their properties, dogs aren't allowed. The name, incidentally, commemorates the career of local girl Nancy Perriam who, unusually for a woman, worked on the naval ships as a powder monkey (ie someone who filled shells and cartridges with powder – a task usually done by boys.) Nancy lived nearby in Tower St where she died in 1865 aged 98.

Pub-wise, you're not exactly short of choices and there are a couple of good ones right on the path. Almost as soon as you step off the Starcross Ferry you come to *The Beach* (☎ 01395 272090, 🖳 www.the beachpub.co.uk; daily noon-2pm & 6.30-9pm; 🐾), a vibrant place with some good food and a great atmosphere. Dogs are welcome (which is quite unusual for Exmouth) and no standard main dish is more than £8, with West Country ham, double egg & chips just £6.95.

Continuing along the Esplanade, *The Grove* (☎ 01395-272101; food daily noon-10pm; 🐾), part of the Young's chain, offers a similar menu with few surprises – with mains £7.95-£13.50 – though the vegetarian sweet potato curry with steamed rice and naan bread for £9.95 is a quirky option. Dogs are very welcome here too.

Heading into town, don't be too put off by the exterior of *The Heavitree* (☎ 01395-263640, 🖳 www.theheavitree.co.uk; food

served Mon-Fri 10am-2.30pm & 6-9pm, Sat 10am-7pm, Sun 10am-5pm; 🐾) on the central roundabout, which is a little noisy and lairy but nevertheless very good value with steaks from just £8.50; it also has WI-FI and is one of the few pubs in the centre that allows dogs.

There is the usual range of international cuisines. On High St you'll find *Ganges* (☎ 01395-263800; daily from 6pm) for Indian food, the Thai *Lemongrass* (☎ 01395-269306, 🖳 www.lemongrassthai.co .uk; Tue-Sat noon-2.30pm & 5.30-10.30pm, Sun & Mon eves only; curries £6.95-9.95) and the Italian *Avanti* (☎ 01395-224546; Mon-Sat 6-10pm), with *pollo milanese* (breaded chicken breast with tomato and herb spaghetti) for £8.95. Nearby on The Beacon you'll find *Golden Dragon* (☎ 01395-264027; Fri, Sat & Sun noon-2pm, daily 6-11.30pm) with crispy seaweed (£3.70) and chicken in oyster sauce (£5.20).

Back down on The Parade you'll also find *The Mexican* (☎ 01395-223388, 🖳 www.eatmexican.co.uk; Mon-Thur 11am-2pm & 6-10pm, Fri & Sat 11am-2pm & 6-10.30pm, Sun 6-9.30pm; winter hours vary so call in advance) where mains cost £9.95-14.95. Back on The Strand, *The Bamboo Restaurant* (☎ 01395-267253; Mon-Sat noon-2.30pm & 5.30-11pm, Sun noon-2.30pm & 5.30-10.30pm) is a large but discreet place, with the usual tantalising Asian dishes including sliced duck, fresh ginger & spring onions (£8.30).

There are some good fine-dining options too, our favourite being *The Chronicle* (☎ 01395-488015, 🖳 www .chroniclerestaurant.co.uk; Wed-Mon 6-9pm), 3 Chapel Hill, named after the building in which it sits which once housed the offices of the local *Exmouth Chronicle* newspaper. The cuisine is influenced by all four corners of the world and, while often fancy, is not excessively expensive: seared lamb's liver, for example, with sweet onions, smoked bacon & creamy mash is only £10.70.

Finally, a rundown of the eating options in Exmouth wouldn't be complete without mention of *River Exe Café* (☎

07761-116103, ☐ riverexecafe.com; Mar/
Apr-Sep, opening times change throughout
the season but are approx 10am-10pm), the
town's most unusual eatery. Situated on a
barge floating on the River Exe, you have
to get a water taxi to get to it (£4 from the
Marina, leaving at half-past each hour and
taking 20 minutes). The menu changes regularly but surely the most appropriate food
to try would be their Exe mussels steamed
in Devon cider, bacon, tarragon & cream
(or pernod, white wine, tomatoes and saffron) for £13.95.

Transport
[See also pp55-60] Stagecoach's 57 **bus**
connects the town with Exeter via Topsham
and Lympstone; their 56 service goes to
Exeter via Woodbury and Lympstone.
Meanwhile, their No 157 and 357 services
travel to Budleigh Salterton; the 157 goes
via Sidmouth.
   Trains run approximately twice an
hour to Exeter.
   For a **cab** try AJ Taxi (☎ 01395-
222655).

EXMOUTH TO SIDMOUTH   [MAPS 40-46]

Today's **12½-mile (20km; 4hrs 25 mins)** stage begins with a saunter through
Exmouth on what, at approximately two miles, is said to be the longest seafront
in Devon, and ends within the borders of a World Heritage Site (see box below).
   The cliff-top-walking involved in this stage is pretty relentless at times, and
there are a couple of moderately strenuous climbs. However, the views from
West Down Beacon and Brandy Head more than make up for any aches and
pains, while Otter Estuary Nature Reserve and the spectacular sea-stacks at
Ladram Bay add plenty of wonder and variation to the day.
   In addition, in Budleigh Salterton there are a couple of cafés (albeit both
linked to monstrous caravan parks), which are a good spot for lunch and provide a chance to replace any lost fluids, and plenty of options for a cream tea or
evening meal once you arrive in the elegant Regency town of Sidmouth.

❏ The UNESCO Jurassic Coast World Heritage Site
The Jurassic Coast World Heritage Site (aka the Dorset and East Devon Coast World
Heritage Site) stretches for 95 miles (155km) from Orcombe Point, just outside
Exmouth in East Devon, to Studland Bay and the chalk stacks of Old Harry Rocks in
Purbeck, Dorset.
   In order to get some sort of handle on the complicated geology of this region, it's
useful to remember that, if walking from west to east along the coast path, the rocks
on which you tread are getting ever younger the further you go. Starting with the red
rocks of the **Triassic Period** (from 250 million years old) between Exmouth and Lyme
Regis, the coast path then clambers over the younger stones of the **Jurassic Period**
(from 200 million years old) between Pinhay Bay and White Nothe, before finally
entering the **Cretaceous Period** (from 145 to 65 million years old) as you climb round
Ringstead Bay. (As you probably expect, the division isn't quite as neat as this – many
of the cliffs between Durdle Door and Studland, for example, are often still Jurassic
due to various geological folds and the land tilting in the mid-Cretaceous Period (see
pp74-5) – but for non-geologists this simple rule is a good place to begin.
   It is due to this incredible and – unusually – very visible geology that the coastline was designated England's first UNESCO World Heritage Site in 2001, thereby
placing it alongside sites such as the Great Barrier Reef and the Grand Canyon.

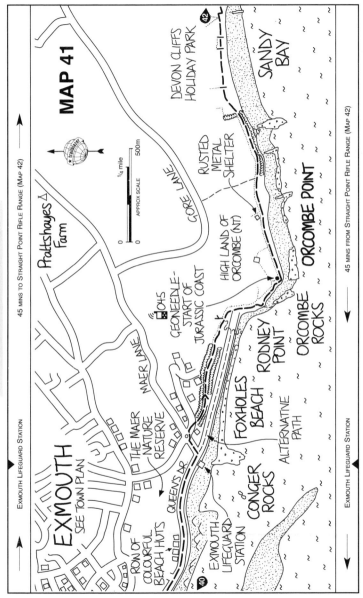

MAP 41

EXMOUTH
SEE TOWN PLAN

EXMOUTH LIFEGUARD STATION

45 MINS TO STRAIGHT POINT RIFLE RANGE (MAP 42)

Prattshayes △ Farm

DEVON CLIFFS HOLIDAY PARK

SANDY BAY

RUSTED METAL SHELTER

GORE LANE

MAER LANE

GEONEEDLE - START OF JURASSIC COAST

HIGH LAND OF ORCOMBE (NT)

ORCOMBE POINT

THE MAER NATURE RESERVE

QUEEN'S DR.

ROW OF COLOURFUL BEACH HUTS

EXMOUTH LIFEGUARD STATION

FOXHOLES BEACH

RODNEY POINT

ORCOMBE ROCKS

ALTERNATIVE PATH

CONGER ROCKS

45 MINS FROM STRAIGHT POINT RIFLE RANGE (MAP 42)

EXMOUTH LIFEGUARD STATION

¼ mile

500m

APPROX SCALE

The route

Disembarking from the ferry in Exmouth, follow the promenade (Esplanade) parallel with the road all the way along the seafront. It's quite a pleasant stretch, with seawall, beach, windsurfers and volleyballers to your right and **The Maer**, a nature reserve, on the opposite side of the road. If it's windy beware the gusts blowing sand off the beach and directly into your eyes. On your way look out

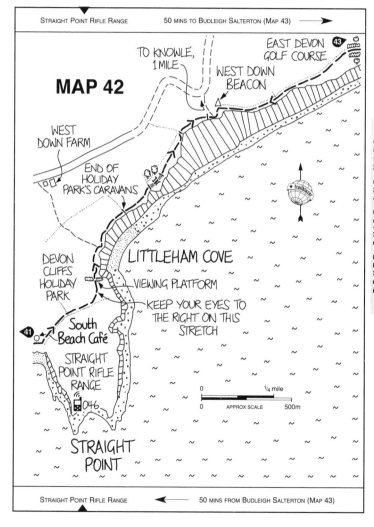

STRAIGHT POINT RIFLE RANGE   50 MINS TO BUDLEIGH SALTERTON (MAP 43) ⟶

TO KNOWLE,
1 MILE

EAST DEVON 43
GOLF COURSE

WEST DOWN
BEACON

MAP 42

WEST
DOWN FARM

END OF
HOLIDAY
PARK'S CARAVANS

trailblazer

DEVON
CLIFFS
HOLIDAY
PARK

LITTLEHAM COVE

VIEWING PLATFORM

KEEP YOUR EYES TO
THE RIGHT ON THIS
STRETCH

41 South
Beach Café

STRAIGHT
POINT RIFLE
RANGE

046

0   ¼ mile

0   APPROX SCALE   500m

STRAIGHT
POINT

STRAIGHT POINT RIFLE RANGE   ⟵   50 MINS FROM BUDLEIGH SALTERTON (MAP 43)

ROUTE GUIDE AND MAPS

for the **Allen Williams turret**, like a dalek's 'head', a relic not of time-travel but of WWII.

At Exmouth Lifeguard Station you have two options: turn left up to the roundabout then right to walk above the beach; or continue along the seafront to virtually the end of the tarmac and **Foxholes Beach**, where a steep path zig-zags upwards to rejoin the other path.

The trail is easy as it crosses the pastures of the National Trust-owned **High Land of Orcombe** and the views of the sea and back along the coast are occasionally magnificent. The strange **Geoneedle monument** marks the beginning of the **Jurassic Coast** which now spreads out, daunting and yet inviting in equal measure, in front of you.

The path hugs the coast through **Devon Cliffs Holiday Park** (caravans only), where you can stop at *South Beach Café* (Mar-Oct daily 8am-9pm), before reaching **Straight Point Rifle Range**. Guns crack, waves crash and the wind whistles (and people say that what they love most about the coast path is the tranquillity it provides). Below you to your right as you pass along the edge of the park is **Littleham Cove** – home to swallows, falcons, kittiwakes and grey seals.

Leaving the caravan park, the trail clambers over the spectacular terracotta cliffs to reach **West Down Beacon** (129m/423ft), from where you descend along foliage-enveloped trails through **Jubilee Park** (keep your eyes open for linnets, falcons and clouded yellow butterflies) to the Promenade in Budleigh Salterton.

BUDLEIGH SALTERTON [map p213]

Situated at the mouth of the River Otter, the genteel town of Budleigh Salterton was appropriately called Ottermouth until the name was changed to reflect what, at the time, was the town's primary industry: salt-panning.

Apart from picking up a sandwich or resting on the town's quiet little seafront there is little to keep you in Budleigh Salterton today. The thatched **Fairlynch Museum** (☎ 01395-442666, 🖳 www .devonmuseums.net/Fairlynch; Apr-Sep & October half-term Sun-Fri 2-4.30pm; free) is the main attraction, with Bronze Age and geological displays and an impressive collection of some 4000 items of clothing, some dating back to the early 18th century.

Perhaps its most curious possession, however, actually lies chained up outside: a log apparently gnawed by a beaver that washed up on the banks of the River Otter, which is a mystery as there are no beavers in this river, nor indeed supposedly in England. (The most plausible explanation is that one of the Otter's tributaries, the Tale, runs through the private Escot Estate where apparently they do keep beavers – and it must have washed down from there.)

The only other site of note is the blue plaque that adorns a wall on Fore St celebrating the fact that the house features in the background of John Everett Millias's painting *The Boyhood of Raleigh*. The great adventurer Walter Raleigh, the subject of

---

❏ Important note – walking times
Unless otherwise specified, **all times in this book refer only to the time spent walking**. You will need to add 20-30% to allow for rests, photography, checking the map, drinking water etc. When planning the day's hike count on 5-7 hours of actual walking.

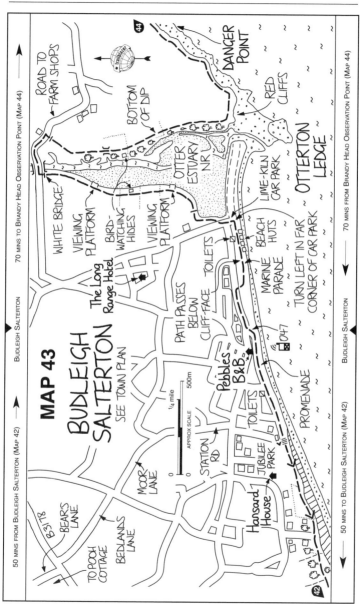

❏ **A pebble's tale**
Budleigh Salterton is known for its Lower Triassic pebble beds. For thousands of
years the predominantly oval shaped and extremely hard pebbles have been spilling
out from the local cliffs as sea and time take their toll. Four hundred million years
old, they are identical to rocks found in Northern France, both being made of hard
quartzite. They are thought to have been transported to their two respective homes via
one of the giant rivers that flowed through the Triassic period's arid and scorching red
deserts (see Geology pp72-7).

---

the painting, was actually born a couple of
miles inland in East Budleigh.

Budleigh Salterton Jazz Festival (🖥
www.budleighjazzfestival.org) is held here
in April and the **Literary Festival** (🖥
www.budlitfest.org.uk) in September.

Services
Though it has several services there is little
accommodation here for walkers wanting a
single-night stay; as a result, most trekkers
continue to Sidmouth where more beds are
available. However, there is a **tourist information office** (☎ 01395-445275, 🖥 www
.visitbudleigh.com; summer Mon-Sat
10am-4pm, sometimes to 5pm in the peak
season; winter Mon, Wed, Fri & Sat 10am-
4pm though they may close earlier), on
Fore St, as well as a Co-op **supermarket**
(6am-10pm), in the middle of the High St,
which has a **post office** (Mon-Fri 9am-
5.30pm, Sat 9am-12.30pm) housed within
it, and a Lloyds **Pharmacy** (Mon-Fri 9am-
6pm, Sat 9am-4pm). There are **cash
machines** on the High St.

Where to stay
Camping is available relatively nearby at
Pooh Cottage Holiday Park (off Map 43;
☎ 01395-442354, 🖥 www.poohcottage.co
.uk; £7-9pp for hiker & tent; 🐾 free; mid
Mar to Oct) which is just over 1½ miles
(approximately half an hour's walk)
inland.

Suitable **B&Bs** are rather thin on the
ground. *The Pebbles* (☎ 01395-442417, 🖥
www.bedandbreakfastbythebeach.com; 3D
or T; ☞; WI-FI; £50-60pp, sgl occ £89-110),
16 Fore St, has marvellous rooms with
tremendous views and although expensive

is worth the price. Breakfast is taken in the
conservatory overlooking the rear garden,
which virtually backs onto the path itself.

Meanwhile, also close to the path, the
luxurious *Hansard House Hotel* (☎ 01395-
442773, 🖥 www.hansardhousehotel.co.uk;
1S/4D/5T/1F; ☞; 🐾 £5; WI-FI; £45-48pp,
sgl £48-52, sgl occ £65-75), 3 North View
Rd, welcomes dogs and is also popular with
walkers.

Up towards the top of the High St, *The
Feathers* (☎ 01395-442042, 🖥 www.feath
ers-hotel.co.uk; 4D; WI-FI; £30-35pp, sgl
occ £55-65) is a traditional pub, originally
dating back to the 16th century though it's
been heavily worked on since.

Finally, *The Long Range Hotel* (☎
01395-443321, 🖥 www.thelongrangehotel
.co.uk; 2S/3D/3T; ☞; WI-FI; £47.50-
59.50pp, sgl £59.95-69.75) is out of town
on Vales Rd but only a few hundred metres
from the coast path. It's a friendly and effi-
ciently run place with a lovely conservatory looking over the Otter Valley.

Where to eat and drink
Near the path, *Slice of Lyme* (☎ 01395-
442648; Mon 10am-3:30pm, Tue-Fri
10am-3.30pm & 6-9pm, Sat 10am-4pm &
6-9pm, Sun 10am-4pm) does some very
acceptable food during the day, with cream
teas at £4.65, while its evening menu is
equally tempting: try the roasted
Mediterranean vegetable lasagne at £10.95.
It also has an ice-cream kiosk next door,
which is handy, though true ice-cream affi-
cionados are advised to try *The Creamery*
which boasts over 30 ice-cream flavours;
true gluttons can add clotted cream for even
more calories.

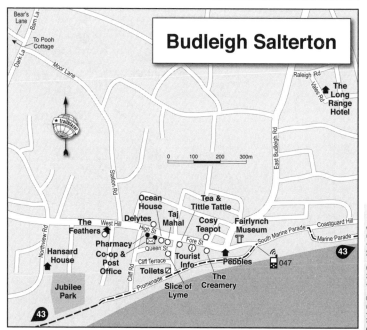

Delytes (☎ 01395-443182, 🖥 www
.delytes.co.uk; Mon-Thur & Sat 9am-4pm,
Fri 9am-5pm), a delicatessen, has a good
selection of sandwiches and baguettes starting at £2.50, though the home-cooked local
free-range beef with horseradish or mustard
and salad is 20p more. It also has a wonderful bread selection and offers meals such
as a quiche of the day with salad for £5.65.
On the opposite side of the road, *Ocean
House* (☎ 01395-442676, 🖥 www.ocean
house.biz; Mon-Sat 10am-4pm) is a much
smarter, swisher affair, a café and deli combined that also hosts the occasional themed
evening (eg pizza nights or rustic supper
nights). The menu is varied and appetising,
including Welsh rarebit for £6.75 or homemade fish cakes for £8.95.

Up at the top of the road, *The Feathers*
(see Where to stay; food Mon-Sat noon-
2.30pm & 6-9pm, Sun lunchtimes only)
offers a fairly standard pub-grub menu

including 8oz gammon steak with egg or
pineapple for £8.25 and a light-bite menu
for £5.25 (though this is not available Sat
evening or Sun lunch).

On Fore St, *Tea and Tittle Tattle* (☎
01395-443203; Tue-Sat 10am-4.30pm, Sun
noon-4.30pm) does some substantial meals
such as steak & kidney pudding for £7.95.
Cosy Teapot (☎ 01395-444016; daily
10am-4.45pm) is a very traditional lace-
and-doily affair that sells the odd antique as
well as a varied selection of cakes, with
mince pies for £1.

Lastly, there's an Indian takeaway, *Taj
Mahal* (☎ 01395-446093; daily noon-2pm
& 5.30-11pm), on the High St.

Transport
[See also pp55-60] For **buses**,
Stagecoach's 157 and 357 connect the town
with Exmouth and Sidmouth. **Budleigh
Taxis** can be reached on ☎ 01395-446000.

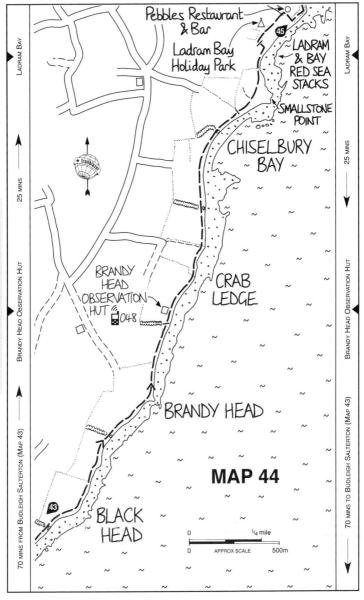

LADRAM BAY

25 MINS

BRANDY HEAD OBSERVATION HUT

70 MINS FROM BUDLEIGH SALTERTON (MAP 43)

LADRAM BAY

25 MINS

BRANDY HEAD OBSERVATION HUT

70 MINS TO BUDLEIGH SALTERTON (MAP 43)

Pebbles Restaurant & Bar

Ladram Bay Holiday Park

45

LADRAM & BAY RED SEA STACKS

SMALLSTONE POINT

CHISELBURY ~ BAY ~

trailblaze

CRAB LEDGE

BRANDY HEAD OBSERVATION HUT ☎048

BRANDY HEAD ~

MAP 44

43

BLACK HEAD

0   ¼ mile
0   500m
APPROX SCALE

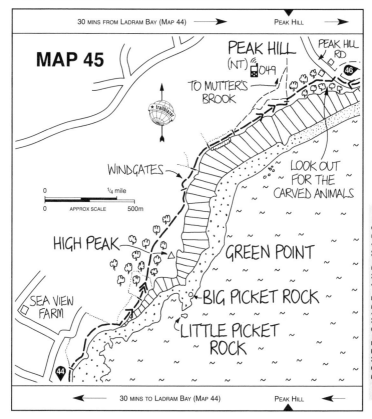

MAP 45

PEAK HILL
(NT) 🔔049

PEAK HILL
RD

46

TO MUTTER'S
BROOK

WINDGATES ←

LOOK OUT
FOR THE
CARVED ANIMALS

0   ¼ mile
0   APPROX SCALE   500m

HIGH PEAK

GREEN POINT

SEA VIEW
FARM

BIG PICKET ROCK

LITTLE PICKET
ROCK

44

ROUTE GUIDE AND MAPS

30 MINS TO LADRAM BAY (MAP 44) ←   PEAK HILL ←

Leaving Budleigh Salterton along the Promenade, past seemingly endless commemorative benches, eventually you hit the River Otter and there is a brief but pleasant sojourn round **Otter Estuary Nature Reserve**. Don't get too excited by the name, however, for mink are more common than otters and any paw prints you come across are more likely to belong to a Jack Russell. As compensation, however, in the skies above soar merlins and red kites.

Having left the reserve and rejoined the coast, you are now confronted by the ominously named cliffs **Danger Point** and **Black Head**, the trail here making for a majestic stroll on a sun-soaked summer's afternoon. **Brandy Head**, named after the contraband that was smuggled here, is topped by an **Observation Hut** that was used to test weapons and gun sights during the Second World War. Continuing past **Chiselbury Bay** and **Smallstone Point**, you soon come to **Ladram Bay** with its impressive display of red sandstone sea stacks and the gigantic ***Ladram Bay Holiday Park*** (☎ 01395-568398, 🖳 www.ladrambay.co.uk; Easter to early Nov; in peak season minimum booking four nights so accept walk-ins only if they have space; £15-35 per pitch for two adults and tent; 🐾 £3-5; WI-FI), home to ***Pebbles Restaurant*** (daily noon-2pm & 6-9pm) and ***Pebbles Bar*** (daily 10am-9pm); both are open to 9.30pm in school summer holidays. In addition they have ***Coast Café*** (school summer holidays daily 9am-9pm, rest of season days/hours vary), a ***takeaway*** (school summer holidays noon-11pm) and ***Wave Bar*** (school summer holidays noon-midnight, rest of season 6-11pm) and a ***supermarket*** (school summer holidays 8am-8pm, rest of season 8am-5pm).

Following Ladram Bay you arrive at what initially appears to be a daunting climb. This is **High Peak** (157m) and the haul is initially quite lenient; it becomes less so, however, once you enter the woods.

Once at the top take a deep breath; the reward for your efforts is a gradual descent through the trees and a dramatic view of the coastal cliffs ahead before you need to climb again, this time up the steeper slopes of **Peak Hill**. Descending through woodland once more (look out for the rabbits and mice carved into tree stumps) you arrive with some relief at **Peak Hill Road**. Leaving it to inspect the ranks of **commemorative benches**, you soon come to a right turn leading down to **Jacob's Ladder Beach**. As you round the cliff, *Clock Tower Café* (☎ 01395-515319, 🖳 www.clocktowercafesidmouth.co.uk; daily 10am-5pm, to 6pm in school summer holidays) stands above you, a restored 17th-century lime kiln and pseudo-fort that serves such delicacies as deep-fried whitebait (£6.25) and homemade cakes.

Clifton Walkway and its rockfalls are now all that separate you from the end of the stage. Survive and you'll soon be strolling on Sidmouth seafront with all the other sunkissed sightseers.

SIDMOUTH [map p219]
'A town caught still in a timeless charm'
John Betjeman
Nestling quietly in the Sid Valley, with red cliffs soaring on either side, Sidmouth is, as the former poet laureate suggests, a lovely place. Winner of numerous awards for its gardens, floral displays abound throughout the town centre. A touch too old-fashioned and genteel for some, for the average walker who simply seeks sustenance and sleep Sidmouth has plenty to offer on both counts.

Featuring in the Domesday Book as 'Sedemuda', Sidmouth began life as a small fishing community. Its geographical location prevented the town from successfully constructing a decent harbour, as a result of which Sidmouth didn't really grow in earnest until tourism took off during the

Georgian and Regency eras (1720-1840); much of the town's architecture still dates from this time. The young Queen Victoria holidayed in the town as a baby in 1819 (Royal Glen Hotel bears a plaque celebrating the visit) and the town's growth and popularity as a resort continued throughout her reign.

Sidmouth Museum (☎ 01395-516139, 🖳 www.sidvaleassociation.org.uk; Apr-Oct Mon 1-4pm, Tue-Sat 10am-4pm; free), on Church St, houses exhibitions describing the town's development from a fishing village through to Regency and Victorian times as well as an exhibition on the Jurassic Coast. They also offer free guided walks to various parts of the town, each informative amble lasting approximately two hours.

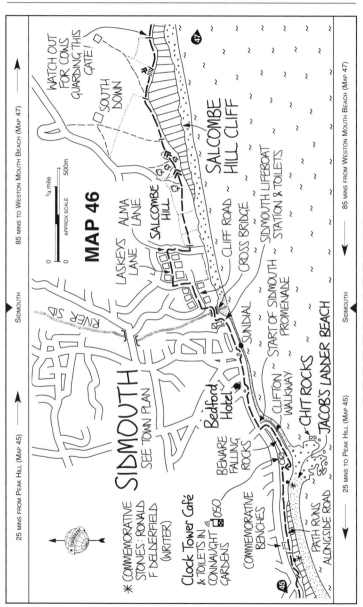

Sidmouth Folk Week (🖵 www.sidmou thfolkweek.co.uk) is held here in August.

Services

The **tourist information centre** (☎ 01395-516441, 🖵 www.visitsidmouth.co.uk; Apr-Oct Mon-Sat 10am-5pm, Sun 10am-4pm, Nov-Feb Mon-Sat 10am-1pm, Mar-Apr Mon-Thur 10am-4pm, Fri & Sat 10am-5pm) stands at the eastern end of town on Ham Lane. For **internet** they will direct you to the **library** (Mon & Fri 9am-6pm, Wed & Thur 9am-5pm, Sat 9am-1pm) on Blackmore Drive, just west of the High St.

There are two **trekking/camping shops** on Fore St, one that's a national chain – Mountain Warehouse (Mon-Sat 9am-5pm, Sun 10am-4pm) – and one that's not: Sidmouth Outdoor Co (☎ 01395-579988; Mon-Sat 10am-1pm & 2-5pm). Nearby there's the **chemist**, Boots (Mon-Sat 9am-5.30pm, Sun 10am-4pm).

Much of what a trekker traditionally needs lies back from the front at the top end of Fore St (by which point it's actually called High St), including a Co-op **super-market** (Mon-Sat 7am-9pm, Sun 10am-4pm) and the **post office** (Mon-Fri 8.45am-5.30pm, Sat 8.45am-4.30pm). There are also some **banks** with **ATMs**.

Where to stay

Oddly, all of Sidmouth's **bed and break-fasts** are a short jaunt from the centre. Closest, on Salcombe Rd, are: pristine *The Hollies* (☎ 01395-514580, 🖵 www.hollies guesthouse.co.uk; 5D; WI-FI; £32.50-45pp, sgl occ £45-55), though they are not keen on one-night bookings in peak periods; *Canterbury House* (☎ 01395-513373, 🖵 www.Canterbury-House.com; 1S/4D/1D or T/2T; WI-FI; £33-37pp, sgl occ £45); and *Berwick House* (☎ 01395-513621, 🖵 www .berwick-house.co.uk; 4D/2T; WI-FI; £34-38pp, sgl occ £44-50) where kippers, por-ridge, and scrambled egg with salmon are on the breakfast menu; in fact, the latter two both dish up award-winning breakfasts.

A little further from the centre and all in a row along Vicarage Rd are *The Groveside* (☎ 01395-513406, 🖵 www.the groveside.co.uk; 1S/5D/3T; WI-FI; £40pp),

an Edwardian boutique guest-house that serves locally purchased and organic food on its breakfast plates; *Southcombe* (☎ 01395-513861, 🖵 www.southcombeguest house.co.uk/home.html; 5D/2T/1Tr; WI-FI; £35pp, sgl occ £40), where it is possible to add a four-course dinner (£17) to your bill and belly; and *Bramley Lodge* (☎ 01395-515710, 🖵 bramleyowner@btinternet.com; 2S/2D/1T/1F; ✆; £34-38pp, sgl occ from £60; Mar-Oct). The last in the row, *Lynstead* (☎ 01395-514635, 🖵 www.lyn steadguesthouse.co.uk; 1S/1T/2D/2Tr; ✆; 🐾; WI-FI; £30-32pp, sgl occ £40-45), is dog friendly and also has a pleasant garden in which to relax.

Fifteen minutes from the town centre and on Cotmaton Rd, *Glendevon* (☎ 01395-514028, 🖵 www.glendevon-hotel .co.uk; 4S/3D/1D or T; WI-FI; £40pp) has lovely big airy rooms; evening meals are available by agreement.

Though not home to any B&Bs the seafront is lined with **hotels**. Two of the first that you come to are *The Bedford Hotel* (☎ 01395-513047, 🖵 www.bedford hotelsidmouth.co.uk; 40 flexible rooms; ✆; WI-FI; 🐾 £5; £53-90pp for dinner, bed and breakfast), where £10pp will be deducted if you don't want an evening meal; and *Hotel Riviera* (☎ 01395-515201, 🖵 www.hotel riviera.co.uk; 26 flexible rooms; ✆; 🐾 £13.50 inc a meal; WI-FI; £112-193pp), where an evening meal (restaurant open daily 12.30-2pm & 7-9pm) is also avail-able, although the room prices alone will perhaps deter most walkers.

Remaining on The Esplanade, there are three hotels owned by the same company, Sidmouth Hotels (toll free ☎ 0800-048 1731; 🖵 www.hotels-sidmouth.co.uk). Both *The Kingswood & Devoran Hotel* (☎ 01395-516367; 11S/ 15D/15T/7F; ✆; 🐾 in private rooms only £7; WI-FI; B&B £61-86pp, B&B £51-76pp) and *Hotel Elizabeth* (☎ 01395-513503; 1S/11D/16T; ✆; WI-FI; DB&B £63-86pp, B&B £53-76pp) offer dinner (five-course meal), bed and break-fast; if an evening meal is booked separate-ly it costs £25.

Cheaper than the above but with rates that do not include such a lavish evening

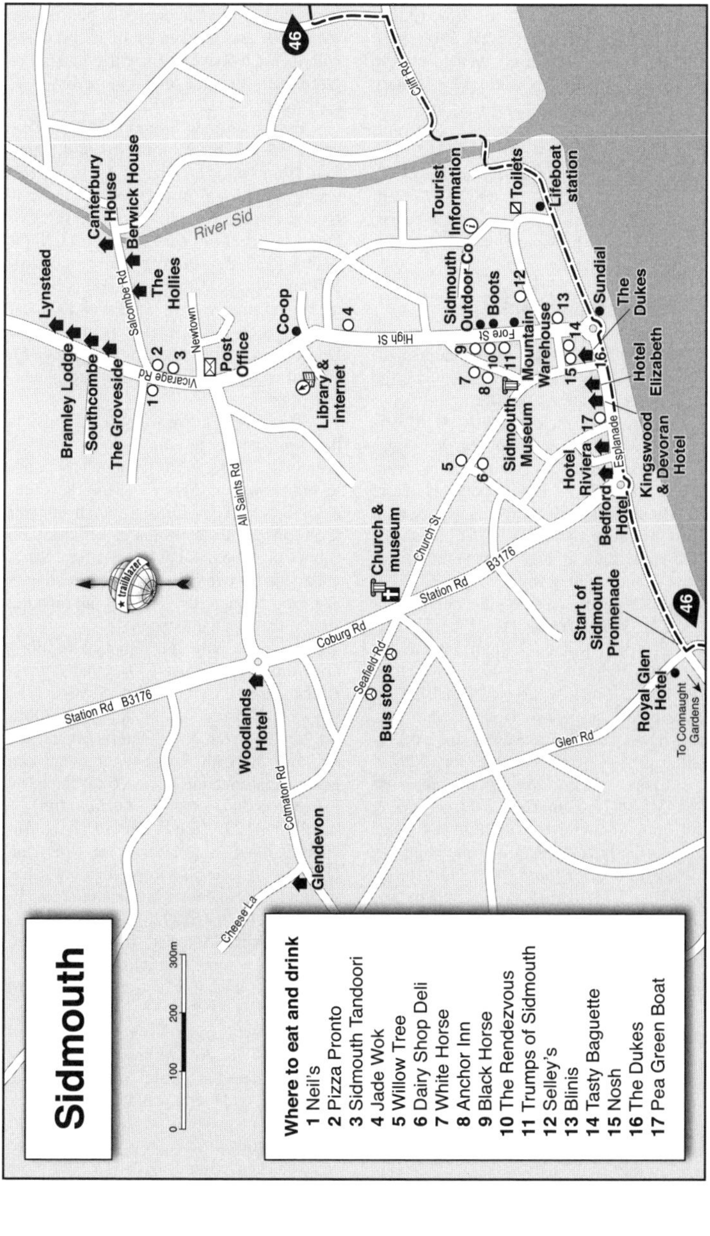

Sidmouth

0 100 200 300m

Where to eat and drink
1 Neil's
2 Pizza Pronto
3 Sidmouth Tandoori
4 Jade Wok
5 Willow Tree
6 Dairy Shop Deli
7 White Horse
8 Anchor Inn
9 Black Horse
10 The Rendezvous
11 Trumps of Sidmouth
12 Selley's
13 Blinis
14 Tasty Baguette
15 Nosh
16 The Dukes
17 Pea Green Boat

ROUTE GUIDE AND MAPS

meal, *The Dukes* (☎ 01395-513320; 3S/1T/4D/5F; ☛; WI-FI; B&B £40-66pp). The Dukes is open all year but the Kingswood and Elizabeth close for January and part of February.

Finally, away from the seafront, *Woodlands Hotel* (☎ 01395-513120, 💻 www.woodlands-hotel.com; 3S/2S or T/ 8D/7D or T; ☛; WI-FI; 🐾; £37-70pp; closed mid Dec to mid Jan), on the corner of Station Rd and Cotmaton Rd, is a 10-minute walk inland.

Where to eat and drink

It's surprising more people in Sidmouth don't suffer from obesity, given the temptation placed before them every day by the huge range of eateries on offer.

Takeaways include *Nosh* (☎ 01395-514724; Mon-Sat 8am-5pm, Sun 9am-3pm) a sandwich kitchen (with sarnies from £2.90) as well as jacket potatoes (from £2.90) on Market Place, and its nearest rival *Tasty Baguette* (☎ 01395-577575; Mon-Sat 8am-3pm, Sun in high season only), on Dove Lane, with tortilla wraps (£2.50-3) and jacket potatoes also on the menu.

The White Horse (☎ 01395-514271; July-Sep daily 8.30am-7.30pm, June & Oct 8.30am-6.30pm, to 3 or 4pm in winter), on Old Fore St, may sound like a pub but it's more of a local fast-food place, with fish, burger and pasties to take away, and a decent turkey & stuffing pie and chips for £5.95.

There is also *Sidmouth Tandoori* (☎ 01395-579944; Sun-Thur 5-11pm, Fri & Sat 5pm to midnight), on Radway Place (the northerly continuation of the High St), the nearby *Pizza Pronto* (☎ 01395-516319; Sun-Thur 5-11.30pm, Fri & Sat 5pm to late) and the Chinese *Jade Wok* (☎ 01395-514720; Sun-Thur noon-2.30pm & 5-11pm, Fri & Sat noon-2.30pm & 5-11.30pm) on the High St.

For sit-down food there are several good **cafés** – the following being just a small selection. The best known is *Trumps of Sidmouth* (☎ 01395-512416; Mon-Sat 9am-5pm, Sun 11am-4pm), on Fore St, which has existed in one form or another since 1813, its longevity probably due at least in part to its great sandwich selection

(eg duck liver paté in orange & plum sauce for £2.50) and the beauty of its premises with its old wooden fittings; it's the kind of place that's almost a tourist attraction in its own right.

For a traditional tearoom, *Willow Tree* (☎ 01395-514890; Mon-Sat 10am-4.30pm, Sun 11am-4pm), on Church St, is perfect; amongst the usual suspects on the menu is a good cottage pie with roast veg (£6.95). Opposite is *The Dairy Shop Deli* (☎ 01395-513018; summer daily 8.30am-5.30pm, winter 9am-4pm) serving lovely meals and snacks, most made with the local produce they sell in the shop including a Devon ham sandwich with mustard (£4.95), as well as plenty of vegetarian and gluten-free options.

The only problem with all the above is their reluctance to allow dogs on their premises. There is a solution for dog-lovers, however: *Selley's* (Mon-Sat 9am-4.30pm, Sun 10am-4pm; to 6pm in summer if custom demands; 🐾) is tucked away on Libra Court (behind Fat Face on Fore St). A cream tea for two is just £6 here. Seating is al-fresco though they've got an awning should the weather close in.

Even the pubs are reluctant to allow dogs on their premises. One that does is *Black Horse* (☎ 01395-513676, 💻 www.blackhorseinn-sidmouth.co.uk; Mon-Fri 9am-9pm, Sat & Sun 9am-9.30pm; 🐾) on Fore St, with a non-fussy menu and good pizza selection (from £6 for the basic 9" cheese and tomato). *Anchor Inn* (☎ 01395-514129; food served Mon-Sat 10am-9.30pm, Sun 11am-9pm; WI-FI), on Old Fore St, doesn't accept dogs but it has wi-fi and it also does a fair fish pie (£6.25). *Blinis* (☎ 01395-572920, 💻 www.blinis-cafe-bar.co.uk; Mon-Sat 10am-6pm, lunch noon-4pm) is more of a swish bar-café than a pub but it does a lovely crab paté on hot buttered toast (£6.95).

For **restaurants** there are two good choices: *The Rendezvous* (☎ 01395-516724; Tue-Sat 11am-3pm, Thur-Sat 6-8.30pm), on Fore St, has a Mediterranean-influenced menu with everything from sandwiches (during the day only; about £4.95) to pesto chicken, pasta dishes and a 10oz rump steak (£16.95). *Neil's* (☎ 01395-519494, 🖥 www.neilsrestaurant.com; Tue-Sat from 6pm) is beyond the northern end of the High St, on Radway Place. As they justifiably put it, they turn seafood into great food (though other, non-fishy dishes are also available). The cuisine is adventurous and tasty – try the Brixham sea bass on a seafood risotto – and the menu changes according to that day's catch. Nor is it too expensive, their early evening set menus costing £12.95 for two courses, £15.95 for three.

If all the above sounds a little too 'inland', our favourite place on the seafront is *Pea Green Boat* (☎ 01395-514152; Mon-Fri 9am-10pm, Sat 10am-10pm, Sun 10am-4pm), which does mezze platters for £10, pizzas from £7.50 and good vegetarian options including courgette penne with peppers, chilli and garlic (£8). They also

do, uniquely in our experience, a great champagne cream tea (£11).

Also worth recommending is *The Dukes* (see Where to stay; food served Sun-Thur noon-9pm, Fri & Sat noon-9.30pm), on The Esplanade, offering a good selection of homebaked pizzas (from £8.95 for 9", £10.25 for 12") and ploughman's platters (£7.50).

Transport

[See also pp55-60] Stagecoach's 157 **bus** travels east to Budleigh Salterton and Exmouth; the No 52A meanwhile connects the town with Seaton and Exeter and the 52B with Honiton and Exeter. Axe Valley's 899 also journeys between Sidmouth and Seaton stopping at Branscombe and Beer en route. For a **taxi** try Peak Taxis (☎ 01395-513322).

SIDMOUTH TO SEATON   [MAPS 46-50]

Today's 10¼-mile **(16.5km; 4hrs 10 mins)** stage is tough. As far as Branscombe Mouth it is a trail of steep and largely wooded pathways, where the lucky walker crosses pretty combes on the way to barren and sparsely populated beaches. True, only the occasional periods of level cliff-top walking offer any mercy on the knees. But the rewards, particularly gorgeous Lincombe, are ample.

There is also a decent café at Branscombe Mouth, whereafter the terrain changes drastically as you begin a spectacular walk below Hooken Cliffs, formed by a landslip in 1790. At windy Beer Head there are great views over Seaton Bay, where one finds both the friendly, photogenic fishing village of Beer, offering plentiful food and accommodation, and Seaton, this stage's destination. With the distance between Beer and Seaton being only 1½ miles, the former is a viable overnight stop, especially as tomorrow's stage is relatively short.

Finally, note that apart from the places mentioned above there is nowhere for the walker to get food or drink.

The route

Your first task, having left Sidmouth, is to climb up steep **Salcombe Hill Cliff**, an ascent that bears more than a passing similarity to a couple of yesterday's climbs: the path begins gently in a field before winding up the steep slope to some woods that sits on the summit like a toupé.

Following the path along the cliff-tops into **Salcombe Mouth**, round the edge of **Maynard's Cliff** and skirting **Combe Wood**, note the colours of the cliffs with the pastel reds and dirty oranges of the Triassic era topped, on occasion, with the lighter hued Cretaceous Upper Greensand – the Jurassic-era rock having been eroded away entirely (a phenomenon that geologists call an 'unconformity'). *(continued on p224)*

ROUTE GUIDE AND MAPS

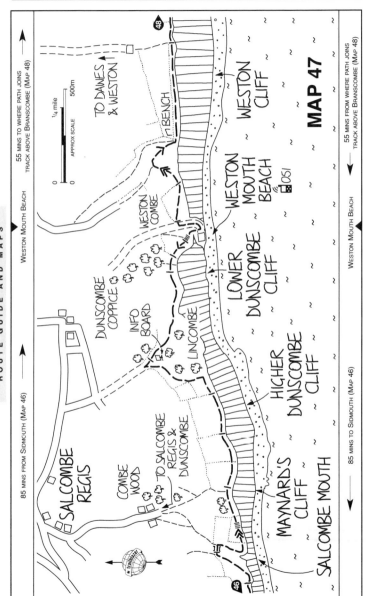

85 MINS FROM SIDMOUTH (MAP 46) →

WESTON MOUTH BEACH

55 MINS TO WHERE PATH JOINS TRACK ABOVE BRANSCOMBE (MAP 48) →

← 85 MINS TO SIDMOUTH (MAP 46)

WESTON MOUTH BEACH

55 MINS FROM WHERE PATH JOINS TRACK ABOVE BRANSCOMBE (MAP 48)

MAP 47

APPROX SCALE
¼ mile
500m

TO DANES & WESTON

BENCH

WESTON CLIFF

WESTON COMBE

WESTON MOUTH BEACH

051

LOWER DUNSCOMBE CLIFF

DUNSCOMBE COPPICE

INFO BOARD

LINCOMBE

HIGHER DUNSCOMBE CLIFF

SALCOMBE REGIS

COMBE WOOD

TO SALCOMBE REGIS & DUNSCOMBE

MAYNARD'S CLIFF

SALCOMBE MOUTH

Trailblazer

46

48

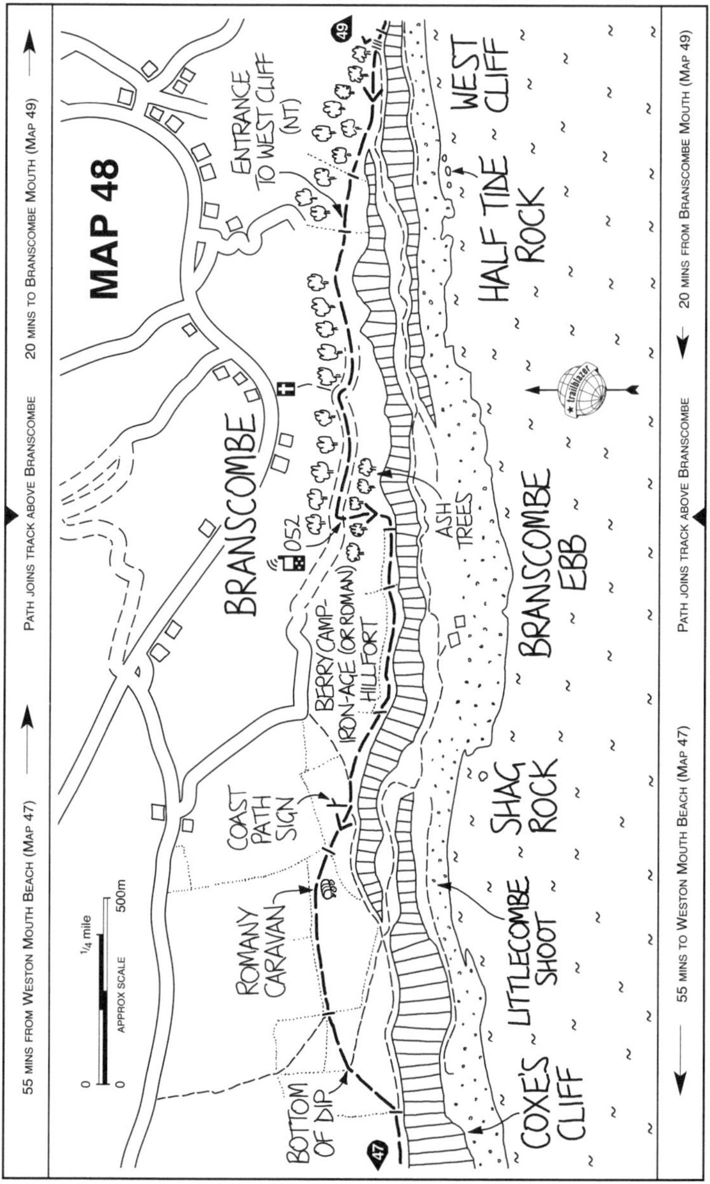

MAP 48

ENTRANCE TO WEST CLIFF (NT)

BRANSCOMBE

BERRY CAMP—
IRON-AGE (OR ROMAN)
HILLFORT

COAST PATH SIGN

ROMANY CARAVAN

BOTTOM OF DIP

COXES CLIFF

LITTLECOMBE SHOOT

SHAG ROCK

ASH TREES

BRANSCOMBE EBB

HALF TIDE ROCK

WEST CLIFF

¼ mile

500m

0

APPROX SCALE

ROUTE GUIDE AND MAPS

(continued from p221) The arduous ascent of Salcombe Hill Cliff proves to be a mere taster of what is to come, the trail climbing even higher to surmount **Higher Dunscombe Cliff**.

Afterwards, the path flirts with **Lincombe**, the calf muscles enjoying a lucky escape as the trail for once passes around the back of the combe rather than dropping into it. Keep your eyes peeled for green woodpeckers, painted lady butterflies and the rare marsh helleborine (*Epipactis palustris*) orchid as the trail continues to tackle the undulations before descending through **Dunscombe Coppice** to **Weston Mouth**'s undisturbed pebble beach. Climbing out, you soon find yourself amongst the wild flowers on the rim of **Weston Cliff**, the way sticking to the cliff edge before heading inland across farmland on **Coxe's Cliff**. Passing the site of **Berry Camp**, an Iron-age (or possibly Roman) hill-fort, you now follow a wooded path with ash trees to your right heading above the small village of **Branscombe** to the National Trust owned **West Cliff**, from where you continue through the steep woods to Branscombe Mouth.

BRANSCOMBE MOUTH   [MAP 49]

Branscombe Mouth reached the headlines back in 2007 when a container ship, *MSC Napoli*, ran aground offshore while being towed to Portland, having been badly damaged in a storm off Lizard Point. The cargo that was subsequently washed ashore – including brand-new BMW motorbikes, perfumes, nappies and car parts – was gratefully (and illegally, as it turned out) taken by scavengers, who had collected on the beach, until the police intervened a few days later.

Though there aren't any motorbikes on offer these days, there's just enough to Branscombe Mouth to keep walkers happy. For **food**, *The Sea Shanty Beach Café & Restaurant* (☎ 01297-680577, ☐ www.the seashanty.co.uk; food served Apr-Oct daily 10am-5pm, winter weekends only; 🐾) has some great outdoor seating. It is not overly cheap but their sandwiches (£5.80-7.25) are substantial, tasty and filling; or you could

try a Shanty burger (£8.50) or half-pint of prawns (£5.30). There is a **shop** (Apr-Oct; daily 8.30am-5.15pm) that sells basics such as newspapers and pasties; their stock is sold via the café at weekends in winter. If you have a desperate need for WI-FI access go to The Sea Shanty Caravan Park's office behind the café. However, the minimum charge is £5 (for 24 hours).

Less than two hundred metres (about 180 yards) up the road from Branscombe Mouth, **B&B** is provided at *Great Seaside* (☎ 01297-680470, ☐ www.greatseaside.co .uk; 2D/T or F; 🐾; WI-FI; £42.50-47.50pp, sgl occ £75) which resides in a 16th-century National Trust farmhouse, the first written evidence of which dates from 1339!

Axe Valley's 899 **bus service** (from Branscombe Village Hall) travels between Sidmouth, Beer and Seaton; see pp55-60 for details.

From Branscombe Mouth head up **East Cliff** to follow the path through Sea Shanty Caravan Park. (Alternatively, you can climb up over the top of **Hooken Cliffs**, the two paths reconvening shortly before Beer Head.) Time spent amongst the caravans is brief and you're soon back on a pleasant if rugged path that twists and turns its way through foliage sandwiched between Hooken Cliffs and Hooken Beach. A steep climb presents marvellous views back over a collection of chalk pinnacles before a field takes you to **Beer Head** – and the most westerly chalk cliffs in England. From here you then skip down to and over **Arratt's Hill** before a short road walk into the pretty fishing village of Beer.

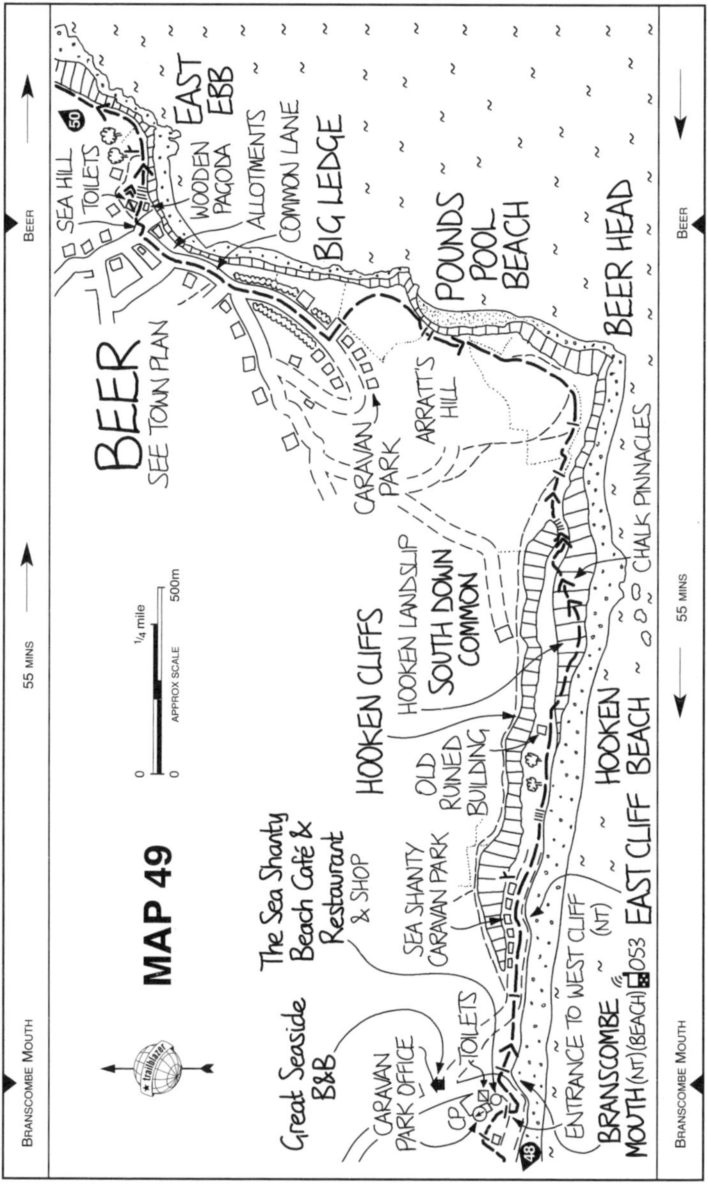

BRANSCOMBE MOUTH

BEER

55 MINS

MAP 49

Great Seaside B&B

The Sea Shanty Beach Café & Restaurant & Shop

CARAVAN PARK OFFICE

TOILETS

Sea Shanty CARAVAN PARK

HOOKEN CLIFFS

OLD RUINED BUILDING

¼ mile

0

0   500m

APPROX SCALE

HOOKEN LANDSLIP

SOUTH DOWN COMMON

BEER

SEE TOWN PLAN

CARAVAN PARK

ARRATT'S HILL

SEA HILL

TOILETS

WOODEN PAGODA

ALLOTMENTS

COMMON LANE

BIG LEDGE

EAST EBB

50

POUNDS POOL BEACH

BEER HEAD

ENTRANCE TO WEST CLIFF (NT)

BRANSCOMBE (NT)(BEACH) 1053

EAST CLIFF BEACH

HOOKEN BEACH ~ ~ ~ CHALK PINNACLES

48

BRANSCOMBE MOUTH

BEER

55 MINS

BEER

Devon villages don't come much more quintessential than cosy Beer, an ancient thatched village nestled on the county's south coast. Along with the village called Hope, Beer seems to be one of those places that was named after something that most trekkers need to function properly. However, the name actually derives from the Anglo-Saxon word 'Bearu', meaning 'Grove', referring to the woodlands that originally cloaked the area.

The village made the front pages of the tabloids briefly in the summer of 2011 thanks to a dolphin, George, that took up residence offshore. However, once George had had enough of swimming with locals and holidaymakers, he took off back to deeper waters, thereby allowing the village to return to being – as the locals like to proclaim – Devon's best-kept secret.

The main joy of Beer can be had simply by strolling along its lovely main street, or taking in such sights along the way as **Beer Heritage Centre** (free entry) at the bottom of Sea Hill, opposite an old World War II **gun-position**, and 16th-century **Starre House**, the village's oldest, built from local stone. If that thrill begins to pall, there are also the **Beer Quarry Caves** (☎ 01297-680282, 🖳 www.beerquarrycaves .co.uk; Easter to Sep daily 10am-5pm, Oct 11am-4pm; £6.80) which have a history stretching back over two millennia. 'Beer stone' was used in the construction of Exeter, Winchester and St Paul's cathedrals as well as Westminster Abbey and the Tower of London – where no doubt some of those smugglers who hid contraband in this vast underground complex feared they may end up. The Quarry Caves are a stop on Axe Valley's 899 bus service; see pp55-60.

Beer Rhythm & Blues Festival (🖳 www.steppinout.info) is held here in October.

Services

Assuming you have an account accepted by the post office you can withdraw money at the **post office** (Mon-Fri 9am-5.30pm, Sat 9am-12.30pm) for free. If not, there are **cash machines** at both The Anchor Inn and The Dolphin (both charge around £1.85 to withdraw cash), too. There's also a **chemist** (Mon-Wed & Fri 9am-1pm & 2-5.30pm, Thur & Sat 9am-1pm) and Beer Village **Store** (Mon-Sat 8am-6pm, Sun 9am-1pm).

Where to stay

Beer is certainly not short of accommodation. *YHA Beer* (☎ 0845-371 9502, 🖳 www .yha.org.uk/hostel/beer; 38 beds, one dorm room is en suite; dorm beds from £15.40, 4-bedded room from £66) provides meals and has 24-hr access. The hostel is a short way out of town at the bottom of Bovey Lane. To get there follow Causeway until you get to a crossroads of sorts; keep left here and follow Townsend; turn right down Bovey Lane and the hostel is on your right.

Close to the beach you'll find a bed in a **pub** at *The Anchor Inn* (☎ 01297-20386, 🖳 www.anchorinn-beer.com; 4D/2T; ☛; WI-FI; £30-47.50pp, sgl occ £60-95) where all rooms have a sea view though they don't accept one-night bookings at weekends in the main season.

There are also some particularly impressive **B&Bs** in the village. Centrally, on Fore St, the cheapest you're likely to find is *Bank House* (☎ 01297-625562, 🖳 www.bankhouseatbeer.co.uk; 2D/1F; 🐾; £30pp). Only a short walk further along you'll find both the delightful *Colebrooke House* (☎ 01297-20308, 🖳 www.cole brookehouse.com; 4D/2F; ☛; WI-FI; £37-40pp, sgl occ from £45), who unfortunately for the lone traveller do not do a single occupancy rate over the summer, and *Durham House* (☎ 01297-20449, 🖳 www .durhamhouse.org; 7D/1T; WI-FI; £32-37pp; sgl occ £45-65; closed Jan), where breakfast options include cinnamon French toast and eggs Benedict.

Just off Fore St and with the most competitive rates that we came across in the whole village, *Ashdale House* (☎ 01297-20683, 🖳 www.ashdalehouse.co.uk; 3D; WI-FI; £27.50-35.50pp, sgl occ £40) stands at 6 Gordon Terrace. Meanwhile, next door – though with an address on Dolphin Rd – is the more upmarket *Belmont House* (☎

01297-24415, ⌨ www.belmonthousebed
andbreakfast.co.uk; 5D; ☕; WI-FI; £35-
50pp, sgl occ £48-60) who offer a pick-up
and drop-off service from different points
on the path and from Axminster railway station and Exeter Airport, as well as operating
their own walking company (see p30).

Hotel accommodation is available at
Dolphin Hotel (☎ 01297-20068, ⌨ www
.dolphinhotelbeer.co.uk; 3S/13D/3T/3F; ☕;
WI-FI; 🐾 £10; £36-49pp, sgl occ negotiable), on Fore St. Rates include a full-
English breakfast and their restaurant
serves some delightful food (see Where to
eat). In fact, the only downside to the hotel
is its popularity and bookings for one-night
stays are generally not available at the
weekends over summer.

Where to eat and drink
Almost everything is on Fore St, where
you'll find a surprisingly wide choice of
cuisines to cater for all budgets. For takeaway food, **Woozie's Deli** (summer Mon-
Sat 9am-5.30pm, Sun 10am-5pm; winter
10am-5pm) does a good line in pasties (eg
beef and stilton pasty £2.25). **Beer Fish &
Chips** (☎ 01297-625774; Mon-Fri noon-
2.30pm & 5-8.30pm, Sat noon-9pm, Sun
noon-7.30pm; Nov-Jan closed Sun & Mon)
next door is the local chippy. Just up the
road, **Spice Merchant** (☎ 01297-22203;
summer noon to midnight, winter noon-
2.30pm & 5.30-11.30pm) is an Indian, and
there's a pizzeria, too, a few metres further
up: **Gina's** (☎ 01297-21121; Thur-Sun 6.30-
9pm) does a spicy pizza with salami, pepperoni, ham and peppers for £8.80.

For **cafés**, **Captain's Cottage** (☎
01297-20942; summer daily 11am-5pm,
winter hours weather dependent) does our
favourite cream tea (£5.25) in the village as
well as tasty crab sandwiches (£5.95). The
surroundings are relaxed and the welcome
very friendly. There are also **seasonal cafés**
on the beach.

Pub-wise, there are two good choices.
Dolphin Hotel (see Where to stay; food
served daily noon-2pm & 6-9pm) offers
few surprises though their signature dish of
Lyme Bay scallops fried with smoked
bacon and spring onions is a delicious one

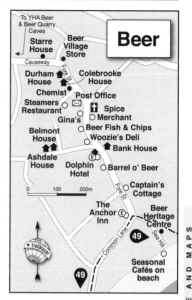

(£14.25). There is also regular live entertainment on Friday nights. **The Anchor Inn**
(see Where to stay) has a nice beer garden
which is separated from the main building
by the coast path. It serves food throughout
the day (breakfast daily 8.30-9.30am, lunch
Mon-Sat noon-2.30pm, Sun noon-3pm,
dinner Sun-Thur 6-9pm, Fri & Sat 6-
9.30pm) with some interesting options in
the evening including smoked mackerel fillet with wasabi mayo and bread for £5.50 as
a starter, and calamari with a sweet chilli
dip for £11 for mains.

For **restaurants**, fish and seafood is a
speciality at **Barrel o' Beer** (☎ 01297-
20099, ⌨ www.barrelobeer.com; summer
Mon-Sat 11.30am-11pm, Sun noon-10pm,
winter 11.30am-2.30pm & 6pm to about
9pm; 🐾 OK) which, despite the name, is a
fine restaurant rather than a pub; their River
Exe mussels in a white wine sauce and fries
costs £10.50. **Steamers** (☎ 01297-22922,
⌨ www.steamersrestaurant.co.uk; Tue-Sat
coffee 10.30am-noon, lunch noon-2pm,
dinner 7-9pm; Sun lunch 11.45am-
2.15pm), just off Fore St on New Cut, gets

its name from the building's original use as a steam bakery. The food is inventive and tasty (mains £12-19), with such treats as baked veg and goat's cheese in filo pastry with tomato and basil concasse (£12).

Transport

[See pp55-60] First's X53 **bus** stops here (Beer Cross) en route between Exeter and Weymouth. Axe Valley's No 899 calls here en route between Sidmouth and Seaton.

To continue to Seaton, there are two routes – one with steps, one designed to avoid them – that lead up **East Ebb** and out of Beer. The path takes you around East Ebb's white cliffs and along a minor road which ends at the base of **Beer Hill**. There are further alternatives here: at low tide turn right to walk along **Seaton Hole Beach**. At high tide, continue to follow the road as far as Wessiter's Rd where, on your left opposite Wessiter's Rd, there's a well-signed public footpath. This brings you back to the seafront near the seasonal *Chine Café* (Mar-Oct daily 10am-4.30pm) and toilets. Turn left to pass another seasonal café, *Jane's Kiosk* (where there are some toilets), some beach huts and olde-worlde lampposts, to the sleepy seaside town of Seaton.

SEATON   [map p231]

While lacking the Regency splendour of Sidmouth or the olde-worlde charm of Beer, Seaton's plentiful amenities and accommodation make it a good option for a stop. Known as Fleet ('Creek') in Saxon times, its location near the mouth of the Axe River once made it an important port, and so it remained up until about the 14th century, when fierce storms caused parts of Haven Cliff to subside into the estuary and a shingle bank to form. The town has also dabbled in shipbuilding and salt-panning down the years, the latter having been practised since the Iron Age.

The banks and flood plains that flank the Axe Estuary now host a number of nature reserves. **Seaton Tramway** (☎ 01297-20375, 🖳 www.tram.co.uk; daily Apr-Oct 10am-4/5pm, check web at other times of year; Seaton to Colyton return £9, all-day explorer £10, 🐾 £1 each way; allow two hours) is a good way to see them as it meanders for three miles through the Axe Valley to Colyton, following the old Seaton & Beer Railway line that closed in 1967.

Other notable sites in town include **Seaton Labyrinth** in **Cliff Field Gardens** – a 60ft diameter spiral. Its half-a-mile turf pathways are lined with stones taken from different areas of the Jurassic coast, to help explain the region's fascinating 185-million-year-old geological history. Residing on the top floor of the Town Hall in Fore St, **Seaton Museum** (☎ 01297-24227, 🖳 www.seatonmuseum.co.uk; late May to Oct Mon-Fri 10.30am-12.30pm & 2.15-5pm; free) has an interactive display on the Jurassic coastline as well as an old smuggler's shawl from the mid 19th century.

Services

The **tourist information centre** (☎ 01297-21660, 🖳 www.seaton.gov.uk; daily May-Sep 10am-3.15pm, Oct to 3pm, Nov, Dec & Mar Fri & Sat 10am-2pm, Apr 10am-3pm) is only about 15 metres from the Tramway office. They'll point you in the direction of the library on Queen St if you ask about **internet access**; you need to become a member but it doesn't take a minute to join and then you get 30 minutes free; after that it's £2.20.

Other facilities in town include the **post office** (Mon-Fri 9am-5.30pm, Sat 9am-12.30pm), two **chemists** – Lloyds (Mon-Sat 9am-5.30pm) and Boots (Mon-Sat 9am-3pm) on the corner of Harbour Rd and Fore St – a **launderette**, Launderama (7am-7pm), at the top of Fore St, as well as a huge Tesco **supermarket** on Harbour Rd and a Co-op (Mon-Sat 8am-10pm, Sun 10am-4pm) on Harepath Rd. There are also some **banks** with **ATMs**.

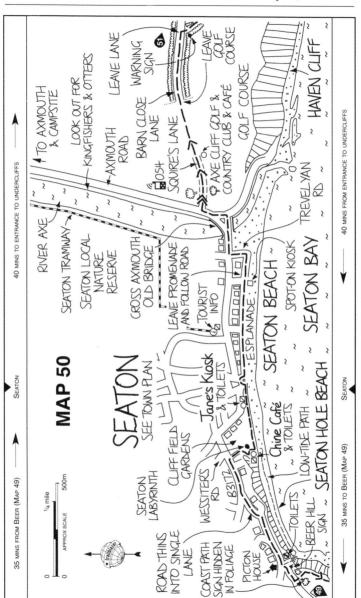

MAP 50

SEATON
SEE TOWN PLAN

51

TO AXMOUTH & CAMPSITE

LOOK OUT FOR KINGFISHERS & OTTERS

LEANE LANE

WARNING SIGN

AXMOUTH ROAD

LEANE GOLF COURSE

BARN CLOSE LANE

SQUIRE'S LANE

AXE CLIFF GOLF & COUNTRY CLUB & CAFÉ

GOLF COURSE

HAVEN CLIFF

RIVER AXE

SEATON TRAMWAY

SEATON LOCAL NATURE RESERVE

CROSS AXMOUTH OLD BRIDGE

LEANE PROMENADE AND FOLLOW ROAD

TOURIST INFO

TREVELYAN RD

SPOT-ON KIOSK

SEATON BAY

SEATON BEACH

ESPLANADE

JANE'S KIOSK & TOILETS

CLIFF FIELD GARDENS

SEATON LABYRINTH

WESSITER'S RD

B3172

CHINE CAFÉ & TOILETS

LOW-TIDE PATH

SEATON HOLE BEACH

TOILETS

BEER HILL SIGN

ROAD THINS INTO SINGLE LANE

COAST PATH SIGN HIDDEN IN FOLIAGE

PICTON HOUSE

49

¼ mile
500m
APPROX SCALE
0
0

trailblazer

ROUTE GUIDE AND MAPS

Where to stay
Campers should head for Axmouth and *Axe Farm Campsite* (off Map 50; ☎ 01297-24707; £5 per hiker and tent; 🐾; Mar-Oct) which is just under three-quarters of a mile from where the path leaves Axmouth Rd (the road that leads to the site). There is a **shop** and **launderette** on site. The shop is always open 8-10am but otherwise the hours are variable depending on business.

Seaton has plentiful **B&B** accommodation, all of which is within a few hundred metres of the path. On the town's western edge opposite the top of Old Beer Rd near the high-tide route is the dog-friendly *Picton House* (☎ 01297-22771, 🖳 www .pictonhouse.co.uk; 3D; 🐾 £5-6; WI-FI; £30-35pp, sgl occ about £50; Mar-Oct), Beer Rd, the only downfall being that it is a short walk from the town itself.

More central, and dotted about by Jubilee Gardens and the Clock Tower, you will find: *Baytree* (☎ 01297-24611, 🖳 www.baytreeguesthouse.co.uk; 1S/1T/2D/2F; single has shared bathroom; ☛; WI-FI; £35-40pp, sgl £45-50), 11 Seafield Rd; *Holmleigh House* (☎ 01297-625671, 🖳 www.holmleighhouse.com; 4D/1T; ☛; WI-FI; £35pp, sgl £55), Sea Hill, who will pre-pare packed lunches (£5); and *Beaumont* (☎ 01297-20832, 🖳 www.smoothhound.co .uk/hotels/beaumon1; 2D/1T/2F; WI-FI; £32.50-35pp, sgl occ £50), Castle Hill, which is right on the seafront with the park to its rear.

Just across The Esplanade from the path, *Pebbles* (☎ 01297-22678, 🖳 www .pebbleshouse.co.uk; 1D/2F; WI-FI; £37.50-42.50pp, sgl occ £50-75; closed mid Dec-Feb), 2 Sea Hill, doesn't generally accept one-night bookings at the weekend. Nor does *Mariners* (☎ 01297-20560, 🖳 www .marinershotelseaton.co.uk; 1S/7D/2T; ☛; WI-FI; £40-44pp, sgl £50, sgl occ £55-70) on the seafront's eastern side. In the same vicin-ity you will find *Beach Belles* (☎ 01297-23198, 🖳 www.beachbelles.yolasite.com; 1T/1D/one room with bunk-beds which can be connected to either room; ☛; WI-FI; £30pp), 3 Beach Rd, and *Blue Waters* (☎ 01297-23245, 🖳 www.bluewatersseaton.co

.uk; 4D; WI-FI; £27.50-37.50pp, sgl occ £45-55), 52-54 Harbour Rd.

For pub-based B&B consider *Eyre Court Hotel* (☎ 01297-21455, 🖳 eyre courthotel.co.uk; 4D/1T/3F; WI-FI; £27.50-34.50pp, sgl occ £45-49) on Queen St.

Where to eat and drink
Our favourite place for a coffee is *Terrace Arts Café* (Tue-Thur 10am-3pm, Fri 10am-4pm, Sat 10am-9pm, Sun 11am-3pm), a dog and human-friendly place with a good selection of teas and smoothies as well as some decent food (with a few vegetarian options including courgette and potato frit-ters on a bed of salad with sour cream for £5.50). As the name would suggest, there is also local art for sale.

The Terrace is just one of several cafés in Seaton. On the front, *The Galley Café* (daily 8.30am-6.30pm, to 4pm in winter depending on the weather) does great little sandwich baps as well as larger meals such as crab cakes with sweet chilli dip (£6.50). Head inland and you'll find a couple of sizeable places: *Finishing Touches* (☎ 01297-24951; Mon-Sat 9am-4.30pm), on Harbour Rd, has, unusually, a hairdressers attached to it, though there is little else that's unusual about its fairly standard breakfast menu. Of a similar size, *Temptations* (daily 9am-4pm, weekends in summer to 8pm), on Fore St, is a popular place doing a roast of the day for £5.95. For a feed-up, try *Trotters* (☎ 01297-21411; Mon-Sat 8am-3pm, Sun 9am-3pm; in win-ter sometimes closed on Wed), on Marine Place, with its vague Fools And Horses theme and some big breakfasts (eg work-man's breakfast, containing all the usual components, for £6.25).

Eyre Court (see Where to Stay; food Mon-Sat noon-2pm & 6-9pm, Sun lunch noon-3pm & 6-8.30pm) does a sausage baguette with tea or coffee for £5.95.

There are several **takeaways** in Seaton too. *Foley's Four C's* (Mon-Thur 11am-7pm, Fri & Sat 11am-8pm, Sun 11am-6pm; takeaway closes an hour later every evening) is a classy place that offers imagi-native marine meals such as swordfish & chips for £9.75; shark is also often seen

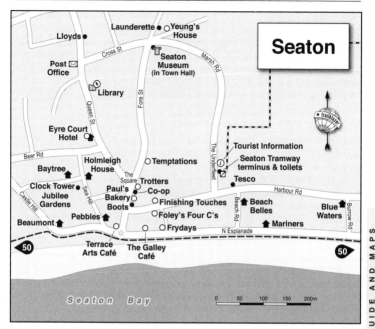

Seaton

Launderette • ○ Yeung's House
Lloyds •
Cross St
Seaton Museum (in Town Hall)
Marsh Rd
Post ⊠ Office
Library
Queen St
Fore St
trailblazer
Eyre Court Hotel ○
Beer Rd
Tourist Information
The Underfleet
Seaton Tramway terminus & toilets
Holmleigh House
○ Temptations
Baytree
The Square Trotters
Tesco
Clock Tower
Sea Hill
Paul's Bakery ○ Co-op
Harbour Rd
Castle Hill
Jubilee Gardens
Boots ○ Finishing Touches
Beach Belles
Blue Waters
Burrow Rd
Beaumont
Pebbles
○ Foley's Four C's
Beach Rd
○ ○ Frydays
Mariners
50
Terrace Arts Café
The Galley Café
N Esplanade
50

Seaton Bay

0   50   100   150   200m

ROUTE GUIDE AND MAPS

basking on the menu. *Frydays* (Sun-Thur 11.30am-8.30pm, Fri & Sat to 9pm) is its closest rival, in a less prominent position but with some lip-smacking fare such as monkfish goujons and chips £6.90. There's also a Chinese restaurant, *Yeung's House* (☎ 01297-625559, 🖳 www.yeungshouse .co.uk; Mon & Tue 5-10pm, Wed & Thur noon-1.30pm & 5-10pm, Fri & Sat noon-1.30pm & 5-10.30pm) on Fore St.

Finally, for those on a real budget you can often buy a bag of three pasties or sausage rolls, left over from the day before,

for £2 from *Paul's Bakery* (Mon-Fri 9am-4pm, Sat 8am-4pm) at the bottom of Fore St.

Transport
[See pp55-60] For **buses**, Stagecoach's No 52A connects the town with Sidmouth and Exeter while First's X53 stops here en route between Exeter and Poole. First's X54 also stops here; Axe Valley's 899 service also goes to Sidmouth.

For a **taxi** try Pete's Taxis (☎ 01297-20999).

SEATON TO LYME REGIS   [MAPS 50-53]

This **7-mile (11.5km; 3hrs)** section of the coastal path is like no other and will, without any doubt, will be one the highlights of your walk. The day mainly comprises walking through the remarkable Axmouth to Lyme Regis Undercliffs National Nature Reserve (see box p236), shaped and moulded by landslides and, left to its own devices, that most unique and wonderful of landscapes: an English jungle. However, as with all jungles the terrain underfoot may cause problems, added to which there are some steep ascents to be tackled.

Furthermore, the trail winds constantly up and down and back and forth, and is pockmarked with roots and interrupted by the odd fallen tree, so it is a day to be wary of your ankles. It's also a day for carrying supplies as refreshments are not available in the reserve. That said, and despite the tribulations, for most people this day is one of unfettered joy. But should you struggle against all these difficulties, at least comfort yourself in the knowledge that at the end of this stage lies Lyme Regis, a smashing town that's used to catering – from royalty downwards – for those in need of a well-earned rest.

The route
Leaving Seaton via the Esplanade – where, once upon a time, both a Tudor fort and a Martello tower stood – you make your way to **Axmouth Old Bridge**, a pedestrian bridge which was built in 1877 and is thought to be the oldest concrete bridge in Britain. Lying one mile inland, the village of Axmouth and the harbour were of great importance during Roman times and are situated at the end of a Roman road, The Fosse Way, which, running from Lincoln to Exeter was, following the Roman invasion in AD43, the western frontier of the Roman Empire.

A bit of tarmac-treading follows as you make your way to – and then up – Squire's Lane before bisecting **Axe Cliff Golf & Country Club** (☎ 01297-21754, 🖥 www.axe-cliff-golf.co.uk), where there is a walker-friendly **café** (daily 8am-5.30pm-ish but closed to non members during events, matches and tournaments), to join **Barn Close Lane**. The turn-off to the nature reserve is marked by a notice warning visitors of the strenuous and remote nature of the path; approach the cliff-edge by negotiating your way along hedgerows and across fields.

After an unspectacular stroll over the fields atop **Haven Cliff**, what follows next is nothing short of extraordinary as you enter an area where nature, as a rule, is definitely in charge: welcome to **Axmouth to Lyme Regis Undercliffs** (see box p236).

Apart from the occasional information board and the odd ruined building camouflaged amongst the leaves and vines – such as **Landslip Cottage** near **Downlands Cliff**, from which the Victorian owners used to sell afternoon teas to tourists, or the **old chimney** (part of a 19th-century freshwater pumping station) at the approximate halfway point – there is nothing to distract you away from the natural beauty of the forest. At **Pinhay Cliff** things get a little more civilised as you join a sealed track; but the moment is brief and soon the wilds embrace you once more. From the viewpoint below Pinhay Cliff, Portland Bill can be seen as – on occasion – can peregrine falcons.   *(continued on p236)*

❏ **Important note – walking times**
Unless otherwise specified, **all times in this book refer only to the time spent walking**. You will need to add 20-30% to allow for rests, photography, checking the map, drinking water etc. When planning the day's hike count on 5-7 hours of actual walking.

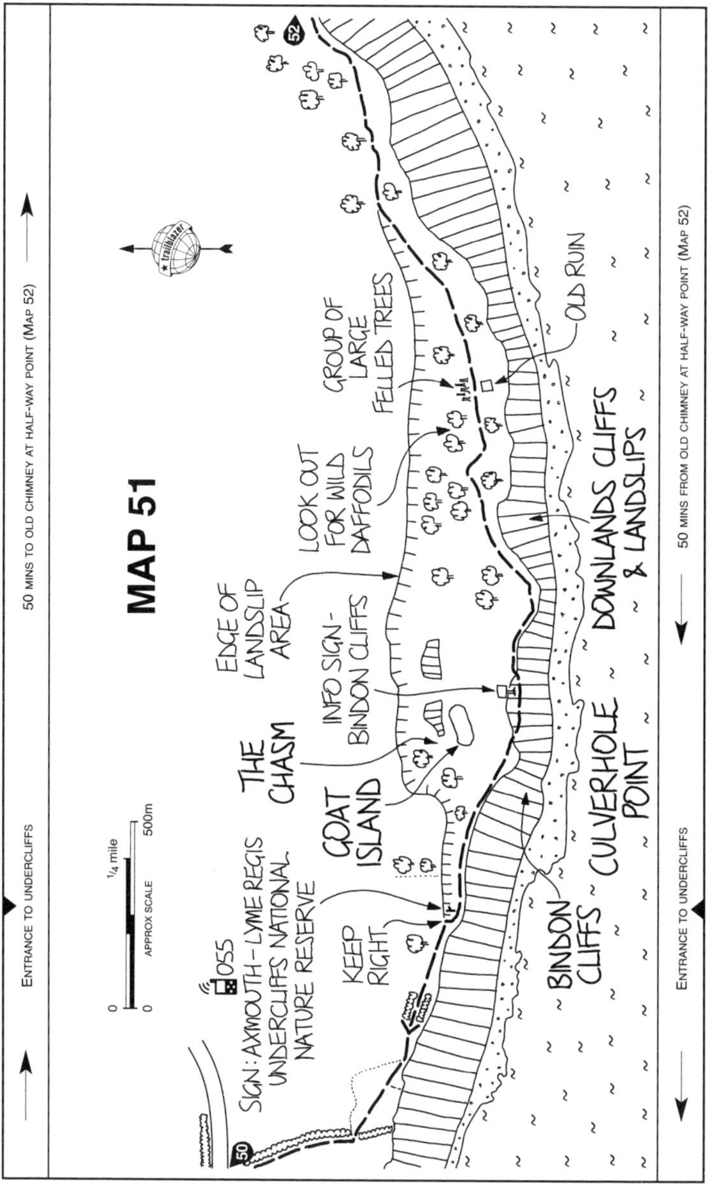
MAP 51
50 MINS TO OLD CHIMNEY AT HALF-WAY POINT (MAP 52)
ENTRANCE TO UNDERCLIFFS
0
0
APPROX SCALE
1/4 mile
500m
trailblazer
50
52
SIGN: AXMOUTH-LYME REGIS UNDERCLIFFS NATIONAL NATURE RESERVE
055
KEEP RIGHT
GOAT ISLAND
THE CHASM
EDGE OF LANDSLIP AREA
INFO SIGN- BINDON CLIFFS
LOOK OUT FOR WILD DAFFODILS
GROUP OF LARGE FELLED TREES
OLD RUIN
DOWNLANDS CLIFFS & LANDSLIPS
CULVERHOLE POINT
BINDON CLIFFS
ENTRANCE TO UNDERCLIFFS
50 MINS FROM OLD CHIMNEY AT HALF-WAY POINT (MAP 52)

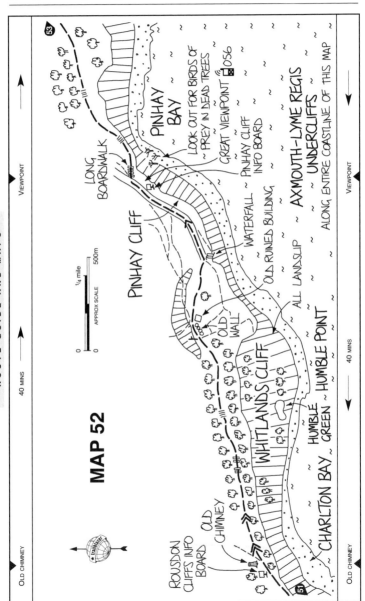

MAP 52

OLD CHIMNEY — 40 MINS — VIEWPOINT

OLD CHIMNEY — 40 MINS — VIEWPOINT

¼ mile

APPROX SCALE

500m

ROUSDON CLIFFS INFO BOARD

OLD CHIMNEY

WHITLANDS CLIFF

CHARTON BAY ~ HUMBLE GREEN ~ HUMBLE POINT

OLD WALL

PINHAY CLIFF

LONG BOARDWALK

PINHAY BAY

LOOK OUT FOR BIRDS OF PREY IN DEAD TREES

GREAT VIEWPOINT 056

PINHAY CLIFF INFO BOARD

WATERFALL ~ OLD RUINED BUILDING

ALL LANDSLIP

AXMOUTH-LYME REGIS UNDERCLIFFS

ALONG ENTIRE COASTLINE OF THIS MAP

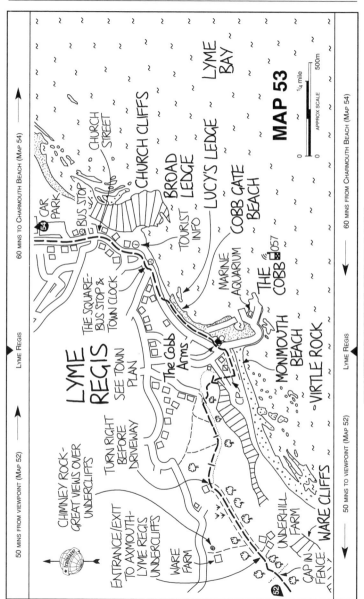

❏ Axmouth–Lyme Regis Undercliffs National Nature Reserve

Designated a National Nature Reserve in 1955, the Axmouth–Lyme Regis Undercliffs are the result of numerous landslips. They are just one of many areas along the south coast to have suffered from this natural phenomenon, which occurs when long spells of wet weather saturate permeable Cretaceous rocks. As these rocks lie on impermeable clay, they eventually give way to the pressure exerted on them by the sheer volume of water and break away from the cliffs, leading to great scars in the landscape called undercliffs.

The 750-metre-wide **Whitlands Undercliff** (Map 52, p234) is actually the result of two landslips, in 1765 and 1840. However, the vicinity's most spectacular geological collapse happened at **Bindon Cliffs** (Map 51, p233), to the west of Whitlands, on Christmas Eve 1839, when what became known as The Great Landslip occurred. The first landslide ever to be scientifically documented – having been witnessed by the vicar of Axminster, William Conybeare, and William Buckland, a professor of geology at Oxford – where once there had been pasture there was now a gigantic chasm, 100m wide, 50m deep and 1km long. In the process, **Goat Island**, a piece of land forced off the top of the cliffs, formed a new plateau closer to the sea – the wheat and turnips that were grown on it surviving to produce another crop the following year which became popular souvenirs. Following such a remarkable event, the Undercliffs became a Victorian tourist attraction, regularly visited by paddle steamer; they even inspired a piece of music, *Landslide Quadrille*, which would be played on the boats as they passed.

What makes the Undercliffs so special is the way the land has since been left to its own devices during the 20th century, having been deemed too dangerous to graze sheep. Myxomatosis, too, has lent a hand, culling most of the local rabbits. As a result, the Lyme Regis Undercliffs are now one of the most significant wilderness areas in Britain, protected as part of the West Bay Special Area of Conservation and the East Devon AONB. A safe habitat for much **flora and fauna**, the Undercliffs provide sanctuary to green woodpeckers, bullfinches and Dartford warblers amongst many other birds. Many variations of flower thrive here too, including the pink pyramidical and the autumn ladies tresses orchid. Shrews and mice, lizards, grass snakes and newts scurry and slither in the undergrowth, whilst butterflies such as the wood white, silver-washed fritillary and chalk-hill blue flit from plant to plant. And all the while, flying high above you, ravens and peregrine falcons menacingly eye the ground. It's a magical place – and a splendid arena for the walker.

(Cont'd from p232) Continuing on, and having left the convoluted pathways near **Underhill Farm**, you eventually arrive at **Ware Cliff**, from where a wide grass path is followed that leads, eventually, to **The Cobb** – Lyme Regis's harbour.

LYME REGIS   [map p241]

Following the granting of a royal charter by King Edward I in 1284, the port-town that had previously simply been known as Lyme added the term 'Regis' in celebration ('regis' merely signifying that it has some sort of royal connection or endorsement). 'The Pearl of Dorset', as Lyme likes to be known, sits just inside the county border

and has all that the walker could desire including several sights and attractions.

The town's main landmark is its harbour-wall, **The Cobb**, built in a curved shape in the 13th century to protect the resident boats. It famously features in Jane Austen's *Persuasion* and the book (and, subsequently, film) of John Fowles' *The*

French Lieutenant's Woman. Austen and the crooked harbour aside, what Lyme Regis is best known for is fossils, with famed local palaeontologist Mary Anning making numerous discoveries of great importance hereabouts in the early 19th-century (see box pp238-9). **Lyme Regis Museum** (☎ 01297-443370, 🖥 www.lyme regismuseum.co.uk; Easter to Nov Mon-Sat 10am-5pm, Sun 11am-5pm, Nov-Easter Wed-Sun 11am-4pm; £3.75) is built on the site of Anning's birthplace and includes exhibits and displays explaining the local geological and paleontological finds. The town celebrates Mary Anning Day in September each year when there are talks and displays of recently discovered fossils.

Fossils are also a major component of **Dinosaurland** (☎ 01297-443541, 🖥 www .dinosaurland.co.uk; mid Feb to end Oct daily 10am-5pm, check opening hours in winter; £5) on Coombe St. With over 8000 specimens, the museum is housed in a Grade I listed building in what was once a church.

For more animated exhibits, **Lyme Regis Marine Aquarium** (Map 53; ☎ 01297-22106, 🖥 www.lymeregismarine aquarium.co.uk; Mar-Oct daily 10am-5pm,

contact them for details of winter hours; £5) has starfish and sea scorpion as well as a display on the history of The Cobb on which it is situated.

Finally, **The Town Mill**, just off the main strip at the bottom of the hill, is mentioned in the Domesday Book (1086) and the mill (admittedly a more recent reincarnation) can be visited (Tue-Sun 11am-4pm; £2.50). The area, though small and tucked away, is developing fast, with a tearoom, restaurant, bakers and brewers all establishing themselves here.

Both **Lyme Regis Fossil Festival** (🖥 www.fossilfestival.com; mostly free) and **Lyme Regis Jazz Festival** (🖥 www.lyme regisjazzfestival.co.uk) are held here in May.

Services

The **tourist information centre** (☎ 01297-442138, 🖥 www.westdorset-weymouth.gov .uk; Apr-Oct Mon-Sat 10am-5pm, Sun 10am-4pm, Nov-Mar Mon-Sat 10am-3pm) is on Bridge St, the eastern extension of Broad St. Contact them to get the latest news about any possible changes to the path due to landslips between Exmouth and Portland as they have up-to-date information. Also worth looking at is: 🖥 www.lymeregis.org.

❏ The Lassie of Lyme Regis

Most people are familiar with Lassie, the collie dog who, in a succession of hugely popular films and TV series from the '40s right up to the '70s (and there was even a remake as recently as 2006), saved various hapless humans from the bottom of wells/cliff-faces/disused mine shafts, usually by barking at her owner who, somehow, managed to understand exactly what the problem was and help Lassie to effect a rescue. What is less well-known, however, is that the fictional bitch who first appeared in a novel in 1940 called *Lassie Come Home* by Eric Knight, was based on a real-life rough-haired crossbreed whose owner was the landlord of the Pilot Boat Inn in Lyme Regis. Though the breed may have been different, the heroic qualities that made the fictional Lassie so endearing were very much in evidence. According to popular legend, in the First World War the Royal Navy battleship *HMS Formidable* was struck by a torpedo off the coast of South Devon with the loss of over 300 men. One of the life rafts was eventually washed up on the coast off Lyme Regis. Having been brought ashore, it was found that everybody within had seemingly perished too, and the corpses of the sailors were laid on the tables of the Pilot Inn.

Lassie, curious to see what was going on, started to lick at the feet of one of the cadavers – and the landlord noticed that the body responded! The man was revived, his life was saved – and thus a legend was born.

There's an **internet café** (☎ 01297-444570; Mon-Fri 9.30am-5.30pm; 15 mins £1, one hour £2.80 with a maximum charge of £5) in the old school in Poole's Court off Church St. Just about everything else is at the top of Broad St including the **post office** (Mon-Sat 8.30am-5.30pm), Co-op (daily 8am-10pm) and Tesco Express (daily 6am-11pm) **supermarkets** and a branch of Boots the **Chemist** (Mon-Sat 9am-5.30pm). There are a couple of banks with **ATMs** on Broad St. The street also plays host to Sanctuary (☎ 01297-445815, 🖳 www.lyme-regis.com; daily 10.30am-5.30pm), a secondhand **bookshop** that is full of character.

Where to stay

Although it's not possible to camp within Lyme Regis itself, *Wood Farm Caravan & Camping Park* (Map 54; ☎ 01297-560697,

🖳 www.woodfarm.co.uk; pitch £11-13 plus £5-7.50pp; 🐾 £2-2.50; WI-FI £1.50/60 mins; Easter to early Nov) is only a short distance off the path (though approximately two miles from Lyme Regis, between the town and Charmouth). There is a **café** and a shop on the site, both being generally open daily 8.30am until 6.30pm when the park is open.

A night above one of the local **pubs**, all of which are dog friendly, is an option. The first you arrive at on your way into town is *The Cobb Arms* (☎ 01297-443242, 🖳 www.lymeregis.com/cobbarms; 3F; 🐾; WI-FI; 🐾 £10 per stay; £40-45pp, sgl occ £60-80), Marine Parade, which also serves food (see Where to eat).

Meanwhile, high up on Silver St and at the back of the town is *The Nag's Head* (☎ 01297-442312, 🖳 www.nagsheadlymereg is.co.uk; 1S/1T/3D/1F; 🐾; WI-FI; £35pp,

❏ Mary Anning and the fossil coast

Born in Lyme Regis in 1799, Mary Anning developed from a poor and uneducated background to become one of the world's leading and most revered fossil collectors and palaeontologists. Introduced to fossil-hunting by her father, who sold his locally collected curios to tourists to supplement his income as a cabinetmaker, his early death in 1810 at the age of 44 forced Mary and the rest of her large family to continue his work not so much out of scientific curiosity as the need to put food on their plates.

Mary's extraordinary ability to make significant discoveries, however, and her increasing knowledge on the subject coincided with the 19th-century's fledgling obsession with geology and evolution. In fact, Charles Darwin was a student of one of her earliest customers and some of her discoveries assisted in proving the extinction of some species – an idea previously given little credence as it suggested that God's Creation was somehow imperfect.

Anning collected her fossils along the coastal cliffs that surround Lyme Bay and some of her finds remain some of the most significant in the palaeontological field. She made the first of several important discoveries with her brother Joseph

Ichthyosaurus

in 1811 at the tender age of 12, unearthing a 17ft-long ichthyosaurus ('fish lizard') under the cliffs between Lyme and Charmouth. The family sold it for £23 and it was soon exhibited in London, the skull remaining the property of the Natural History Museum to this day. Down the years, Anning's reputation grew with each spectacular new find; in 1823 she discovered a complete plesiosaurus ('Near lizard') and in 1828 a pterodactyl skeleton, the first of its type to be found outside Germany. By the age of 27 she

Plesiosaurus

sgl occ negotiable), No 32. There is live music most Saturday nights and if there's an event on Sky Sports that brings in a crowd the owners may well light the barbecue. A more central option is the *Ship Inn* (☎ 01297-443681; 2D with a shared bathroom; ✇; WI-FI; 🐾; £22.50-25pp, sgl occ £45-50), on Coombe St, opposite the fish bar; incidentally, one of the barmaids has herself completed the whole of the coastal path. The rate includes a continental-style (help yourself) breakfast.

The most centrally located **B&B** is *Old Lyme Guest House* (☎ 01297-442929, 🖳 www.oldlymeguesthouse.co.uk; 5D; ✇; WI-FI; £40-45pp, sgl occ £70-80; Feb-Nov), at 29 Coombe St, which is ideal for access to the town's many restaurants and shops.

Others that are just as close to the amenities can be found on Pound St,

including the delightful *Blue Sky* (☎ 01297-442339. 🖳 www.bluesky-lymeregis.co.uk; 5D; WI-FI; 🐾 £5; £37.50-42pp; sgl occ £50-55), at No 8, and the modern *Cleveland* (☎ 01297-442012, 🖳 www.lymeregisbandb.co.uk; 3D; WI-FI; £42.50-47.50pp, sgl occ £80-90).

Still further, though still within a stroll of the centre of Lyme Regis too, are *Manaton* (☎ 01297-445138, 🖳 www.ManatonLymeRegis.co.uk; 3D/1T/1F; WI-FI; £35-43.75pp, sgl occ £45-57.50), on Hill Rd, and *Lucerne* (☎ 01297-443752, 🖳 www.lymeregis.org/lucerne; 1S/2D/1T; £32-38pp) on View Rd.

Moving towards the town's outskirts, *Lewesdon* (☎ 01297-442884, 🖳 www.lewesdon.co.uk; 1D/2T; ✇; WI-FI; £32.50-34pp, sgl occ £40) sits on Silver St and can provide gluten-free breakfasts; while

had opened Anning's Fossil Depot in which she exhibited and sold her finds. Visiting geologists from all over Europe and America flocked to the shop. Unfortunately, the great social inequality of the time meant that a woman of her background was never going to be given the plaudits she deserved; indeed, many of her finds were credited to (male) palaeontologists who had purchased the items from her. However, in 2010 she was included in a list of the 10 British women to have most influenced the history of science and she is also thought to have been the inspiration for the tongue twister 'She sells seashells on the seashore'.

Fossil hunting today Although a few ichthyosaur skeletons are still discovered each year, it seems rather unlikely that you will find one whilst strolling along the coastal path. However, the Jurassic coast is still a treasure trove for fossil-hunters and there are many great sites for hunting and collecting along the way. Most accessible are the beaches at Seatown and Charmouth but there are several other great spots including Church Cliffs (accessed from Lyme Regis harbour), Thorncombe Beacon, Burton Bradstock, Kimmeridge Bay and Eype. Note that **you must always be wary of the tides.** You should also always **be aware of the stability of any cliffs and do your hunting from the beach**; do not hammer into the cliffs themselves. (Anning herself lost her faithful dog Tray in a landslip in 1833.)

The most common finds are **ammonites** – the spiral-shaped shells of extinct marine molluscs (some of which can be up to a metre in diameter) – and **belemnites** – once called 'Devil's thunderbolts' due to their shape but in reality part of an internal shell in what was a squid-like animal. Occasionally hunters do discover more significant finds including the brown or black bones of an extinct marine reptile.

A good website to consult, particularly if you want to know where to look, and whether there is any specific safety advice, is 🖳 www.ukfossils.co.uk/dorset.htm; you can also pick up free pamphlets in the local tourist offices. Charmouth Heritage Coast Centre (see p244) and Lyme Regis Museum (see p237) also have good displays on the fossils unearthed nearby.

charming, octagonal *The Thatch* (☎ 01297-442212, 🖥 www.thatchatlymeregis .co.uk; 1D/1T; 🐾; £37.50pp, sgl occ £65) is on Uplyme Rd.

On the eastern edge of town – and all actually on the path – are *The London* (☎ 01297-442083, 🖥 www.londonlymeregis .co.uk; 2D/1D or T/2F; 🐾; WI-FI; £35-47.50pp, sgl occ £60-85), at 40 Church St, a thatched 17th-century former coaching inn serving a buffet-style continental breakfast; and *Albany* (☎ 01297-443066, 🖥 www.albany-lymeregis.co.uk; 1S/2D/1T/ 1F; WI-FI; £35-41pp and sgl £45). Both are on Charmouth Rd and have magnificent views out to sea.

Those wishing to add a little style to their stay may like to opt to go a **hotel**. Centrally located and hard to miss as you walk up Broad St is the *Royal Lion Hotel* (☎ 01297-445622, 🖥 www.royallionhotel .com; 4S/17D/12F; 🐾; WI-FI available but not in rooms; 🐾 £6 in patio rooms only; B&B £52.50-77.50pp, sgl £75, DB&B £76-101pp, sgl £98); this old coaching inn, built in 1601, is so regal it even has a swimming pool!

Further up the hill, on Silver St, is *Mariners Hotel* (☎ 01297-442753, 🖥 www.hotellymeregis.co.uk; 1S/10D/2T/1F; 🐾; WI-FI; £52.50-72.50pp, sgl £65-75), which was also built in the 17th century as a coaching inn.

Where to eat and drink

Always a pretty genteel and civilised place, over the past couple of decades Lyme Regis has also become rather trendy and sophisticated. As a result, the town now boasts several good delis for takeaway food and a wide variety of cuisines offering food from all over the world.

On the way in, *Lyme Bay Sandwich Bar* (☎ 01297-444299; Easter-Oct daily 11am-4pm) does sarnies from £2.95, including a local crab sandwich for £4.25 (as a baguette it is £5.25).

Almost opposite, *Good Food Store* (Mon-Sat 8.30am-5pm, Sun 10am-4pm) offers a steak baguette for £3.95, a brie and grape sandwich for £4.95 and also has a café with WI-FI; while *Cottage Bakery* (☎ 01297-445515; Mon-Sat 9am-5pm) claims to have the cheapest prices in town with tea for just £1 and a slice of Dorset apple cake with clotted cream for £2.45.

Back on Broad St, *Lyrinda's* (Mon-Sat 8am-5pm, Sun 10am-5pm; daily to 4pm in winter) offers a subcontinental twist to their food, with bhajis (95p) and samosas (£1.25) for sale as well as a fine selection of cheese, olives, artichokes etc. They also do traditional sandwiches, starting at £3.55 for hummus and salad. A little further down, *The Whole Hog* (Apr-Oct Fri-Mon 10.30am-4pm) has a simple formula: roast meat, stuck in a bun or between two slices of bread, smothered with an appropriate sauce – and off you go. Perfect for those just passing through – the shop is a mere few metres off the path and the service is quick – a roast pork roll with apple sauce in a sandwich is £3.50.

Café-wise, round the corner from The Whole Hog, *Bell Cliff* (daily 9am-6pm, June-Sep to 8.30 or 9pm) is a pleasant place with some lovely outdoor seating and a member of staff whose smile is so wide it almost meets at the back. It also boasts a fair and filling menu with such uncomplicated delights as a jacket potato with chilli for £6.25. They are also one of the very few eateries in town where dogs are allowed. *Aroma* (Mon-Sat 10am-4pm, Sun 11am-4pm) is a popular place with locals despite its location on a busy corner and the fact dogs aren't welcome. It also offers a good selection of light bites including a bagel with cream cheese and bacon for £3.90.

For a **takeaway** supper there's a Chinese, *Hong Kong* (☎ 01297-445182; Tue-Sun 5.30-11pm), on Church St; an Indian on Broad St, *Lal Qilla* (☎ 01297-442505, 🖥 www.lalqillalyme.co.uk; daily noon-2.30pm & 6-11.30pm), which is a restaurant too; a *Pizza & Steak House* (☎ 01297-444778, Mon-Sat from 6pm) tucked away between Broad St and the Town Mill (Old Mill) Area which doubles up as a pizza joint, with 12" thin-crust pizzas from £6.95; and *Lyme's Fish Bar* (☎ 01297-442375; school holiday periods daily noon-9pm; rest of year Mon-Fri noon-2.30pm & 5-9pm, Sat & Sun noon-9pm),

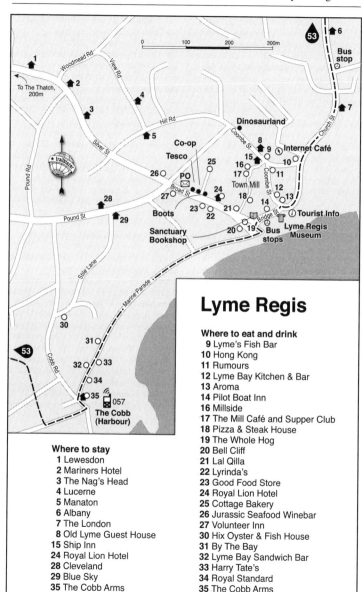

Lyme Regis

Where to eat and drink
9 Lyme's Fish Bar
10 Hong Kong
11 Rumours
12 Lyme Bay Kitchen & Bar
13 Aroma
14 Pilot Boat Inn
16 Millside
17 The Mill Café and Supper Club
18 Pizza & Steak House
19 The Whole Hog
20 Bell Cliff
21 Lal Qilla
22 Lyrinda's
23 Good Food Store
24 Royal Lion Hotel
25 Cottage Bakery
26 Jurassic Seafood Winebar
27 Volunteer Inn
30 Hix Oyster & Fish House
31 By The Bay
32 Lyme Bay Sandwich Bar
33 Harry Tate's
34 Royal Standard
35 The Cobb Arms

Where to stay
1 Lewesdon
2 Mariners Hotel
3 The Nag's Head
4 Lucerne
5 Manaton
6 Albany
7 The London
8 Old Lyme Guest House
15 Ship Inn
24 Royal Lion Hotel
28 Cleveland
29 Blue Sky
35 The Cobb Arms

in our opinion the best of several chippies in town. They also have a stand on the beach which is open daily noon-9pm.

International cuisine isn't confined to the takeaways, however, with Lyme Regis also boasting a couple of Italians, the best in our opinion being *Lyme Bay Kitchen and Bar* (☎ 01297-445371; daily 5.30-9pm), a traditional Italian with a fine selection of liqueurs and dishes such as *gamberetti avocado* (tiger prawns cooked in white wine, butter and garlic and served with avocado, tomato and lemon and topped with North Atlantic crevette and olive oil for £14.95). Furthermore, *Harry Tate's* (☎ 01297-445793, 🖥 www.harry tates.co.uk; Mon-Fri noon-12.30pm & 6-9pm, Sat & Sun 9.30am-9.30pm) offers standard British fare as well as a Spanish tapas menu and they do a good paella (£10.50).

Lyme Regis also boasts some very good **restaurants**. Most celebrated and decorated of all, *The Mill Cafe & Supper Club* (☎ 01297-445757, 🖥 www.millcafe andsupperclub.co.uk; Tue-Sun approx 10am-5pm & Thur-Sat 7.30-10pm) is housed in the renovated Town Mill. The food is described as Italian home cooking. During the day they serve gourmet sandwiches as well as pasta and other dishes and in the evening they have a set menu; three courses for £19.50-22.50.

In the same area, *Millside Restaurant* (☎ 01297-445999, 🖥 www.themillside.co .uk; daily coffee 10.30am-noon, lunch noon-2.30pm, dinner 6.30-9pm, closed Sun eves and all day Mon) is a worthy alternative and a great place to sit outside on a sunny afternoon with a beer. Food-wise, their salmon fishcakes with wilted spinach, soft-poached eggs and a homemade herb mayo is light and fair value at £12.50. In the summer they are open for afternoon tea (2.30-5.30pm).

Beyond the Old Mill, near the chippy, is *Rumours* (☎ 01297-444740, 🖥 www .rumours-restaurant.co.uk; Thur-Tue 6.30-9.30pm), a formal restaurant with some succulent meat and fish dishes (mains £11.25-18.50), including John Dory pan-fried in an orange cream sauce for £15.95.

Finally, at the top of Broad St just as you leave the shops behind there's *Jurassic Seafood Winebar* (☎ 01297-444345, 🖥 www.lymeregis.com/jurassic-seafood-wine -bar; food from 6pm) with an impressive dinosaur-themed mural on the back wall and mains (£11.95-15.95) such as prawn, scallops and langoustines served with herb rice and salad for £17.95.

Even though it takes a bit of effort to walk (the best way is to go through the gardens) up to *Hix Oyster and Fish House* (☎ 01297-446910; 🖥 www.hixoysterandfish house.co.uk; daily noon-10pm), on Cobb Rd, the views, let alone the food, make it worthwhile. Crumpets and tea are served 10-11.30am & 3-5pm; snacks are also available Mon-Fri 3-5pm); oysters are £2.25 each and main courses from £14.75-24.

For **pubs and inns** you have several choices: *Pilot Boat Inn* (☎ 01297-443157; daily noon-10pm) is the original home of Lassie the wonder dog (see box p237), where £9.25 will get you fish such as coley, salmon and smoked haddock. *The Royal Lion Hotel* (see Where to stay; daily breakfast 8-10am, bar food noon-3pm & 6-9pm but all day in summer, restaurant 6.45-9pm) exudes venerability with its wood-panelled walls, oak beams and log fire. They offer some good set menus, with two courses for £22.95 or three for £28.95, from a menu that changes daily.

The Volunteer Inn (☎ 01297-442214; summer daily noon-3pm & 6-9pm, winter Tue-Sat noon-3pm & 6-9pm, Sun & Mon lunch only; 🐾) is one of the few eateries in town that isn't anti-dog. The food is pretty varied (home-made sausages for £10, crab on toast £6.50) and they focus on local produce. *The Cobb Arms* (see Where to stay; food daily summer noon-9pm, winter noon-7pm, hours may differ slightly depending on business) has a good menu including several gluten-free options and, according to some locals at least, is the place to go in the winter months for Sunday lunch (£9.50). Nearby, *Royal Standard* (☎ 01297-442637, 🖥 www.theroyalstandard lymeregis.co.uk; food daily 10am-9pm; WI-FI; 🐾) is another 400-year-old-plus establishment with a relaxed attitude to dogs. In the evening main courses cost £9.45-11.95; the menu includes a pint of prawns with Mary Rose sauce for £9.95.

Not too far away, though providing a contrast with all these venerable old inns, is *By the Bay* (☎ 01297-442668, 🖥 www.bythebay.co.uk; summer daily 10am-9pm, winter Wed-Sun 10am-5pm, Fri & Sat to 9pm), a shiny metal-and-glass affair overlooking the sands with a good selection of teas and cakes as well as mains

(£9.95-15.95), with a superb smoked salmon risotto just £10.95.

Transport
[See also pp55-60] The most useful **bus** service throughout the Dorset section of the coast path is First's X53: running from Exeter to Poole it stops at numerous locations useful to walkers. Their No 31 (Axminster–Weymouth) service also stops here and at Charmouth and Chideock.

LYME REGIS TO SEATOWN (& CHIDEOCK)   [MAPS 53-56]

Very different from yesterday – but just as dramatic – today's **7¼-mile (11.75km; 3hrs)** stage has much to offer including some wonderful cliff-top walking and an ascent to the highest point of the UK's southern coast: Golden Cap (191m/627ft). Landslides on leaving Lyme Regis have forced the official trail to divert inland, only rejoining the coast at Charmouth (which is also the last place to pick up any supplies that you may need). A very steep lane-walk leads you away from the village but once back on the cliffs and out in the elements the scenery is mesmerising, the views from the summit of Golden Cap and the long descent from it rounding off a fantastic day's walk. Seatown has limited accommodation so it may be worth planning for a night in Chideock, a three-quarters of a mile stroll inland.

Note that it is possible to walk to Charmouth from Lyme Regis straight along the beach, which may appeal to fossil hunters. However, this is not the official route and a **tide-timetable must be closely consulted** before embarking on such an adventure. It is also imperative not to walk too close to the cliffs due to the danger of falling rocks.

The route

From Lyme Regis's tourist information centre, head up Church St as far as Lyme Regis Football Club; just beyond, a gate on the right takes you into the first of a series of fields on the edge of **Timber Hill** that you cut across to arrive at a patch of woodland. A sign here states 'Charmouth: 2¼ miles'; walk about 20 metres further on and you come to a second sign stating that Charmouth is now 1½ miles! Congratulate yourself on your superhuman speed and continue through the woods, climbing steeply upwards to a diversion (caused by further landslips). The path now goes left to continue amongst the trees, descending leisurely to a B-road where you turn right to pass the entrance to Lyme Regis Golf Club & Course, before arriving at the A3052. It's a road you flirt with a couple of times, deserting it on the first occasion to follow the **white markers** through the golf course and the rhododendron wood at **Fern Hill**; and, secondly, by walking down the driveway that leads past Fernhill Hotel on the way down to the roundabout.

If camping, ***Wood Farm Caravan & Camping Park*** (see p238) is signed to your left. Should a night under the tarp not be in your itinerary, carry straight on, following the pavement past the blue Charmouth sign. Soon enough the village will rise to greet you. The path through Charmouth is not well signed so follow Map 54 closely: you need to take **Higher Sea Lane**. Eventually you'll arrive at **Charmouth Beach**, the path then turning off by **Charmouth Heritage Coast Centre** (see below).

CHARMOUTH   [map p246]

For those not too taken by the idea of a night in Lyme Regis, the village of Charmouth has the necessary amenities to make a stop possible and also provides an ample head-start for those wishing to get to Seatown (not to be confused with Seaton) or beyond the next day.

The centre of interest for tourists in the village – and on the coast path – is the **Charmouth Heritage Coast Centre** (☎ 01297-560772, ☐ www.charmouth.org; Apr-Oct daily 10.30am-4.30pm, winter Wed-Sun 10.30am-4.30pm), which organises 'fossil' and rockpooling events.

As for **services** in the village, most supplies can be found on The Street, the main road running along the back of Charmouth. **Provisions** are available from Charmouth Stores (Mon-Sat 7am-9pm, Sun 8am-9pm), and there is also a **chemist** (Mon-Fri 9am-1pm & 2-5.30pm) and **post office** (Mon-Fri 9am-1pm, Sat 9am-12.30pm, Mon, Wed & Fri 2-5.30pm) with **ATM** (not free).

Internet access is provided at the library (☎ 01297-560640; Wed 10.30am-12.30pm & 2-5pm, Fri 2.30-5.30pm, Sat 10.30am-12.30pm), costing £1 per half hour, the first 30 minutes being free to all.

There are a few **B&Bs** scattered about the village although finding one willing to do a one-night stop during peak times may be an issue.

Close to the junction of Higher Sea Lane and The Street is *Melville* (☎ 01297-561207, ☐ www.charmouthbandb.co.uk; 1D; £37.50pp, sgl occ £40-50). They may accept bookings for a one-night stay.

Further along the path and in close proximity to the beach, *The Beach Rooms* (☎ 01297-560030, ☐ www.thebeachrooms .co.uk; 1D or F; ☞; WI-FI; £65pp, sgl occ

£130) offers a double suite with its own living room and an extra sofa bed. To locate it turn left off Lower Sea Lane into Hammonds Mead and look for the sign at the end of the first driveway on your left. Although they generally don't accept one-night bookings in advance, call on the day and you may land on your feet.

Also off Lower Sea Lane, but in the opposite direction along Riverway, is *Swansmead* (☎ 01297-560465, ☐ www .swansmead.co.uk; 1D/1F; ☞; Easter to Sep; £35-37.50pp, sgl occ £63-68). There are great views and airy and clean rooms but unfortunately for the walker there is also a two-night minimum stay policy.

Hotel-wise, *The White House Hotel* (☎ 01297-560411, ☐ www.whitehouseho tel.com; 4D/2D or T; ☞; ✖; WI-FI; £45-85pp, sgl occ £60-90), 2 Hillside, The Street, is a fine establishment with decent rooms and wonderful food and all within a fine Regency-era building. One-night bookings are not always possible at the weekend but during off-peak times a speculative call may discover a gap in the diary.

Hensleigh House (☎ 01297-560830, ☐ www.hensleighhotel.co.uk; 1S/2T/3D; ☞; ✖ £10 per stay; WI-FI; £45-65pp), Lower Sea Lane, is another option for those with savings to spend.

As for **food**, on The Street *The Old Bank Café* (☎ 01297-561600; summer Thur-Tue 10am-5pm to 8.30pm on Fri & Sat, winter Fri-Tue 10am-4pm) dishes up decent lunches focusing on traditional English food; on a Sunday a roast, with pudding and coffee is £9.50.

Meanwhile, fish 'n' chips are available from *Charmouth Fish Bar* (Tue-Sat noon-2pm, Mon-Sat 5-9.30pm). Pub meals can be enjoyed at *The George* (☎ 01297-560280;

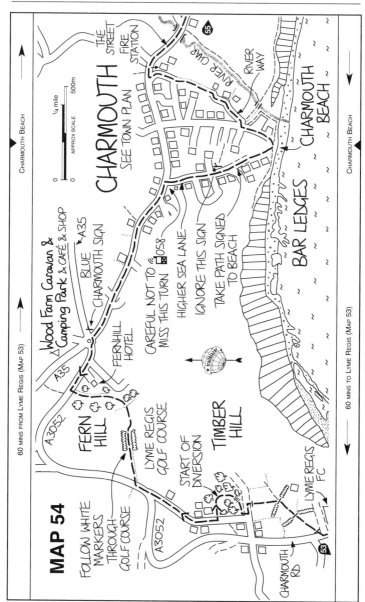

MAP 54

FOLLOW WHITE MARKERS THROUGH GOLF COURSE

← 60 MINS FROM LYME REGIS (MAP 53) →

A3052

A3052

FERN HILL

LYME REGIS GOLF COURSE

START OF DIVERSION

TIMBER HILL

LYME REGIS FC

CHARMOUTH RD

53

CHARMOUTH BEACH

Wood Farm Caravan & Camping Park & CAFÉ & SHOP

A35

BLUE CHARMOUTH SIGN

FERNHILL HOTEL

CAREFUL NOT TO MISS THIS TURN ⌂058

HIGHER SEA LANE

IGNORE THIS SIGN

TAKE PATH SIGNED TO BEACH

CHARMOUTH
SEE TOWN PLAN

¼ mile

APPROX SCALE

0   500m

THE STREET

FIRE STATION

55

RIVER CHAR

RIVER WAY

CHARMOUTH BEACH

BAR LEDGES

CHARMOUTH BEACH

← 60 MINS TO LYME REGIS (MAP 53) →

ROUTE GUIDE AND MAPS

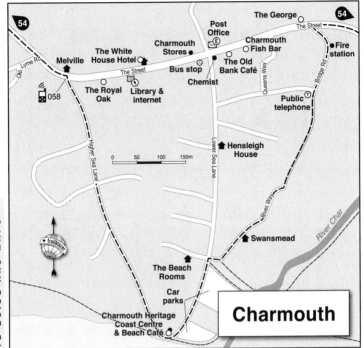

Charmouth

Tue-Sun noon-2pm & 6.30-9pm), where you can sample their award-winning steak & kidney pie (£8), and *The Royal Oak* (☎ 01297-560277, 💻 www.theroyaloakcharmouth.co.uk; food Mon-Sat noon-3pm & 6-9pm, Sun noon-2.30pm), with dishes such as pork and caramelised onion sausage and mash (£8.95) and beer-battered cod goujons (£7.95). Finally, below the Heritage Centre and right on the path and the shore is the *Beach Café* (Mar-Oct daily from 9.30am).

In the evenings the restaurant at *The White House Hotel* (see Where to stay; food Tue-Sat 8pm one sitting, weekends only in winter) may also be worth a try. Much of the food is locally sourced and some of the ingredients even originate from the owners' own garden and their chickens.

First's 31 and X53 **bus services** (see pp55-60) stop regularly in Charmouth on its way to or from Lyme Regis, Abbotsbury and Weymouth.

From Charmouth Heritage Centre, with Portland Bill in the distance – you can clearly make out a path that leads off up the next cliff. However, due to landslips, this has been closed, thus necessitating a further diversion via Lower Sea Lane, River Way, Bridge Rd and The Street, past the fire station to **Stonebarrow Lane** and the **hill** of the same name, surmounted by a National Trust car park. Take the footpath on the right, signed 'Golden Cap: 2¼ miles';

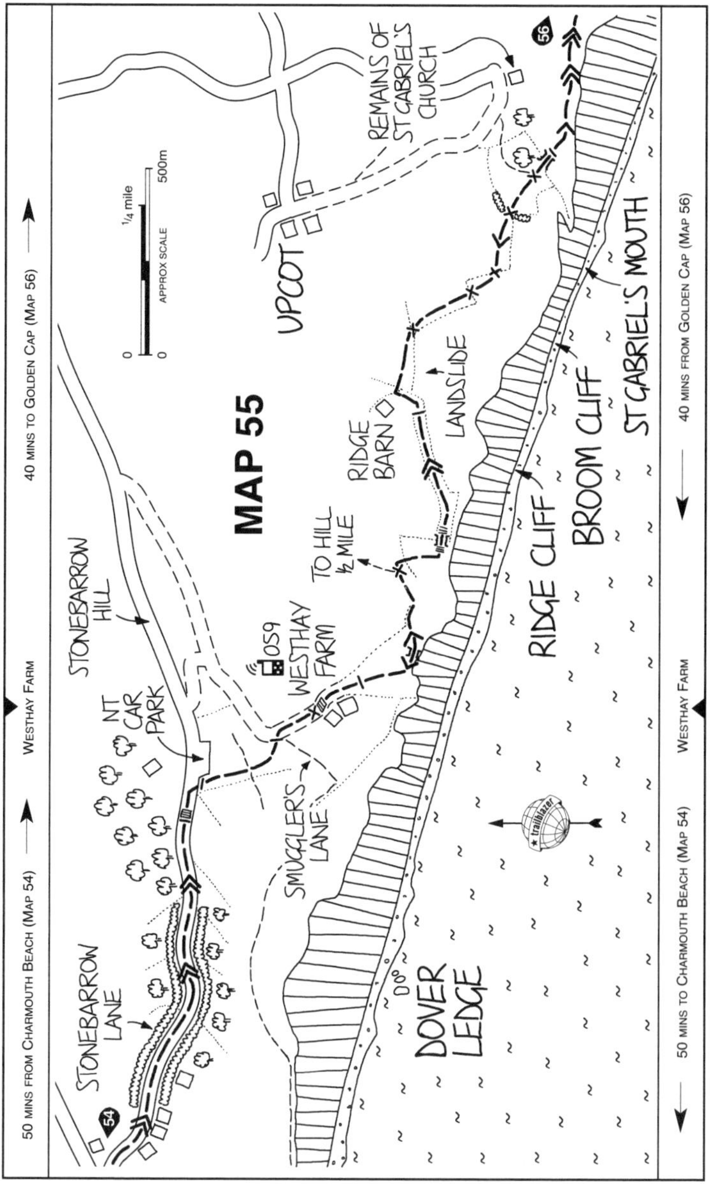
50 mins from Charmouth Beach (Map 54)
Westhay Farm
40 mins to Golden Cap (Map 56)
MAP 55
0
0
APPROX SCALE
1/4 mile
500m
54
STONEBARROW LANE
STONEBARROW HILL
NT CAR PARK
059
WESTHAY FARM
SMUGGLER'S LANE
TO HILL ½ MILE
RIDGE BARN
LANDSLIDE
UPCOT
REMAINS OF ST GABRIEL'S CHURCH
56
DOVER LEDGE
RIDGE CLIFF
BROOM CLIFF
ST GABRIEL'S MOUTH
trailblazer
50 mins to Charmouth Beach (Map 54)
Westhay Farm
40 mins from Golden Cap (Map 56)

a grassy path now leads you, via the National Trust's **Westhay Farm**, back to the cliffs.

The path undulates dramatically, at times perilously close to the cliff-edge, before you ascend the mighty **Broom Cliff**, with the ruins of 13th-century **St Gabriel's Church** (which lies on The Monarch's Way – see p37) lying to your left. A few hundred calf-popping paces further and you arrive atop that star of book covers and photoshoots, **Golden Cap** (191m/627ft) – the south coast's highest point. With Portland Bill to the east and the cliffs of Devon to your west, you now descend. Should you do this at dusk, the waning sun will turn the eastward cliffs a brilliant orange – it's just marvellous.

A brief dalliance with both woods and farmland eventually brings you to a road that bends down to **Seatown**.

SEATOWN   [Map 56]

Regarded as one of Dorset's prime fossil-collecting spots, Seatown has little to offer save for a great pub, a campsite (with a small shop) and some precious tranquillity. However, Chideock (see below) is only a 15- to 20-minute stroll inland, where there is (slightly!) more on offer. To walk there either take the bridleway, Mill Lane, to the east of Golden Cap Holiday Park, or follow Sea Hill Lane to the site's west. Details on both places can be found at 🖳 www.chideockandseatown.co.uk.

Unusually, in Seatown **campers** are the ones who have the shortest walk to find their accommodation. At the back of the beach, *Golden Cap Holiday Park* (☎ 01308-426947, 🖳 www.wdlh.co.uk;

£15.90-30.50 per pitch based on two sharing and a car; 🐾) is certainly worth a stop and has a **shop** (summer daily 8.30am-9pm, winter 8.30am-6pm) that is well stocked and sells camping gas as well as hot drinks and snacks. WI-FI (£1.50/hr) can also be purchased and the showers are tremendous!

For **food**, *The Anchor Inn* (☎ 01297-489215, 🖳 www.theanchorinnseatown.co.uk; food summer daily noon-9pm, winter Mon-Thur noon-2.30pm & 6-9pm, Fri noon-2.30pm & 5.30-9pm, Sat noon-9pm, Sun noon-5.30pm) is a lovely old smugglers' haunt with a great menu; if it's on the specials board try their lobster salad with lemon mayo (£14.95).

CHIDEOCK   [map p250]

Up in Chideock (pronounced Chidock) there is also a Londis (Mon-Fri 7am-8pm, Sat & Sun 8am-8pm) **store** which also has a **post office** (Mon-Sat 9am-1pm).

Chideock is also the place to look for a B&B. On Main St, at *Warren House* (☎ 01297-489996, 🖳 www.warren-house.com; 2D/1T/1F; 🌢; WI-FI; £35-40pp, sgl occ £50), a 17th-century Grade-II Dorset Longhouse (a longhouse is a long thatched cottage); *Chideock House* (☎ 01297-489242, 🖳 www.chideockhouse.co.uk; 2D/1T; 🌢; 🐾; WI-FI; £32.50-35pp, sgl occ £65-70) which is open March to May and July to early September only, and the lovely *Rose Cottage* (☎ 01297-489994, 🖳 www.rosecottage-chideock.co.uk; 1T/1D;

WI-FI; £39pp, sgl occ rate negotiable), which offers luggage transfer as far as either Abbotsbury or Seaton (£16-18). *Bay Tree House* (☎ 01297-489336, 🖳 www.baytreechideock.co.uk; 1T/1D; 🌢; WI-FI; £40pp, sgl occ £59) is a good choice, the noise of the main road pretty successfully kept to a minimum. Unfortunately they don't take advance bookings for one night in the summer season, though it's always worth trying them if you turn up without a booking.

If these are all full, set in a beautiful location (albeit around a mile along the A35) is *Frogmore Farm* (off Map 56; ☎ 01308-456159, 🖳 www.frogmorefarm.com; 2D/1T; 🌢; 🐾; WI-FI; £35pp, sgl occ

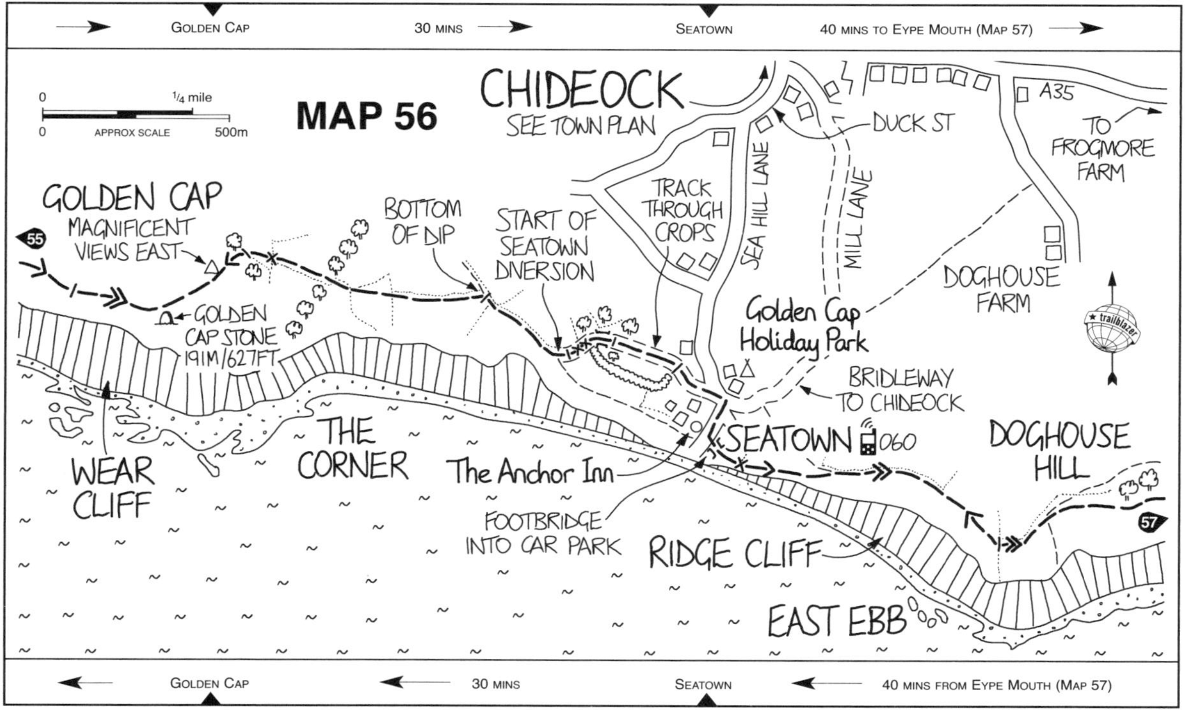
Golden Cap
30 mins
Seatown
40 mins to Eype Mouth (Map 57)
0
¼ mile
0
APPROX SCALE
500m
MAP 56
CHIDEOCK
SEE TOWN PLAN
A35
DUCK ST
TO FROGMORE FARM
TRACK THROUGH CROPS
SEA HILL LANE
MILL LANE
GOLDEN CAP
MAGNIFICENT VIEWS EAST
55
BOTTOM OF DIP
START OF SEATOWN DIVERSION
DOGHOUSE FARM
GOLDEN CAP STONE 191M/627FT
Golden Cap Holiday Park
trailblazer
BRIDLEWAY TO CHIDEOCK
SEATOWN
060
DOGHOUSE HILL
THE CORNER
The Anchor Inn
WEAR CLIFF
FOOTBRIDGE INTO CAR PARK
57
RIDGE CLIFF
EAST EBB
Golden Cap
30 mins
Seatown
40 mins from Eype Mouth (Map 57)

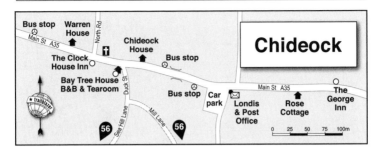

£38). The next morning you can walk across paths to Thorncombe Beacon (see Map 57, p253) rather than going back along the road.

For **food** there are some particularly quirky options that won't disappoint. The tearoom at *Bay Tree House* (see Where to stay) has limited opening hours (Easter-Oct 2-5pm) but does a good cream tea (£4.95).

Home to approximately 150 clocks, *The Clock House Inn* (☎ 01297-489423, 🖳 www.clockhousechideock.co.uk; food daily summer noon-2.30pm & 5-9pm, hours may be extended at peak times, winter noon-2.30pm & 6-9pm; 🐾 welcome in the bar) is a thatched 16th-century village freehouse that serves a significantly proportioned gammon steak (£8.95-11.95) as well as their 'speciality bangers, mash, veg & onion gravy served in a Yorkshire Pudding' (£9.95). Their sausages are made by a local butcher; the choice varies but may include:

kangaroo & cranberry (delicious!); wild boar; duck and orange; and venison, as well as more standard tastes. They also have a Pricebuster menu (£6) which has slightly smaller portions but which are large enough for most appetites.

Also thatched, *The George Inn* (☎ 01297-489419, 🖳 www.georgeinnchideock .co.uk; food daily noon-2.30pm & 6-9.30pm; 🐾 on a lead and in the bar/on the terrace; free WI-FI) is a 'traditional Dorset pub' where all the food is locally sourced: you'll get a Chideock egg – a homemade chorizo scotch egg – for £4.75, or a Taste of the West beefburger for £8.95. There is a log-fire, real ales and often live entertainment. Thursday night is pizza night.

For **buses**, First's 31 and X53 (see pp55-60) services stop regularly in Chideock, connecting the village with Lyme Regis, Abbotsbury and Weymouth.

SEATOWN TO ABBOTSBURY   [MAPS 56-62]

This is a stage of two halves: initially consisting of undulating cliff-top walking (with some steep climbs), this **12½-mile (20km; 4hrs 10 mins)** stage passes through several small coastal hamlets on its way to Burton Freshwater and the outer extremities of Chesil Beach. From here, however, things get much flatter and easier as you pass by nature reserve, mere and common before turning inland to circle Chapel Hill and arrive at one of Dorset's many highlights: the village of Abbotsbury. Refreshments are available every couple of miles or so, as is accommodation should it become required.

(Note that those who are either running out of time to complete their trek, don't fancy walking through Weymouth, or just want a change of scenery from all this seaside, should consider taking the South Dorset Ridgeway. This leaves the main coast path at West Bexington; details can be found on pp260-3.)

The route
The first ascent of the day occurs on leaving Seatown and the climb up **Ridge Cliff**. This is quickly followed by an even more strenuous one which takes you up the interestingly named **Doghouse Hill**, where the path leads you along the top of a ridge, traversing rolling cliffs until arriving at **Thorncombe Beacon**.

From the beacon the official path initially turns left and heads inland briefly. However, many people go straight down from the beacon as it is more direct. If you follow the official route you will see signs for *Downhouse Farm* (☎ 01308-421232, 🖳 www.downhousefarm.org), which offers **camping** (£15 per pitch for two people in their higher field and £10 in the lower field; toilet and shower facilities available behind the café) and also has a *Garden Café* (Mar to end Oct Tue-Sun 10am-6pm, daily in peak season; 🐾, water bowl provided). Breakfast is served 10-11.30am and main meals for the rest of the day; a delicious farm-house cream tea costs £4.95 and a gluten-free brownie £2.75. They also provide newspapers so you can take a well-earned rest. The farm/café is about an 8-minute walk from where a track leaves the path; it is well signposted.

The official path turns back towards the cliffs at **Hope Corner**. There's a spring here, situated in a giant dip and surrounded by a stone wall. The path then descends to **Eype Mouth**.

EYPE MOUTH [Map 57, p253]
Situated in the dip between two cliffs ('Eype' meaning 'A Steep Place' in Old English) at the mouth of the River Eype, there are limited amenities for walkers. The Boathouse by the entrance to the car park has some leaflets regarding local tourist attractions.

Camping can be arranged just off Mount Lane at *Eype House Caravan & Camping Park* (☎ 01308-424903, 🖳 www.eypehouse.co.uk; £14-21 per pitch and two adults, 🐾 £2 but not allowed late July to end Aug; campsite open Easter to early Oct). They also have a **log pod** which sleeps up to four people; bedding is not provided and there is a minimum two-night booking (£30-40 per night). Their *Tea Gardens* and **Shop** are generally open daily 9am-5pm; the shop stocks basic necessities

and camping gas and the tea garden serves cream teas, ice-creams and snacks.

Hotel-style recuperation can be had a little further up the lane at *Eype's Mouth Country Hotel* (☎ 01308-423300, 🖳 www.eypesmouthhotel.co.uk; 3S/10D/3T/1F; ➘; 🐾; WI-FI; £52.50-62.50pp, sgl £75, sgl occ £100). Note that the hotel is unlikely to accept bookings for one-night stays at weekends between March and October.

Food is also available at the hotel downstairs in their restaurant, *The Smuggler's Bar* (food Apr-Oct daily noon-2pm & 6.30-8.30pm), where delights such as seafood platters (£11.95) grace the menu. In the winter months (Nov-Mar same hours) food is served in the hotel itself.

Crossing a stream by the beach, you again take off upwards to conquer **West Cliff** (another strenuous climb), at the top of which to the left is *Highlands End Holiday Park* (☎ 01308-426947, 🖳 www.wdlh.co.uk; pitch and two people is £13.70-25.40; 🐾 £3.20; mid Mar-Nov). There is a **shop** (daily 8.30am-6pm) on site which stocks a good range of basic foods and has a **tourist information point**.

The path then goes downhill to **West Bay** – an unprepossessing town that resembles, from this aspect, something out of the old Soviet Union. Continue towards it, however, and you'll find it is actually an amiable little place with a decent harbour.

WEST BAY   [Map 57; Map 58, p255]

At the furthest western point of Chesil Beach, West Bay (🖳 www.westbay.co.uk) is a working harbour but one that also thrives on the passing tourist trade, with several places to stay and eat. The town used to be known as Bridport Harbour and actually falls within the boundaries of Bridport, a couple of miles away. The arrival of the railway in Bridport caused the name change when, in an early example of rebranding, the harbour was renamed West Bay to make it sound more attractive to tourists.

Fans of classic television comedies may want to stand on the beach, remove all their clothes and walk into the sea in homage to the memorable opening scene of *The Life and Times of Reginald Perrin*, which was shot here.

Services

With most services located in Bridport, a couple of miles up the road, there is little in West Bay for the walker though it does boast a **post office** as well as a couple of **stores** including Costcutter (Map 57; Mon & Fri-Sun 8am-6pm, Tue-Thur to 7pm; sometimes closed 1-2pm) and, more convenient for the path, Harbour Stores (Map 58; Mon-Sat 7am-5pm, Sun 7.30am-5pm); the left-hand side is a shop and the right a **newsagent** which also sells ice-cream. On the right side of the door to the newsagent look out for the sign 'Unattended children will be given espresso and a free kitten'.

There is an **ATM** (£1.85 per transaction) in Harbour Amusements.

Where to stay

Much of the accommodation in West Bay can be found on West Bay Rd, the lengthy thoroughfare which runs all of the way to Bridport. Unless specified, the places listed below are on or off Map 58.

In July and August only **campers** are in luck as *Britt Valley Campground* (☎ 01308-897232, 🖳 www.brittvalley.co.uk;

about £10 for a hiker & tent inc use of shower; 🐾) occupies two of the local fields. Follow the West Bay Rd out of town and the site will soon appear on your left.

One of the nearest **B&Bs** to the path is *Durbeyfield House* (☎ 01308-423307, 🖳 www.durbeyfield.co.uk; 1T/7D; 1T/1D share facilities; ➼; 🐾; WI-FI; £31.50-45pp, sgl occ £33-48; deduct £5 if breakfast not required) at 10 West Bay Rd. Happy to take one-night bookings and with their own licensed restaurant, for convenience in West Bay you won't do much better. *Seacroft* (Map 57; ☎ 01308-423407, 🖳 www.seacroftbandb.co.uk; 2D/1F; ➼; WI-FI; £40-45pp), 24 Forty Foot Way, is also conveniently placed for the path and for an evening meal, if you like fish & chips, as it is next to Seasider (see Where to eat).

Also taking one-night bookings and with their prices open to negotiation – albeit a fair old jaunt along West Bay Rd – is *Fleet Cottage* (☎ 01308-458698, 🖳 www.fleetcottage.co.uk; 2D/1T/1F; 1D/1T share bathroom; ➼; 🐾; WI-FI; £30-32.50pp, sgl occ £40, family room £69-100 depending on number of occupants) at No 152. Next door at No 154, *Britmead House* (☎ 01308-422941, 🖳 www.britmeadhouse.co.uk; 5D/2T/2F; ➼; WI-FI; 🐾; £22-40pp, sgl occ £44-60) is a professionally run establishment that is popular with walkers. They will transfer luggage (£10-15) onwards to either Abbotsbury or Lyme Regis but be aware that in summer one-night bookings in advance may not be accepted.

Other options on or near this road include *Eypeleaze* (☎ 01308-423363, 🖳 www.eypeleaze.co.uk; 1D/1T; ➼; WI-FI; £28-32pp, sgl occ £35-45), No 117, who are willing to accept one-night stops depending on other bookings; and the majestic *Roundham House* (☎ 01308-422753, 🖳 www.theroundhamhouse.com; 1S/2T/5D; ➼; 🐾; £4; WI-FI; £47-62.50pp,

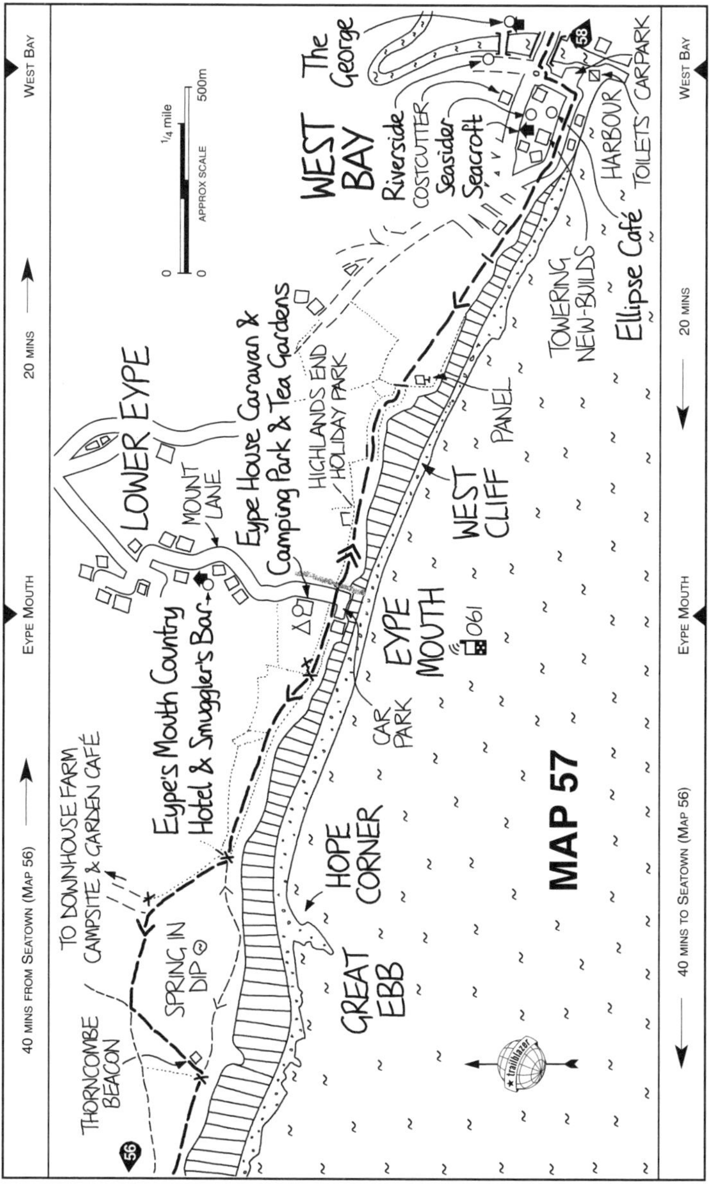

WEST BAY

The George

WEST BAY

Riverside
COSTCUTTER
Seaside
Seacroft

HARBOUR
TOILETS CAR PARK

Ellipse Café

TOWERING
NEW-BUILDS

HIGHLANDS END
HOLIDAY PARK

Eype House Caravan &
Camping Park & Tea Gardens

LOWER EYPE

MOUNT
LANE

WEST
CLIFF

PANEL

EYPE
MOUTH

061

Eype's Mouth Country
Hotel & Smuggler's Bar

CAR
PARK

HOPE
CORNER

MAP 57

GREAT
EBB

TO DONNHOUSE FARM
CAMPSITE & GARDEN CAFÉ

SPRING IN
DIP

THORNCOMBE
BEACON

56

40 MINS FROM SEATOWN (MAP 56)

EYPE MOUTH

20 MINS

WEST BAY

40 MINS TO SEATOWN (MAP 56)

EYPE MOUTH

20 MINS

WEST BAY

¼ mile

500m

0

0

APPROX SCALE

ROUTE GUIDE AND MAPS

sgl £58, sgl occ £75; June-Oct) on
Roundham Gardens – a cul-de-sac on your
right approximately three-quarters of a mile
along West Bay Rd; First's X53 bus service
(see pp55-60) stops at the end of the road.

The **hotels** in West Bay tend to be
more convenient for the path.
Accommodation doesn't come more central
than the ***Bridport Arms Hotel*** (☎ 01308-
422994, 🖥 www.bridportarms.co.uk; 1S/
2T/10D; ☞; 🐾 £10; WI-FI; £60-77.50pp,
sgl £85), a 16th-century flower-fronted inn
right on the harbour with some smart
rooms, some with four-poster beds.
Haddon House Hotel (☎ 01308-423626,
🖥 www.haddonhousehotel.co.uk; 2S/5T/
7D; ☞; WI-FI; 🐾; £44.75-60pp, sgl £79.50-
89.50), allow one-night bookings except on
a Saturday night in summer and is one of
the smarter places in town, a Regency-style
pile at the near end of West Bay Rd by the
roundabout.

Finally, there's ***The George*** (Map 57;
☎ 01308-423191, 🖥 www.george-westbay
.co.uk; 1T/3D/2F; ☞; £35-52.50pp, sgl occ
£55-65). Note, however, that they offer a
continental breakfast.

Where to eat and drink
There is a surprisingly large number of
eateries in West Bay. On the way into the
village, don't be put off by the glass-fronted
shiny exterior of ***Ellipse*** (Map 57; ☎
01308 459221, 🖥 www.ellipsewestbay.co
.uk; daily 9am-6pm, lunch noon-3pm, Fri &
Sat 7-11pm), for the place has a decent simple menu of sandwiches (from £4.25), paninis (all £4.95; 🐾), pasta dishes from £6.75
at lunch-time, hot & cold drinks as well as
ice-cream. They also allow dogs – unlike
some of their scruffier rivals nearby.

Dominating the harbour, ***Bridport
Arms Hotel*** (see Where to stay; food served
daily noon-2.30pm & 6-9pm Aug weekends
noon-9pm) has mains ranging from £10.50
(for the vegetarian options) rising to £17.95
for sirloin steak served with peppercorn butter, hand-cut chips, beef tomato and baked
field mushrooms; they also do fish specials.
Behind it, right on the sand, ***Watch House
Café*** (☎ 01308-459330, 🖥 watchhouse
cafe.co.uk; summer Sun-Thur 9am-5pm, Fri

& Sat 9am-9pm, winter daily 9am-5pm) is
an unusual place, serving the kind of dishes
you'd expect to find on a beachfront menu
(eg sandwiches from £4, burgers from
£8.50) amongst more surprising items (eg
crispy salt and pepper squid for £8.95).
They also have a varied breakfast menu
(eggs benedict £6.50), and freshly baked
cream teas after 2pm. They also have a
pizza oven (Sun-Thur 4-8pm; £6.50-11).

As with the accommodation, some of
the best – or at least quirkiest – options lie
inland along West Bay Rd. ***The Tea Station***
(Mon-Fri noon-4pm, Sat & Sun noon-
4.30pm) is just one of several pleasant tearooms in town, housed in the now defunct
train station. A ploughman's lunch here is
good value at £4.20.

Nearby, the ***West Bay Tea Rooms*** (☎
01308-455697; summer daily 10am-5pm,
winter 11am-3pm) has a wide tea selection
and a good choice of baguettes (£3.95-6.50)
and sandwiches; note that dogs are not
allowed here. Almost opposite, ***Sladers
Yard Art Café*** (☎ 01308-459511, 🖥 www
.sladersyard.co.uk; daily 10am-5pm) is an
organic café with sandwiches for £5.95-
8.95, as well as a Wessex cheese board (£8,
or £15 for two people).

Virtually next door, ***Quarterdeck at
Durbeyfield*** (see Where to stay; daily
noon-8.30pm) is good value with most
mains for £8.50. The food is homemade
and includes stews, curries and belly of
pork. Just up the road, ***Haddon House
Hotel*** (see Where to stay; daily 7.45-
9.15am, noon-2pm & 6.15-8.45pm) offers
one of the more refined dining experiences
in the village, with some sophisticated dishes including escalope of milk-fed free range
rose veal (£16.50).

Even smarter, ***Riverside Restaurant***
(Map 57; ☎ 01308-422011, 🖥 www.the
fishrestaurant-westbay.co.uk; Tue-Sun
noon-2.30pm, Tue, Wed, Fri & Sat 6.30-
9pm) is a lovely place with windows overlooking the village and waterway and an
excellent menu of fine food, not cheap
(mains on the specials board £20-30) but
certainly worth investigating; try their
grilled brill with a celeriac, coriander &
horseradish remoulade for £23.95.

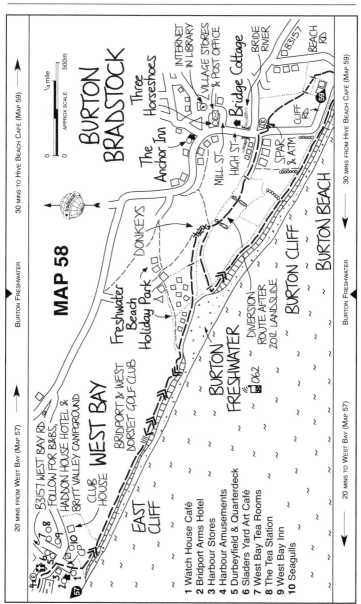

MAP 58

BURTON BRADSTOCK

Three Horseshoes

INTERNET IN LIBRARY

Village Stores & Post Office

Bridge Cottage

BRIDE RIVER

B3157

BEACH RD

The Anchor Inn

MILL ST

HIGH ST

SPAR & ATM

CLIFF RD

59

CLIFF RD

BURTON BEACH

BURTON CLIFF

DONKEYS

Freshwater Beach Holiday Park

BURTON FRESHWATER

DIVERSION ROUTE AFTER 2012 LANDSLIDE

062

¼ mile

500m

APPROX SCALE

0

0

Trailblazer

B3157 WEST BAY RD, FOLLOW FOR B&Bs,

HADDON HOUSE HOTEL & BRITT VALLEY CAMPGROUND

WEST BAY

BRIDPORT & WEST DORSET GOLF CLUB

CLUB HOUSE

EAST CLIFF

57

20 MINS FROM WEST BAY (MAP 57)

BURTON FRESHWATER

30 MINS TO HIVE BEACH CAFÉ (MAP 59)

30 MINS FROM HIVE BEACH CAFÉ (MAP 59)

BURTON FRESHWATER

20 MINS TO WEST BAY (MAP 57)

1 Watch House Café
2 Bridport Arms Hotel
3 Harbour Stores
4 Harbour Amusements
5 Durbeyfield & Quarterdeck
6 Sladers Yard Art Café
7 West Bay Tea Rooms
8 The Tea Station
9 West Bay Inn
10 Seagulls

ROUTE GUIDE AND MAPS

Across the river, *The George* (see Where to stay; daily noon-2.30pm & 6-9.30pm) serves more traditional pub food (mains up to £13.50) though very good value and with some surprises such as coq au vin for £9.

Moving across the harbour to the eastern side of the village, *West Bay Inn* (☎ 01308-422157; Mon-Fri noon-2pm & 6-9pm; Sat noon-2.30pm & 6-9.30pm, Sun noon-3pm only) is a traditional pub but with a good specials board and such unexpected delights as duck breast with hoisin sauce (£15.95). Virtually opposite, at the *Seagulls* (☎ 01308-425099, 🖥 www.seagullsrestaurant.co.uk; Tue-Sat noon-2pm & 6.30-11.30pm, Sun noon-2pm & 6.30-10.30pm) you'll find fish, unsurprisingly, is the speciality; mains start at about £5 (for prawn salad), and include skate wings in a balsamic glaze for £14 rising to £19.95 for the poached monkfish medallions.

Finally, there is of course a chippy: *Seasider* (☎ 01308-42778; Apr to mid Nov Tue-Sat 11.30am-2.30pm, Mon-Wed 5-8pm, Thur-Sun 5-9pm; late Nov to Apr Thur-Sat 5-8/8.30pm, Fri & Sat noon-2.30pm) has both a restaurant and a take-away. The fish is fresh and the batter crunchy. A large cod & chips costs £7; they also have whitebait (£13.15).

There are also plenty of **snack kiosks** all around the harbour selling fish & chips or burgers and the like.

Transport
[See pp55-60]   First's coastal X53 **bus** service stops off en route between Exeter, Weymouth and Poole via Abbotsbury and Lyme Regis.

At the eastern end of West Bay there's more climbing to be done to get over **East Cliff**. With a golf course on your left and Portland getting ever closer, there are great views ahead of Burton Beach and the sand-coloured cliffs before it. A perambulation on the pebbles at **Burton Freshwater** (see below for details about camping at the holiday park here) follows before the climb up **Burton Cliff**, atop which, by gazing inland, the Saxon settlement of Burton Bradstock comes into view. Straight ahead, the terrain flattens out, the ominous edge of Portland's Underhill getting ever closer.

To access **Burton Bradstock** turn left up Cliff Rd (see Map 58, p255).

BURTON BRADSTOCK
[Map 58, p255]
This unspoilt old stone village is very pleasant and one can't deny that it's got a lot of lovely old buildings, many of them, inevitably, topped with thatch. That's particularly true of the old cottages around St Mary's Church, a number of which date back to the 16th and 17th century. That said, it is probably not worth diverting from the path just to see the village unless you plan to take advantage of its services. If you decide to do so, hopefully you'll find it charming enough to justify your trudge inland.

Many of the events in **Burton Bradstock's Festival of Music and Art** (🖥 www.burtonbradstockfestival.com), held in August, take place in the church.

Regarding the facilities available here, dotted about Burton Bradstock are the **Village Stores** (Mon-Fri 8am-1pm & 2-5.30pm, Sat 8am-12.30pm, Sun 8-11am) which houses the **post office** (Mon-Fri 9am-1pm & 2-5.30pm, Sat 9am-12.30pm); and a Spar **supermarket** (Mon-Sat 7.30am-8pm, Sun 8am-8pm) with an **ATM** in the petrol station before crossing the Bride River. For **internet access**, the village has a cute little library (Mon 3-5pm, Tue 10am-noon, Wed 3-5pm, Thur 3-5pm, Fri 3-5pm, Sat 10am-noon).

Should you wish to **camp** in the area *Freshwater Beach Holiday Park* (☎ 01308-897317, 🖥 www.freshwaterbeach.co.uk; mid Mar to mid Nov; £5-17 for a tent and two people, 🐾 £2.50; WI-FI

£4/day) is the huge family-orientated caravan metropolis at the back of Burton Freshwater.

Bed and breakfast is provided at *Bridge Cottage* (☎ 01308-897222, 🖳 www .bridgecottagebedandbreakfast.co.uk; 1D/ 1T/2F; ✆; WI-FI; 🐾; £32.50-42.50pp, sgl occ £45-85), 87 High St. Note that in July and August they have a minimum two-night stay policy at the weekends. For B&B in a pub try *The Anchor Inn* (☎ 01308-897228, 🖳 www.anchorinnburtonbradstock.co.uk; 2D, en suite £42.50-50pp, sgl occ £75).

Alternatively, beyond the village, *Chesil Beach Lodge* (Map 59; ☎ 01308-897428. 🖳 www.chesilbeachlodge.co.uk; 1D/2D or T; 🐾 £10; WI-FI; £45-55pp, sgl occ £80-105) is on the coast road (B3157). The best way for walkers to reach it is to continue along the coast path for just under half a mile before turning inland before Old Coastguard Holiday Park and following the footpath. They do not take one-night bookings at the weekend over the summer months.

For **food**, the two pubs on the main road in the centre are the places to go. The menu at *The Anchor Inn* (see Where to stay; food Mon-Sat noon-2pm & 6-9pm, Sun noon-3pm & 6-8.30pm) changes regularly but focuses on fish and shellfish – dived West Bay scallops are £17.95 – but they also have meat and vegetarian options.

Just down the hill, *Three Horseshoes* (☎ 01308-897259, 🖳 www.three-horse shoes.com; daily noon-2pm & 6-9pm) is very dog friendly and offers good home-made food with a particular flair for desserts.

First's coastal X53 **bus service** (see pp55-60) calls in en route between Exeter, Weymouth and Poole via Abbotsbury and Lyme Regis.

ROUTE GUIDE AND MAPS

The walking is easy as you pass Burton and then **Hive Beach** where *Hive Beach Café* (☎ 01308-897070, 🖳 www.hivebeachcafe.co.uk; daily 10am-3pm depending on season, check web for details) is a far cry from your average seasonal establishment – try the Loch Fyne kippers (£8.95) and keep an eye out for vacationing rock stars! More caravan parks and cliffs follow.

Cogden Beach soon spreads out on your right and **Burton Common** appears bleak and endless to your left, looking in many ways like Dartmoor (its tors are around 50 miles south-west). The path slices between the two, their contrasting charms changing with each season.

Passing behind **Burton Mere**, you walk through scrub and farmland along the back of a pebble ridge – the sea isn't always visible but the sound of the waves remains therapeutic enough.

Having passed through **West Bexington Nature Reserve** – of importance due to the rare shingle habitat that thrives here – you arrive at the car-park at **West Bexington Beach**, where there is a café. It is also the start of the **South Dorset Ridgeway** (see pp260-3). For the continuation of the main route see p263.

WEST BEXINGTON [Map 60, p259]

It is hard to imagine that contemporary West Bexington was once, before the Romans came, inhabited by the feared and belligerent Durotriges tribe that once occupied much of Dorset; indeed, what with a French raiding party burning and pillaging the tiny village (and destroying its church) in the 15th century, it's fair to say that this sleepy hamlet has had more than its fair share of excitement down the centuries. All this violence in such a tranquil location is worth contemplating at *Blue Anchor* (☎ 01308-897810; Easter-Nov daily 10.30am-6pm), a café at the end of Beach Rd.

(Continued on p260)

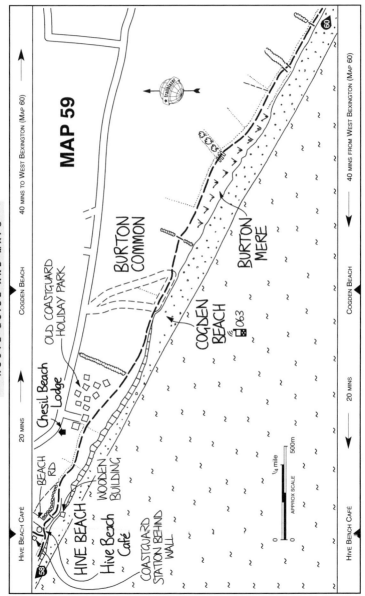

MAP 59

40 MINS TO WEST BEXINGTON (MAP 60)

COGDEN BEACH

20 MINS

HIVE BEACH CAFÉ

BURTON COMMON

BURTON MERE

OLD COASTGUARD HOLIDAY PARK

Chesil Beach Lodge

BEACH RD

WOODEN BUILDING

HIVE BEACH

Hive Beach Café

COASTGUARD STATION BEHIND WALL

COGDEN BEACH

063

40 MINS FROM WEST BEXINGTON (MAP 60)

COGDEN BEACH

20 MINS

HIVE BEACH CAFÉ

¼ mile

500m

APPROX SCALE

0

0

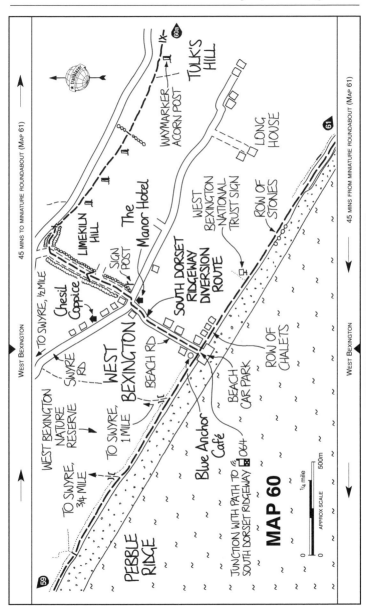

(Continued from p257) There is only one **B&B** – and at certain times of year, not even that: *Chesil Coppice* (☎ 01308-897351, 🖥 www.chesil-coppice.co.uk; 1D or T in self-contained flat; ☞; WI-FI; 🐾; £30pp for B&B, £45 for the whole flat on a self-catering basis; Apr-Oct) is on Swyre Rd.

More luxurious accommodation can be found at *Manor Hotel* (☎ 01308-897660, 🖥 www.manorhoteldorset.com; 9D/4D or T; ☞; WI-FI in public areas; up to medium-sized 🐾 £15; £55pp, sgl occ £85; restaurant daily noon-2pm, Mon-Sat

6-9pm, Sun 6-8pm), one of the older buildings in the village.

The nearest **bus stop** is at Swyre, about 1¼ miles/2km from Blue Anchor café. First's coastal X53 **bus** service (see pp55-60) stops off by The Bull Inn there, linking it with Exeter, Weymouth, Poole, Abbotsbury and Lyme Regis. The route is also very handy for the South Dorset Ridgeway (aka The Inland Coastal Route), which follows the course of the B3157 road for much of its length.

The South Dorset Ridgeway (aka Inland Coastal Route)
[Map 60, p259; Map 60a & 60b; Map 60c, p263; Map 73, p291]
At its most basic, this walk could be seen as nothing but a short cut, saving the weary trekker about 19¼ miles on the standard route via Weymouth and Portland. Thus those short on stamina and shoe leather, the fatigued and the fed-up, may appreciate this reducing of their expedition. But this **17-mile (27.4km; 5 hrs 10 mins)** saunter, **which has been part of the SWCP since its inception in 1978** (and thus 25 years before Portland), offers so much more than just a saving of time. For the South Dorset Ridgeway takes you through one of the most ancient landscapes in the UK. Very few – if any – walks in the UK will take you past such a wealth of **Neolithic, Bronze Age and Roman sites**, from burial chambers and barrows to stare holes and stone circles, not to mention a rash of tumuli like geological pimples pockmarking the ground. (For details of these various sites, see Appendix B, p323.)

It is an incredibly beautiful walk too. Those who have walked on the South Downs Way will find several similarities as they stroll along a chalk ridge with gigantic sweeping views over a terrain that falls away on either side of the trail; indeed, curiously, there are more views of the sea on this route than on the coast path! There is the wildlife, too, particularly birdlife, with raptors especially ubiquitous, including an abundance of buzzards, kestrels and even the odd kite soaring and swooping. There are skylarks aplenty, too, performing a vertical lift-off from the fields as if powered, seemingly, by nothing but song.

Of course, the 'official' coast path is not without its attractions too, and we recognise that most people will stick to the seaside route, especially as it takes in the idiosyncratic isthmus of Portland which was added to the official trail in 2003. But we do urge you, if you have the time, to try to fit in at least a section of the Ridgeway as well. You'll find that Weymouth is a good base, with buses from there to West Bexington in the morning and buses back from Osmington in the late afternoon and evening; see pp55-60 for details.

Note that there are **no refreshments** on the South Dorset Ridgeway until Osmington, less than a mile from the end of the trail, though a side-trip to Abbotsbury, three-quarters of a mile down the hill, is a viable option. Note, too, that just about the entire trek is on an **exposed ridge** so bring suitable raingear and sunblock to cover all weather possibilities.

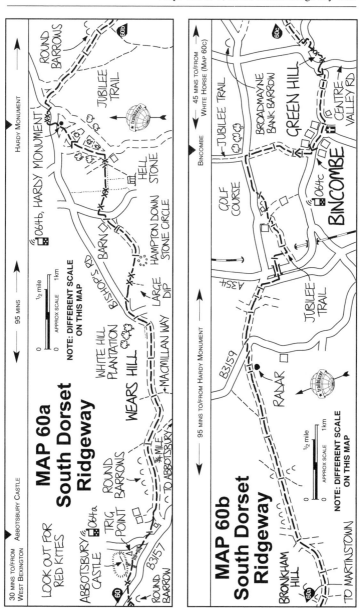

The route

Leave West Bexington from the beach car park next to the Blue Anchor and follow the road up the hill, passing The Manor Hotel on your right. Where the road bends away keep heading straight up on a farm track to the summit of **Limekiln Hill** where the path meets and follows the B3157. Crossing several fields, you are soon passing the first of a myriad of tumuli, or barrows, on the trail.

Traversing **Tulk's Hill**, you cross the road to climb the western end of the ridge up to **Abbotsbury Castle**. Sitting proudly above the surrounding landscape, this triangular hill-fort is the most prominent of the Iron Age sites on the route, one of a string of such fortfications that include nearby Eggardon Hill Fort and much larger Maiden Castle, both of which are visible from here. Excavations have also yielded evidence of a Roman signal tower that was situated here and the site was, for centuries, the location for a warning beacon, used, for example, during the nation's wait for the arrival of the Spanish Armada.

Crossing a minor road after the castle, the trail dodges through numerous barrows as it heads to the summit of **Wears Hill**, with the western side of The Fleet ever increasing in size below you. St Catherine's Chapel comes into sight and a path offers access to Abbotsbury.

Cross the Macmillan Way and continue past **White Hill Plantation** to Bishop's Rd from where you should follow the path to **Hampton Down Stone Circle**, an ancient monument thought to have been used for rituals and constructed around 2000BC.

An even more impressive prehistoric site lies nearby, just south of the path after Hampton Barn Farm. This is the dramatically named **Hell Stone**, a burial chamber or dolmen built around 6000 years ago that was restored, incorrectly by all accounts, in the 19th century. Hell Stone stands just to the south of the path: just before you enter the woods leading up to the Hardy Monument, turn south through the farm gate and walk across the field to the dolmen.

From here it's only a woodland walk to **The Hardy Monument** (Apr-Sep Sat & Sun 11am-5pm; £2). If you were looking forward to seeing a monument to the writer of *Tess of the d'Urbervilles*, *Far from the Madding Crowd*, *The Mayor of Casterbridge* etc you're going to be in for a bit of a disappointment. The Hardy commemorated by this huge memorial is actually Rear Admiral Sir Thomas Masterman Hardy (1769-1839), captain of *HMS Victory*, part of the fleet that won the Battle of Trafalgar in 1805 and, more famously, the man from whom Admiral Nelson requested a kiss as he lay dying from his wounds (Hardy complied with his friend's wishes, kissing his dying friend on the forehead). Built in 1844-5 the monument stands 22 metres (72ft) high and is owned by the National Trust.

After the monument the Ridgeway joins the Jubilee Trail (see p37) to reach **Bronkham Hill**, passing yet more prehistoric earthworks, before a 3¼-mile stroll amongst numerous barrows brings you to the Roman Rd between Dorchester and Weymouth, now known, more prosaically, as the **A354**. Excavations near here uncovered a mass grave of some 50 decapitated Scandinavians dating back to the Saxon Age.

Crossing the busy road via a bridge, you follow a gravel path before the Jubilee Trail is again joined briefly, the two trails following the same route as they make their way to a minor road. The spell on tarmac is brief and you soon leave the road, turning right – and south – on to a farm's driveway, finally

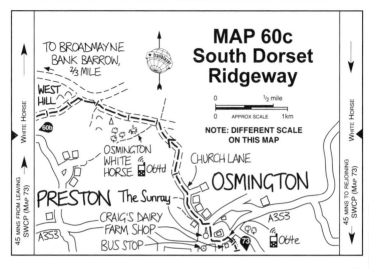

MAP 60c
South Dorset
Ridgeway

0 ½ mile
0 APPROX SCALE 1km

NOTE: DIFFERENT SCALE
ON THIS MAP

TO BROADMAYNE
BANK BARROW,
⅔ MILE

WEST
HILL

60b

OSMINGTON
WHITE
HORSE

PRESTON The Sunray

CRAIG'S DAIRY
FARM SHOP

A353

BUS STOP

CHURCH LANE

OSMINGTON

A353

73

WHITE HORSE

WHITE HORSE

45 MINS FROM LEAVING SWCP (MAP 73)

45 MINS TO REJOINING SWCP (MAP 73)

ROUTE GUIDE AND MAPS

leaving the Jubilee Trail behind as it veers away to the north. The path descends to the end of another minor road and on to the settlement of **Bincombe**, leaving it after the church to go through more fields to **Green Hill**. Carrying on to **West Hill** and back on to the ridge, tumuli again rise peacefully from the earth as you pass a trig point and above the famous **Osmington White Horse** (see p288).

From here you make your last descent to pass through farmland leading to the end of Church Lane in **Osmington**, home of *The Sunray* (☎ 01305-832148, 🖥 www.the-sunray.co.uk; Mon-Sat noon-2pm & 6-9pm, Sun noon-8.30pm) proffering a lunchtime carvery (£5.65, Sun £10.50). On the way out of the village, *Craig's Farm Dairy Shop* (Mon-Fri 9am-5pm, Sat 9am-4.30pm, Sun 10am-4pm) is a decent little farm shop that sells fruit, cheeses, meats and ice-cream.

To reach the SWCP from here, head east along the A353, turning right off the road and passing through four fields on your way to **Osmington Mills** and a reunion with the coast path (see p288).

(Main route continued from p257) After more horizontal hiking the pebbles disappear and you're left to stroll on a four-wheel drive track, the scrub hemming you in on both sides. Having passed **The Old Coastguards**, once a haunt of Thomas Hardy, a minor road (complete with pill-box) ensues, the epic expanse of **Chesil Beach** now beginning to dominate the view in front of you.

Before you hit the western end of The Fleet (the lagoon behind Chesil Beach), the path takes a left and climbs as if heading towards the 15th-century **St Catherine's Chapel**. St Catherine, incidentally, is the patron saint of spinsters and women are said to visit the church in desperate search of husbands. Gentlemen trekkers – you have been warned. *(continued on p266)*

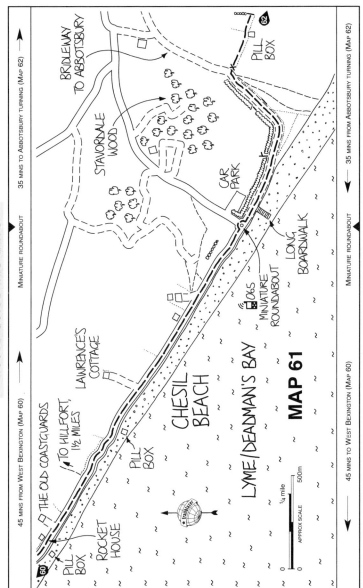

45 MINS FROM WEST BEXINGTON (MAP 60)

MINIATURE ROUNDABOUT

35 MINS TO ABBOTSBURY TURNING (MAP 62)

BRIDLEWAY TO ABBOTSBURY

62

PILL BOX

STAVORDALE WOOD

CAR PARK

LONG BOARDWALK

065 MINIATURE ROUNDABOUT

LAWRENCE'S COTTAGE

TO HILLFORT, 1½ MILES

PILL BOX

THE OLD COASTGUARDS

ROCKET HOUSE

PILL BOX

60

CHESIL BEACH

LYME/DEADMAN'S BAY

MAP 61

trailblazer

¼ mile   500m

APPROX SCALE

0   0

35 MINS FROM ABBOTSBURY TURNING (MAP 62)

MINIATURE ROUNDABOUT

45 MINS TO WEST BEXINGTON (MAP 60)

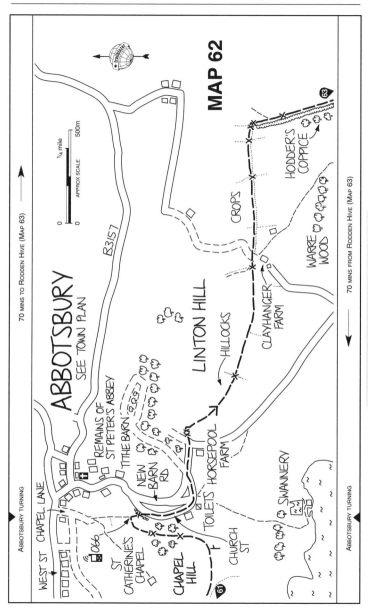

MAP 62

ABBOTSBURY
SEE TOWN PLAN

70 MINS TO RODDEN HIVE (MAP 63)

B3157

WEST ST   CHAPEL LANE

REMAINS OF ST PETER'S ABBEY

TITHE BARN

NEW BARN RD

ST CATHERINE'S CHAPEL

1066

CHAPEL HILL

CHURCH ST

TOILETS

HORSEPOOL FARM

LINTON HILL

HILLOCKS

CLAYHANGER FARM

SWANNERY

WARRE WOOD

CROPS

HODDER'S COPPICE

APPROX SCALE
¼ mile
0   500m

ABBOTSBURY TURNING

ABBOTSBURY TURNING

70 MINS FROM RODDEN HIVE (MAP 63)

ROUTE GUIDE AND MAPS

(continued from p263) The climb towards the chapel affords your first views of **West Fleet** – and, if you're lucky, the mute swans of **Abbotsbury Swannery** (see below). Rounding the hill, the path veers off to the right and you arrive at a junction: turn left for the village or turn right to arrive at a stile next to an impressive plane tree. Turning left here will lead you into **Abbotsbury** itself; or you can turn right and follow the road onwards along the coastal path. To walk every inch of the coastal path take the second turning left after the plane tree, following Church St into the village.

ABBOTSBURY

Rich in English history, the pristine little village of Abbotsbury (🖳 www.abbotsbury .co.uk) is one of the highlights of the whole walk – there's nowhere else along the whole of the coast path quite like it. There is plenty of accommodation and it's a great place to stop; however, it is also very popular so booking ahead, especially in summer, is advisable.

Sight-wise, the most important buildings are the remains of the Benedictine **Abbey of St Peter**, which was founded in the 11th-century; the accompanying **Tithe Barn**, at 272ft the longest in England (indeed, when they rethatched the roof in 2006, so enormous was the task that it took three years to complete!); and **St Catherine's Chapel** (see p263) – the latter two being 15th-century additions to the village. Having survived the Black Death and other invasions, the abbey finally met its match in the Dissolution under Henry VIII and was destroyed in 1538. The barn, however, supposedly resisted the same fate due to its multitude of uses, while the chapel survived due to its importance as a navigational aid to those sailing in Lyme Bay.

Dotted amongst them are several **cottages** that date back to the 16th century or earlier, with many of them incorporating materials from the demolished abbey.

The monks were also responsible for the **Swannery** (☎ 01305-871858, 🖳 www .abbotsburyswannery.co.uk; Mar-Oct daily 10am-5/6pm; £10.50; NO dogs!), established in the 11th century to supply the fare for their tables. The swans are somewhat luckier today and hundreds reside here. If you're a sucker for a cygnet plan your trip for between mid-May and late June when they are hatching.

In the centre of the village, the 14th-century **Church of St Nicholas** remains scarred by the English Civil War – the Grade-I listed tower still bearing the marks of musket fire, shot whilst the Cavaliers had the Roundheads under siege within its walls.

Finally, the **Subtropical Gardens** (☎ 01305-871387, 🖳 www.abbotsburygardens .co.uk; Mar-Oct daily 10am-5pm, July-Aug to 6pm, Nov-Mar to 4pm; 🐾 if on a lead; £10.50), on Bullers Way about three-quarters of a mile from the village, were originally established in 1765 as the first Countess of Ilchester's kitchen garden. Today the 20 acres are filled with rare and exotic plants – and an eatery, *The Colonial Restaurant* (☎ 01305-871732; hours as for the gardens but they close about half an hour earlier).

Services

There is a **tourist information point** (ie a table piled with leaflets) in Bellenie's Bakehouse (see Where to eat). The **post office** (Mon, Tue, Thur & Fri 9am-3pm & 4-5pm; Wed & Sat 9am-1pm) is just round the corner, while the other way on the same street is **Chapel Lane Stores** (summer 7am-7pm, Sun 8am-6pm, winter closing earlier).

Where to stay

Abbotsbury is fairly stuffed with holiday accommodation, including several **B&Bs**; furthermore some of it, for an area that you'd expect to be exorbitant, is very reasonably priced. For those aiming to save a buck and also house a dog for a night both *Cowards Lake Farmhouse* (☎ 01305-871421, 🖳 cowards-lakebandb@btconnect .com; 1D/1T; 🛏; 🐾; WI-FI; £35pp, sgl occ

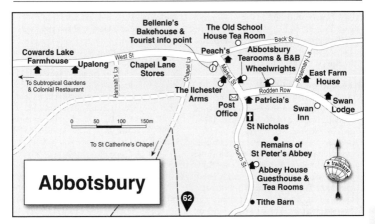

Abbotsbury

£50) and **Upalong** (☎ 01305-871882, 🖥 www.upalongwestdorset.co.uk; 1D/1D or T, shared facilities; 🛏; 🐕 downstairs only; WI-FI; £27.50pp, sgl occ £35) can be found on West St.

Abbey House Guest House (☎ 01305-871330, 🖥 www.theabbeyhouse.co.uk; 2T/3D; 🛏; WI-FI; £37.50-55pp, sgl occ £75-110) is typical of the kind of accommodation available in the village, being both gorgeous and ancient. The place actually dates back to the 15th century when it was part of the abbey's infirmary and overlooks the abbey today, its grounds (parts of which are now given over to the tearoom – see Where to eat) sloping down to the duck-filled millpond. Do settings get any better? Rooms are individual, as you'd expect, with one attic room and others with king-size or half-tester beds.

Another couple of eateries-cum-B&Bs that come recommended are **Abbotsbury Tearooms** (☎ 01305-871143, 🖥 www.abbotsbury-tearooms.co.uk; 2D/1F; 🛏; WI-FI;

£37.50pp, sgl occ £50-75; mid Mar-Oct), 26 Rodden Row, and **Wheelwrights** (☎ 01305-871800, 🖥 www.wheelwrights .co.uk; 1D or T; WI-FI in tearoom; £40pp, sgl occ £65), 14 Rodden Row.

Still central, at 6 Market St, is the lovely **Peach's** (☎ 01305-871364, 🖥 www .abbotsburybandb.co.uk; 1S/1D; £35pp, sgl £40pp).

Further east the 17th-century Dorset longhouse at **East Farm House** (☎ 01305-871363, 🖥 www.eastfarmhouse.co.uk; 2D/1T; 🐕; WI-FI in public areas; £65pp, sgl occ £50-65) is now an equine-centric farm on the edge of the village centre. On the eastern extremity of the village is **Swan Lodge** (☎ 01305-871249, 🖥 www.swan-inn.net; 2T/3D; 🐕; £37.50pp, sgl occ £55) across the road from – and owned by – the Swan Inn (see Where to eat).

Hotel-wise, with a long and interesting history (an arch that can be seen in the hotel's wall is thought by some to date back as far as the 11th century!), *The Ilchester*

❏ **Where to stay: the details**
Unless specified, B&B-style accommodation is either en suite or has private facilities; 🛏 means at least one room has a bath; 🐕 signifies that dogs are welcome in at least one room but always by prior arrangement, an additional charge may also be payable; WI-FI means wi-fi is available in the property, though not always (reliably) in every room.

Arms Hotel (☎ 01305-871243, 💻 www
.ilchester-arms.co.uk; 7D/2T; ☞; WI-FI;
£40.50-48pp, sgl occ £71) is on Market St
in the very heart of the village. Food is also
provided (see Where to eat).

Where to eat and drink
It probably won't come as any surprise to
find that there is no shortage of **tearooms**
in Abbotsbury. One of the smartest is *Abbey
House Tea Rooms* (see Where to stay; Mar-
Oct 10am-5pm), with excellent cream teas
to gorge on while watching the ducks frolic
in the pond below. Nor is it the only B&B
with a tearoom attached, with both
Abbotsbury Tearooms (see Where to stay;
mid Mar-Oct Thur-Tue 11am-5pm) and
Wheelwrights (see Where to stay; Feb-Nov
Sat-Wed 2-5.30pm) operating a nice little
sideline in baked comestibles. At the latter
they offer teas and homemade cakes, with
cream teas a speciality (two scones: £5.50).
Note, however, they are shut in the morn-
ings as this is when the baking is done for
the afternoon's customers.

Two more tearooms face each other in
the centre of the village. *The Old School
House Tea Room* (☎ 01305-871808; Tue-
Sun 10am-5/5.30pm; 🐾) is known for its
'set teas' that include sandwiches, scone,
cake and a pot of tea, the exact price
depending on the filling in the sandwich
(£8.95-12.95). It has a lovely little patio

garden out back, a delightful hostess, dogs
are welcome and there is also a great selection of cakes.

Bellenie's Bakehouse & Tea-Room
(☎ 01305-871990; Feb to mid Dec Wed-
Mon 8am-4.30pm) proudly boasts of its
award-winning cakes such as a delicious
farmhouse fruitcake for £2.40 or a magnificent four-scone cream tea for £7.50; as
hosts of the village's tourist information
point, they also have a good selection of
brochures to browse while you tuck in.

The pubs and inns are the most reliable
source of food in the evenings. On the outskirts of town, *Swan Inn* (see Swan Lodge,
Where to stay; food summer daily 11am-
9pm, winter 11.30am-2.30pm & 6-9pm)
has a wide range of fairly simple but filling
fare such as braised pork in cider and apple
sauce with veg (£11.95). Right in the centre, *The Ilchester Arms* (see Where to stay;
food daily noon-3pm & 6-9pm) has an à la
carte restaurant with fish specialities.

Transport
[See pp55-60] First's coastal X53 **bus**
service passes through en route between
Exeter and Poole. If you happen to be here
on a Wednesday First's 61 (operated by
Damory Coaches) calls here en route
between Wyke Regis and Dorchester. It
also stops at Chickerell, Langton Herring,
Portesham and Winterborne Abbas.

ABBOTSBURY TO FORTUNESWELL [MAPS 62-68]

This **13-mile (21km; 4hrs 20 mins)** day starts with a 3-mile hike along a ridge
and through fields that, at times, can feel a long way from the sea. It is however, good walking. There are great views over the surrounding countryside as you
make your way through the farmland, eventually arriving at the western end of
The Fleet – the great expanse of water that separates the mainland from the
large pebble ridge of Chesil Beach, and also a nature reserve.

The rest of the stage is largely spent on the flat. Following the lakeshore,
interrupted only by Chickerell Rifle Range (should target practice forbid your
passing there is an easy alternative), you eventually arrive at Ferrybridge in
Wyke Regis, from where you can either cross the tombolo (sand bar) to the Isle
of Portland (2 miles/3.2km; 40 mins), or continue on into Weymouth (3
miles/5km; 1hr 10 mins). There is accommodation in both places and to get to
both there are buses.

This may not be the most exciting stage and the lack of any refreshments until you reach the suburbs of Weymouth/Portland is irksome. Luckily, there are plenty of places along the banks of The Fleet that make great locations for a picnic. Accommodation-wise, there are a couple of options for campers but little else.

The route
To leave the little village head down Church St, passing St Nicholas Church and Tithe Barn, before turning off down a minor road – Grove Lane – signed to The Swannery. Carry on straight down the lane and you are soon on the coastal path again by the gorgeous plane tree.

Passing the entrance to the Swannery (see p266), you leave the road on a bend to cross a stile, following the path up over fields with St Catherine's Chapel watching your progress from the rear and the western end of **The Fleet** now clearly visible to your right. The path follows a ridge with an idyllic pastoral landscape to the right that gently recedes towards Chesil Beach. This ridge is followed until a sharp turn sends you down and right, briefly along the outskirts of **Hodder's Coppice**, before more fields take you to the edges of **Wyke Wood**. Having briefly followed Bridge Lane you pass a house marked 'private' on your right and, crossing a few more fields, you reach **Rodden Hive** and **Fleet Lagoon Nature Reserve**.

Despite the path's occasional brief diversion away from the water's edge (such as at **Herbury**) you never stray too far from The Fleet and its flapping feathery frequenters. Much of the walking is along the edge of farmland, interrupted only by the odd field boundary. **Campers** can find a pitch at either *West Fleet Holiday Farm* (☎ 01305-782218, 🖳 www.westfleetholidays.co.uk; 🐾; £9-19 for walker and tent, additional person £4-5; 🐾; 🐕 £2-3 but must be on lead at all times; Easter-Sep); or *Sea Barn Farm* (phone as for West Fleet; 🖳 www.seabarnfarm.co.uk; 🐾; £8-17 for walker and tent, additional person £4-5; 🐾; 🐕 £2-3 but must be on lead at all times; Mar-Oct) which is slightly cheaper and the views are better. Follow the signs from the coast path.

A little further along, *East Fleet Farm Touring Park* (off Map 63; ☎ 01305-785768, 🖳 www.eastfleet.co.uk; £14-22 for 2 people & tent; 🐕 £1-2; mid Mar-Oct).

Chickerell Rifle Range is eventually reached. **If the red flags are flying do not enter** but follow the short detour to the north instead. You then pass by a caravan park before heading towards an **army training centre**, after which the path turns east by the water's edge to cross level grassland and pasture with the eastern end of Chesil Beach in your sights and with Portland becoming ever clearer. Strolling past chalets on your left you arrive at a minor road that leads you onwards to **Ferrybridge**. Here a choice needs to be made; for Portland and the continuation of the path, turn right and continue along the tombolo on a dreary 2-mile roadside trudge – although watching the kite surfers in Portland Harbour can be entertaining. Three roundabouts are crossed, the third furnished with a bus-stop and The Little Ship pub. *(continued on p272)*

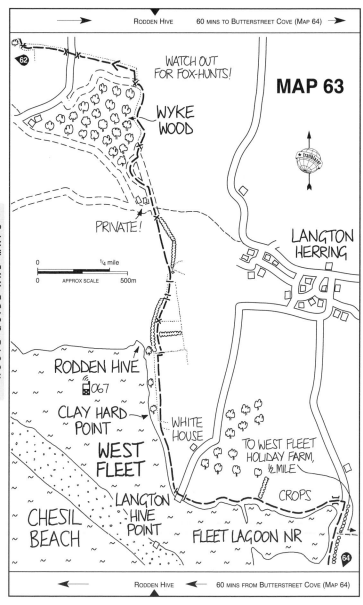

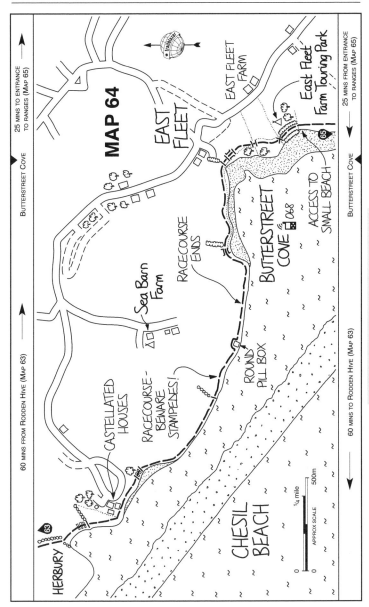

MAP 64

25 MINS TO ENTRANCE TO RANGES (MAP 65)

BUTTERSTREET COVE

25 MINS FROM ENTRANCE TO RANGES (MAP 65)

BUTTERSTREET COVE

EAST FLEET FARM

EAST FLEET

East Fleet Farm Touring Park

65

ACCESS TO SMALL BEACH

BUTTERSTREET COVE ⌂ 068

60 MINS FROM RODDEN HIVE (MAP 63)

60 MINS TO RODDEN HIVE (MAP 63)

Sea Barn Farm

RACECOURSE ENDS

CASTELLATED HOUSES

RACECOURSE - BEWARE STAMPEDES!

ROUND PILL BOX

CHESIL BEACH

HERBURY

63

¼ mile

500m

APPROX SCALE

0

0

ROUTE GUIDE AND MAPS

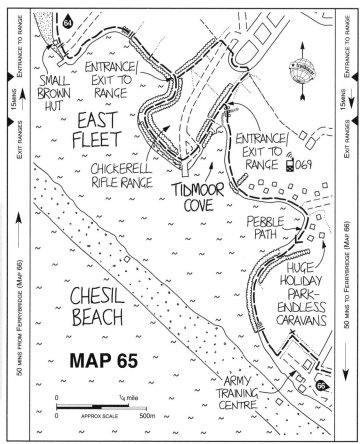

MAP 65

(*continued from p269*) Continue along this road before turning right into Pebble Lane, following it as far as **Chiswell** and *The Cove House Inn* (Map 67; ☎ 01305-820895, 🖥 www.thecovehouseinn.co.uk; Mon-Fri noon-2.30pm & 6-9pm, Sat & Sun noon-9pm; open all day in school summer hols). The menu is pretty standard (sandwiches £4.75-7.25, mains £7.95-14.95) but includes, for gluttons, a good mixed grill of lamb chop, steak, bacon and sausage topped with a fried egg and served with chips and peas (£14.25). From there continue to **Fortuneswell** (see p274).

The alternative to crossing to Portland is to continue onwards, crossing the road and heading into Weymouth. There are **buses**, too, to both Portland and Weymouth from Ferrybridge: First's 6 (Weymouth–Wyke Regis), their No 1

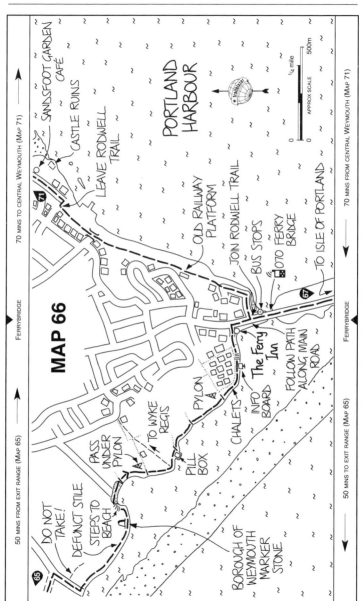

MAP 66

50 MINS FROM EXIT RANGE (MAP 65)

FERRYBRIDGE

70 MINS TO CENTRAL WEYMOUTH (MAP 71)

70 MINS FROM CENTRAL WEYMOUTH (MAP 71)

FERRYBRIDGE

50 MINS TO EXIT RANGE (MAP 65)

SANDSFOOT GARDEN CAFÉ

CASTLE RUINS

LEAVE RODWELL TRAIL

PORTLAND HARBOUR

OLD RAILWAY PLATFORM

JOIN RODWELL TRAIL

BUS STOPS

TO FERRY BRIDGE

TO ISLE OF PORTLAND

The Ferry Inn

FOLLOW PATH ALONG MAIN ROAD

CHALETS

INFO BOARD

PYLON

TO WYKE REGIS

PASS UNDER PYLON

PILL BOX

STEPS TO BEACH

DEFUNCT STILE

DO NOT TAKE!

BOROUGH OF WEYMOUTH MARKER STONE

APPROX SCALE

¼ mile

500m

ROUTE GUIDE AND MAPS

(Weymouth–Portland) and 10 services (Dorchester–Portland), the open-top No 501 (Weymouth–Portland Bill) and South West Coaches Nos 205, 206 and 210 services all call in at the bus stops here.

For the route guide for the trek into Weymouth, see p280.

FORTUNESWELL   **[Map 68]**
Scruffy Fortuneswell isn't the most charismatic of stops on the path but for a night or two it's fine. Services on Fortuneswell (the road that runs through the village) include a

Co-op **supermarket** (Mon-Sat 7am-10pm) with a free **ATM**, a Boots the **Chemist** (Mon-Fri 9am-5.30pm, Sat 9am-1pm) and a **post office** (Mon-Fri 9am-1pm & 2-5.30pm, Sat 9am-12.30pm).

ROUTE GUIDE AND MAPS

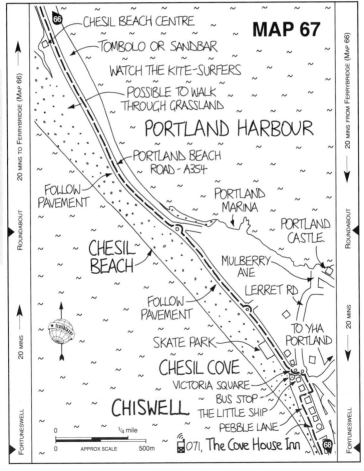

MAP 67

CHESIL BEACH CENTRE

TOMBOLO OR SANDBAR

WATCH THE KITE-SURFERS

POSSIBLE TO WALK THROUGH GRASSLAND

PORTLAND HARBOUR

PORTLAND BEACH ROAD - A354

FOLLOW PAVEMENT

PORTLAND MARINA

PORTLAND CASTLE

CHESIL BEACH

MULBERRY AVE

LERRET RD

FOLLOW PAVEMENT

SKATE PARK

TO YHA PORTLAND

CHESIL COVE

VICTORIA SQUARE

CHISWELL

BUS STOP

THE LITTLE SHIP

PEBBLE LANE

071, The Cove House Inn

20 MINS TO FERRYBRIDGE (MAP 66)

20 MINS FROM FERRYBRIDGE (MAP 66)

ROUNDABOUT

ROUNDABOUT

20 MINS

20 MINS

FORTUNESWELL

FORTUNESWELL

0   ¼ mile

0   APPROX SCALE   500m

66

68

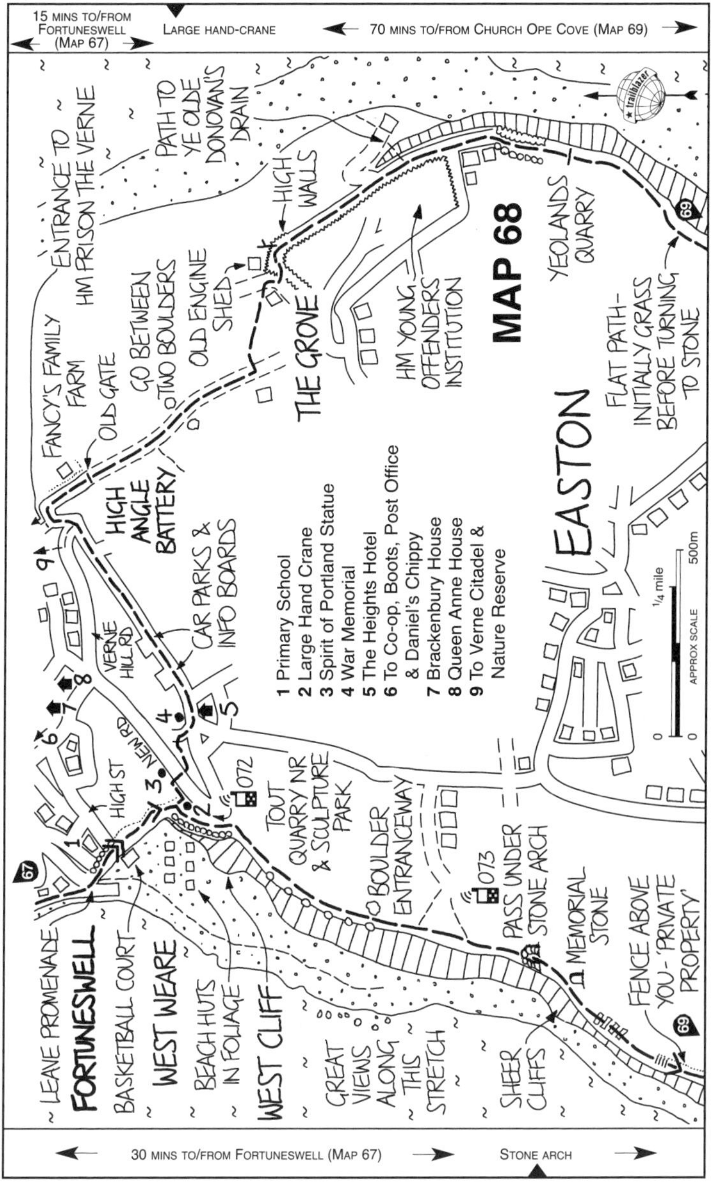

15 MINS TO/FROM FORTUNESWELL (MAP 67)

LARGE HAND-CRANE

70 MINS TO/FROM CHURCH OPE COVE (MAP 69)

PATH TO YE OLDE DONOVAN'S DRAIN

HIGH WALLS

ENTRANCE TO HM PRISON THE VERNE

GO BETWEEN TWO BOULDERS

OLD ENGINE SHED

MAP 68

THE GROVE

HM YOUNG OFFENDERS INSTITUTION

YEOLANDS QUARRY

FANCY'S FAMILY FARM

OLD GATE

FLAT PATH – INITIALLY GRASS BEFORE TURNING TO STONE

HIGH ANGLE BATTERY

CAR PARKS & INFO BOARDS

EASTON

VERNE HILL RD

NEW RD

HIGH ST

TOUT QUARRY NR & SCULPTURE PARK

TO BOULDER ENTRANCEWAY

1 Primary School
2 Large Hand Crane
3 Spirit of Portland Statue
4 War Memorial
5 The Heights Hotel
6 To Co-op, Boots, Post Office & Daniel's Chippy
7 Brackenbury House
8 Queen Anne House
9 To Verne Citadel & Nature Reserve

APPROX SCALE

500m

¼ mile

0

PASS UNDER STONE ARCH

MEMORIAL STONE

FENCE ABOVE YOU – 'PRIVATE PROPERTY'

LEANE PROMENADE

FORTUNESWELL

BASKETBALL COURT

WEST WEARE

BEACH HUTS IN FOLIAGE

WEST CLIFF

GREAT VIEWS ALONG THIS STRETCH

SHEER CLIFFS

30 MINS TO/FROM FORTUNESWELL (MAP 67)

STONE ARCH

ROUTE GUIDE AND MAPS

Accommodation is quite limited on Portland but to save you travelling to and from Weymouth it is worth considering stopping on the isle. There is a hostel, *YHA Portland* (☎ 0845-371 9339, 🖳 www.yha .org.uk/hostel/portland; 28 beds; dorm beds from £13.40, 4-bedded room from £57) in Hardy House on Castle Rd.

On Fortuneswell Rd there are two **B&Bs**, both welcoming walkers. Approximately halfway up the hill, *Brackenbury House* (☎ 01305-826509, 🖳 www.brackenburyhouse.co.uk; 3D/2D or T; 2D share toilet; 👅; 🐾; WI-FI but only available for some networks; £27pp, sgl occ £30) is a more than decent place to spend a night and the proprietors pay careful attention to detail and value is one of their by-words. More upmarket and a little more pricey, *Queen Anne House* (☎ 01305-820028, 🖳 www.queenannehouse .com; 4D; 👅; WI-FI; £37.50-47.50pp, sgl occ £48-75), 2-4 Fortuneswell, is a couple of doors further along. Finally, overlooking Fortuneswell, as well as the surrounding area, is a **hotel** with wonderful views: *The Heights Hotel* (☎ 01305-821361, 🖳 www .heightshotel.com; 66D or T; 👅; WI-FI in public areas but not guaranteed in all rooms; £40-85pp; sgl occ £80-150) on Yeates Rd is a modern place with a restaurant (daily noon-2pm & 6-9pm) and panoramic windows to make the most of the great views.

Food-wise, *The Cove House Inn* (see p272) is the most popular place on Underhill even though it's down in Chiswell, a 10-minute walk away from most of the island's accommodation. There's a chippy, *Daniel's* (Mon-Thur noon-1.30pm & 5.9.30pm, Fri & Sat noon-2pm & 5-10pm, Sun 5-9pm) on Fortuneswell. *The Heights Hotel* (see above; food daily 7am-9pm; WI-FI), which does decent food such as Chesil chicken (£10.95).

For **buses**, First's Nos 1 and 10 services regularly travel between Weymouth and Portland. In summer First also operates an open-top bus (501) between Weymouth and Portland Bill. South West Coaches 205 and 210 services stop here and connect Portland with Weymouth via Wyke Regis. See pp55-60 for details.

FORTUNESWELL TO WEYMOUTH (VIA THE ISLE OF PORTLAND CIRCUIT) [MAPS 68-71]

Today's multifaceted **14¾-mile (23.75km; 5hrs 25mins)** walk around the wild and intriguing Isle of Portland (see box opposite) feels like an adventure like no other on this trek. Connected to the mainland by two miles of road, the isle feels somehow estranged from the rest of Dorset as if cast away – without ever truly being able to free herself from the mainland's grasp. With a landscape that encompasses lonely clifftops, disused quarries, housing and industrial estates, MoD compounds, prisons and institutions, nature reserves, a 13th-century church and three lighthouses, there is little likelihood of you becoming bored on this great slab of limestone. Wildlife abounds too, with over half of Britain's 57 butterfly species in residence and birdlife visiting the isle in such numbers that one of the three lighthouses has been turned into a bird observatory. Basking sharks, dolphins and seals also inhabit the waters offshore.

The path is generally easy on the legs but with a couple of short ascents around the Underhill area, and there are a number of places to stop for food, including one near the isle's southern tip, close to the halfway point. To return to the mainland, the coast path suggests you need to walk the tombolo twice – though buses also cross the tombolo frequently between Fortuneswell and Ferrybridge.

The route

From The Cove House Inn the path now briefly follows the edge of Chesil Cove, turning left and then right to head up the steep path to **West Cliff**, with the beach huts and boulders of **West Weare** below you. At the very top of the steps turn back for a great view over Portland Harbour: one of the largest man-made harbours in the world, it was formed by the construction of huge stone breakwaters between 1848 and 1905.

The path now heads through disused **Tout Quarry**, a nature reserve and sculpture park. As you walk alongside the boulders, under stone archways and with some sheer drops to your right, there are marvellous views back down along the whole of Chesil Beach. This exposed cliff-top path contrasts starkly with yesterday's agrarian amble.

The path gradually bends south and widens, with housing estates interrupting the scenery on the left and a **business park** doing similar work straight ahead. Passing this, you descend gradually across grasslands; watch out for the odd sprouting of barbed wire lying in wait in the scrub to snare the unwary.

❏ The Isle of Portland

Six kilometres long, two-and-a-half kilometres wide and made of limestone, the Isle of Portland is what is known as a **tied island**, connected to the mainland by a sandbar, or tombolo – which, in Portland's case, is better known as the A354. The island today is most famous for Portland stone, a durable, good-looking material used in the building of Buckingham Palace and St Paul's Cathedral (the latter, incidentally, designed by Christopher Wren who was once MP for Weymouth and controlled the quarries on Portland). The stone was also used for thousands of gravestones during the two world wars.

The isle is divided into two main areas: the northern, steeply sloping Underhill (which has been visible for many miles) and the flatter, plateau-like southern expanse of **Tophill**. The isle slopes down from approximately 150 metres above sea-level near **The Verne**, atop Underhill, to just above sea-level by the time that you reach Portland Bill. There are eight settlements, the two most relevant to the walker being Chiswell (see p272) and Fortuneswell (see p274). Although close enough to be almost indistinguishable, Chiswell consists of the flatter area near Chesil Cove and the sea (ie the home of The Cove Inn) whilst Fortuneswell is made up of the sloping streets that lead up from the hill.

The most prominent tourist attraction on the island – save, perhaps, for the lighthouse at Portland Bill – is **Portland Castle** (Map 67; ☎ 01305 820539, 🖳 www.port landcastle.co.uk; daily Apr-Jun 10am-5pm, July & Aug 10am-6pm, Sep 10am-5pm, Oct-early Nov 10am-4pm; £4.30). Known as a Device Fort or Henrician Castle, it was constructed (using Portland Stone, of course) on the orders of Henry VIII in 1540 in order to defend Weymouth from attack by the French and Spanish. Possibly due to the quality of the stone it is one of the best preserved castles from this era. The fortress can be visited easily enough from Fortuneswell.

One final tip: whilst a guest on the isle be wary of using the word 'rabbit'. Records suggest that superstitious quarry workers would always see a bunny emerging from its burrow immediately before a rockfall. Such was their superstition, they often refused to work if one was spotted! The unusual moniker 'underground mutton' is how the locals are said to refer to our furry friends.

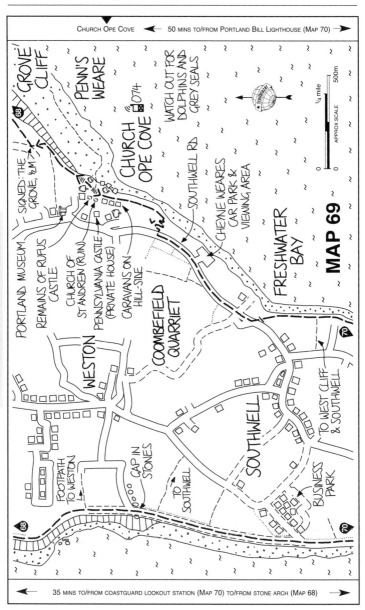

CHURCH OPE COVE ◄ 50 MINS TO/FROM PORTLAND BILL LIGHTHOUSE (MAP 70) ►

GROVE CLIFF

PENN'S WEARE

SIGNED 'THE GROVE, ½M'

CHURCH OPE COVE

SOUTHWELL RD

WATCH OUT FOR DOLPHINS AND GREY SEALS

CHEYNE WEARES CAR PARK & VIEWING AREA

FRESHWATER BAY

MAP 69

PORTLAND MUSEUM

REMAINS OF RUFUS CASTLE

CHURCH OF ST ANDREW (RUIN)

PENNSYLVANIA CASTLE (PRIVATE HOUSE)

CARAVANS ON HILL-SIDE

WESTON

COOMBEFIELD QUARRIET

SOUTHWELL

TO WEST CLIFF & SOUTHWELL

FOOTPATH TO WESTON

GAP IN STONES

TO SOUTHWELL

BUSINESS PARK

APPROX SCALE

0   ¼ mile

0   500m

ROUTE GUIDE AND MAPS

◄ 35 MINS TO/FROM COASTGUARD LOOKOUT STATION (MAP 70) TO/FROM STONE ARCH (MAP 68) ►

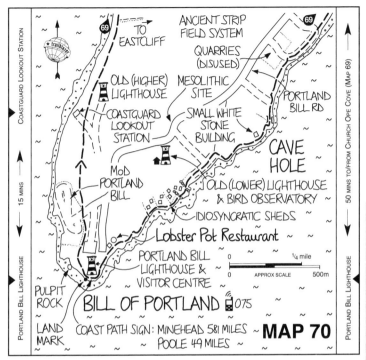

On the way you come to a **coastguard's lookout station** and the **Old (Higher) Lighthouse** – the light from which first guided sailors in 1716. The younger, bigger **Portland Bill Lighthouse** (☎ 01305-861233, 🖥 www.trinity house.co.uk/lighthouses/lighthouse_list/portland_bill.html; generally Apr-Sep Sun-Thur 11am-4.30pm but check website), which was built between 1905 and 1906 and now houses Portland's **Visitor Centre** (Apr-Sep daily 11am-5pm), is but a short stroll away, with **Pulpit Rock**, a remarkably square stone, formed during quarrying in the 1870s, on the right. A few strides away, ***Lobster Pot Restaurant*** (☎ 01305-820242, 🖥 www.lobsterpotrestaurantportland.co.uk; daily 9.30am-5pm) is a decent spot for lunch.

A little further along the path, the old (lower) lighthouse, built in 1789, houses a **bird observatory** and also provides hostel-type ***accommodation*** (☎ 01305-820553, 🖥 www.portlandbirdobs.org.uk; 9 bunk-bed rooms each with 2-4 beds, sleeps 20; £20pp) for ramblers, twitchers, naturalists and artists. Meals are not provided but cooking facilities are available. There is also a self-contained lighthouse keeper's cottage (1T/1 room with bunk bed; shower; 🐾; £80 for up to four people). Booking is recommended in the spring and autumn as they are the best seasons for birdwatching.

Keeping to the right of Portland Bill's idiosyncratic 'sheds', you pass through disused and deserted quarries and out of sight of any civilisation. The path gradually rises away from the shoreline to a road, until a second path winds downwards through rocks and scrub to the remains of **Rufus Castle** – also known as Bow and Arrow Castle and built in the late 15th century. The ruins now constitute a Grade-I listed building and unfortunately are deemed too fragile for the public to freely wander. Close by (though off the path) is the site of the 13th-century **Church of St Andrew**, Portland's parish church until the 18th century. Its graveyard remains, however, the eternal resting place of seafarers; the grave-stones, made of course of local stone, are worth a look. Not too far away (and also off the path), **Portland Museum** (☎ 01305-821804, 🖥 www.portland museum.co.uk; Easter-May & Sep Thur-Tue 10.30am-4pm, June, Jul & Aug daily 10.30am-4pm, Oct weekends only and half-term, Nov-Easter closed apart from half-term; check website as hours differ every year!) has display sections that include Stone, Sea and Shipwrecks and Famous Portland People.

The path continues through the scrub, above the quarries and boulders of **Penn's Weare** and **Grove Cliff** and through a gate at the far end of the huge **Yeolands Quarry**, with Portland goats grazing nearby. This leads to a Young Offenders Institution and the **Old Engine Shed**, that housed the locomotives that were used in the quarries. Continue onwards along the road passing **Fancy's Farm** and the entrance to **HM Prison The Verne**: formerly a fortress and a barracks for a thousand troops, the Verne Citadel became a prison in 1949, the interior being completed by prisoners themselves. The prison holds an unwanted record thanks to ex-inmate John Hannan who, having escaped (by tying bedsheets together to make a rope) in 1955, was still on the run in 2001 – at 46 years a record for evading recapture. (Hannan was actually serving only a 21-month sentence in the first place.) Behind you is **High Angle Battery**, built in 1892 to defend Portland Harbour.

The path follows the road to the left, passing car-parks, information boards and a war memorial on the right and **The Heights Hotel** (see p276) on the left.

The path now follows a combination of tarmac and trails to the large **hand crane** and stone marked 'Portland, Home of Portland Stone'. The path now drops back to the top of West Weare, with the well-known **Spirit of Portland Statue** just a couple of steps away from the trail.

All that's left to complete your Portland Odyssey is to retrace your footsteps back down into Fortuneswell and across the tombolo.

Into Weymouth

For the walk to the centre of Weymouth you join **The Rodwell Trail**, which begins opposite The Ferry Inn (see Map 66, p273). The coast path leaves the Rodwell just before *Sandsfoot Garden Café* (weather permitting summer daily approx 9am-5pm; winter weekends only) near **Sandsfoot Castle** (🖥 www.san dsfootcastle.org.uk), one of Henry VIII's fortifications which, together with Portland Castle (over on the island but away from the coast path), defended the harbour. Most of the ruins have now fallen into the sea but some remain and lottery funding has enabled it to be opened to the public.

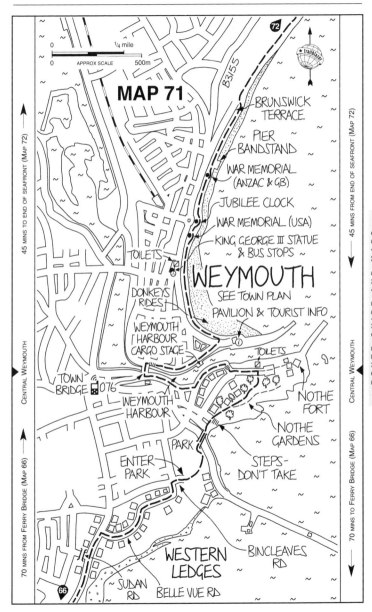

From the café follow the road for a distance to **Belle Vue Rd**, where you turn right, then Bincleaves Rd where another right turn and then an almost immediate left leads you into a park. That leads, via a bridge, to **Nothe Garden**, passing the Victorian **Nothe Fort** (☎ 01305-766626, 🖳 www.nothefort.org.uk; May-Sep daily 10.30am-5.30pm, Easter school holiday and Oct half-term daily 10.30am-4.30pm; £6) on your right. The gardens lead around the pretty little **harbour** where, crossing the **Town Bridge**, you follow the coast path signs down the steps and along the eastern edge of the harbour. You then take up the tram lines, passing **Weymouth Harbour Cargo Stage** on the right, the smell of fish pungent in the air. At the end of the road there's the Pavilion and tourist office in front of you to the right – and the promenade (Esplanade) along Weymouth seafront ahead.

It's a lovely stroll along the seafront, with arcades and fairground rides on your left and kid-laden donkeys panting in the sun to your right. The promenade is adorned with statues and memorials aplenty to the great and the good: the grand **George III statue** (situated by the bus-stops) is followed by a **Jubilee Clock**, a tribute to Queen Victoria, and then the more solemn ones to American GIs, ANZAC forces and home-grown Tommys who perished in World War II. From the Pier Bandstand, follow the blue Coast Path signs and continue along Brunswick Terrace and out of town.

WEYMOUTH   [map p285]

In 2012 Weymouth enjoyed a degree of fame as the host of the Olympic sailing events. This is, by all accounts, a good thing, not least because, prior to this, the town, Dorset's fourth largest, was best known as the favourite holiday destination of his Royal Highness George III following the decision of his brother, the Duke of Gloucester, to build a huge residence here. Though the townsfolk didn't follow the lead of their fellow south-coast resorts Lyme and Bognor (and, indeed, Wyke) in changing their name to celebrate the royal patronage bestowed upon them, there is no doubting they are just as proud of their regal links. Not only are there plaques and place names aplenty in Weymouth that commemorate George's visits, but there's also the rather gaudy statue of him in the centre and a large white chalk depiction of him atop a horse etched into the hillside just outside the town near Osmington (see p288). It does seem an awful lot of fuss to make over a monarch who is best known for having purple urine and a tendency to slip into insanity (both, incidentally, being symptoms of the blood disease porphyria, from which the king suffered).

Perhaps, given that Weymouth's prior claim to fame was as the place where the Black Death entered the country in 1348, the locals' desire to celebrate the king's choice of holiday destination is understandable. And it is in this light that we must view the Olympics: that regardless of whether one considers them a success or not, and whether it proved to be a boon for the town – or bankrupts it – the games have, at least, given Weymouth something else to shout about in the coming years.

There's plenty for walkers to enjoy in the town – including a wonderful sweep of sand that stretches for miles, a great harbour with some lovely restaurants as well as facilities galore. **Wessex Folk Festival** (🖳 www.wessexfolk.co.uk) is held here in June and **Dorset Seafood Festival** (🖳 www.dorsetseafood.co.uk) in July. The latter is opened by a rather bizarre race in which participants swim across the harbour before downing oysters and champagne!

Services

Weymouth's **tourist information office** (☎ 01305-785747, 🖳 www.visitweymouth.co.uk; daily Mar-Oct 9.30am-5pm, Nov-Mar to 4pm) is one of the largest on the trail. As is usual, the town's library has **internet access** (Mon & Thur 10am-7pm, Tue & Fri 9.30am-5.30pm, Wed 9.30am-1pm, Sat 9am-4pm), where the first half-hour is free and after that it's just £1 for every extra 30 minutes. Just bring some form of ID. An alternative is the internet café *Cobwebs* (🖳 www.ecobwebs.co.uk; Mon-Fri 10am-8pm, Sat 10am-6pm, Sun noon-6pm), on Great George St, though it's more expensive at £3 for an hour. Nearby is the **post office** (Mon-Fri 9am-5.30pm, Sat 9am-2pm) and there are plenty of **banks** with **ATMs** around town.

The town centre also has a branch of Boots the **chemist** (Mon-Tue 9am-5.30pm, Wed-Sat 8.30am-5.30pm, Sun 10am-4pm), on St Thomas St with another entrance on St Mary St. **Camping suppliers** Mountain Warehouse and Trespass are within a couple of hundred yards of each other on St Mary St and both have the same opening hours (Mon-Sat 9am-5.30pm, Sun 10am-4pm); and a Tesco Metro **supermarket** (Mon-Sat 7am-10pm, Sun 10am-4pm) on nearby St Thomas St. Finally, there's a **launderette**, Park Laundry (☎ 01305-772573), in the town centre on Brownlow St.

Where to stay

There's a **hostel** in Weymouth. *Bunkhouse Plus* (☎ 01305-775228, 🖳 www.bunkhouseplus.co.uk; mix of 2- & 4-bed rooms totalling 18 beds and 2D en suite; WI-FI; £16.50-19pp) is a facility-packed place with a large guest kitchen (with free tea, coffee and toast) and no curfew.

Weymouth has approximately 150 **B&Bs** so unless you're waltzing into town during a visit from the Queen, Pope or an alive-and-well Elvis there shouldn't be too many issues with finding a bed. They can be fairly helpfully divided into three separate categories: those that will allow people to book well in advance for one night only; those that do so but not at weekends; and those that don't. Ever. That said, most will

accept people for just one night if they have availability and you turn up on the day looking for a bed. One that belongs in the first category, on the way into town and perfectly located by two of Weymouth's great harbour-side pubs, *Old Harbour View* (☎ 01305-750828, 🖳 www.oldharbourviewweymouth.co.uk; 1D/1T; WI-FI; £48pp, sgl occ £72) is not cheap but the location is ideal.

Moving north to the almost unbroken string of establishments on The Esplanade, two more places that accept one-night bookings can be found here with *The Roundhouse Hotel* (☎ 01305-761010, 🖳 www.roundhouse-hotel-weymouth.com; 1T/4D; 🖤; WI-FI; £47.50-£80pp, sgl occ £85) at No 1 and, at No 2, *Aaran House* (☎ 01305-766669, 🖳 www.aaranhouse.co.uk; 1S/4D/2T; 1S/D share facilities; 🖤; WI-FI; £30-36pp, sgl occ plus £45-61). Their neighbour at No 3, however, *Beach View Guest House* (☎ 01305-549038, 🖳 www.beachviewguesthouse.com; 1S shared facilities/5D/1F; 🐾; WI-FI in guest lounge; £30-38pp; sgl £25-30; sgl occ £45-61) does not accept bookings for one-night stops in the summer; however, a gap in the diary could always lead to them providing a last-minute deal.

Still on Esplanade, dogs and their owners should point their paws towards *The Anchorage* (☎ 01305-782542, 🖳 www.theanchorageweymouth.co.uk; 2S shared shower facilities/3D/1T/2F; WI-FI; 🐾 £5 per stay; £32-36pp, sgl occ £48-55) at No 7, which accepts one-night bookings except in summer. *The Bedford* (☎ 01305-786995, 🖳 www.thebedfordweymouth.co.uk; 2S/4T/2F; WI-FI; £34-38pp, sgl £40), at No 17, accepts one-night bookings except in August.

Still good value are *The Bourneville* (☎ 01305-784784, 🖳 www.bournevillehotel.co.uk; 2S/3D or T/2T/6D/3F; 🖤; WI-FI; £25-44pp, sgl occ £40-70 but negotiable) at No 31-32, which has a licensed bar, and *Bay View Hotel* (☎ 01305-782083, 🖳 www.bayview-weymouth.co.uk; 7D/1F; WI-FI; £27.50-30pp, sgl occ £30-60), No 35, which provides fridges in its rooms. Alas, neither of these is likely to take a one-night booking in July or August though both are worth a call on the day if you're stuck.

Equally reluctant to take one-night bookings are *The Edenhurst* (☎ 01305-771255, 🖳 www.edenhurstweymouth.com; 2S/4D/2T/4F; WI-FI; £34-44pp, sgl occ £34-59), No 122 The Esplanade, and *The Langham* (☎ 01305-782530, 🖳 www.langham-hotel.com; 4D/3T/5F; ☛; WI-FI; £34-44pp, sgl occ £68-88), at No 130; the latter provides evening meals (3 courses £11.95) if booked in advance. In contrast and before leaving The Esplanade altogether, right at its heart sits *Gloucester House* (☎ 01305-785191, 🖳 www.gloucesterhouseweymouth.co.uk; 3S/6D/2T/4F; ☛; WI-FI; £35-45pp, sgl occ £55-60) at No 96, where one-night bookings are generally allowed except for bank holiday weekends.

The Esplanade isn't the only street stuffed with accommodation; at the opposite end of town there is another string of B&Bs on Brunswick Terrace. Most of them are great value and several accept one-night stops, at least outside the peak seasons of July and August. Cheap and dog-friendly are *Whitecliff* (☎ 01305-785554, 🖳 www.whitecliff-guesthouse.co.uk; 1S/4D/1T/2F; the single and double share bathroom; ☛; 🐾 £variable; £20-50pp, sgl occ depends on season), at No 7, a decent and well-run place where you'll get a bed for as little as £20 in winter, albeit without breakfast; and, with better rooms, *Sunnyside* (☎ 01305-786358, 🖳 www.sunnysideweymouth .com; 1D/1T/3F; the double and twin share a shower; 🐾; WI-FI; £30-40pp) at No 15.

Also very good value are *Lichfield House* (☎ 01305-784112, 🖳 www.lichfieldhouse.net; 3D/2T/1F; ☛; £30-33pp, sgl occ maybe slightly more), at No 8, and *Seaspray* (☎ 01305-786943, 🖳 www.seaspray-guesthouse.co.uk; 1S/2D/1D or T/2F; £25-40pp, sgl £30-40) at No 6.

Further down the street, *The Redcliff* (☎ 01305-784682, 🖳 www.redcliffweymouth.co.uk; 2S/4D/5D or T/1T; 1S/1T share shower facilities; WI-FI; £28-45pp, sgl £28), at No 18-19, do not accept bookings for one-night stays in summer; while *Horizon* (☎ 01305-784916, 🖳 www.horizonguesthouse.co.uk; 1S/1T/1D/1D or T/1F; £30-40pp; sgl £30), at No 16, are also unlikely to take one-night bookings between mid July and the whole of August. Meanwhile, *Spindrift* (☎ 01305-773625, 🖳 www.spindriftweymouth.co.uk; 1S/2D/1T/2F; ☛; WI-FI; £37.50-42.50pp, sgl £35-50, sgl occ £55; closed Jan), No 11, whilst not overly cheap, their breakfasts include their own homemade jam and bread. They also do a reduced rate for those not requiring breakfast (£30-32pp).

One block behind Brunswick Terrace, and fronted with a busy road rather than the sea, Waterloo Place is home to another line of B&Bs. *Oliver's Guest House* (☎ 01305-786712, 🖳 www.oliversguesthouse.co.uk; 2S/4D/1T; the twin, a double and one single share a shower room; WI-FI; £25-35pp, sgl occ same rate), at No 12, though they may not accept a one-night booking in July/August; *The Bay* (☎ 01305-786289, 🖳 www.thebayguesthouse.co.uk; 2D/3D or T; WI-FI; £30-40pp, sgl occ £42-65) at No 10; and *The Seaham* (☎ 01305-782010, 🖳 www.theseahamweymouth.co.uk; 5D; WI-FI; £34-45pp, sgl occ £50-70) at No 3. This last, incidentally, has kippers, haddock and salmon on their breakfast menu.

There are several **hotels** at the northern end of The Esplanade. Both *Hotel Mon Ami* (☎ 01305-786917, 🖳 www.hotelmonami.co.uk; 20S or T/20D; ☛; WI-FI on lower floors; £30-45pp), No 143-145, and *Marina Court* (☎ 01305-782146, 🖳 www.marinacourt.co.uk; 1S/9D/4T; WI-FI; £33-42pp, sgl occ £37-45), No 142, provide

---

❏ **Where to stay: the details**
Unless specified, B&B-style accommodation is either en suite or has private facilities; ☛ means at least one room has a bath; 🐾 signifies that dogs are welcome in at least one room but always by prior arrangement, an additional charge may also be payable; WI-FI means wi-fi is available in the property, though not always (reliably) in every room.

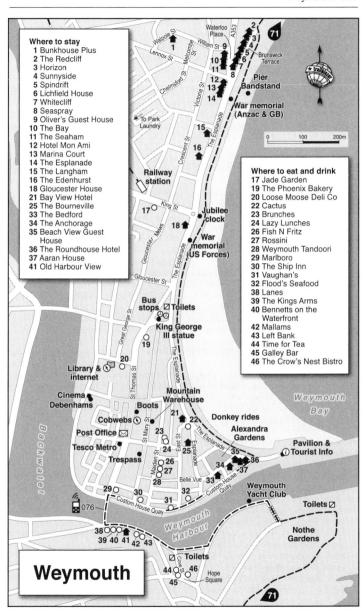

Where to stay
1 Bunkhouse Plus
2 The Redcliff
3 Horizon
4 Sunnyside
5 Spindrift
6 Lichfield House
7 Whitecliff
8 Seaspray
9 Oliver's Guest House
10 The Bay
11 The Seaham
12 Hotel Mon Ami
13 Marina Court
14 The Esplanade
15 The Langham
16 The Edenhurst
18 Gloucester House
21 Bay View Hotel
25 The Bourneville
33 The Bedford
34 The Anchorage
35 Beach View Guest House
36 The Roundhouse Hotel
37 Aaran House
41 Old Harbour View

Where to eat and drink
17 Jade Garden
19 The Phoenix Bakery
20 Loose Moose Deli Co
22 Cactus
23 Brunches
24 Lazy Lunches
26 Fish N Fritz
27 Rossini
28 Weymouth Tandoori
29 Marlboro
30 The Ship Inn
31 Vaughan's
32 Flood's Seafood
38 Lanes
39 The Kings Arms
40 Bennetts on the Waterfront
42 Mallams
43 Left Bank
44 Time for Tea
45 Galley Bar
46 The Crow's Nest Bistro

Waterloo Place
Walpole St
Lennox St
William St
A353
Melcombe St
Brunswick Terrace
Chelmsford St
Pier Bandstand
Victoria St
War memorial (Anzac & GB)
Crescent St
The Esplanade
To Park Laundry
0   100   200m
Railway station
King St
Jubilee clock
Gloucester Mews
War memorial (US Forces)
Gloucester St
Great George St
Bus stops Toilets
King George III statue
The Esplanade
Library & internet
St Thomas St
Cinema
Debenhams
Boots
Mountain Warehouse
Weymouth Bay
Cobwebs
St Mary St
Donkey rides
Alexandra Gardens
Post Office
23
East St
Pavilion & Tourist Info
Tesco Metro
24
The Esplanade
Trespass
Maiden St
26
27
28
Belle Vue
Backwater
29
30
31
32
Custom House Quay
Weymouth Yacht Club
076
Toilets
Weymouth Harbour
Nothe Gardens
38
39 40 41 42 43
Cove St
Toilets
44   46
45
Hope Square

Weymouth

71

evening meals (June-mid July). Finally, on this strip you'll also find ***The Esplanade Hotel*** (☎ 01305-783129, 💻 www.theesplanadehotel.co.uk; 1S/6D/1T/3D, T or F; all en suite; ♥; WI-FI; £40-55pp, sgl £50-60; sgl occ £75-90; Mar-end Oct) at No 141, an award-winning place run by a highly amiable chap; it offers haddock, kippers, porridge, and a veggie alternative for breakfast. Will accept one-night stops in the peak season if booked on the day. In the winter months they operate walking tours (see p31).

Where to eat and drink

The Phoenix Bakery (Mon-Fri 9.30am-5pm, Sat 8.30am-5pm, Sun 10am-4pm) is one of the best bakeries on the path in our opinion with really delicious freshly baked goods. Their breads are smashing, their pies and flans marvellous and as for one of their bruschettas (£2.50) ... simply scrumptious. They also have a café upstairs.

There are several other good-value delis and snack places around including ***Loose Moose Deli Co*** (☎ 01305-774941; Mon-Fri 7am-4.30pm, Sat 9am-4pm), on School St just off Thomas St; the absurdly cheap sandwich bar ***Lazy Lunches*** (☎ 01305-782187; Mon-Sat 9am-4pm, Sun 10.30am-3pm), on St Alban St, with baguettes for just £2 – including crisps, a drink and a cake(!); nearby, the family-friendly ***Brunches*** (Mon-Sat 8.30am-4.30pm, Sun 10.30am-3pm) where a tea-cake, toast and a pot of tea is £1.99; and ***Cactus*** (☎ 01305-778933; Mon-Fri 10.30am-5.30pm, Sat 10am-5.30pm), which has been going for 15 years and does a lovely Dorset apple cake (£2.50).

Of the plethora of **fish & chip shops**, a few stand out: ***Fish N Fritz*** (Mon-Sat noon-10pm, Sun noon-9pm) is our favourite, one that has signed up to Hugh's fish fight (a campaign led by TV chef Hugh Fearnley-Whittingstall to promote less popular fish to try to save the diminishing stocks of cod and other favourites) and offers a tasty mackerel bap for £2.70. ***Bennetts on the Waterfront*** (☎ 01305-781237; Sun-Thur 11.30am-10.30pm, Fri & Sat to 11.15pm) is also a friend of Hugh's and has some similarly quirky items on the menu including mackerel in a bap and chips for £5.20; while ***Marlboro*** (☎ 01305-785700; daily 11.30am-10pm) is one of the most established in town and has been going since 1974; haddock and chips £6.75.

For a sit-down meal in the evening, the harbour area is definitely a happy hunting ground. ***Flood's Seafood*** (☎ 01305-772270, 💻 www.floodsrestaurant.co.uk; Mon-Sat 6.30-9.30pm) brings you seafood straight from net to plate, with today's catch on the blackboard. Mains (£13-18), include such complicated treats as monkfish wrapped in cured parma ham alongside scallops, all flavoured with pesto and given a balsamic glaze.

Two outstanding pubs face each other across the harbour: ***The Kings Arms*** (☎ 01305-770055, 💻 www.kingsarmsweymouth.co.uk; food noon-3pm & 5-9.30pm) is an old-school pub, very friendly and very good value too – with their surf & turf just £11.50. ***The Ship Inn*** (food daily noon-9pm; 🐕) is a Hall & Woodhouse place and, typically, a more modern, swish affair. Nevertheless, dogs are still allowed and you can't fault the food, with mains (many of them delicious) generally less than £10. On the same side, ***Vaughan's*** (☎ 01305-769004, 💻 www.vaughansbistro.co.uk; Tue-Sat 10.30am-2.30pm & 7-9.30pm, Sun 10.30am-2.30pm) offers a good selection of light bites (£2.25-8.75) such as a local crab salad for £8.75.

Back across the water near the Kings Arms, ***Left Bank*** (☎ 01305-785799, 💻 www.leftbankweymouth.com; daily noon-2.30pm & 6.30-9pm), focuses on seafood with mains ranging from £17 (for line-caught cod, prawns, maple syrup and smoked bacon salad) to a 'Fruits de Mer' for sharing (£80). Also on Trinity Rd, ***Mallams*** (☎ 01305-776757, 💻 www.mallamsrestaurant.co.uk; Mon-Sat 6-9.30pm; two courses £24.99) is another popular spot; the menu changes regularly but mains usually include lamb cutlets, beef, loin of cod and roast fillet of wild bass. A fourth option on Trinity Rd, ***Lanes*** (☎ 01305-772073; Tue-Sat noon-2.30pm & 6-9pm, Mon 6-9pm), has main dishes ranging from £10.95 to £15.95 and does a great bowl of

ROUTE GUIDE AND MAPS

mussels, cooked with chilli, lime and coriander with coconut milk for just £10.95.

There are some interesting options around Hope Square, south of the harbour. *Galley Bar* (☎ 01305-784059, 🖳 www.the galleybistro.co.uk), has, on occasion, been known to serve, I kid you not, zebra steaks (£15.95) amongst more usual fare. The *Crow's Nest Bistro* (☎ 01305-786930, 🖳 www.crowsnestweymouth.com; Mon-Sat 9am-5pm, food 9am-3pm, Thur-Sat 7-10pm) is unusual in that it offers many of its mains as tapas-sized dishes for around half the price (eg five sardines served with lemon for £6.95, or three of them for £3.75). They also do some good pizzas (8" for £3.95-4.95, 12" for £6.95-7.95).

Time for Tea (☎ 01305-777500; Wed-Mon 9.30am-5pm) serves nothing but home cooking, much of it French (the owner hails from Paris) and specialises in dishes such as 'Cassoulet Au Canard Confit' (duck cassoulet), though doesn't ignore the cuisine of his new homeland either, baking cakes and scones daily and conjuring up a mean Dorset apple cake.

Nearby on Maiden St, *Rossini* (☎ 01305-789406, 🖳 www.rossinis.co.uk; Mon-Sat from 6pm) offers some great Mediterranean cuisine (from pasta to paella is how they term it) though they also serve some North African dishes such as lamb tagine for £14.95.

For food from further-flung corners of the world, try *Weymouth Tandoori* (☎ 01305-776744, 🖳 www.weymouthtandoori .co.uk; daily noon-2pm & 5.30-11.30pm) on Maiden St, or *Jade Garden* (☎ 01305-778844, 🖳 www.jadegardenweymouth.co .uk; Sun-Thur 5-11:30pm, Fri & Sat 5pm-midnight) on King St, a Chinese restaurant that also offers dishes from Malaysia and Thailand.

Transport

[See pp55-60] Weymouth is very well-connected by **bus**: both First (Nos 1, 6, 8, 10, 31, X53 & 501) and South West Coaches (205, 206 & 210) operate numerous services year-round and throughout the day.

To access Durdle Door and Lulworth you would need to catch Damory Coaches' summer-only X43. Outside peak times you would need to catch the X53 to Wool and then take Damory Coaches Nos 103 or 104 services to Lulworth. Note that other than in peak season there are very few services and taking public transport between Weymouth and Lulworth will require some planning, making walking a far more attractive – and possibly less time consuming – option.

Trains (First Great Western and South West Trains) connect Weymouth with Poole, Bournemouth, London and Bristol. To get to Exeter, Torquay or Plymouth by train you need to change in Castle Cary.

WEYMOUTH TO LULWORTH COVE   [MAPS 71-76]

This **11-mile (17.75km; 4hrs 40 mins) stage** is as splendid as it is strenuous. Reckoned by many to be the most beautiful on the trail, it takes you to the pure white chalky cliffs leading to Lulworth Cove – similar to the chalky cliffs prevalent further east at Beachy Head and the South Downs of Sussex.

Apart from their distinctive colour, the other characteristic of this type of cliffs is the way they rise and fall, sometimes relentlessly so – and this is certainly true of this trail, which starts off with an iron-flat walk along Weymouth seafront (complete with several places serving refreshments) and ends with a real rollercoaster along the cliffs leading to Durdle Door – perhaps the Dorset coastline's most iconic feature. From there it's a comparatively small hop to Lulworth Cove – one of the county's more famous olde-worlde villages, where even the bus shelter is thatched!

The route

The first gradient on this strenuous stage is a small one. Having finally diverted from the seafront at Weymouth, passing Oasis Café and after The Lookout Café the path climbs **Bowleaze Coveway** over Jordan Hill, which is topped by the remains of a **Roman temple**. Not much is known about this once-sacred place other than that it was built in around the 4th century; there's not much now save for the simple square outline of the temple's foundations in the ground. The road continues down to another temple of sorts, this one dedicated to the practice of sun worshipping – Beachside Leisure Centre (🖳 www.bowleaze .co.uk) and its **Beach Café** (summer daily 9am-10pm, winter 9am-5pm with its own **ATM** (£1.75).

Climbing out of the dip, the path passes the Art Deco splendour of **Riviera Hotel**, which looks particularly spectacular at night when lit up in a subtle blue lighting, and on into the fields at the end of the road. Look to your left for the best view from the path of the **Osmington White Horse** (see Map 60c, p263) at Osmington Hill. The figure on the horse is George III and was done in the early 1800s. Notices by the signposts suggest that the path across the fields here is but a temporary diversion to keep you away from some cliffside erosion. A quick glance to your right as you rejoin the cliffs will show why they've had to do this – and why it will be many years, if ever, before they reroute the path back along the tops again!

The path now does saunter along – or near – the cliffs, below the perimeter of an activity centre, before dropping, after some simple meandering, to a reunion with the South Dorset Ridgeway (see pp260-3), just before it meets the road running down to **Osmington Mills**.

OSMINGTON MILLS [Map 73, p291]

There's little to the village save for a place to have lunch but it's perfectly located – and there are a couple of options for accommodation should you wish to linger longer.

For **campers**, *Rosewall Camping* (☎ 01305-832248, 🖳 www.weymouthcamping .com; Mar/Apr-Oct, weather dependent; 🐾 £2; hiker & tent £10-15) has a **shop** (Mar/Apr to end Oct approx 9am-5pm; limited hours rest of year) which is well stocked in the high season but has a more limited selection in the low season; the site is right on the path. There's also a **B&B**, No 1 Old Coastguards (☎ 01305-832663, 🖳 www.heritagecoastbandb.co.uk; 1S/1D; share facilities; £35-40pp, sgl occ £50), offering pleasant adjoining rooms. It's tucked away nicely down a quiet little lane, close to both the path and the pub.

At the bottom of the village – and yet also its very heart – is the charming

Smugglers Inn (☎ 01305-833125, 🖳 www .smugglersinnosmingtonmills.co.uk; 4D; ☻; WI-FI; 🐾 £5; £42.50-50pp, sgl occ £70), a lovely thatched place with origins dating back to the 13th century. It's another Hall & Woodhouse place and bears the same smart-traditional style of the others in the chain. It's also good value and boasts some great **food** (summer Mon-Sat 11.30am-9.30pm, Sun to 9pm; winter Mon-Sat noon-9.30pm, Sun to 9pm) with mains from £8.95 (for the burgers) up to £14.95 for the fish mixed grill.

As for **transport**, First's X53 coastal **bus** service stops in Osmington village (see Map 60c) – a 15-minute walk from Osmington Mills – en route between Poole and Weymouth. In summer Damory Coaches operate the X43 service between Weymouth and Lulworth Cove. See pp55-60 for details.

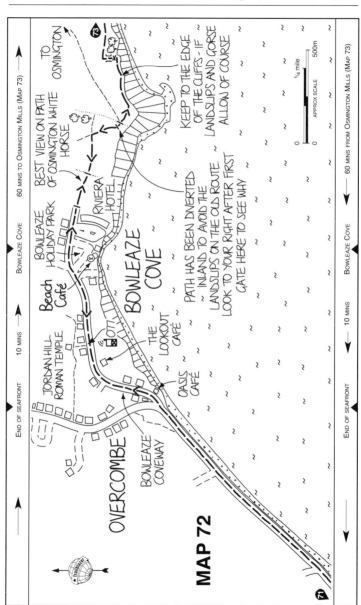

MAP 72

OVERCOMBE

BOWLEAZE COVEWAY

JORDAN HILL ROMAN TEMPLE

Beach Café

OASIS CAFÉ

THE LOOKOUT CAFÉ

BOWLEAZE COVE

Bowleaze Holiday Park

RIVIERA HOTEL

BEST VIEW ON PATH OF OSMINGTON WHITE HORSE

TO OSMINGTON

PATH HAS BEEN DIVERTED INLAND TO AVOID THE LANDSLIPS ON THE OLD ROUTE. LOOK TO YOUR RIGHT AFTER FIRST GATE HERE TO SEE WHY

KEEP TO THE EDGE OF THE CLIFFS - IF LANDSLIPS AND GORSE ALLOW OF COURSE

APPROX SCALE

0 ¼ mile

0 500m

End of Seafront — 10 MINS — Bowleaze Cove — 60 MINS TO OSMINGTON MILLS (MAP 73)

END OF SEAFRONT — 10 MINS — BOWLEAZE COVE — 60 MINS FROM OSMINGTON MILLS (MAP 73)

Heading round behind Smugglers Inn, more field walking follows, the path squeezed between fence and cliffs, a couple of brick shelters the only significant features before the path cuts through the houses of **Ringstead Bay**, heading round the back of them and on, up past the landslips that lie to your right like scruffy terracing, and the tiny wooden **chapel dedicated to St Catherine**, to the remote houses at **White Nothe**. (Note you can also walk along the landslips, known as **Burning Cliff**, though you do so at your own peril and you may not be able to ascend to White Nothe so you'll have to return before continuing on the path! The cliff is so-named after a band of bituminous shale caught fire in 1826.)

The tough stuff begins here. Most of the climbs on this section to Durdle Door are both lengthy and steep. The first descent, down to **Middle Bottom**, is typical. Passing a **stone obelisk** (which, along with a second obelisk nearby, is yet another 19th-century navigational aid used by sailors, examples of which we have seen all along this trek), the path descends quickly along the cliffside before climbing, equally rapidly, out of it.

A second descent down to the beach by the **Bat's Hole** rock formation and a third to the wonderfully named **Scratchy Bottom** (which features in the book *Rude Britain: The 100 Rudest Place Names in Britain* by Ed Hurst and Rob Baile) follow in short order before finally the view of the natural arch at **Durdle Door** (see box below) comes into view. If planning to camp at Durdle Door Holiday Park (see p294) turn left here. There's still one more climb, however, over **Hambury Tout**, before the elegant arc of lovely **Lulworth Cove** is reached.

❏ Durdle Door

Geologically speaking, Durdle Door is nothing more than an arch of limestone rock set out at sea but joined to the mainland by a narrow sliver of land or isthmus. Derived from an Old English word thirl meaning 'to drill', the door is part of the 12,000-acre Lulworth Estate. Though it appears to have been here forever, the arch was of course formed by the tides eroding the rock away – the same force that now threatens to destroy it, and which UNESCO are now attempting to counteract to prevent it falling into the sea altogether. (Incidentally, to see what Durdle Door might have looked like once upon a time, neighbouring Stair Hole is an 'infant' cove, the waves having broken through to form an arch and the Wealdon clays behind that which were once protected are now rapidly being eroded.)

So far, so prosaic. Plenty of artists down the years have been inspired by Durdle Door, however, and this curiously carved lump of rock features in many works, from music videos (step forward Billy Ocean, Cliff Richard and Tears for Fears who all shot promotional videos here), to films (Emma Thompson's *Nanny McPhee* and *Wilde*, the biopic of Oscar Wilde starring Stephen Fry, both had scenes filmed here), and, perhaps most famously, it was also used as a location for the 1967 film adaptation of Thomas Hardy's novel *Far from the Madding Crowd*, starring Julie Christie.

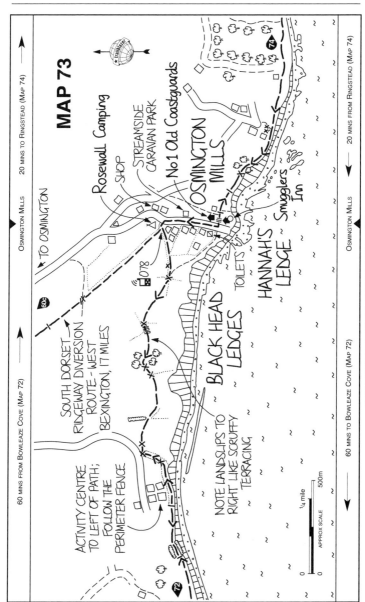

OSMINGTON MILLS

MAP 73

TO OSMINGTON

Rosewall Camping

SHOP

STREAMSIDE CARAVAN PARK

No 1 Old Coastguards

OSMINGTON MILLS

Smugglers Inn

HANNAH'S LEDGE

TOILETS

BLACK HEAD LEDGES

SOUTH DORSET RIDGEWAY DIVERSION ROUTE – WEST BEXINGTON, 17 MILES

ACTIVITY CENTRE TO LEFT OF PATH; FOLLOW THE PERIMETER FENCE

NOTE LANDSLIPS TO RIGHT LIKE SCRUFFY TERRACING

1/4 mile

500m

0

0

APPROX SCALE

OSMINGTON MILLS

ROUTE GUIDE AND MAPS

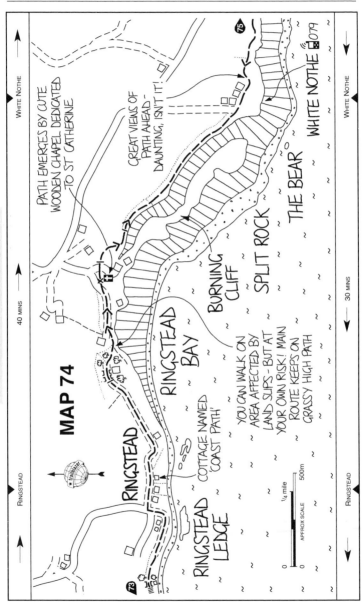

MAP 74

PATH EMERGES BY CUTE WOODEN CHAPEL DEDICATED TO ST CATHERINE

GREAT VIEWS OF PATH AHEAD - DAUNTING, ISN'T IT!

WHITE NOTHE ᵈ079

WHITE NOTHE

40 MINS

30 MINS

RINGSTEAD

THE BEAR

SPLIT ROCK

BURNING CLIFF

RINGSTEAD BAY

COTTAGE NAMED 'COAST PATH'

YOU CAN WALK ON AREA AFFECTED BY LAND SLIPS - BUT AT YOUR OWN RISK! MAIN ROUTE KEEPS ON GRASSY HIGH PATH

RINGSTEAD

RINGSTEAD LEDGE

¼ mile

500m

APPROX SCALE

0   0

trailblazer

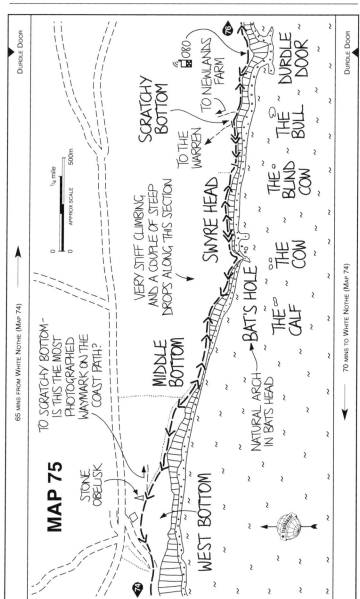

DURDLE DOOR

MAP 75

65 MINS FROM WHITE NOTHE (MAP 74)

TO SCRATCHY BOTTOM –
IS THIS THE MOST
PHOTOGRAPHED
WAYMARK ON THE
COAST PATH?

APPROX SCALE

¼ mile

500m

SCRATCHY
BOTTOM

TO NEWLANDS
FARM

TO THE
WARREN

VERY STIFF CLIMBING,
AND A COUPLE OF STEEP
DROPS ALONG THIS SECTION

SWYRE HEAD

MIDDLE
BOTTOM

STONE
OBELISK

BAT'S HOLE

THE
CALF

THE
COW

THE
BLIND
COW

THE
BULL

DURDLE
DOOR

NATURAL ARCH
IN BATS HEAD

WEST BOTTOM

70 MINS TO WHITE NOTHE (MAP 74)

DURDLE DOOR

LULWORTH COVE AND WEST
LULWORTH [Map 76 & map p297]

One of the most picturesque coves on the
south coast, inland of which is one of the
walk's most idyllic villages, Lulworth
Cove and its accompanying village, West
Lulworth, virtually demand that you spend
a night here. Add some wonderful nearby
scenery, a couple of fantastic pubs, some
great B&Bs and an absorbing **Heritage
Centre** (daily 10am-4pm) that almost suc-
ceeds in explaining to these rather dim-
witted authors about the complicated
geology of the Jurassic Coast, and it's a
strange trekker indeed that decides to
breeze through. Indeed, it's lucky that the
next stage is so magnificent (whatever
route you take) and that the tourist hordes
can overwhelm both the cove and Durdle
Door sometimes – otherwise it would be
pretty difficult to find reasons to move on!

Services

There isn't much in the way of amenities in
either the cove or the village. There is a
shop, Hambury Stores, on Church Rd on
the edge of the village, that doubles up as
the **post office** (Mon-Fri 9am-1pm). The
Heritage Centre has a **cash machine**
(approx £1.50).

For **tourist information** the website
🖳 lulworthonline.co.uk is kept reasonably
up to date.

Where to stay

There is **camping** just a few minutes back
from Durdle Door, immediately behind the
car park at the top of the hill. *Durdle
Door Holiday Park* (☎ 01929-400200, 🖳 www
.lulworth.com/holiday/holiday_park.htm;
Mar-Oct) has a café/bar, shop and, of
course, a wonderful location. A pitch for
walkers is £10-16 (hiker and tent); booking
is recommended. There's also a charge of
£3 per dog. It's a nice place, though spend
a night here and you'll understand why a
collection of crows is called a murder,
because that's exactly what you'll want to
do with them at 5am when they wake up.

Lulworth also boasts a **hostel**, though
it's a little way out of the village. *YHA*

Lulworth Cove (☎ 0845-371 9331, 🖳 www
.yha.org.uk/hostel/lulworth-cove; 34 beds;
dorm beds from £13.40, 4-bedded room
from £57) is a pleasant place with helpful
staff. They also plan to have **camping**
(£10pp) and free **WI-FI**. To get here follow
the road to West Lulworth to a signpost on
the right pointing the way to the hostel;
thereafter, see Map 76.

Other accommodation includes highly
recommended *The Castle Inn* (☎ 01929-
400311, 🖳 www.lulworthinn.com; 9D/1T/
1F; ♥; ✖; WI-FI; £49.50pp, sgl occ £89), a
beautiful, thatched 16th-century establishment that also dishes up tremendous food
(see Where to eat). It's the heart of the village and a wonderfully atmospheric place.

Meanwhile, Main Rd (aka B3070) is
lined with fine and quirky **bed and breakfasts**. Some of these have street numbers
while others have house names; those with
numbers are the village's original cottages,
whilst those which are number-less are
more recent builds. Built over 470 years
ago and Grade-II listed, *Amy Cottage* (☎
01929-400264, 🖳 www.amycottage.co.uk;
2D, shared bathroom; ♥; WI-FI; £32.50-
35pp, sgl occ £50), 25-26 Main Rd, was the
first in the village to provide shelter and
food and, retaining most of its original features, it is a quaint and homely place to
spend a night.

Within a relatively similar price range
you'll also come across *Forge Cottage* (☎
01929-400445; 2D; ♥; WI-FI; £35pp, sgl
occ £45-50), No 31, and *Downalong* (☎
01929-400300, 🖳 down-along.co.uk; 1D/
1T; WI-FI; £35pp, sgl occ £50). Also on
Main Rd are *The Old Barn* (☎ 01929-
400305, 🖳 www.theoldbarnlulworthcove
.com; 3D/2T; ♥; ✖; internet access; £35-
42.50pp, sgl occ £40-55; Mar-Oct), who do
not accept bookings for one-night stays at
the weekend in summer, and *Abilee
Cottage* (☎ 01929-400406, 🖳 www.abilee
cottage.co.uk; 1T; ♥; ✖ £5; £35pp, sgl
occ £58), where a continental breakfast is
served; they can also provide packed
lunches (£5).

Another place that serves only a continental breakfast, this time on School Lane

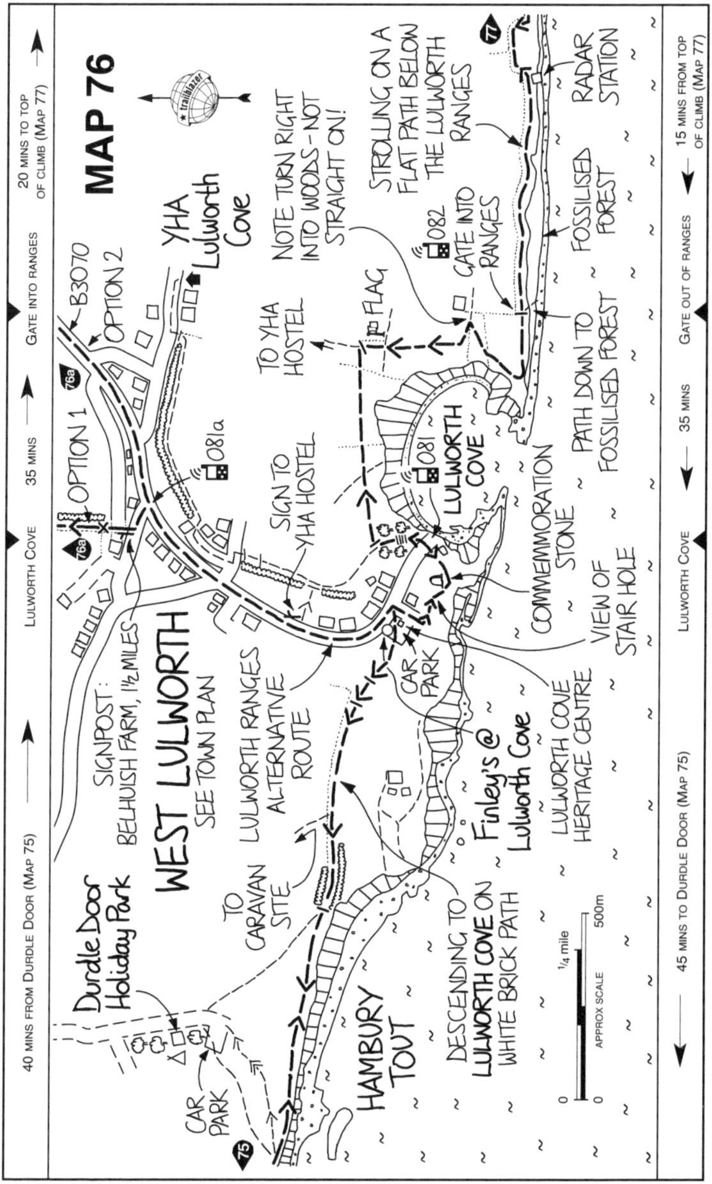

MAP 76

Durdle Door Holiday Park

WEST LULWORTH
SEE TOWN PLAN

SIGNPOST:
BELHUISH FARM, 1½ MILES

SIGN TO YHA HOSTEL

TO CARAVAN SITE

LULWORTH RANGES
ALTERNATIVE ROUTE

CAR PARK

Finley's @ Lulworth Cove

LULWORTH COVE HERITAGE CENTRE

DESCENDING TO LULWORTH COVE ON WHITE BRICK PATH

HAMBURY TOUT

CAR PARK

1/4 mile
APPROX SCALE
500m

COMMEMORATION STONE

VIEW OF STAIR HOLE

LULWORTH COVE

PATH DOWN TO FOSSILISED FOREST

FOSSILISED FOREST

RADAR STATION

STROLLING ON A FLAT PATH BELOW THE LULWORTH RANGES

GATE INTO RANGES

NOTE TURN RIGHT INTO WOODS – NOT STRAIGHT ON!

YHA Lulworth Cove

TO YHA HOSTEL

B3070
OPTION 2

OPTION 1

just off Main Rd, is *The Copse* (☎ 01929-400581, 🖳 www.copse-lulworth.co.uk; 1D/1T; ◗; WI-FI; £27.50-35pp, sgl £50-65).

The following four B&Bs are all reluctant to accept one-night stays at the weekend and over summer but may do if there is space in their diary. Those with slightly looser purse strings may wish to investigate the 400-year-old dog-friendly *Tewkesbury Cottage* (☎ 01929-400561; 2D/1T; shared bathroom; ◗; 🐾; £35-39pp, sgl occ £50-55), 28 Main Rd, or *Bindon Bottom* (☎ 01929-400256, 🖳 www.bindonbottom.com; 4D/1T; ◗; WI-FI; £42.50-50pp, sgl occ £75-90), a large Victorian country house built in 1871 opposite the junction of Church Rd and Main Rd, from which there are great views over the surrounding countryside. The ingredients for breakfast are locally sourced and where possible organic. Next door you will find *Cove House* (☎ 01929-400137, 🖳 www.covehouse.net; 3D/1T; WI-FI; £45pp, sgl occ £90). At the time of research new owners were expected to take over and open for B&B in February 2013. However, contact them for details.

On Sunny Side is *Gatton House* (☎ 01929-400252, 🖳 www.gattonhouse.co.uk; 6D/1T/1F; ◗; WI-FI; £40-48pp, sgl occ £60; Apr to mid Sep), set back from the main road. They only accept bookings for a two-night stay at weekends.

Hotel accommodation can be found down in Lulworth Cove itself, just a couple of hundred metres or so from the path. *Cromwell House Hotel* (☎ 01929-400253, 🖳 www.lulworthcove.co.uk/The_Cromwell House_Hotel; 1S/16D or T/3F; ◗; WI-FI; 🐾 £6; £52-60pp, sgl occ £55-75) offers an evening meal (7-9pm; main course £15; discount for prebooking), with sustainable seafood on the menu, though snacks are available all day. The hotel also has Sky Sports. Contact them for details of their self-catering flat (1D/1T and a futon), though this can't be booked for a single-night stay on a Saturday.

Even nearer the path, *Lulworth Cove Inn* (☎ 01929-400333, 🖳 lulworth-cove inn.co.uk; 12D; WI-FI; £40-50pp; £60-100) has some lovely rooms, many with sea view, and accepts one-night bookings except at weekends and on bank holidays. Opposite, *The Gift Shop* (☎ 01929-400272; 2D, shared bathroom; ◗; small 🐾; £35-42.50pp, sgl occ full room rate) does not accept bookings for one-night stays – but by Lulworth's standards it's very reasonable value.

Finally, also down at the Cove, *Lulworth Mill House* (☎ 01929-400404, 🖳 www.lulworthbeachhotel.com; 8D/4D or T; ◗; WI-FI; £49.50-64.50pp, sgl oc £89) is situated where the old mill once stood and has some of the best views of the cove of any accommodation; food is available here at Dandelion (see Where to eat).

Where to eat and drink

Round the back of the Heritage Centre, the *Secret Garden/Sunnyside* and *Parlour* are three places sharing the same premises (summer holidays 9am-7pm, 10am-4.30 or 5pm at other times, Nov-Easter 10am-4pm). The last is an ice-cream parlour, while the other two are characterful tearooms with some nice food.

Across the way, don't be put off visiting *Finley's @ Lulworth Cove* (summer daily 9.30am-6pm, winter 10am-4pm), just because it is the stop of choice for the tourist busloads. Their food occasionally achieves excellence: their wraps, for example, in particular their cheese-steak wrap (just £5.25), are especially scrumptious.

Also down in the Cove, *Dandelion* (🖳 dandelioncafe.co.uk; Tue-Sat 8.30am-11pm, Sun 8.30am-8pm) is a new place owned by the holiday giant HF Holidays and one of several in a chain of establishments situated in various beauty spots dotted around the country. It is also one of the few places in Lulworth Cove that's open for breakfast – good for those camping up the hill who want to set off early-ish. Their breakfast choice is good too and includes eggs benedict and a cup of coffee for £8.20.

For supper there are, in our opinion, two stand-out choices: in West Lulworth *The Castle Inn* (see Where to stay; food served Mon-Fri noon-2pm, Sat & Sun to

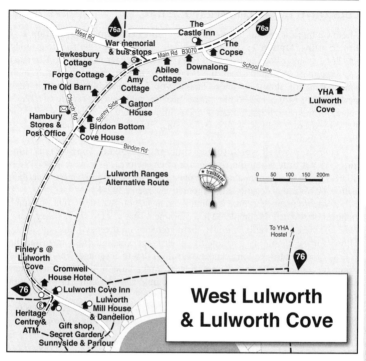

West Lulworth & Lulworth Cove

2.30pm, & daily 6-9.30pm, from 7pm in winter; 🐕) has a large menu scrawled on blackboards including sirloin steak (£16.90) and, for true gluttons, the enormous Mexican or Indian chip butties (garlic bread with chips on top covered in chilli con carne/curry and then grilled with cheese on top for around £10). They boast a decent variety of ciders and real ales and the setting is full of character too. It's also one of those places where dogs aren't just allowed but are made to feel positively welcome, with treats on the bar.

Down at the Cove, their nearest rival in terms of quality (though not geographically), is *Lulworth Cove Inn* (see Where to stay; food daily noon-9pm), a typically smashing Hall & Woodhouse place with the usual reasonably priced yet high-quality

food, an 8oz rump steak served with blue cheese and mushroom sauce only £12.95, and gourmet burger £8.95. The Castle Inn may shade it in terms of atmosphere, but this place has, in our opinion, better food.

Transport
[See pp55-60]   In summer, Damory Coaches' X43 **bus** service travels between Weymouth and Swanage via Durdle Door, West Lulworth and Lulworth Cove. Out of season, to access either Weymouth or Swanage you would need to take one of Damory Coaches' irregular 103 or 104 services to Wool or Wareham and travel onwards from there. First's 102 service goes to Dorchester (Sundays only).

For a **taxi** try Silver Car (☎ 07811-328281 or ☎ 01929-400409).

LULWORTH COVE TO KIMMERIDGE BAY   [MAPS 76-79]

There's a bit of a military theme to this **7¼-mile (11.75km; 3hrs; Option 1: 4 hrs 55 mins. Option 2: 4½ hours)** stage. In addition to the fact that today you'll be visiting both an Iron-Age fort (which was later used by the Romans) and various fortifications from the Second World War, there is also the small matter that, for almost its entire length, **you'll be walking through a very active firing range**. Indeed, the ranges provide the greatest obstacle to today's stage, for the path through them is open only occasionally. This is a shame, for the ranges are a delight, with fortifications, fossilised forests and fascinating flora abounding.

In short, **it's well worth timing your walk to ensure your arrival coincides with a time when the ranges are open** (before you leave call ☎ 01929-404819 to check when the ranges are open); and this is the trek we've described below. (We've also described the alternatives; see pp302-4.)

If you do manage to hike through the ranges, you'll actually find this stage rather short – it can be completed in a morning. (That's not to say it's easy, however, for there are several painfully sharp gradients on the way.) This, of course, allows for the possibility – for the fit, at least – of combining this stage and the following one into one long (and exhausting) day to Swanage. This is no bad thing, for accommodation at Kimmeridge is both a little off the trail and in short supply. However, only the fit and fanatical should consider doing this – it's a lot of miles and gradients to squeeze into one day.

If you do decide to combine the two stages, you should certainly consider bringing lunch with you from Lulworth, unless you're willing to trek uphill to Kimmeridge village from the bay.

The route through the ranges

The day begins with a relatively untaxing stroll around the cove that brings you to the no-nonsense fence surrounding the firing range. Once through the **gate**, a short diversion on entering the range also brings you to one of the most unusual of sights on the trail: a **fossilised forest**.

Don't expect to see stone trees 'growing' out of the cliff-ledge; instead, look for **thrombolites**, which are fossilised rings of algae that thrived around tree trunks when the forest was flooded 150 million years ago. The area used to be known as 'Vairy Vances' or Fairy Dances, in reference to these thrombolite rings.

The walk within the ranges can best be described as two very stiff climbs and one long but gentle one, separated by some surprisingly unchallenging sections, all set amongst some fascinating (particularly if rusting military vehicles are your thing) and beautiful scenery.

The first of the big climbs we mentioned lies about a mile from the fossilised forest; it's an exhausting haul up **Bindon Hill**, usually done to a soundtrack of crashing waves and whistling wind. That climb conquered, a lovely bit of gentle ridge-top rambling follows before a sharpish descent to **Arish Mell** – from

> ❑ **KEEP TO THE PATH!!**
> More than anywhere else on the coast path, it is absolutely vital that you keep to the
> signposted path through Lulworth Military Range (the yellow-topped posts tradition-
> ally point the way). As you can probably tell by all the metalware rusting in the fields,
> there's a fair bit of unexploded ordnance left lying hereabouts. So keep to the path –
> and make sure your dog keeps to the path too.

where the lengthier climb up to **Flowers Barrow** begins. It's a wearying climb
– you can see why Iron-age man chose the summit of this hill as the location for
a **fort** – and why the Romans subsequently used it for their own military
purposes. The unexcavated remains of the fort explain the existence of the
unusual bumps and folds in the summit.

Amongst these remains are a couple of hut circles and a few ramparts;
sadly, however, where the hill forts were designed to protect the inhabitants
from invaders, they are helpless against the depredations of the elements, and
much of the site has fallen victim to erosion.

Also on the Barrow, an old **WWII gun emplacement** shows that, while
weaponry and warfare may have changed in the 2500 years since the Iron Age
fort was built, a hilltop location is still regarded as invaluable when it comes to
looking out for enemy advances. Further down the slopes, the rust-coloured
metal ball is actually a WWII **Allen Williams Steel Turret** – of which we've
already seen an example in Exmouth.

The path passes more ruins at **Worbarrow** and its accompanying **Tout**, or
hill, which resembles a giant geological apostrophe punctuating the sea. You
then climb for a third time (though mercifully less steeply now) towards
Tyneham Cap which, unusually, the path contours round rather than conquers,
dropping gently via unconcerned sheep to the gate at the end of the ranges.
Incongruously, next-door is a small **oil well** – indeed, it's said to be the site of
the oldest continually working oil well in the world!

From here it's but a short stroll round to **Kimmeridge Bay**. At first sight
there doesn't seem to be much here save for a large car park, some public toilets and a couple of old sheds down on the water's edge. However, these sheds
provide the answer to why so many people come to this bay for they house the
Fine Foundation Marine Centre (Apr-Sep term time Wed, Thur, Sat & Sun
10.30am-5pm, school hols Tue-Sun and bank hols 10.30am-5pm, Oct-Mar Sun
noon-4pm) which provides an interactive explanation on the neighbouring bay,
its ledges and rockpools, waters that together make up the **Purbeck Marine
Nature Reserve** – Britain's longest-established Voluntary Marine Nature
Reserve – home to sea anemones, crabs, wrasse, mullet, lobster and blennies.
For the amenities of Kimmeridge (see p304) you have to walk for 10-15 minutes up the hill from the bay.

See p306 for the continuation of the route.

ROUTE GUIDE AND MAPS

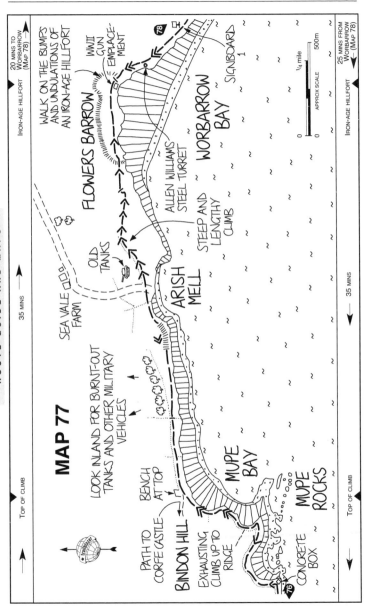

MAP 77

◄ TOP OF CLIMB   ← 35 MINS →   IRON-AGE HILLFORT   20 MINS TO WORBARROW (MAP 78) →

PATH TO CORFE CASTLE

BINDON HILL

BENCH AT TOP

LOOK INLAND FOR BURNT-OUT TANKS AND OTHER MILITARY VEHICLES

SEA VALE FARM

OLD TANKS

FLOWERS BARROW

WALK ON THE BUMPS AND UNDULATIONS OF AN IRON-AGE HILLFORT

WWII GUN EMPLACE-MENT

EXHAUSTING CLIMB UP TO RIDGE

CONCRETE BOX

MUPE ROCKS

MUPE BAY

ARISH MELL

ALLEN WILLIAMS STEEL TURRET

STEEP AND LENGTHY CLIMB

WORBARROW BAY

SIGNBOARD 1

APPROX SCALE

0   500m
0   ¼ mile

◄ TOP OF CLIMB   ← 35 MINS →   IRON-AGE HILLFORT   25 MINS FROM WORBARROW (MAP 78) →

★ trailblazer

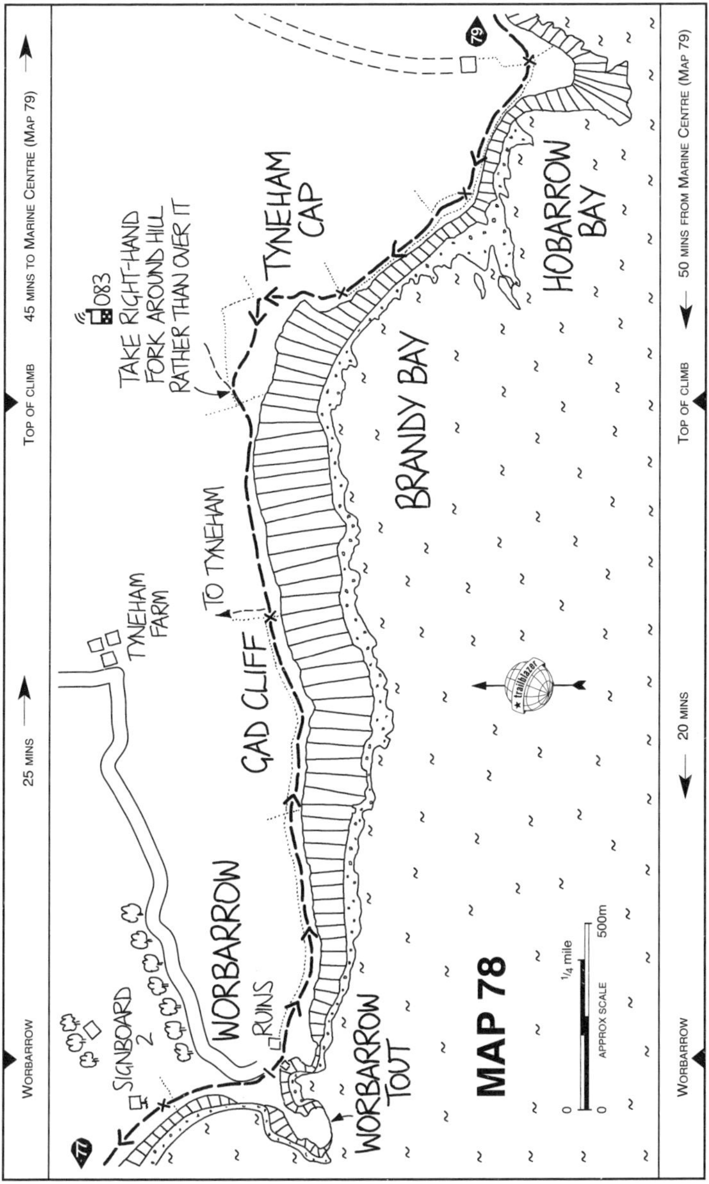

MAP 78

WORBARROW

ROUTE GUIDE AND MAPS

SIGNBOARD 2

TYNEHAM FARM

WORBARROW RUINS

WORBARROW TOUT

CAD CLIFF

TO TYNEHAM

TAKE RIGHT-HAND FORK AROUND HILL RATHER THAN OVER IT

083

TYNEHAM CAP

BRANDY BAY

HOBARROW BAY

trailblazer

¼ mile

APPROX SCALE

500m

0

79

70

WHEN THE RANGES ARE CLOSED   [Map 76a; Map 76b, p305]
Option 1
Yes, the walk through the ranges is the kind of stroll that causes writers to write, poets to eulogise, and atheists to not only believe in the existence of a God but to also believe that he loves us dearly and clearly wants us to be happy. But if the ranges are shut when you arrive, there's no need to plunge headlong into a pit of despair and self-loathing. Because, simply put, this **13½-mile (21.75km; 4hr 55mins)** yomp has more than enough compensations. It's much easier (though longer), with fewer of those roller-coaster undulations that are so characteristic of the coastal route.

The scenery, too, is often exquisite (and if you've followed this book from the start – and especially if you began at the beginning of the coast path in Minehead – your eyes and ears will probably be grateful to gaze upon something other than the sea), with sumptuous bluebell woods, sweeping country estates, neatly cultivated fields, ancient farmhouses and some whopping great country manors to titillate the senses.

There's also more wildlife on this path too, with deer (both roe and the rarer sika, an immigrant from East Asia, thrive in the ranges), hares, pheasants and raptors all dropping by now and again to see who's passing. And overlaying everything is this comforting, life-affirming tranquillity and isolation. It's just lovely. And yes, while there is a good amount of this walk that is undertaken on roads (approximately four miles), much of it is on quiet country lanes edged with lovely cottages or rhododendron forests, where traffic is infrequent and there are grassy verges to hop onto if necessary.

So cease your wailing, silence those gnashing teeth, dry those tears from your eyes and wipe your nose on your Gore-Tex; because you have a lovely walk to complete – and you need to get going...

The route The day begins with a stroll from the official path up to West Lulworth (assuming you haven't already visited it), from where the first of the steep climbs begins up through fields to a brief union with the **Purbeck Way** (see p37), a route that you very quickly betray for the Hardy Way which leads you down past hare-inhabited pastures to **Belhuish Farm**. Reaching the end of their drive, after the B3071 the path then follows the edge of gorgeous Burngate Wood, filled with deer and bluebells, which you leave by its most easterly point to saunter eastwards on a rough track to **Park Lodge**, with Lulworth Castle (see p304) and its domed chapel to your right.

More woodland skirting occurs after crossing another road, with the idyllic looking lake and its '**fort**' to your left. Following a hedge-lined country track, it's not long before you hit the range (the border, as you'll soon discover, being marked by a red flag). Follow the path round the ranges' edge and you soon reach **Coombe Heath Nature Reserve** and from there more woodside wandering leading to a small country lane which, in turn, leads to Bindon Lane. Not far from where you hit the tarmac you'll come to *Luckford Wood House & Campsite* (☎ 0788-871 9002, ☎ 01929-463098, 💻 www.luckford leisure.co.uk; contact them for rates but expect to pay around £7pp based on two people sharing a tent; firewood £3-7pp; generally open Easter to November; booking essential), a relaxed place where they still allow open fires. They also offer **B&B** (8D, T or F; WI-FI; 🐾 £variable; from £75pp).

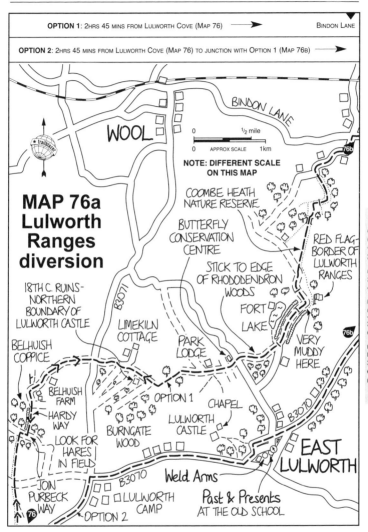

While it's never a blessing to feel the thud of sole on tarmac, the road is pleasantly quiet and the bucolic views to Holme Priory – after you've passed the crossroads at **West Holme** – are distracting. You eventually leave this road for a bridleway leading, via an unsightly quarry, to Dorey's Farm and yet more sylvan strolling – at least until the road to Kimmeridge is reached. There now follows the least pleasant couple of miles on this walk, though with some love-ly little cottages and giant **Grange Farm** on the way, it isn't entirely horrid. The road-rambling ends with a steep, uphill gradient, your reward for con-quering it being some wonderful sweeping views north and south over lovely, voluptuous Purbeck. A steep descent, some more road walking, a bisection of *Steeple Leaze Farm* and its **campsite** (see below), another small climb and descent and a traverse of four or five fields follows before Kimmeridge Bay is reached – and a reunion with the official trail.

Option 2

Definitely the inferior of the three routes, basically on this **12-mile (19.3km; 4½hrs)** option you are treading tarmac the whole way. The road in question is the B3070 which is the same road that you join when you hit Lulworth Cove and which passes through West Lulworth and the ranges (but is open even when the ranges are usually shut). Given all the pavement-pounding, you should really consider this option only if you are after a pub, an internet café, or Lulworth Castle – all of which can be found in East Lulworth.

The route From West Lulworth continue on the B3070 to East Lulworth. The pub here, *The Weld Arms* (☎ 01929-400211; 🖳 www.weldarms.co.uk; food daily noon-3pm & 6-9pm) is a goodie. It does a great minute steak in ciabatta with garlic sauce & chips (£7.95) for lunch, as well as mains in the evening such as a hearty and traditional fish pie, with beetroot purée and buttered leeks (£13.50). They also have a lovely beer garden. The only problem with it is that it is probably too near West Lulworth to consider it a lunchtime option; though if you visit the castle first it could fit in with your day's schedule. The **internet café** is at Past & Presents at the Old School (☎ 01929-400637; 🖳 www .pastandpresents.co.uk; daily summer 10am-5pm, winter 10am-4pm) with internet £1 for 15 mins/£3 per hour).

The road passes the entrance of **Lulworth Castle** (Sun-Fri 10.30am-5pm; £5, English Heritage members free); the castle was originally built as a hunt-ing lodge in the early 17th century by Thomas Howard, 3rd Lord Bindon, to entertain hunting parties for the king and his court. Gutted by a fire in 1929, it was restored and is still maintained by English Heritage. **Camp Bestival** (🖳 www.campbestival.net), held here in July, is the little sister of the far larger Bestival, held on the Isle of Wight.

From Lulworth Castle walk along the B3070 to **West Holme** where the road meets Option 1 (see p303); the route passes a path to Kimmeridge (see below) before reaching the sea and joining up with the official path.

KIMMERIDGE   [Map 76b]

There isn't much to this village, however, other than a **B&B**, a **campsite** – and a very good **café**: *Clavell's* (☎ 01929-480701, 🖳 www.clavellscafe.co.uk; Easter-Oct daily 10am-5.30pm, Thur fish & chips 5.30-7.30pm, July-Sep daily 6.45-8.30pm, Nov-Easter closed Mon & eves except Thur & Sat eve) has a good selection of sandwich-es and baguettes (£6.75), meals and cakes.

Their evening menu is particularly good (mains £8.95-16.95), including such delights as lamb Wellington and monkfish king prawn kebab.

The **campsite**, *Steeple Leaze Farm* (☎ 01929-480733; £5pp; Easter till Sep/Oct depending on weather; 🐾 £1), is about 20 minutes out of Kimmeridge on the alterna-tive route (see above). It's a simple place

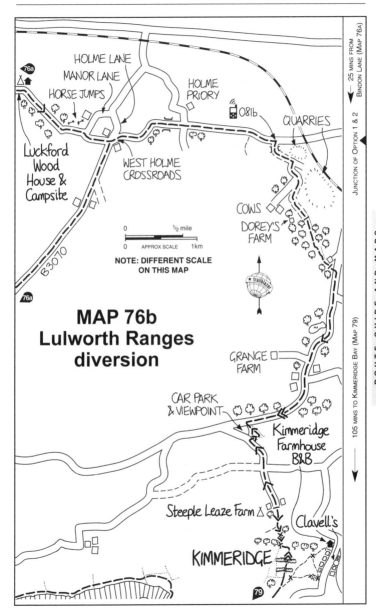

76a

HOLME LANE

MANOR LANE

HORSE JUMPS

HOLME
PRIORY

081b

QUARRIES

Luckford
Wood
House &
Campsite

WEST HOLME
CROSSROADS

B3070

0   ½ mile

0   APPROX SCALE   1km

NOTE: DIFFERENT SCALE
ON THIS MAP

COWS

DOREY'S
FARM

76a

★ trailblazer

MAP 76b
Lulworth Ranges
diversion

GRANGE
FARM

CAR PARK
& VIEWPOINT

Kimmeridge
Farmhouse
B&B

Steeple Leaze Farm △

Clavell's

KIMMERIDGE

79

25 MINS FROM
BINDON LANE (MAP 76A)

JUNCTION OF OPTION 1 & 2

105 MINS TO KIMMERIDGE BAY (MAP 79)

ROUTE GUIDE AND MAPS

with no showers and no food available on site, but it does allow open fires. It gets popular in season particularly with people looking to party, so don't expect a quiet night.

Kimmeridge Farmhouse (☎ 01929-480990, 🖳 www.kimmeridgefarmhouse.co.uk; 1D/2D or T; ☛; WI-FI; £40-42.50pp, sgl occ £65-75) is a great big 14th-century pile owned by the same lady who runs Clavell's – so this will be the only option for food in the evenings! Note that they do not accept credit cards.

Damory Coaches' No 275 **bus service** connects the village with Swanage, Corfe Castle and Wareham – albeit once a week on a Thursday!

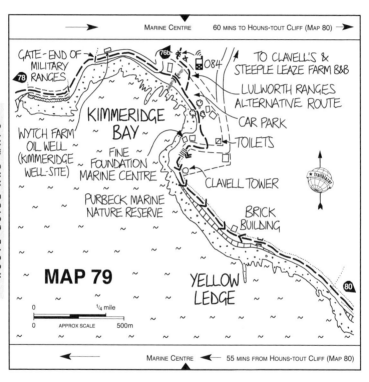

KIMMERIDGE BAY TO SWANAGE [MAPS 79-84]

Just two stages to go, but by now it should have become clear that the coast path is not going to let you complete your trek without a struggle. For though in mileage terms the trek is not too daunting at **13½ miles (21.75km; 4hrs 50 mins)**, those bald statistics hide a couple of pretty hamstring-hammering, calf-creaking, buttock-berating ascents. But there are compensations – as always – in the form of some delicious views, an ancient and remote chapel, the penultimate lighthouse on the path, a diverting nature reserve and the touristy

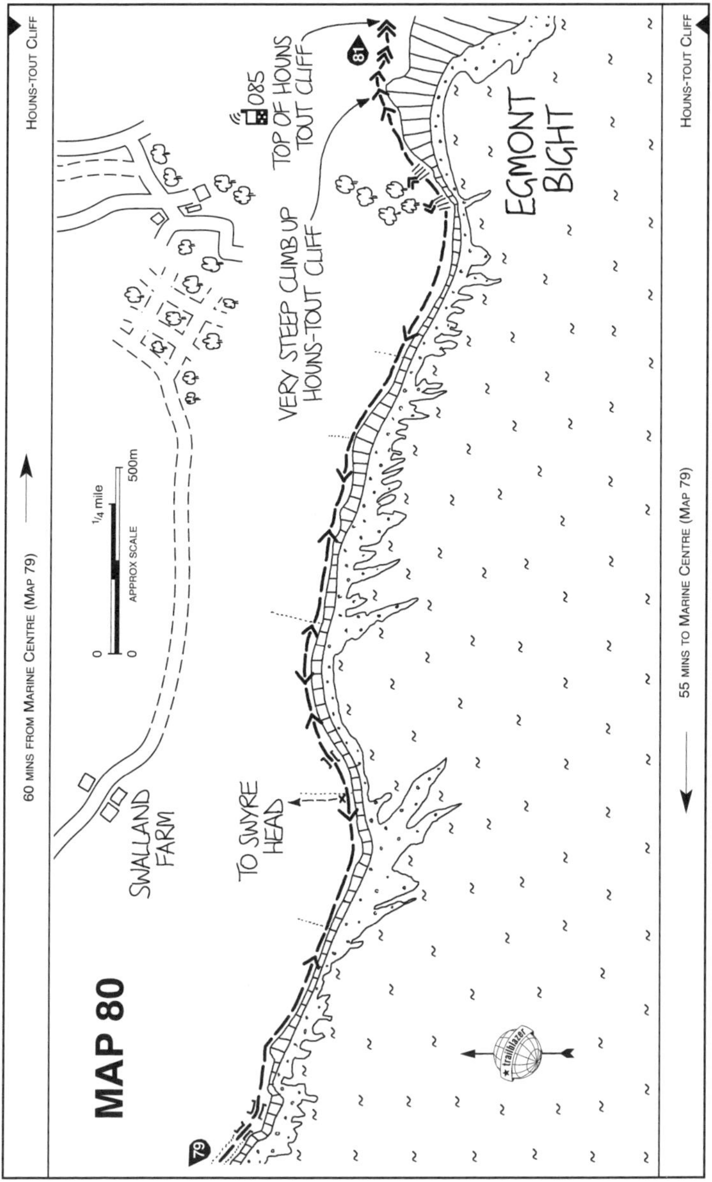
MAP 80
60 MINS FROM MARINE CENTRE (MAP 79)
HOUNS-TOUT CLIFF
55 MINS TO MARINE CENTRE (MAP 79)
HOUNS-TOUT CLIFF
APPROX SCALE
0
1/4 mile
0
500m
SWALLAND FARM
TO SWYRE HEAD
VERY STEEP CLIMB UP HOUNS-TOUT CLIFF
TOP OF HOUNS TOUT CLIFF
085
EGMONT BIGHT
79
81
trailblazer

Tilly Whim Caves. The village of Worth Matravers, about a mile inland, is also a sweet place with a great pub and well worth a detour if you're after refreshments. If you're not planning on visiting the village, there's nowhere else to stop for food until Durlston, about a mile before Swanage – so make sure you bring your own!

The route
The path leaves Kimmeridge Bay via the 19th-century **Clavell Tower**, a folly built by the 70-year-old Reverend John Richards Clavell in 1830. It was moved back from the cliff edge at great expense and effort in 2002 to avoid the encroaches of the sea and the slips of land. The tower is now available as accommodation – though it's usually booked out years in advance and costs over £500 for a three-night stay even in winter! Contact The Landmark Trust (🖥 www.landmarktrust.org.uk) if you're interested.

The gradients are rather gentle for the first few miles (especially when compared to some of the giants of the previous two stages) but don't be lulled into a false sense of security. You'll see what we mean when you tackle the hill of **Houns Tout Cliff** – the summit of which is only gained after a tough slog. Following the descent, a simple meander inland of **Chapman's Pool** brings you to the point where you could leave the coast path for Worth Matravers.

WORTH MATRAVERS   [off MAP 81]
Campers in need of somewhere to pitch and lovers of quirky quality pubs will be tempted to the knot of thatched limestone cottages built round a pond known as Worth Matravers.

Weston Dairy Campsite (☎ 0775-715 9749, 🖥 www.worthcamping.co.uk; 🐾; mid July-Aug only; £6pp) lies on the path between Chapman's Pool and the village. Cakes and bacon sandwiches are available from the farmer, which is handy as the food at the **pub** isn't always available. That, however, is one of the few criticisms that can be levelled at *The Square & Compass* (☎ 01929-439229, 🖥 squareandcompasspub .co.uk; summer daily noon-11pm; winter Mon-Thur noon-3pm & 6-11pm, Fri-Sun noon-11pm). Their recipe for success is simple: pasties and pies served until they run out, washed down with real ales or homemade cider, served inside in an atmospheric low-ceilinged pub or outside on some monolithic garden furniture (they hold a week-long stone-carving festival every year; see p16), to the backdrop of regular live music and the hum of lively chatter. Oh, and they've got a **fossil museum** attached. As you've probably gathered, it's one of those pubs whose fame stretches way beyond the boundaries of the county.

Worth Matravers can also be reached from Map 82.

The slog up Houns Tout Cliff was not the last for, having climbed **Emmett's Hill**, a near-vertical descent and ascent follows to **St Aldhelm's Head** – home to a coastguard, a house or two, a radar research monument, and a 12th-century chapel dedicated to the eponymous saint that's made of local Purbeck stone. If you missed the turning to Worth Matravers earlier it is also accessible by taking the track due north from St Aldhelm's Chapel.

It is with no small relief to find that the haul up to St Aldhelm's really is the last major climb of the day, and though five miles separate you from Swanage, none of them, thankfully, is that taxing. *(Continued on p312)*

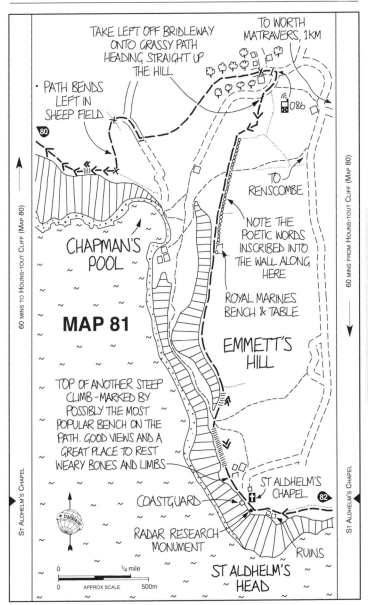

TO WORTH
MATRAVERS, 1KM

TAKE LEFT OFF BRIDLEWAY
ONTO GRASSY PATH
HEADING STRAIGHT UP
THE HILL

· PATH BENDS
LEFT IN
SHEEP FIELD

086

80

TO
RENSCOMBE

NOTE THE
POETIC WORDS
INSCRIBED INTO
THE WALL ALONG
HERE

CHAPMAN'S
POOL

ROYAL MARINES
BENCH & TABLE

MAP 81

EMMETT'S
HILL

TOP OF ANOTHER STEEP
CLIMB - MARKED BY
POSSIBLY THE MOST
POPULAR BENCH ON THE
PATH. GOOD VIEWS AND A
GREAT PLACE TO REST
WEARY BONES AND LIMBS

ST ALDHELM'S
CHAPEL

82

COASTGUARD

trailblazer

RADAR RESEARCH
MONUMENT

RUINS

0   ¼ mile

0   500m
APPROX SCALE

ST ALDHELM'S
HEAD

60 MINS TO HOUNS-TOUT CLIFF (MAP 80)

60 MINS FROM HOUNS-TOUT CLIFF (MAP 80)

ST ALDHELM'S CHAPEL

ST ALDHELM'S CHAPEL

ROUTE GUIDE AND MAPS

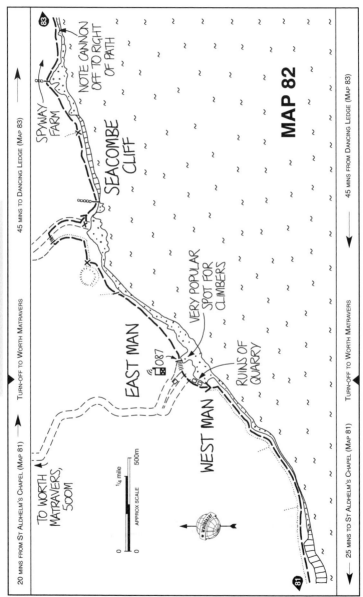

MAP 82

83

20 MINS FROM ST ALDHELM'S CHAPEL (MAP 81) → TURN-OFF TO WORTH MATRAVERS ← 45 MINS TO DANCING LEDGE (MAP 83) →

45 MINS FROM DANCING LEDGE (MAP 83) → TURN-OFF TO WORTH MATRAVERS ← 25 MINS TO ST ALDHELM'S CHAPEL (MAP 81) →

NOTE CANNON OFF TO RIGHT OF PATH

SPYWAY FARM

SEACOMBE CLIFF

VERY POPULAR SPOT FOR CLIMBERS

EAST MAN

RUINS OF QUARRY

WEST MAN

☐ 087

TO WORTH MATRAVERS, 500M

¼ mile

500m

APPROX SCALE

0

0

81

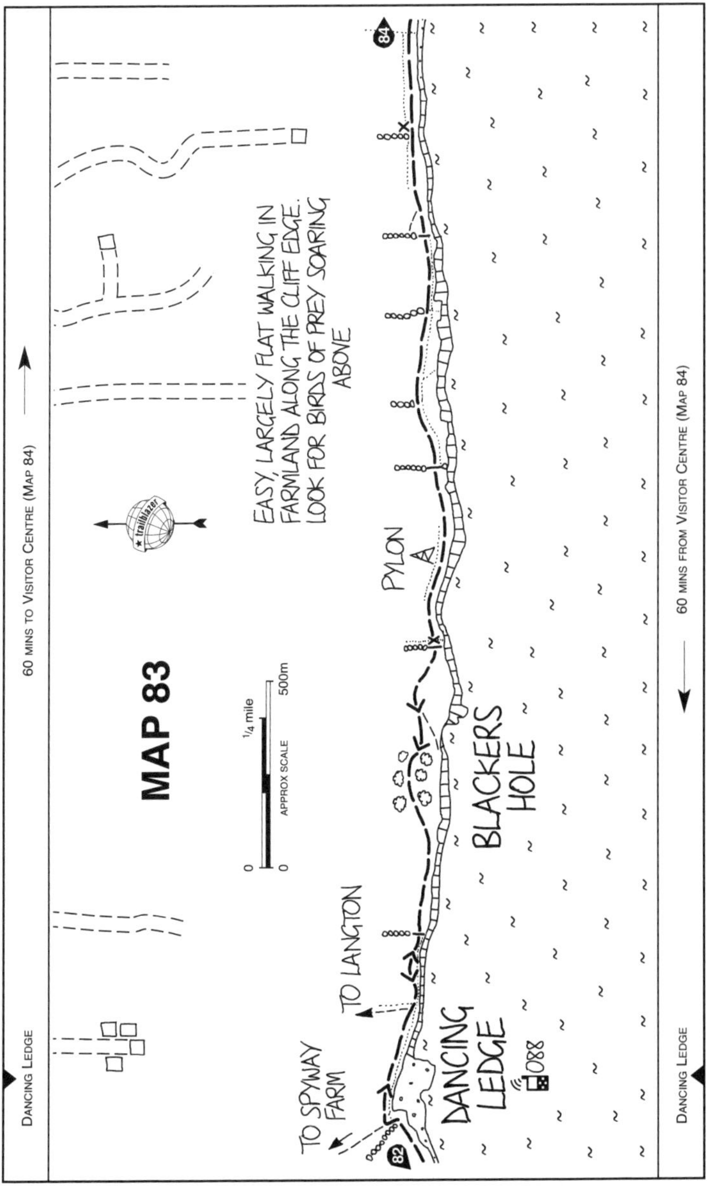
DANCING LEDGE
60 MINS TO VISITOR CENTRE (MAP 84)
MAP 83
trailblazer
0
1/4 mile
0
APPROX SCALE
500m
EASY, LARGELY FLAT WALKING IN FARMLAND ALONG THE CLIFF EDGE. LOOK FOR BIRDS OF PREY SOARING ABOVE
TO SPYWAY FARM
TO LANGTON
PYLON
84
82
DANCING LEDGE
088
BLACKERS HOLE
DANCING LEDGE
60 MINS FROM VISITOR CENTRE (MAP 84)

(Continued from p308) The path meanders past old quarries and cliffs – the latter a real draw for local climbers, for whom the region has plenty – and on via **Dancing Ledge** to the lighthouse at **Anvil Point** and so on to **Durlston National Nature Reserve**, home of butterflies, birds and plants galore.

From here the path descends on pretty **Isle of Wight** Rd (yes, that is the island you can see ahead of you on a clear day) and out into the outskirts of **Swanage**, which you reach via a short detour along **Peveril Point**.

SWANAGE [map p315]

The final town on the Jurassic coastline is actually rather a small and unassuming place. With a population of around 10,000 and lacking any major sights or attractions, Swanage is nevertheless the largest settlement on the Isle of Purbeck and another place that survives – and in high summer thrives – on the tourist hordes. What these tourists find when they arrive is a pleasant place with amiable people, a great sweeping arc of sand, the 'Pier of the Year 2012' – and with just about every amenity a trekker could need.

Swanage Jazz Festival (🖳 www .swanagejazz.org) is held here in July and the **Folk Festival** (🖳 www.swanageff.co .uk) in September.

Services

Swanage centre is a compact place with everything in easy reach. The **tourist information office** (☎ 01929-422885, 🖳 www .visitswanageandpurbeck.co.uk; Easter-Oct daily 10am-5pm, Nov-Easter Mon-Sat 10am-5pm) is on the seafront overlooking the sands. On High St you'll find the library with **internet** (Mon 10am-6.30pm, Wed 9.30am-5pm, Fri 9.30am-5pm, Sat 9.30am-4pm), the local **launderette**, Purbeck Valet (Mon-Wed & Fri 9am-4pm, Thur & Sat 9am-1pm) and, at its eastern end, the **camping outlet** Jurassic Outdoor (☎ 01929-424366, 🖳 www.jurassicoutdoor .com; summer Mon-Fri 10am-5pm, Sat 9am-5pm, Sun 10am-4pm, winter Mon-Fri 10am-4pm, Sat to 5pm).

Moving to Station Rd you'll find the **chemist** Boots (9am-5.30pm, Sun 10am-4pm) and the **supermarket** Budgens (Mon-Sat 7am-9pm, Sun 11am-5pm), while at the end of the road, by the station, is a second

and larger supermarket, Co-op (Mon-Sat 8am-8pm, Sun 10am-4pm). Opposite here is the **post office** (Mon-Fri 9am-5.30pm, Sat 9am-12.30pm). There are also some **banks** with **ATMs** around town.

Where to stay

Swanage is blessed with two **hostels**. The first is **YHA Swanage** (☎ 0845-371 9346, 🖳 www.yha.org.uk/hostel/swanage; 101 beds; WI-FI; dorm bed from £17.40, 2-bedded bunk room from £42), on Cluny Crescent. In our opinion, however, it is bettered by **Swanage Auberge** (☎ 01929-424368, 🖳 www.swanageauberge.co.uk; 15 beds; WI-FI; 🐾; from £18pp), 45 High St, which is smart, clean, central and friendly. Both hostels provide meals and packed lunches.

There are several particularly decent **B&Bs** scattered about town and also in New Swanage (see p317). However, note that during festivals (see box pp15-16) many require a two-night minimum stay.

Climbing the hill on Park Rd you will find the upmarket, award-winning *Clare House* (☎ 01929-422855, 🖳 www.clare-house.com; 5D/1D or T; 🐾; WI-FI; £42.50-49pp, sgl occ full rate in summer, negotiable in winter) at No 1; *Ocean Lodge* (☎ 01929-422805, 🖳 www.oceanlodge swanage.co.uk; 2D/1D or T/2F; 🐾; WI-FI; £25-50pp, sgl occ £40-60), at No 3, who will not accept one-night bookings in advance during the summer holidays; and the dog-friendly *The Limes* (☎ 01929-422664, 🖳 www.limeshotel.net; 3S/6D/3F; 🐾; 🐾; WI-FI; £46pp, sgl £41-52) at No 48, which is also licensed.

In the same vicinity but on Manor Rd, *Hermitage Guesthouse* (☎ 01929-423014,

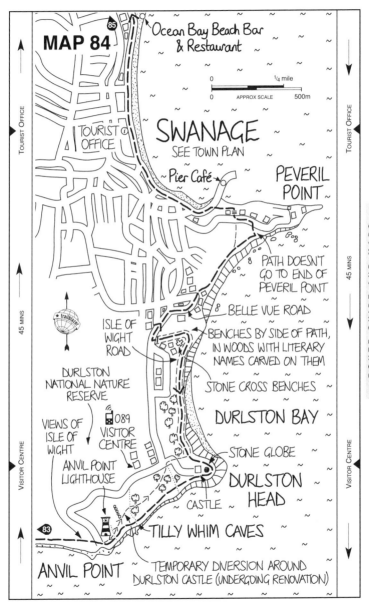

MAP 84

85

Ocean Bay Beach Bar
& Restaurant

TOURIST
OFFICE

TOURIST OFFICE

0   1/4 mile
0   500m
APPROX SCALE

SWANAGE
SEE TOWN PLAN

~ Pier Café ~

PEVERIL
POINT

PATH DOESN'T
GO TO END OF
PEVERIL POINT

BELLE VUE ROAD

BENCHES BY SIDE OF PATH,
IN WOODS WITH LITERARY
NAMES CARVED ON THEM

ISLE OF
WIGHT
ROAD

DURLSTON
NATIONAL NATURE
RESERVE

STONE CROSS BENCHES

DURLSTON BAY

VIEWS OF
ISLE OF
WIGHT

089
VISITOR
CENTRE

STONE GLOBE

ANVIL POINT
LIGHTHOUSE

DURLSTON
HEAD

CASTLE

83

TILLY WHIM CAVES

ANVIL POINT ~

TEMPORARY DIVERSION AROUND
DURLSTON CASTLE (UNDERGOING RENOVATION)

ROUTE GUIDE AND MAPS

www.hermitage-online.co.uk; 2D/2T/3F, shared facilities; ✉; WI-FI; £30pp, sgl occ £45; Mar-Nov) overlooks the town.

Moving to the centre of town and closer to the bus and railway stations is *Firswood* (☎ 01929-422306, ⌨ www.firs woodguesthouse.co.uk; 1S/2D or T/4D; ✉; WI-FI; £31-33pp, sgl occ full room rate), 29 Kings Rd, though they don't take credit or debit cards.

A short stroll away from the centre and opposite St Mary's Church on Kings Rd are *Millbrook* (☎ 01929-423443, ⌨ www.mill-brookswanage.com; 4D/3T/ 1F, 1D/1T share facilities; WI-FI; £29-32.50pp, sgl occ £40-65; Feb-Oct), No 56, who do not accept bookings for a one-night stays on a Saturday; and *Rivendell Guesthouse* (☎ 01929-421383, ⌨ www .rivendell-guest-house.co.uk; 1S/8D or T; ✉; WI-FI; £41.50-46pp, £45 sgl), No 58, who will take one-night bookings throughout July and August only if their diary allows.

Where to eat and drink

The quirkiest place to enjoy a coffee is on Swanage's award-winning **pier** (☎ 01929-425806, ⌨ www.swanagepiertrust.com; daily Apr-Sep 7am-7pm, Oct-Mar 9am-4pm), where the walls of *Pier Café* (see Map 84) are adorned with an exhibition of saucy seaside postcards from the mid-20th century by Donald McGill, and even has its own underwater camera with a screen in the adjoining pier shop! Note there is a 70p charge to walk on the pier.

Back on dry land but almost as unusual, *Gee Whites* (☎ 01929-425720, ⌨ www .geewhites.co.uk; Easter-Oct 9am-9pm) is an unusual place, a thatched open-sided affair that wouldn't look out of place on the white sands of the Caribbean. If you fancy celebrating the end of your trek early, they do six oysters for £6 including a couple of glasses of cava. It can look bleak in overcast conditions, of course, but pick a hot day in August and it's a lovely, bubbling place.

No less quirky, hidden away amongst the alleyways in the heart of town is the *Purbeck Chocolate Co* (Mon-Sat 9.30am-

5.30pm, Sun 11am-4pm), aka Cocoa Central or Chococo, with a range of great hot chocolates (£2.50) from cinnamon to chilli which are real revivers in wet weather.

Purbeck Deli (☎ 01929-422344, ⌨ www.thepurbeckdeli.co.uk; Mon-Fri 9.30am-5pm, Sat to 5.30pm, Sun Mar-Dec 11am-4pm), on Institute Rd, is a good-looking shop in the heart of the town bursting with cheeses and chutneys, where you can build your own baguette from the produce on offer for just £3. For those unfortunate enough not to be staying in Swanage, this place is convenient and delicious enough to demand a visit.

For somewhere to sit down and eat, very close by is *Brook Tea Room* (Mon-Thur & Sun 9am-5pm, Fri & Sat 9am-9pm) which has a good selection of pasties and pies (eg spinach and feta pasty £3.50) as well as a good crab sandwich.

Round the corner on High St, *Earthlights* (01929-422266, ⌨ earthlights cafe.co.uk; Mon-Wed 9.30am-6.30pm, Thur-Sun to 7.30pm and sometimes later) is a pleasant place for a tea or coffee and they also do a decent line in paninis (with brie, grape & walnut currently their most popular at £4.95). They open in the evenings a couple of days a week, serving some good-value meals (£5.95-8.95).

For **takeaway food**, two fish places stand close to each other: *Fish Plaice* (☎ 01929-423668; daily 11.30am-9pm) serves the usual battered fare – as well as some renowned homemade fishcakes – that has 'em queuing out of the door.

The Parade (☎ 01929-423578; Mon-Wed 11.30am-2pm & 5-10pm, Thur-Sat 11.30am-2.15pm & 4.30-10pm, Sun 5-9pm) offers a more formal piscine-eating experience with great views over the sea from some tables. Their seafood sampler at £8.45 is pretty good value.

Masala (☎ 01929-427299; 11am-2pm & 5.30-11.30pm; curries £7.95-11.95), on High St, is a fairly standard Indian that does takeaway (though not deliveries); and close by is *Rainbow Kebab* (☎ 01929-427373; Sun-Wed 3pm-1am, Thur-Sat to 1.30am).

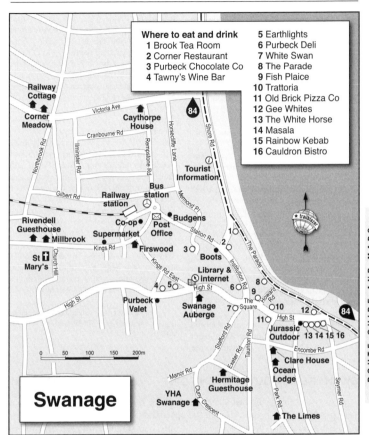

Where to eat and drink
1 Brook Tea Room
2 Corner Restaurant
3 Purbeck Chocolate Co
4 Tawny's Wine Bar
5 Earthlights
6 Purbeck Deli
7 White Swan
8 The Parade
9 Fish Plaice
10 Trattoria
11 Old Brick Pizza Co
12 Gee Whites
13 The White Horse
14 Masala
15 Rainbow Kebab
16 Cauldron Bistro

Swanage

ROUTE GUIDE AND MAPS

The High St is also the place to come for **restaurants**. *Old Brick Pizza Co* is an upmarket pizza place with decent stone-baked pizzas from £8.85 up to £11.45 for the 'Inferno', a carnivorous concoction of meatballs, pepperoni, and pancetta topped with both chilli and jalapeno peppers.

Cauldron Bistro (☎ 01929-422671; Thur-Sun from 6.30pm) is a long-established place serving fairly fancy British/European fare (mains £9.75-14) such as organic salmon, linguine and parmesan cheese (£13.95).

The White Horse (☎ 01929-422469, 🖳 www.thewhitehorseinnswanage.co.uk; daily noon-3pm & 6-9pm) is the place for your pub classics (mains £6.95-11.50) such as steak and ale pie (£7.45). It's a friendly place and has Sky TV for the football.

Also on this strip, *Trattoria* (☎ 01929-423784; Mon-Fri 10am-9pm, Sat & Sun from 9am) is the restaurant arm of Fortes Café next door, with some standard but good-value Italian dishes including pasta for £7.95-9.75 (the most expensive being for canelloni).

White Swan (☎ 01929-423804, 🖳 www.whiteswanswanage.com; daily noon-9pm) is a deceptively large place in the centre of town, a real-ale pub and the home of Piddle Beer that's so popular with locals and tourists alike that they even operate their own loyalty-card system! Part of this popularity is to do with their friendliness and willingness to please – as exemplified by the fact they allow you to charge your mobile phone for free while you drink. Food-wise, they serve baguettes for £6.45-6.95, the delicious chicken, bacon and honey mustard coming in at the cheaper end of this range. It's a different menu in the evenings, including stir fry for £6.95 (for the vegetarian option) up to £8.45.

There is another good option towards the other, western, end of the High St, where it turns inland. *Tawny's Wine Bar* (☎ 01929-422781, 🖳 www.tawnyswinebar.co .uk, Mon-Sat noon-2.30pm, daily 6.15-9.30pm) is a friendly place with some good value, hearty lunches (around £5.95) and evening dishes (£12.25-19.50) such as local crab in chilli, lime, ginger and cream sauce with linguine (£14.95).

Moving back towards the sea and north to Institute Rd, *Corner Restaurant* (☎ 01929-424969, 🖳 www.thecorner restaurant.co.uk; Wed & Thur from 6.30pm, Fri & Sat from 6pm) boasts a fine cocktail list and has mains starting from £16 (for a vegetarian risotto) up to £21 (for locally reared strip loin of beef with blue cheese or garlic butter).

For additional options for a meal see New Swanage, p318.

Transport

[See pp55-60] Wilts & Dorset's No 40 **bus** travels to Poole via Wareham whilst their No 50 travels to Bournemouth via Sandbanks and South Haven Point, and their No 44 goes to Worth Matravers.

In summer, Damory Coaches X43 service travels between the town and Weymouth stopping at Lulworth Cove en route. Swanage is also connected by Damory's No 275 to Kimmeridge, albeit once a week on a Thursday only. To access Weymouth out of peak times you would need to take Wilts & Dorset's No 40 to Wareham where you connect with First's X53 coastal service to Weymouth and beyond.

For a **taxi**, try Swanage Associated Taxis (☎ 01929-421122 or ☎ 01929-425350).

SWANAGE TO SOUTH HAVEN POINT [MAPS 84-88]

And so you come to the last stage – and, at **7½ miles (12km; 2hrs 40 mins)** a very pleasant one it is too. After all the ups and downs of the previous few days, it's also a relatively painless one, with only one simple climb, an even more gentle descent – and then, for the first time in the book, a lengthy stretch of beachcombing along the flat sands of South Haven.

It's a lovely, serene end to your journey as you pick your way amongst the sun seekers, sand strollers, naked naturists and other daytrippers to South Haven Point and the finish line, where any aches and niggles that have haunted you for the past few days are suddenly soothed by the most effective balm known to man – the overwhelming sense of achievement and self-satisfaction.

The route

The stage begins with a simple stroll along Swanage seafront, the path eventually abandoning the coast to strike through the suburbs of **New Swanage**.

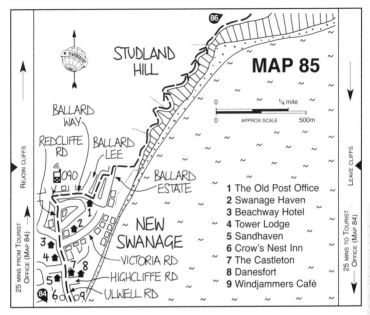

STUDLAND HILL

MAP 85

BALLARD WAY

REDCLIFFE RD

BALLARD LEE

BALLARD ESTATE

NEW SWANAGE

VICTORIA RD

HIGHCLIFFE RD

ULWELL RD

REJOIN CLIFFS

LEAVE CLIFFS

25 MINS FROM TOURIST OFFICE (MAP 84)

25 MINS TO TOURIST OFFICE (MAP 84)

0   ¼ mile
0   APPROX SCALE   500m

1 The Old Post Office
2 Swanage Haven
3 Beachway Hotel
4 Tower Lodge
5 Sandhaven
6 Crow's Nest Inn
7 The Castleton
8 Danesfort
9 Windjammers Café

NEW SWANAGE   [Map 85]
Where to stay

If you don't find anywhere that suits in Swanage it is worth considering staying in New Swanage. Two places willing to accept bookings for one-night stays are *Corner Meadow* (☎ 01929-423493, 🖳 www.cornermeadow.co .uk; 2D/1T/1F; WI-FI; £40pp, sgl occ £60; Mar-mid Oct), at 24 Victoria Ave, and the dog-friendly *Railway Cottage* (☎ 01929-425542, 🖳 www.rail waycottagehotel.co .uk; 3D/1T/1F; ➷; WI-FI; 🐾; £30-40pp, sgl occ £40-55) at No 26.

An amble towards the seafront will bring you to *Caythorpe House* (☎ 01929-422892, 🖳 www.caythorpehouse.co.uk; 2S/2T/3F, the two singles and twin share shower facilities; ➷; 🐾; WI-FI; £25-36pp, sgl occ £25-72), No 7 Rempstone Rd, situated a mere 100 metres from the sands.

Heading to the east of town, just after the path leaves the beach, are three more options, all on Ulwell Rd: *Beachway Hotel* (☎ 01929-423077, 🖳 beachway.helen2@bt internet.com; 3S/3D/1T or F/1F; most share facilities; ➷; 🐾; £25-34pp) at No 19; *Tower Lodge* (☎ 01929-422887, 🖳 www .towerlodgehotel.co.uk; 1S/2D/1T/5F; ➷; WI-FI; £35-40pp) next door at No 17; and *Sandhaven* (☎ 01929-422322, 🖳 www .sandhaven-guest-house.co.uk; 1S/4D/1T/ 2F; ➷; WI-FI; £37.50-42.50pp, sgl occ £60-85) at No 5. All accept one-night stops, although not necessarily during school summer holidays in July and August.

Nearby on Highcliffe Rd, *The Castleton* (☎ 01929-423972, 🖳 www.the castleton.co.uk; 1S/6D or T/2F; ➷; WI-FI; £42.50-60pp, sgl £50-55; Mar-Oct) at No 1, and *Danesfort* (☎ 01929-424224, 🖳 www .danesforthotel.co.uk; 1S/6D/1T/1F; ➷; WI-FI; £32.50-42.50pp, sgl 40-50 sgl occ £50-85) at No 3, are also decent options. The latter can supply evening meals (£22.50 for three courses) if pre-arranged although a one-night stay in July or August may prove difficult.

A couple of blocks north resides the luxurious 'boutique' *Swanage Haven* (☎ 01929-423088, 🖥 www.swanagehaven .com; 7D; ☛; WI-FI; £32.50-55pp, sgl occ £60-105), No 3 Victoria Rd, which – delightfully – offers massage (£40 for the standard full-body massage) and pampering at their Swanage Day Spa. One-night stops are an option but as ever it is unlikely they'll take a solitary night's booking too far in advance.

Finally, heading out of town on the coast path will lead you to the cliff-top *The Old Post Office* (☎ 01929-422041, 🖥 www .oldpostofficeswanage.co.uk; 1D/1T en suite; ☛; WI-FI; £37.50pp, sgl occ £55), No 4 Ballard Estate, which still has a red postbox set in the wall (although for personal letters only). Unfortunately, it has a minimum two-night stay policy though they offer to pick you up from South Haven Point – and the Wilts & Dorset No 50 bus is also easily accessed from both the Point and from Redcliffe Rd (see Map 85) – making a

two-night stop here a distinct possibility. As a further incentive, should you have completed the whole 630 miles of the SWCP and choose to spend an extra night with them, a special treat awaits!

Where to eat and drink
Those staying in New Swanage or at the far northern end of Swanage have two good options, both of which, conveniently, also sit on the path. *Windjammers* (Mon-Thur 9am-5pm, Fri & Sat 9am-11pm, Sun 10am-4pm) is a fairly standard café though one with some unusual breakfasts such as blueberry oats, maple syrup, yoghurt and juice (£3.25) in addition to the standard cooked breakfast (£6.50). On Fri and Sat evenings they also open to serve tapas (£2.95-4.25). Up the hill, *Crow's Nest Inn* (☎ 01929-422651; food served Mon-Sat noon-2pm & 6-8pm) offers a surprisingly sophisticated menu with mains as little as £9.95 (for a wild mushroom chestnut gnocchi) though prices can rise to £15.75.

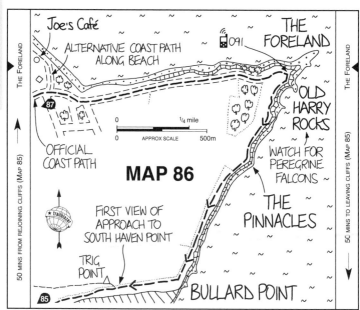

ROUTE GUIDE AND MAPS

Joe's Café

THE FORELAND

ALTERNATIVE COAST PATH ALONG BEACH

THE FORELAND

091

87

OLD HARRY ROCKS

OFFICIAL COAST PATH

MAP 86

WATCH FOR PEREGRINE FALCONS

0   ¼ mile
0 APPROX SCALE 500m

FIRST VIEW OF APPROACH TO SOUTH HAVEN POINT

THE PINNACLES

trailblazer

TRIG POINT

50 MINS FROM REJOINING CLIFFS (MAP 85)

85

BULLARD POINT

THE FORELAND

5C MINS TO LEAVING CLIFFS (MAP 85)

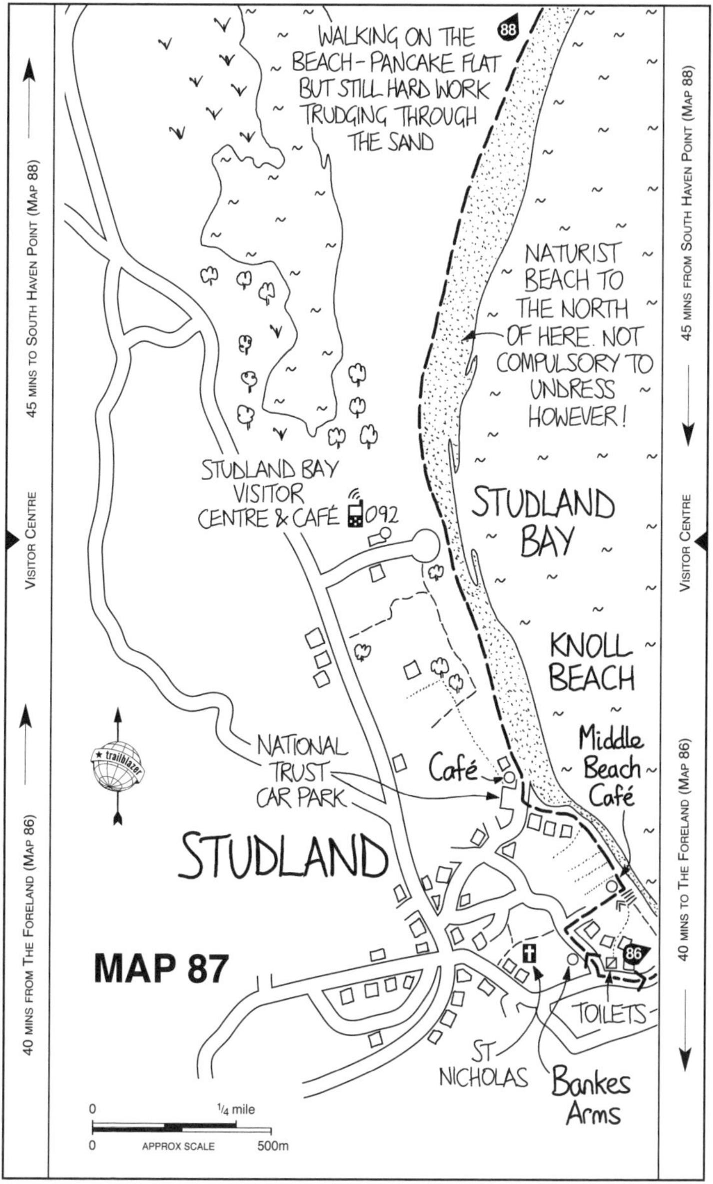

WALKING ON THE BEACH – PANCAKE FLAT BUT STILL HARD WORK TRUDGING THROUGH THE SAND

88

NATURIST BEACH TO THE NORTH OF HERE. NOT COMPULSORY TO UNDRESS HOWEVER!

STUDLAND BAY

STUDLAND BAY VISITOR CENTRE & CAFÉ 092

KNOLL BEACH

NATIONAL TRUST CAR PARK

Café

Middle Beach Café

STUDLAND

MAP 87

86

TOILETS

ST NICHOLAS

Bankes Arms

45 MINS TO SOUTH HAVEN POINT (MAP 88)

VISITOR CENTRE

40 MINS FROM THE FORELAND (MAP 86)

trailblazer

45 MINS FROM SOUTH HAVEN POINT (MAP 88)

VISITOR CENTRE

40 MINS TO THE FORELAND (MAP 86)

ROUTE GUIDE AND MAPS

0   ¼ mile

0   APPROX SCALE   500m

The path then embarks on the gentle climb up breezy **Studland Hill**. You don't stay up there for long, however – just long enough, perhaps, to get your first glimpse of Poole – before the even more gentle descent to **The Pinnacles** and **Old Harry Rocks**, where seagulls soar and falcons swoop.

Your path takes a sharp left here to head eventually into the trees, then splits in two: the right-hand branch takes you to the beach and friendly *Joe's Café* (Easter-Oct daily 10am-4pm up to 8pm depending on weather; Nov-Easter weekends only); by keeping straight on you'll pass some toilets and the road that runs in front of award-winning 16th-century *Bankes Arms* (☎ 01929-450225; 🖳 www.bankesarms.com; 1S/7D/1T/1F; two rooms share a bathroom; ☞; 🐾; £40-44pp, minimum two nights at weekends), the home of the Isle of Purbeck brewery, two log fires, some great food (weekends & school holidays daily noon-9.30pm, weekdays at other times noon-3pm & 6-9pm) and smart rooms. Wonderful, yes – but it's an unusual trekker who stops now when the finishing line is just a long trudge along Studland Beach.

The two paths reunite at *Middle Beach Café* (Apr-Oct daily 10am-4.30pm, winter weekends only) from where your route is pretty self-evident, the path joining the sands of **Studland Bay** to continue its shoreside saunter.

Passing the National Trust 'plaza', home to a visitor centre, *café* (Nov-Mar 10am-4pm, Apr-June 9.30am-5pm, Jul-Aug 9am-6pm, Sep-Oct 9.30am-5pm) and gift shop, the route continues north through the **naturist beach** (the only one in the National Trust's extensive portfolio). Not even the sight of Dorset's finest in the buff can detract you from your task now as you march ever onwards, rounding the bend to see, in the distance ahead, first the large ferry making the short trip between Sandbanks and **South Haven Point**; then, a few steps further on, the point you've probably been dreaming about for the past 217¼ miles (or, indeed, 630 miles if you've walked all the way from Minehead): the **Coast Path Sculpture**, marking the end of this stage, the end of the path – and the end of your walk.

You've made it.

Congratulations!

That was some hike, wasn't it?

❏ **Travelling from South Haven Point**
Wilts & Dorset's No 50 collects passengers from the path's end (Studland) on its way between Swanage and Bournemouth. To get to Poole take the ferry across to Sandbanks and jump on the No 52.

(Opposite) Top: The White Cliffs at Old Harry Rocks, Studland Hill. **Middle**: Shield your gaze on Studland Beach. **Bottom**: The kestrel is a common bird of prey in Britain although it's unusual to be able to get this close to one.

(Overleaf) The end of the road: the Coast Path Sculpture at Sandbanks, near Poole.

The National Trust

NATURISTS
MAY BE SEEN
BEYOND
THIS POINT

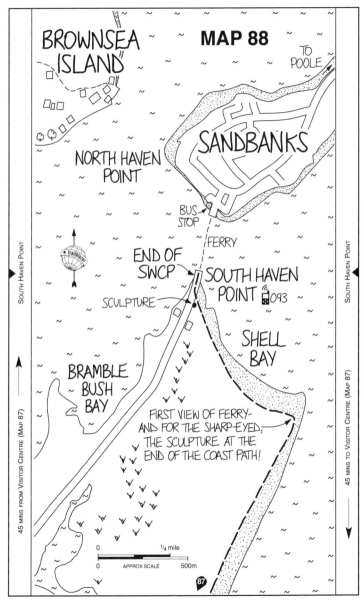

APPENDIX A: POOLE

Though not on the path, there's a fair chance you'll be visiting Poole at some point in your trip – probably at the end – in order to catch transport to/from the start/end of the trail. It's not the most attractive of places, though it *is* big and you'll find all amenities here.

To help you get around pay a visit to The Quay and the **tourist information office** (☎ 0845-234 5560, 🖳 www.pooletourism.com; Apr-June, Sep & Oct daily 10am-5pm, July & Aug daily to 6pm, Nov-Mar Mon-Fri 10am-5pm, Sat 10am-4pm). For most services they'll probably point you in the direction of the Dolphin Centre, home to a **post office** (Mon-Fri 9am-5.30pm, Sat 9am-12.30pm) in WH Smiths, a branch of Boots the **Chemist** (8am-5.30pm, Sun 10.30am-4.30pm), the **camera store** Jessops (Mon-Sat 9am-5.30pm, Sun 10.30am-4.30pm) and, on the top floor, the library, home to the **internet** (Mon-Fri 9am-6pm, Sat 9am to 5pm) which offers up to two hours for free.

The most attractive part of town is the harbour area, where you'll also find some **B&Bs** including *Corkers* (☎ 01202-681393, 🖳 www.corkers.co.uk; 1D/3T/1F; WI-FI; £41.50-47pp, sgl occ £61-77.50), 1 High St, which has some rooms with balconies that overlook the quay and also an à la carte restaurant (Mon-Sat noon-2.30pm, Sun to 3.30pm, daily 6.30-10pm) and café (daily 7am-10pm); and *Quayside* (☎ 01202-683733, 🖳 www.poole-quayside.co.uk; 1S/2D/2T/2F; WI-FI; £35pp, sgl from £50), 9 High St, which is opposite the flashy modern museum.

Nearer to the train and bus stations on Wimborne Rd are *Towngate Guest House* (☎ 01202-668552, 🖳 www.towngateguesthouse.net; 1D or T/1T/1F; WI-FI; £27.50-30pp, sgl occ £45), at No 58, who welcome walkers and are willing to put you up for one night only; and *Arndale Court Hotel* (☎ 01202-683746, 🖳 www.arndalecourthotel.com; 4S/27D/5T/1F; ☕; 🐾; WI-FI; £47.50-52.50pp, sgl £80).

For **food**, *Guildhall Tavern* (☎ 01202-671717, 🖳 www.guildhalltavern.co.uk; Tue-Sat 11.30am-10pm) is a good place for that end-of-trek celebration, pricey and indulgent (mains £18.95-20.95) but with suitably luxurious dishes such as chargrilled whole seabass flambéed in Pernod or monkfish medallions sautéed in a garlic and crayfish butter (£20.95).

Wilts & Dorset's No 52 **bus** (see pp55-60) links Poole with Sandbanks from where you can get a ferry across to South Haven Point. Their No 40 connects the town to Swanage via Wareham. To travel further west, First's X53 coastal service connects Poole with Weymouth, Abbotsbury and Lyme Regis.

Trains connect the town with Weymouth and further afield.

APPENDIX B: THE RIDGEWAY'S PREHISTORIC SITES

Nobody is quite sure why there is such an abundance of prehistoric sites along the Ridgeway. Many think that this chalky ridge provided the easiest way to travel east–west through this part of Dorset, rather than trying to wade through the boggy forested ground present in the valleys below. The Ridgeway also provides a natural 'plinth', a perfect platform for these early people to design and display their temples, tombs and tumuli so their neighbours could see them. Whatever the reasons, the quantity and variety of prehistoric sites on the Ridgeway puts it on a par with the landscape around Stonehenge. Over 3000 sites have now been discovered, many of them only recently.

These sites fall into four main chronological categories. The oldest finds date back to the **Neolithic Age** (4000-2000BC – note the definitions of each of these ages is very fluid and different books may give different start and end dates for the various eras). These were the first farmers, who cleared the Ridgeway of its forests in order to plant crops and cultivate the land. The monuments they built tend to be found at the western end of the Ridgeway, where they had easy access to their building materials – rocks from the Valley of Stones. This valley lies to the west of the Hardy Monument (see Map 60a) and is where early man would source rocks and boulders for their burial chambers and stone circles that dot the landscape. There are only a couple of examples of these within easy reach of the path. The first is **Hampton Down Stone Circle**, constructed around 2000BC – though it has been moved and altered many times since. It is believed that the stone now sits in its original position, though with only 10 of the original stones (a photograph from 1908 indicates there were 16 at that time). On the other side of the Hardy Monument, and a little off the path, is the more impressive **Hell Stone**, a Neolithic stone burial chamber that resembles a kind of mini Stonehenge. Actually, the chamber was only one part of the structure, for from the chamber ran a mound of earth, the whole construction being known as a **long barrow**. Unfortunately, it is widely believed that the 19th-century antiquarians who restored this one rebuilt it incorrectly – though to the laymen it's still a powerful place and the chamber a mighty structure.

In addition to the 17 long barrows on the Ridgeway there are also three **bank barrows**, of which one, **Broadmayne Bank Barrow**, lies around 500m off the path to the north-east of Green Hill. While it is believed the long barrows had some sort of funerary function – the number of bones excavated within the burial chambers suggest they were used as communal burial places – the function of these bank barrows is unknown.

The practice of constructing barrows continued into the **Bronze Age** (2000-500BC) though the style changed as the mounds became more hemispherical. It is these Bronze Age **round barrows** that are the dominant feature of the path. Once again these definitely had a funerary purpose, the corpses of the deceased being placed within the mounds. **Bronkham Hill**, east of the Hardy Monument on the trail, has the finest collection of round barrows on the path. Some important archeological finds have been found in these tumuli including the beautiful Clandon Lozenge, a decorative gold 'plate' that is now on display in the County Museum in Dorset.

By around the 9th century BC the Britons were using a new metal for the first time, heralding in the **Iron Age**. On the Ridgeway, this epoch is best represented by the giant hillforts scattered hereabouts, of which **Abbotsbury Castle** is typical: there's little to cause the layman's jaw to drop when visiting this hilltop site today, though archaeologists will recognise the curves, folds and bumps in the land that are the telltale signs of such a construction. The castle is just one of three in the area, with Maiden Castle, just outside Dorchester, considered to be the most important Iron Age fort in the UK due to its size and history. By the middle of the 1st century AD, however, the Romans had arrived and the Iron Age was ending – and prehistory, too, with the Romans bringing their practice of writing official documents, notes and letters that recorded their time in the UK.

APPENDIX C: MAP KEY

Map key

♠	Where to stay	📖	Library/bookstore	●	Other
○	Where to eat and drink	🕐	Internet	CP	Car park
△	Campsite	🏛	Museum/gallery		Bus station
✉	Post Office	✝	Church/cathedral		Bus stop
£	Bank/ATM	☎	Telephone		Rail line & station
(i)	Tourist Information	☑	Public toilet		Park
		□	Building	082	GPS waypoint

South West Coast Path		Sand dunes		Trees/woodland	
Other path		Cliffs		Bog or marsh	
4 x 4 track		Stone & earth wall		Sand	
Tarmac road		Bridge		Stones	
Steps		Fence		Lighthouse	
Slope		Wall		Golf course	
Steep slope		Hedge		NR Nature Reserve	
Stile		Water		23 Map continuation	
Gate		Stream/river			

APPENDIX D: GPS WAYPOINTS

MAP	REF	GPS WAYPOINT	DESCRIPTION
Map 1	001	SX 48376 54004	Start of walk/Mayflower steps
Map 1	002	SX 48974 53954	Turn-off to Breakwater Hill
Map 2	003	SX 50639 53923	Turn right off road before Oreston Rhino
Map 2	004	SX 50350 52914	Radford Castle
Map 3	005	SX 49140 52394	Jennycliff Café
Map 3	006	SX 49141 50716	Cliffedge Café
Map 4	007	SX 49744 48820	Heybrook Bay
Map 5	008	SX 51786 48489	The Old Mill Café (turn-off to Wembury)
Map 6	009	SX 54021 47711	Ferry at Noss Mayo
Map 6a	009a	SX 52858 49645	Londis in Wembury
Map 6a	009b	SX 55377 52168	Brixton post office
Map 6b	009c	SX 56655 52714	Join lane
Map 6b	009d	SX 57093 51067	Puslinch Bridge
Map 6a	009e	SX 54772 47658	The Ship Inn, Newton Ferrers
Map 7	010	SX 54423 45979	Ruined signal station
Map 8	011	SX 59057 47243	St Anchorite's Rock
Map 9	012	SX 61415 47574	Crossing of Erme, Mothecombe side
Map 10	013	SX 64908 44880	Fryer Tuck, Challaborough
Map 11	014	SX 64853 44022	Pilchard Inn, Bigbury-on-Sea
Map 11	015	SX 66623 44045	Ferry crossing (River Avon)
Map 11a	015a	SX 69261 47236	Roundabout into Aveton Gifford
Map 12	016	SX 67718 41556	Rocky's
Map 13	017	SX 68734 38504	Turn-off to Port Light Inn
Map 14	018	SX 69814 37608	Path left to Bolberry
Map 15	019	SX 72538 36200	Bolt Head
Map 16	020	SX 74148 38087	Mill Bay
Map 17	021	SX 76605 35829	Junction with path by Gammon Head
Map 18	022	SX 79156 36320	Maelcombe House
Map 19	023	SX 80132 37180	Lannacombe Farm B&B
Map 20	024	SX 82456 37221	Turn-off to Start Point Lighthouse
Map 21	025	SX 82334 42016	Torcross
Map 22	026	SX 82888 44346	Slapton Cross
Map 23	027	SX 84075 46876	Strete Post Office
Map 24	028	SX 85935 47962	Take road uphill and to left, not straight on, to Stoke Fleming
Map 25	029	SX 88664 50280	Dartmouth Castle
Map 26	030	SX 90309 49635	Inner Froward Point
Map 27	031	SX 92234 53402	Man Sands
Map 28	032	SX 93514 54677	Sharkham Point
Map 29	033	SX 94030 56163	Entrance to Berry Head NNR
Map 30	034	SX 89516 57606	Seasonal ice-cream stands at Broad Sands
Map 31	035	SX 89460 60284	Paignton Harbour
Map 32	036	SX 89787 62257	Hollicombe Park
Map 33	037	SX 91761 63385	Torquay Marina
Map 34	038	SX 94952 63682	Tip of Hope's Nose
Map 35	039	SX 92154 66031	Join A379

MAP	REF	GPS WAYPOINT	DESCRIPTION
Map 36	040	SX 92656 68475	Maidencombe Beach Car Park
Map 37	041	SX 94041 71961	The Ness
Map 38	042	SX 95496 74828	High- and low-tide routes merge
Map 39	043	SX 97854 78532	Dawlish Warren railway station
Map 40	044	SX 97689 81903	Starcross Ferry
Map 40a	044a	SX 96240 87947	Topsham Ferry
	044b	SX 97633 88244	Turn off to right
	044c	SX 98275 86387	Junction with Station Rd
	044d	SX 98875 84287	Lympstone, cross railway line
Map 41	045	SY 02079 79549	Geoneedle, start of Jurassic Coast
Map 42	046	SY 03594 79851	Straight Point Rifle Range
Map 43	047	SY 06365 81799	Budleigh Salterton
Map 44	048	SY 09047 83638	Brandy Head Observation Hut
Map 45	049	SY 10876 86735	Peak Hill
Map 46	050	SY 11977 86946	Path by Clocktower Café
Map 47	051	SY 16397 87962	Weston Mouth Beach
Map 48	052	SY 19210 88297	Path joins track above Branscombe
Map 49	053	SY 20684 88162	Branscombe Mouth
Map 50	054	SY 25368 90114	Squire's Lane
Map 51	055	SY 27034 89627	Sign: Axmouth–Lyme Regis Undercliffs NNR
Map 52	056	SY 31690 90835	Viewpoint at Pinhay Cliff
Map 53	057	SY 33804 91656	The Cobb, Lyme Regis
Map 54	058	SY 36206 93612	Turn-off to Charmouth
Map 55	059	SY 38315 92966	Westhay Farm
Map 56	060	SY 42011 91776	Seatown
Map 57	061	SY 44782 91079	Eype Mouth
Map 58	062	SY 47487 89729	Burton Freshwater
Map 59	063	SY 50271 88161	Cogden Beach
Map 60	064	SY 53054 86511	Junction with path to South Dorset Ridgeway
		SY 59618 86522	Hampton Down Stone Circle
Map 60a	064a	SY 55071 86596	Abbotsbury Castle
Map 60a	064b	SY 61306 87616	Hardy Monument
Map 60b	064c	SY 68352 84842	Bincombe
Map 60c	064d	SY 71520 84385	White Horse Hill Figure (top of!)
	64e	SY 72839 82931	Turn off road after Craig's Dairy Farm
Map 61	065	SY 55974 84614	Miniature roundabout
Map 62	066	SY 57576 84873	Junction with path to Abbotsbury
Map 63	067	SY 60535 82030	Rodden Hive
Map 64	068	SY 63457 79942	Butterstreet Cove
Map 65	069	SY 64638 78822	Entrance/exit to ranges
Map 66	070	SY 66674 76290	Ferrybridge
Map 67	071	SY 68327 73505	The Cove House Inn
Map 68	072	SY 68639 72928	Large Hand Crane
Map 68	073	SY 68215 72084	Pass under stone arch
Map 69	074	SY 69712 71084	Church Ope Cove
Map 70	075	SY 67711 68279	Bill of Portland
Map 71	076	SY 67882 78756	Bridge over Weymouth Harbour
Map 72	077	SY 69910 81969	Turn-off to Roman temple

MAP	REF	GPS WAYPOINT	DESCRIPTION
Map 73	078	SY 73556 82056	Reunion with South Dorset Ridgeway
Map 74	079	SY 77221 80962	White Nothe
Map 75	080	SY 80595 80302	Path by Durdle Door
Map 76	081	SY 82425 79934	Lulworth Cove
Map 76	081a	SY 82450 80766	Alternative routes divide
Map 76b	081b	SY 90923 85489	Turn off road to quarries
Map 76	082	SY 82975 79720	Gate into Lulworth Ranges
Map 78	083	SY 88895 79777	Take right-hand fork around hill rather than over it
Map 79	084	SY 90803 79304	Stile near end of first alternative route
Map 80	085	SY 94996 77334	Top of Houns-tout Cliff
Map 81	086	SY 96129 77784	Turn-off to Worth Matravers
Map 82	087	SY 97722 76177	Gate at East Man (popular spot for climbers)
Map 83	088	SY 99686 76962	Dancing Ledge
Map 84	089	SZ 03142 77318	Durlston NNR Visitor Centre
Map 85	090	SZ 02989 80264	Turn-off Redcliffe Road to Ballard Way
Map 86	091	SZ 05441 82474	Old Harry Rocks
Map 87	092	SZ 03427 83558	Studland Bay Visitor Centre
Map 88	093	SZ 03620 86653	South Haven Point

INDEX

Page references in bold type refer to maps

334 Other trekking guides from Trailblazer

TRAILBLAZER TREKKING GUIDES
Europe
Corsica Trekking – GR20
Dolomites Trekking – AV1 & AV2
Scottish Highlands – The Hillwalking Guide
Tour du Mont Blanc
Walker's Haute Route: Mt Blanc to the
  Matterhorn

South America
Inca Trail, Cusco & Machu Picchu

Africa
Kilimanjaro
Moroccan Atlas – The Trekking Guide
Australasia
New Zealand – The Great Walks
Asia
Nepal Trekking & The Great Himalaya Trail
Sinai - the trekking guide
Trekking in the Everest Region
Trekking in Ladakh

Kilimanjaro – the trekking guide to Africa's highest mountain
Henry Stedman, 3rd edn, £12.99
ISBN 978-1-905864-24-9, 368pp, 40 maps, 30 photos
At 19,340ft the world's tallest freestanding mountain, Kilimanjaro
is one of the most popular destinations for hikers visiting Africa.
It's possible to walk up to the summit: no technical skills are nec-
essary. Includes town guides to Nairobi and Dar-Es-Salaam, and a
colour guide to flora and fauna. Includes Mount Meru.

Sinai – the trekking guide *Ben Hoffler,* 1st edn, £14.99
ISBN 978-1-905864-41-6, 288pp, 74 maps, 30 colour photos
Trek with the Bedouin and their camels and discover one of the
most exciting new trekking destinations. The best routes in the High
Mountain Region (St. Katherine), Wadi Feiran and the Muzeina
deserts. Once you finish on trail there are the nearby coastal resorts
of Sharm el Sheikh, Dahab and Nuweiba to enjoy. **Due April 2013.**

New Zealand – The Great Walks
Alexander Stewart, 2nd edn, £12.99
ISBN 978-1-905864-11-9, 272pp, 60 maps, 40 colour photos
New Zealand is a wilderness paradise of incredibly beautiful land-
scapes. There is no better way to experience it than on one of the
nine designated Great Walks, the country's premier walking tracks.
Also includes detailed guides to Auckland, Wellington, National
Park Village, Taumarunui, Nelson, Queenstown, Te Anau and Oban.

The Walker's Haute Route – Mt Blanc to the Matterhorn
Alexander Stewart, 1st edn, £12.99
ISBN 978-1-905864-08-9, 256pp, 60 maps, 30 colour photos
From Mont Blanc to the Matterhorn, Chamonix to Zermatt, the
180km (113-mile) Walker's Haute Route traverses one of the
finest stretches of the Pennine Alps – the range between Valais in
Switzerland and Piedmont and Aosta Valley in Italy. Includes
Chamonix and Zermatt guides.

Moroccan Atlas – the trekking guide
Alan Palmer, 1st edn, £12.99
ISBN 978-1-873756-77-5, 268pp, 54 maps, 40 colour photos
The High Atlas in central Morocco is the most dramatic and beautiful section of the entire Atlas range. Towering peaks, deep gorges
and huddled Berber villages enchant all who visit. With 44 detailed
trekking maps, 10 town and village guides including Marrakech.

TRAILBLAZER TITLE LIST

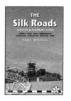

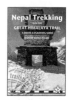

For more information about Trailblazer and our
expanding range of guides, for guidebook updates or
for credit card mail order sales visit our website:

www.trailblazer-guides.com

TRAILBLAZER'S LONG-DISTANCE PATH (LDP) WALKING GUIDES

We've applied to destinations which are closer to home Trailblazer's proven formula for publishing definitive practical route guides for adventurous travellers. Britain's network of long-distance trails enables the walker to explore some of the finest landscapes in the country's best walking areas. These are guides that are user-friendly, practical, informative and environmentally sensitive.

● **Unique mapping features** In many walking guidebooks the reader has to read a route description then try to relate it to the map. Our guides are much easier to use because walking directions, tricky junctions, places to stay and eat, points of interest and walking times are all written onto the maps themselves in the places to which they apply. With their uncluttered clarity, these are not general-purpose maps but fully edited maps drawn by walkers for walkers.

● **Largest-scale walking maps** At a scale of just under 1:20,000 (8cm or $3^1/_8$ inches to one mile) the maps in these guides are bigger than even the most detailed British walking maps currently available in the shops.

● **Not just a trail guide – includes where to stay, where to eat and public transport** Our guidebooks cover the complete walking experience, not just the route. Accommodation options for all budgets are provided (pubs, hotels, B&Bs, campsites, bunkhouses, hostels) as well as places to eat. Detailed public transport information for all access points to each trail means that there are itineraries for all walkers, for hiking the entire route as well as for day or weekend walks.

Coast to Coast *Henry Stedman*, 5th edition, £11.99
ISBN 978-1-905864-47-8, 256pp, 110 maps, 40 colour photos

Cornwall Coast Path (SW Coast Path Pt 2) 4th edition, £11.99
ISBN 978-1-905864-44-7, 352pp, 130 maps, 40 colour photos

Cotswold Way *Tricia & Bob Hayne* 2nd edition, £11.99
ISBN 978-1-905864-48-5, 192pp, 60 maps, 40 colour photos

Dorset & South Devon (SW Coast Path Pt 3) *Stedman & Newton*, £11.99
ISBN 978-1-905864-45-4, 336pp, 90 maps, 40 colour photos

Exmoor & North Devon (SW Coast Path Pt I) *Stedman & Newton*, £11.99
ISBN 978-1-905864-43-0, 192pp, 60 maps, 40 colour photos

Hadrian's Wall Path *Henry Stedman*, 3rd edition, £11.99
ISBN 978-1-905864-37-9, 224pp, 60 maps, 40 colour photos

North Downs Way *John Curtin*, 1st edition, £9.99
ISBN 978-1-873756-96-6, 192pp, 80 maps, 40 colour photos

Offa's Dyke Path *Keith Carter*, 3rd edition, £11.99
ISBN 978-1-905864-35-5, 240pp, 98 maps, 40 colour photos

Peddars Way & Norfolk Coast Path *Alexander Stewart*, £11.99
ISBN 978-1-905864-28-7, 192pp, 54 maps, 40 colour photos

Pembrokeshire Coast Path *Jim Manthorpe*, 4th edition, £11.99
ISBN 978-1-905864-51-5, 224pp, 96 maps, 40 colour photos – due Mar 2013

Pennine Way *Keith Carter & Chris Scott*, 3rd edition, £11.99
ISBN 978-1-905864-34-8, 272pp, 138 maps, 40 colour photos

The Ridgeway *Nick Hill*, 3rd edition, £11.99
ISBN 978-1-905864-40-9, 192pp, 53 maps, 40 colour photos

South Downs Way *Jim Manthorpe*, 4th edition, £11.99
ISBN 978-1-905864-42-3, 192pp, 60 maps, 40 colour photos

West Highland Way *Charlie Loram*, 5th edition, 11.99
ISBN 978-1-905864-50-8, 192pp, 60 maps, 40 colour photos – due Mar 2013

Dorset & S Devon Coast Path

PLYMOUTH – POOLE

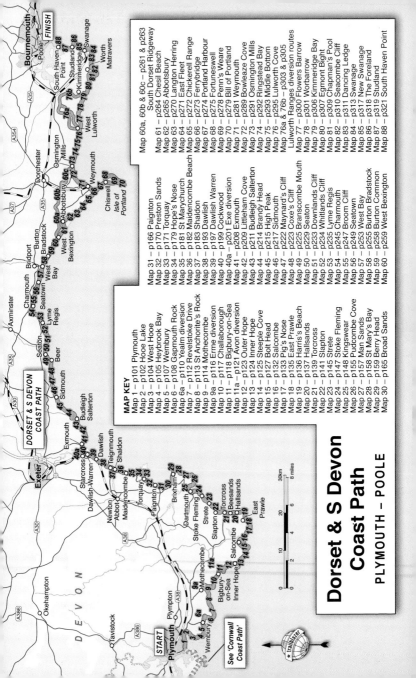